The Church & th

The Church & the World

Understanding the Relevance of Mission

J. Andrew Kirk

Paternoster:
thinking faith

26 25 24 23 22 19 18 17 16 15 14 13 12 11 10 9 8 7 6 5 4 3 2 1

First published 2014 by Paternoster
Paternoster is an imprint of Authentic Media Limited
52 Presley Way, Crownhill, Milton Keynes, MK8 0ES.
www.authenticmedia.co.uk

British Library Cataloguing in Publication Data

A catalogue record for this book is available from the British Library

ISBN 978-1-84227-812-3
978-1-84227-858-1 (e-book)

Cover Design by Paul Airy (www.designleft.co.uk)
Printed and bound by CPI Group (UK) Ltd., Croydon, CR0 4YY

To all members of the International Association of Mission Studies (IAMS), a body committed under the Lordship of Jesus Christ and the leading of the Holy Spirit to the scholarly study of the church's mission and its practice on all continents. May we all continue to strive for intellectual integrity in study and a joyous and passionate engagement in mission, as long as the Lord gives us the strength to fulfil our privileged calling.

Contents

Contents

Acknowledgements

My first debt of gratitude goes to Alan Sell, the general editor of the series of which this volume is a part. When first invited to write on a subject as broad as *The Church and the World* appeared to be, I was hesitant, if not reluctant. However, after much thought and a number of conversations, Alan persuaded me to take on the task.

It has been a challenge, for the subject covers so much diverse ground. However, the assignment has been immensely worthwhile for me. I hope that the result will be of stimulus to those curious and brave enough to read the various chapters. Personally, I have learnt much more about various episodes in the mission of the church about which formerly I only had a hazy notion, particularly those recounted in Part II. I am now convinced of the abiding importance of looking at seminal moments in the life of the expansion of the Christian faith, in order to learn from both the faithfulness and also the errors of past pioneers.

So thank you, Alan, for urging me to respond positively to the request to participate in this particular publishing venture. Thank you also for the latitude you have given to interpret the subject matter and choose the particular topics for study. Such freedom involves responsibility, for inevitably any author will elect events that especially appeal to him or her. In my case, some are familiar, especially those of the latter chapters. At the same time, when I first began to delve into the sources, some were almost unknown to me, except in the most general terms. I hope the selection will also intrigue the reader, and just maybe expand his or her horizons. Finally, thank you for being willing to read each chapter as a first draft became available and make incisive comments. On the whole, I think you may have been too generous in your appraisal of the results.

One or two special friends have most kindly given of their time to read through a chapter related to their area of expertise. Sidney Rooy, a long-time colleague in Latin America and a leading historian of the history of Christianity on the continent, made some judicious comments on Chapter 5. Ian Randall, another colleague, on the staff of the International Baptist

Theological Seminary in Prague, a specialist on early Anabaptist history, read through Chapter 6 and made some most helpful observations on a piece of history and its subsequent consequences that I have grown to appreciate in recent years. Nestor Miguez, a former student of mine in Buenos Aires, who has become a theologian of stature throughout Latin America and beyond, scrutinised Chapter 9, of which the thought of his celebrated father was the subject matter, and suggested some helpful additions. To all these, I am most grateful. Both their assurances and their corrections have been extremely valuable.

Mike Parsons, the Commissioning Editor of Paternoster, has always been easy to work with. Thank you for your patience, support, gentle reminders about the various procedures that have to be followed before a book can be published, and your prompt and clear response to queries.

Lastly, I would like to recognise the many friends and colleagues in the worldwide fellowship of mission theologians, from all continents, who have been such a stimulus and encouragement over so many years. You are too numerous to mention individually. However, I would like to pay tribute especially to the members of the International Association of Mission Studies (IAMS), of which I have been a part for nearly thirty years. The work it has done in advocating, promoting and supporting mission studies has been remarkable. I don't know whether I will have the opportunity to write another major book on Christian mission, so I would like to take this occasion to dedicate this one to IAMS in gratitude for all I have learnt from many of the people who have given time and energy to ensure its continuation and success.

J. Andrew Kirk

General Editor's Preface

Many books are written on the history of Christian doctrine, and volumes of systematic theology never cease to roll from the press. The former may or may not include reflections upon the current 'state of the doctrine'; the latter may or may not pay heed to the history of theological reflection upon the subject in hand. Hence this series entitled, Christian Doctrines in Historical Perspective, the objectives of which are twofold. First, to trace the biblical roots and defining moments in history of major Christian doctrines, with reference to prominent authors and texts (including recent ecumenical texts as appropriate), concluding with an appraisal of the doctrine in current debate. Secondly, to hold together doctrines which belong together but are sometimes, frequently for good reasons, treated in isolation from one another: for example, *The Person and the Work of Christ, Creation and Recreation*.

It is hoped that this series will contribute to that biblical-historical grounding of current theological reflection which is necessary if systematic and constructive theology are to be understood as entailing a conversation between the biblical sources, the heritage of doctrinal thought and the current intellectual environment.

Alan P.F. Sell
Milton Keynes, UK

Projected titles:

Stephen Holmes, *The Holy Trinity* (2011)
Andrew McGowan, *The Person and Work of Christ* (2012)
Robert Pope, *The Church and the Sacraments* (2014)
Andrew Kirk, *The Church and the World* (2014)
Thomas Noble and Jason S. Sexton (eds), *The Holy Trinity Revisited*. Essays in Response to Stephen R. Holmes (2015)

Introduction

At first sight the title of this volume in the series *Christian Doctrines in Historical Perspective* suggests a daunting assignment. As if the task of attempting to offer an account of the doctrine of the church were not complex enough, to add the world into the equation would seem to invite a study of several volumes. Clearly, then, some well-defined limits will have to be set, so that the subject matter does not run out of control.

The Church's Calling to Mission

I shall, then, limit myself to looking at the church in terms of its calling to a mission beyond itself. This means considering the church, not so much in its inner life (*ad intra*), but in its activities outside (*ad extra*). Another book on the church has been prepared for the series (*Church, Ministry and Sacraments*); it will include fundamental elements of the church's life of worship, prayer, discipleship, education and training, structures of leadership, various rites and decision-making processes. The present book will cover aspects of the church's mission agenda as these reflect the growing consensus that Christians of different traditions are reaching.

Whilst the agenda may be phrased in a variety of ways, it generally deals with the church's evangelistic, prophetic and diaconal ministries within the everyday life of human communities. Put another way, it concerns the church's commission to share, in word and action, with a world yet to believe, the good news of Jesus and the kingdom of God: to call all people to believe in the truth of this message; to incorporate them into a fellowship of others who follow Jesus; to be engaged with issues of social justice, human rights and care of the environment; to be involved in care for vulnerable members of society (such as refugees, the homeless, children in need of protection, the lonely, and those suffering from mental traumas, long-term illnesses, substance abuse and bereavement), and in peacemaking actions that bring a resolution of conflict and reconciliation between parties in dispute.[1]

In addition to these various callings, it is part of mission to pay attention to the contextualization of the Christian message and forms of church life in different cultures and social situations. This means considering, in depth, ways in which the faith may be translated into the kaleidoscope of cultures that make up the worldwide human community, in such a manner that, whilst maintaining its own integrity, it may resonate with a broad variety of histories, traditions, customs and perspectives on life.

Mission is also concerned with the necessary task of engaging with other systems of belief, whether they represent religious convictions or emanate from a secular mindset. This activity is usually referred to as dialogue, meaning a respectful conversation with people of other faiths, with a view to gaining an accurate understanding of other people's beliefs and actions, correcting misunderstandings, listening to a critique of one's own faith as perceived by outsiders, collaborating in joint ventures of service and witness (where possible), and giving a testimony to one's own understanding of ultimate truth.

In this latter case, particularly in circumstances where the Christian faith is under attack by people dedicated to destroying its intellectual credibility, Christians have a responsibility to set out the case for its rational coherence and scholarly legitimacy. This task is often referred to as apologetics, meaning the reasoned defence and promotion of Christian belief and living; advocacy would, perhaps, be a better way of describing it. This latter concept indicates 'the recommendation and promotion of a course of action or the defence of a person or cause. This

---

[1] See, for example, the following works on mission: David Bosch, *Transforming Mission: Paradigm Shifts in Theology of Mission* (Maryknoll: Orbis Books, 1991); J. Andrew Kirk, *What is Mission? Theological Explorations* (London: Darton, Longman & Todd, 1999); Samuel Escobar, *The New Global Mission: The Gospel from Everywhere to Everyone* (Downers Grove: IVP, 2003); Michael Nazir Ali, *Mission and Dialogue: Proclaiming the Gospel Afresh in Every Age* (London: SPCK, 1995); Vinoth Ramachandra, *The Recovery of Mission: Beyond the Pluralist Paradigm* (Grand Rapids, MI: Eerdmans, 1997); Steve Bevans and Roger Schroeder, *Constants in Context: A Theology of Mission for Today* (Maryknoll: Orbis Books, 2004); Sebastian Karotemprel, ed., *Following Christ in Mission: A Foundational Course in Missiology* (Boston: Pauline Books, 1996); Risto Ahonen, *Mission in the New Millenium* (Helsinki: Finnish Evangelical Lutheran Mission, 2006); Andrew Walls and Cathy Ross, eds., *Mission in the 21st Century: Exploring the Five Marks of Mission* (London: Darton, Longman & Todd, 2008); Timothy Tennent, *Invitation to World Missions: A Trinitarian Missiology for the Twenty-First Century* (Grand Rapids: Kregel Publications, 2010).

range of meanings adequately covers the significance of the word in its sense of testimony and vindication.'[2]

Finally, the mission of the Christian community is predicated on certain clear ethical principles. It both strives to carry out the tasks it has been commissioned to fulfil with ethical integrity and also engages with non-Christians in debating the key moral issues of the times. As we shall discover in greater depth later in this study, those who claim to take seriously the knowledge of God revealed in the person of Jesus Christ are required to follow a demanding code of ethical rectitude. The beliefs which they declare to be true entail moral consequences. The pattern of their lives, therefore, will either commend those beliefs or cast doubt on them. The non-Christian world, quite rightly, expects Christians to show a consistency between the absolute goodness of the God they worship and the pattern of their lives.

In particular, in the fulfilment of its missionary obligations, the Christian community is required to bring into harmony the ends it seeks to achieve with the means it uses to reach them. This is often a hard lesson to learn, because Christians consider the ends so admirable and urgent that they are tempted to be expedient with the means to carry them out. However, regarding means to be as important as ends is an integral part of their ethical decision-making.

In situations where the Christian faith, though once dominant, is now no longer considered the indispensable ground for guiding moral behaviour, or where Christians represent only a minority of a population, the church's mission is to argue for and demonstrate in practice the coherence that exists between the revealed will of God and human flourishing in all its aspects. So Christians will engage publicly in ongoing debates about ethical issues, however controversial these may be.

As a general guide, in considering ethical dilemmas, the Christian faith is 'pro-life'. This has both negative and positive implications. Negatively, it means that Christians, to be consistent to their beliefs, will oppose all that destroys human life. Thus, for example, they will naturally seek to overturn the liberal laws on abortion, not only because the object in a woman's womb is a baby (not just a foetus, even less just an appendage of the woman's body), but also because abortions often undermine the emotional stability of the pregnant woman and compromise the medical profession's commitment to saving, not destroying, life. They will also campaign against any attempt to legalise euthanasia in any of its forms, because of their respect for the gift of life, the tragedy of premature death and the inviolable dignity of the human person in

---

[2] J. Andrew Kirk, 'Apologetics' in John Corrie, *Dictionary of Mission Theology: Evangelical Foundations* (Nottingham: IVP, 2007), p. 22.

all circumstances. There is no dignity in causing an artificial shortening of human existence.

By the same token, Christians will work for a massive reduction in the worldwide arms trade, which often fuels the destructive violence of war, terrorist activities and state oppression, and also eats up financial resources that should go to tackling endemic poverty. Christians will be pro-life in fighting against political corruption,[3] knowing that neither development aid nor commercial investment will bring a better standard of living to marginalised communities as long as bribery and the misappropriation of funds are regular occurrences. Christians will also seek to reverse the destructive consequences of the manipulation of markets in the interests of the few and struggle for a fairer distribution of the wealth of nations.

Positively, Christians will be involved in advocating policies that promote healthy living, in terms of preventative health care and community development. They will seek to support activities that build good relationships between potentially antagonistic groups, overcome violence, and encourage self-reliance and cooperation. Hence, Christians are already intensely active in facilitating self-sustaining enterprises among poor communities, in promoting programmes of education concerning sexually transmitted diseases and narcotic and alcohol abuse, in caring for orphaned and abandoned children and the physically and mentally damaged. They will work for both equal opportunities and equal respect for women in society, particularly in combating the trafficking of young women in the sex-trade, and the end of bonded labour.

All these activities, and more besides, demonstrate that Christians wish to work for the protection and enhancement of God's gift of a healthy physical, mental and spiritual life. Many other virtues flow from this cardinal centre, such as upholding the dignity of every individual human person, even when a society or culture despises or rejects certain categories – for example, migrants, refugees, travellers, prisoners, the mentally disabled, young offenders, and those who abuse themselves and others through drugs, drink or sexual promiscuity. We will return to the question of how the church becomes involved in matters of ethical principle and practice at a later stage of this study.

The World

Thus far I have been outlining some of the elements that are implicated in the nature of the church as a missionary body. We need now to turn

---

[3] See Daryl Balia, *Make Corruption History* (London: SPCK, 2009).

our attention to the context in which, naturally, it has to operate, namely the world. There may be many different ways of envisaging the term. We may think of the world as one of the planets that circles around the sun in a solar system that constitutes an infinitesimally small part of a vast universe. It is the only planet, known to us, whose conditions sustain complex living organisms. The world, looked at from the outside, is the earth, a solid mass, suspended in space by invisible forces, that moves on its own axis, whilst also moving through space on a circular path, repeated every 365 days. Considered from within, the world is an expanse of land and sea, inhabited by an enormous variety of living species. Principally it is the dwelling of a unique species, *Homo sapiens*, which has organised its existence in a range of complex societies, both to survive and to express its creative capacities through technology, a variety of art forms and organizations. We will be considering the ways in which the Bible makes use of the term, and allow these to guide the shape of this study. Our main concern will be with the world as the humanly inhabited sphere with its attendant natural environment of earth, endowed with a considerable variety of minerals, air and water, and home to a huge diversity of living organisms.

The Church

The church is a distinct community of people of every type and all ages, and from every race, ethnic group, nation and social category, who confess that Jesus of Nazareth, the Messiah, is the Son of God and the only saviour of all humanity. They confirm their belief that this Jesus has called them individually and together into a fellowship of his followers, with the purpose of exhibiting the qualities of a life transformed by the power of God's Spirit, under the rule of God's new order (the kingdom), and of bringing others into the sphere of God's saving actions. The church, though an organization separate from any other, is not detached from the world. It exists in the world. Hence the direction of its mission is not into the world from outside, but rather from one part of the world to another. However, as we shall see, God calls it to be separate from the world in the sense of not accepting beliefs or joining in activities that are at variance with God's blueprint for human wellbeing.

Outline

The first chapter of Part 1 will offer an overview of the way in which the Bible views the world, noticing the characteristic duality of its perception

– both the goodness of the created order and the perversion of its human inhabitants. Chapters 2 and 3 will trace out the meaning and scope of the church's mission, according to a variety of biblical witnesses. The fourth chapter will round off a consideration of the biblical foundations dealing with the relationship between church and world by looking at the ethical expression of its life.

Part II will consist of three chapters that survey different moments in the history of the church, selected in order to give distinct examples of ways in which Christians have interpreted their mission in the world. The intention here is to offer a few models in order to show that the relationship between the church and the world has taken quite distinct forms at different times (even at the same time) and in disparate circumstances.

The final section of the book is dedicated to more recent aspects of the church's engagement with the world. In fact, it will look at the last five decades, when there has been considerable discussion, debate and experimentation in terms of the church's role in the world. Each chapter will consider a particular feature of the church's mission, as these have been highlighted during the last decades of the twentieth century and the beginning of the twenty-first. At the end there will be an attempt to summarise the material, bring together the different threads and draw some provisional conclusions.

The book is intended to present a coherent theme concerning the Christian church's responsibilities in the world in response to the mandate it has from Jesus Christ its head. There is, therefore, an important thread that connects each chapter and ties the subject matter together. The basic question to be answered is, what does the Lord of heaven and earth require of his people (Mic. 6:8) as they seek to follow him faithfully in their daily lives? Various answers have been given in different ages. Lessons for the continuing life of the church can be learnt from all of them.

At the same time, each chapter can be treated as an entity on its own with its own special subject matter. Readers may, therefore, prefer to dip in and out of the book as they are drawn to a particular issue, either historical or contemporary. They will find that the chapters are to a considerable extent self-contained. There are, however, also links between chapters which add a dimension that would otherwise be lost. Thus, for example, to fully understand the religious and secular worlds with which the book concludes, each should be read in the light of the other. Whether you, the reader, wish to start at the beginning (or the end) and work your way through the text chapter by chapter, or whether you prefer to pick out individual chapters is your choice. In either case, I hope that you will find the various discussions fascinating, enriching and stimulating.

Part One

Biblical Foundations

1

'In the World, but Not of the World': A Biblical View of the Cosmos

Human Existence in the World

The title of this chapter points to a paradox. It suggests the possibility that one can be part of the world and deeply immersed in its affairs and yet not belong to it. Although the phrase is not a direct quote from any part of the Bible, it sums up its consistently ambivalent attitude to the whole reality in which human beings find themselves. From birth to death the world is the habitation of all people. It is the setting in which they grow to maturity, form families and nurture the next generation. It is the environment in which, as the psalmist reflects, 'People go out to their work and to their labour until the evening' (Ps. 104:23). There is no escape from the sheer physicality of existence that binds life to the conditions that the planet earth imposes upon all sentient beings.

At the same time, there appears to be implanted in the innermost consciousness of the human species an insistent desire to transcend mere physical being. All humans, however much they may attempt to eradicate it, experience a nagging dissatisfaction with the pursuit of a life absorbed by purely material achievements. The world is at one and the same time our residence, and yet the place where we do not feel entirely at home. It is as if we are seeking another resting-place, which the physical environment is incapable of providing. The Bible gives us the clue as to why we should feel the way we do – caught between the many enjoyments which the world makes possible and the longing for a contentment that is not dependent on the vagaries of having our physical desires met. The teacher of wisdom (Qoheleth) sums up the two realities: 'God . . . has made everything beautiful in its time. He has also set eternity in the hearts of men' (Eccl. 3:10–11, NIV).

The Bible appears to be telling us here, and elsewhere, that, although our life in the world is real (not an illusion as some believe), it is transient and incomplete. It is as if we are on a journey, whose destiny lies beyond the world, and that our ultimate resting-place is elsewhere. So that, if we invest all our hopes and expectations within the confines of physical existence, we are bound to be disappointed. The life that we want to grab hold of, hang on to and control for ourselves always evades our grasp. We are actually constructed to find the true source of comfort and fulfil-ment, to be at ease with ourselves and life around us, beyond the world. The Bible advises human beings to be extremely careful about how they approach their existence in the world:

'Do not store up for yourselves treasures on earth . . . But store up for yourselves treasures in heaven' (Matt. 6:19–20, NIV); 'what will it profit them [those who want to save their life] to gain the whole world and forfeit their life? Indeed, what can they give in return for their life?' (Mark 8:36–7).

What Kind of World?

I will return to the tension between living in the world, yet not fully belonging to it, later in this chapter. There is another apparent discord between two ways of experiencing the world, which the chapter's title calls attention to. The world is, in many ways, a beautiful place. The grandeur and variety of its scenery is awe-inspiring. The diversity of its flora and fauna is astounding: for example, there are over 900 different species of eucalyptus tree and well over thirty different types of banana, growing in the state of Kerala in SW India alone. The intricacy and complexity of the human form is becoming increasingly apparent as new discoveries are made in the field of genetics and the neurosciences. Most human beings, whether they believe that the world has been created by a divine being or evolved by chance from an original formless matter, are constrained to wonder at the exquisite beauty of autumnal leaves turning colour, the variety of hues and tints seen in spectacular sunsets, the form of a snowflake, the amazing exploits of migrant birds or the workings of the human mind in solving intricate mathematical problems – to name but a handful of possible examples. If a person is unable to contemplate certain features of the world with wonderment and admiration, we are inclined to think that there is something lacking in their human make-up.

Yet, at the same time, we also recognise easily the many examples of ugliness and cruelty that exist alongside the lovely and splendid objects we have described. The catalogue of pain, suffering, gratuitous violence, disfigurement, hatred and malice, whether part of life caused by natural disasters or 'man's inhumanity to man', is too obvious to need spelling out in detail. There is a problem of evil abroad in the world that certainly needs much explanation. Either everything we find unattractive, harmful or destructive about the world is a normal constituent of life on this particular planet or somehow, at some time, it has entered into the operations of life on earth. As one might expect, the Bible has much to say about this extraordinary phenomenon of a world at one and the same time beautiful and ugly, good and bad, wholesome and wicked. It is to a review of the variety of affirmations that it makes that I now turn.

A Dialectical Tension: Literal and Metaphorical Uses of the Term

Teresa Okure in a study of mission in the Gospel of John[1] suggests that we should approach this seeming dichotomy by distinguishing between the use of the world in a literal and a metaphorical sense. In the first case, the world is the physical earth and all that lives within it is the creation of God: this is the world ('all things' – *panta*) that 'came into being through [the Word]' (John 1:3,10). In the second case, the world designates the human sphere of unbelief: a world of sin and darkness which rejects God's Word and hates him, his Father and all that belong to him (John 1:5,10c,11; 3:19–20; 15:22–3; 17:14).

The World in the Old Testament

The world is the result of God's creative acts

The contrast described above is seen uniformly throughout the Scriptures. The world is always seen in its foundational relationship to God, the Lord. It has no intrinsic meaning apart from its being the handiwork of the one and only pre-existent deity: 'In the beginning . . . God created the heavens and the earth' (Gen. 1:1). Before the creation of the universe, nothing with physical properties existed. All matter came into being as a result of a decision taken by God to form something outside of himself. Creation happened as an act of speaking: 'Then God said, "Let there be light"; and there was light' (Gen. 1:3); 'By the word of the LORD the heavens were made . . . For he spoke, and it came to be' (Ps. 33:6,9).

Some commentators have interpreted the reference in Genesis 1:2 to 'a formless void', 'darkness' and 'the deep' as an indication that some form of

---

[1] Teresa Okure, *The Johannine Approach to Mission: A Contextual Study of John 4.1–42* (Tubingen: J.C.B. Mohr, 1988), p. 199.

material reality was already there before 'the beginning'. However, this is a highly unlikely supposition, given the overwhelming view of the Hebrew people that God, the Lord, alone was eternal. Thus, the reference to the earth in the shape of a formless void should be taken as the first act of creation. It would be the equivalent to creating the clay from which the potter then goes on to produce all kinds of pottery. Some other commentators have ingeniously suggested that the reference to *tohu* and *bohu* (literally 'waste' and 'void') is a rhetorical way of saying absolute non-being; nothing whatsoever existed. In other words, before God spoke his creative word, there was nothing material,[2] which, as it were, predates the universe. The classical doctrine of *creatio ex nihilo* seems to be implicit in the opening verses of the Scriptures and in the understanding of who God is.

Contemporary cosmologies that seek to explain the origin of the universe, having deliberately excluded God, beg the fundamental question as to why there is something rather than nothing. Thus, Stephen Hawking and Leonard Mlodinow, in a fairly recent book, argue that 'M-theory predicts that a great many universes were created out of nothing. Their creation does not require the intervention of some supernatural being or god. Rather, these multiple universes arise naturally from physical law. They are a prediction of science.'[3]

However, John Lennox[4] points to the fallacy of such a proposition:

Contrary to what Hawking claims, physical laws can never provide a complete explanation of the universe. Laws themselves do not create anything; they are merely a description of what happens under certain conditions. What Hawkins appears to have done is confuse law with agency . . . That is a confusion of category . . . The laws of physics could never have actually built the universe. Some agency must have been involved . . . Hawking's argument appears to me even more illogical when he says that the existence of gravity means the creation of the universe was inevitable. But how did gravity exist in the first place? Who put it there? And what was the creative force behind its birth?[5]

---

[2] For a full discussion of possible alternative interpretations, see Henri Blocher, *In the Beginning* (Leicester: IVP, 1984), pp. 60–67.

[3] Stephen Hawking and Leonard Mlodinow, *Grand Design: New Approaches to the Ultimate Questions of Life* (London: Bantam Press, 2010), pp. 8–9.

[4] John Lennox, Professor of Mathematics in the University of Oxford and author of *God's Undertaker: Has Science Buried God?* (Oxford: Lion Hudson, 2009).

[5] Article written in *Mail Online*, 3 September 2010; see his full discussion of Hawking's views on the scientific meaning of law and the origin of the cosmos in John Lennox, *God and Stephen Hawking: Whose Design Is It Anyway?* (Oxford: Lion Hudson, 2011).

If effects must have satisfactory explanatory causes, it is inconceivable that matter could be spontaneously generated from non-matter without some force intervening from beyond matter. The non-theistic explanation of material existence is simply not an explanation. The intuition, therefore, that the world cannot be comprehended apart from a wholly contingent, gratuitous act of an eternally self-existing and self-defining divine being, who exists beyond time and space, appears to be self-evidently correct. Alternative explanations lack rational plausibility. This is the gist of what has come to be called the *kalam* cosmological argument for the existence of God that states that (a) whatever begins to exist has a cause, (b) the universe began to exist, so (c) it follows logically that the universe has a cause.[6]

First and foremost, then, the world is to be seen in its original and continuing relationship to God. It is part of creation; it is not just nature as an impersonal entity that stands on its own: 'In the Psalms, the world is mainly the created earth and all that is in it – human, animal, mineral and vegetable. The whole world in all these senses was brought into existence by God (33:6–9), is owned by God (24:1), ruled by God (33:10–11), and observed by God both in loving provision and in moral judgment (33:13–15).'[7]

The world belongs to its Creator

The Hebrew Scriptures are emphatic in their insistence that the Creator of all is also the owner of all. In the Abrahamic narrative, for example, both Abraham and Melchizedek, king of Salem, acknowledge that *El Elyon* (God Most High) is the Maker of heaven and earth: 'Blessed be Abram by God Most High, maker of heaven and earth'; 'I have sworn to the LORD (*Yahweh*), God Most High (*El Elyon*), maker of heaven and earth' (Gen. 14:19,22).

The phrase in Hebrew, *qineh samayim waerets* (maker of heaven and earth), has a double meaning, in that the verb *qnh* normally means to buy or acquire, as well as create. Thus it is perfectly valid etymologically to translate the phrase, 'The Lord, God Most High, possessor of heaven and earth'.

---

6   In spite of doubts expressed about the traditional arguments for the existence of God since the writings of Hume and Kant in the eighteenth century, in the absence of credible alternative explanations for existence, they must still be considered rationally powerful; see William Lane Craig, 'The Cosmological Argument' in *The Rationality of Theism* (ed. Paul Copan and Paul K. Moser; London: Routledge, 2003), pp. 112–31.

7   Christopher Wright, 'The World in the Bible', *Evangelical Review of Theology* 34:3 (2010), p. 207.

Hence, in the perspective of the author of Deuteronomy, 'the LORD your God' to whom belong 'the heaven of heavens . . . the earth with all that is in it' (Deut. 10:13–14) is perfectly within his right to give the land to the west of the Jordan to the people he has chosen to inherit it (Deut. 7:13); ultimately he, not the people who live there, is the owner. The clearest expression of ownership is found in the regulations for the Sabbatical Year and Jubilee Year: 'the land is mine: with me you are but aliens and tenants' (Lev. 25.23).[8]

If the term *gerim* is translated 'guests' it gives an admirable picture of the relationship between Yahweh, Israel and the land: 'They [the Israelites] had no ultimate title to the land – it was owned by God. The LORD was the supreme landlord. Israel was his collective tenant. Nevertheless, the Israelites could enjoy secure benefits of the land under the Lord's protection and in dependence on him.'[9]

God was able to promise the land to his specially chosen people, because it belonged to him both before Israel entered into it (Exod. 15:13,17) and subsequently. The people also belonged to Yahweh, for he had redeemed them from slavery in Egypt, in order to make them into a people who would show forth God's mercy and righteousness in every aspect of their daily lives. The land, as belonging to Yahweh, was to be distributed equitably to every household within every clan, so that every family unit possessed the means for subsistence. The portion of land, as it was the sustainer of life, was inalienable to the extended family in perpetuity. Therefore, it could not be treated as a commercial piece of property to be bought and sold for profit.

The world is a gift from its Creator

The regulations of the Jubilee Year were intended to ensure that households did not become alienated from their economic base. One of the most heinous crimes committed by those who prospered economically under the new political regime that arose with the establishment of monarchy (1 Sam. 8:10–17) was the theft of land:

> He [the king] will take the best of your fields and vineyards and olive orchards and give them to his courtiers. (1 Sam. 8:14)

> Ah, you who join house to house, who add field to field, until there is room for no one but you, and you are left to live alone in the midst of the land! (Isa. 5:8)

---

[8]   Also, Ps. 68:9; 79:1 and Jer. 2:7.
[9]   Christopher J.H. Wright, *Old Testament Ethics for the People of God* (Leicester: IVP, 2004), p. 201.

He [the wicked person] has oppressed the poor and left them destitute; he has seized houses he did not build. (Job 20:19, NIV)

They covet fields, and seize them; houses, and take them away; they oppress householder and house, people and their inheritance. (Mic. 2:2)

The land, therefore, was first and foremost to be seen as a gift to be held on trust by the people who acknowledged Yahweh's sovereign right of ownership. It was to be administered, not for individual gain, but in the interests of the whole community (which included the non-Israelites who enjoyed the status of lodgers in the land [Deut. 10:18–19; 24:19; Exod. 22:21; 23:9]).

Given the crucial nature of land to life, it is perhaps not surprising that the primary words translated earth (*adamah* and *erets*) occur so frequently in the Old Testament (some 2,730 times); whereas, the word usually translated world (*tebel*) occurs relatively infrequently (some thirty-six times). It is true that each of them may be used interchangeably, depending on the context. Thus each can refer to the whole inhabited earth, the place where human beings dwell; it is the world made fit for human habitation. Yet, the real interest of the Old Testament narrative is in the world as land, or even soil, that is habitable, because cultivatable.

The world, then, is entirely an act of creation. It is, moreover, a contingent accomplishment, in that God did not have to create. God wished to produce something outside of himself in which he could delight. The world is distinct from God, yet dependent on his continuing presence to sustain its existence moment by moment. He is ever present in its midst to cherish it and provide for all its needs. It reveals the nature and power of God, and thus, in its original goodness, shows God's glory: 'The world belongs to God, submits to God, points to God, is accountable to God and needs God.'[10]

The world was originally good, but is now corrupted

Nevertheless, the world as it has turned out is not as was originally intended. The Scriptures lay the blame for the corruption and destruction that has entered into the world at the door of the first human pair. Although given a beautiful and fertile earth to care for and enjoy, they could not agree to live within the boundaries that God had set. So they yielded to the temptation to set their own rules about what would be permissible, thus violating the regulations that God had put in place to

[10] Christopher Wright, 'World in the Bible', p. 211.

ensure their flourishing. In effect, they set themselves up as the ultimate arbiter of good and evil, thus reversing the relationship of Creator and created. They broke the relationship that would have guaranteed a bountiful life, turning themselves into God's enemies:

> There was one boundary beyond which the pair might not trespass. Their well-being depended upon exercising their considerable freedom within this limitation. Erich Fromm is right, therefore, to point out that sinfulness arose directly from the original misuse of freedom.[11] By going beyond the limit, the first human pair broke the harmony of the created order and the result was a tragic disruption of the harmony of relationships. And so . . . it has been ever since.[12]

So they first ignored, then flouted and finally rewrote the instructions given to them and, as a result, produced a world of disorder and dysfunction.

God's reaction was immediate; it was to make sure that the pair understood both the nature and the consequences of their act of self-assertion. Attempting to gain independence from their Creator and make themselves into the arbiters of their own destiny brought a series of alienations. Humanity from then on has discovered that human life is deformed and distorted. The abnormal has become normal. What should have turned out as a truly glorious blessing has become an affliction.

The Old Testament recognises the ways in which the curse affects the world. From the beginning, the very ground that sustains the life of human beings is put under a malediction, meaning that the soil will only yield crops with a great struggle: 'in toil you shall eat of it [*adamah*/earth] . . . By the sweat of your face you shall eat bread' (Gen. 3:17,19).

This is life outside the garden. God's original plan was that the beings that he had created in his own image would enjoy a land that was exceptionally fertile. They would 'till the ground' (Gen. 2:5) and 'keep it' (Gen. 2:15), i.e. look after it and manage it wisely. Now, however, they have been banished from Eden, to live a life in a different kind of environment, where weeds grow more abundantly than life-sustaining crops (Gen. 3:18; 2:5).

Clearly the contrast between the two situations (inside and outside the garden) is not that of leisure and work; work is part of God's original plan in creating human beings. The contrast is between a work that is blessed and one that is cursed. Instead of humans delighting in and finding full satisfaction in their care of creation, they now find it toilsome, requiring

---

[11] Erich Fromm, *The Fear of Freedom* (London: Routledge & Kegan Paul, 1960), p. 26.

[12] J. Andrew Kirk, *The Meaning of Freedom: A Study of Secular, Muslim and Christian Views* (Carlisle: Paternoster Press, 1998), p. 203.

the kind of extra exertion that produces exhaustion. Whereas in Eden work and leisure were not sharply separated, for the first couple found in work the fulfilment of their nature as created beings, now leisure is experienced as a relief from work; indeed, it is seen as the reward that work makes possible.

The notion of a world under both blessing and curse is frequent in the Old Testament (e.g. Deut. 11:26–8; Ps. 24:1–5; Hag. 1:10–11; Mal. 2:2; 3:9; 4:6). The earth, when God sets his blessing upon it (Deut. 33:13–16a), is still fertile up to a point. The promised land is one flowing with milk and honey 'that the LORD your God looks after. The eyes of the LORD your God are always on it, from the beginning of the year to the end of the year' (Deut. 11:12). The condition for receiving the blessing is heeding every command-ment given by the Lord and 'loving the LORD your God, and serving him with all your heart and with all your soul' (Deut. 11:13). In other words, the curse is mitigated when the people accept a covenant with the Lord to follow his laws. Then they will do what the first pair in Eden failed to do, namely to obey the Lord's command. 'Then he will give the rain for your land in its season, the early rain and the later rain, and you will gather in your grain, your wine, and your oil; and he will give grass in your fields for your livestock, and you will eat your fill' (Deut. 11:14–15).

The world tends to follow false gods

Sin is characteristically understood in terms of idolatry. This is portrayed as a habit of the heart, whereby people turn from following the one true and life-giving Supreme Being and create for themselves substitute 'gods'. The effect of idolatry is that, as the idols are human creations, people are worshipping themselves. The prophet Isaiah, in particular, pours scorn on the senselessness of idolatry. Having described the bare essentials of idol worship – the shaping of metal and wood into objects resembling human beings that are then venerated as if they could influ-ence the course of life and save humans from the vicissitudes of their existence – he mocks and ridicules their efforts:

> All who make idols are nothing, and the things they delight in do not profit . . . They do not know, nor do they comprehend; for their eyes are shut, so that they cannot see, and their minds as well, so that they cannot understand . . . a deluded mind has led him astray, and he cannot save himself or say, 'Is not this thing in my right hand a fraud?' (Isa. 44:9,18,20)

The first stage in idolatry is to lose our sense of preoccupation with God, relating every aspect of life to his loving concern. The second stage is to

pursue our own imaginations, 'following our own devices' (Isa. 65:2). Either
we orientate the whole of life to God's wisdom or we rely on our own (called
in today's jargon 'rational planning').[13]

The problem with idolatry is that it warps the mind and clouds judgement. It points to a spiritual force that deludes people into believing and
acting on a false view of reality. Having abandoned God's world, they
create one of their own, which reflects their evil inclinations. In the Old
Testament, the epitome of idolatry is seen in the book of Judges, when
'the people did what was right in their own eyes' (Judg. 21:25; Deut.
12:8). The latter part of Judges portrays a situation of general lawlessness
(Judg. 17:6; 18:1ff.; 19:1ff.). It is a story of a society that, having turned
relentlessly to idolatry (Judg. 18:14–20), practised a depraved form of
life (Judg. 18:27–31; 19:22–30). It is the inseparable relationship between
idolatry, injustice and immorality that produces God's judgement on the
earth (Isa. 24:4–5; 34:1–2; Jer. 4:23–8; 25:29–32; Zeph. 1:2–3; 3:8).

Idolatry, however subtle and sophisticated it may be in its modern
dress brings certain consequences in its wake:

> Ultimately all corruption springs from idolatry: arrogating to ourselves the
> position that is God's alone. This has led to the belief that natural resources
> belong to us, that they can be exploited for our gratification, that what is
> scientifically possible (embryo research, animal experimentation, gene modi-
> fication) should be allowed, that we are responsible only to ourselves (and
> our shareholders). There is all the difference, however, between freedom *from*
> God and freedom *before* God.[14]

In biblical and theological terms, could it not be said that the current
degradation of the environment (the earth) is the result of policies that
have sprung from a belief that human beings are only accountable to
(supposedly predetermined) economic laws, although, in fact, they have
invented them? In other words, it is the result of idolatry.

The world will be recreated

Idolatry, fortunately, will not be the last word. God's plans to rescue
humanity from its pursuit of false gods and destructive existence by
establishing justice and righteousness through the vicarious suffering of
his servant is strongly hinted at in notable passages in the Old Testament.

[13] J. Andrew Kirk. *What is Mission? Theological Explorations* (London: Darton,
Longman & Todd, 1999), p. 178.
[14] Kirk, *What is Mission?*, p. 178.

God's mission of turning the curse of condemnation into the blessing of salvation is directed towards the nations. This was the essence of God's covenant promise to Abraham that 'all the nations of the earth shall be blessed in him' (Gen. 18:18; also, Gen. 12:3; 22:18). So the nations of the world figure prominently in this plan of salvation. Thus, 'Among those who know me I mention Rahab and Babylon; Philistia too, and Tyre, with Ethiopia' (Ps. 87:4). God's house shall 'be called a house of prayer for all peoples', because 'the foreigners who join themselves to the LORD, to minister to him, to love the name of the LORD, and to be his servants' will be made 'joyful in my house of prayer . . . says the LORD' (Isa. 56:6–8). This universal possibility of salvation is promised as a future event:

'On that day' even Egypt and Assyria will be counted as belonging to God's people, the work of his hand. (Isa. 19:24–5)

'On that day' 'Many nations shall join themselves to the LORD . . . and shall be my people.' (Zech. 2:11)

Because 'God is king over the nations', 'The princes of the peoples gather as the people of the God of Abraham'. (Ps. 47:8–9)

Israel, God's people chosen to be a blessing to the nations, has a specific mission to tell out among its neighbours the good news of God's coming salvation. Thus, 'All the kings of the earth shall praise you, O LORD', because 'they have heard the words of [his] mouth' (Ps. 138:4). They have heard his message, because his people are commanded to 'Declare his glory among the nations, his marvellous works among all the peoples' (Ps. 96:3). What is the message? It is an announcement of peace, salvation and the sovereign rule of Yahweh (Isa. 52:7).

The mission will take the form of both an ingathering – the peoples will come of their own accord to worship the one true God in his place of residence, which is the temple in Jerusalem – and an outreach. Peoples will come from the ends of the earth, singing the praises of the one, true God. Also, God's light, salvation, knowledge and glory will go to the ends of the earth, because Israel has been called to be a missionary force: 'I will give you as a light to the nations, that my salvation may reach to the end of the earth' (Isa. 49:6).[15]

At some point, the curse pronounced on the earth, because of humanity's declaration of independence from its Creator, will be lifted and a

---

[15] I will return to the missionary vocation of God's people in the Old Testament more fully in Chapter 2.

radically different kind of world will be created again. Isaiah conveys the message of Yahweh that he is 'about to create new heavens and a new earth' (Isa. 65:17). The vision is of a transformed social order (Isa. 65:19–23) and a world of nature no longer 'red in tooth and claw' (Isa. 65:25; 11:6–9). God's *shalom* is the ultimate destination of a recreated world. The path to this ideal picture of people and nature living in complete accord is God's gift of reconciliation. This expectation for the future is present fitfully in the Old Testament, but comes to a much more precise expression in the New.

The World in the New Testament

Vocabulary

A range of different words appear in the writings of the New Testament, which are related to or translated by world. The most common is *kosmos*. This is the world which encompasses all the nations on planet earth, or it is the universe as an ordered whole. In classical Greek thought it denotes everything contained within the physical bounds of the different nations and peoples. Unsurprisingly, *kosmos* only occurs in the later writings of the Septuagint (*Wisdom, 2 Maccabees* and *4 Maccabees*), since the Old Testament has a different understanding of the world from that of Greek thought. In Hebrew thinking, the world was always closely associated with God as its Creator. It had no independent existence. The word predominates in the Johannine writings,[16] and therefore these will be treated later in a separate section.

Luke prefers to use the word *oikoumene*, which refers roughly to the then known inhabited world, i.e. the Roman Empire: 'In those days a decree went out from Emperor Augustus that all the *oikoumene* should be registered' (Luke 2:1). In the temptation narrative Luke uses *oikoumene* rather than *kosmos*: 'Then the devil led him up and showed him in an instant all the kingdoms of the *oikoumene*' (Luke 4:5). In Thessalonica, Paul and Silas were accused of 'turning the *oikoumene* upside down' (Acts 17:6). This is a reference to all the various places they had been, proclaiming that Jesus was the Messiah; '[Now they] have come here also.' Again in Acts 19:27 and 24:5, Paul was held responsible for causing trouble among the *oikoumene*, by bringing disrepute on the temple of Artemis in Ephesus and by being 'an agitator among all the Jews throughout the *oikoumene*'.

---

[16] Of the 185 occurrences in the New Testament, 102 appear in the Johannine literature, 47 in Paul, 14 in the Synoptic Gospels and 22 in the rest.

Interestingly, the word only occurs once in the Pauline corpus and that is in a quotation from the Old Testament: 'Their voice has gone out to all the earth (*ge*), and their words to the ends of the *oikoumene*' (Rom. 10:18, quoting Ps. 19:4).

Probably under the influence of Hellenistic Judaism, the spatial notion of world becomes assimilated to the temporal understanding of the Hebrew *olam* (age). So references to 'this age (*aion*)' take on the meaning of all that is happening in the world as it is now constituted. In contrast, 'the age to come' alludes to a new world that is in the process of being formed: 'Yet among the mature we do speak wisdom, though it is not a wisdom of this *aion* or the rulers of this *aion*, who are doomed to perish' (1 Cor. 2:6).

Other expressions are used to represent world. *Ta panta* (all things) is used several times in the hymn or creed found in Colossians 1: 'He himself is before all things (*panton*), and in him all things (*ta panta*) hold together' (Col. 1:17). This is a global term that embraces the visible and invisible parts of all that is created; 'through him God was pleased to reconcile to himself all things (*ta panta*), whether on earth or in heaven' (Col. 1:20). *Ktisis* is usually translated creation, as in this same passage in Colossians: 'He is the image of the invisible God, the firstborn of all creation (*pases ktiseos*)' (Col. 1:15). It is the world seen from the point of view of its creaturely nature. Its first characteristic is that it has come into being by the sovereign act of a divine being who has made everything that could possibly exist, including, were they to exist, multiple universes. *Ktisis* also refers to a new creation that is already present in the old creation in the lives of those who are 'in Christ': 'For neither circumcision nor uncircumcision is anything; but a new creation' (*kaine ktisis*) is everything!' (Gal. 6:15); 'So if anyone is in Christ, there is a *kaine ktisis*' (2 Cor. 5:17); 'the *ktisis* itself will be set free from its bondage to decay' (Rom. 8:21).

The world created through Christ

In some highly significant passages, Christ is spoken of as the agent through whom and for whom the universe has come into existence: 'there is one God, the Father, from whom are all things and for whom we exist, and one Lord, Jesus Christ, through whom are all things (*di hou ta panta*) and through whom we exist (*kai hemeis di autou*)' (1 Cor. 8:6); 'in these last days he has spoken to us by a Son . . . through whom he also created the worlds (*aionas*) . . . of the Son he says, . . . "In the beginning, Lord, you founded the earth, and the heavens are the work of your hands"' (Heb. 1:2,8,10):

What is most distinctive in the New Testament concept of the universe is its christological emphasis. The world was created by God through the Word (John 1:10), and without him nothing that has been made was made (John 1:3). The Christ whom the Gospel proclaims as the agent of redemption is also the agent of God's creation. And he is at the same time the goal toward which all creation is directed (Col. 1:16) and the principle of coherence of all reality, material and spiritual (Col. 1:17).[17]

Christopher Wright speaks of Paul having 'christified' Old Testament monotheism. This is true not only of the original creation, but the creation that is still to come. The scope of the message of the gospel of Jesus Christ, the mystery that has been revealed 'to his holy apostles and prophets by the Spirit' (Eph. 3:5), is that God has a plan for the fullness of time 'to gather up (*anakephalaiosasthai*) all things (*ta panta*) in [Christ]' (Eph. 1:10). The same emphasis on Christ in creation and recreation is found also in the Gospel and Letters of John and in Hebrews. Something similar could be said of the Holy Spirit. In so far as the Holy Spirit is the agent of the new creation, monotheism has also been 'pneumatised'.

The world of material possessions

The world is the place where human beings are required to make a living, in order to be able to support the family they have brought into the world. Work, therefore, is both a necessity and a calling. Able-bodied people should not shirk it. On the contrary, they are to work hard enough to be able to make a surplus over their legitimate daily needs, so that they may be able to contribute to those who, through no fault of their own, are not able to provide for their essential requirements.

Material possessions are part of a normal life. However, people are counselled not to build up large reserves or surpluses. Wealth through accumulation easily becomes a snare: 'those who want to be rich fall into temptation and are trapped by many senseless and harmful desires that plunge people into ruin and destruction' (1 Tim. 6:9); 'the love of money is a root of all kinds of evil' (1 Tim. 6:10), 'For where your treasure is, there your heart will be also' (Matt. 6:21). In other words, the pursuit of riches distorts the meaning of life, for it reverses the true relationship between means and ends: 'You cannot serve God and wealth' (Matt. 6:24). So, the goal of material existence is contentment concerning the provision of what is really needed for living. This will spring from a trust that God will put

---

[17] Rene Padilla, *Mission Between the Times: Essays on the Kingdom* (Grand Rapids, MI: Eerdmans, 1985), p. 2.

us in a place where we can enjoy what is sufficient for life; 'if we have food and clothing, we will be content with these' (1 Tim. 6:8,6; Phil. 4:11).

This attitude towards material goods springs from a proper appreciation of our mortality: the fact that we do not have ultimate control over the span of our lives. 'We brought nothing into the world (*eis ton kosmon*); it is certain that we can take nothing out of it' (1 Tim. 6:7, NRSV margin). Therefore, to people who store up treasures for themselves, who say to themselves, 'You have ample goods laid up for many years; relax, eat, drink, be merry', God says, 'You fool! This very night your life is being demanded of you. And the things you have prepared, whose will they be?' (Luke 12:19–21): 'In the Greek text the phrase "your soul/self/life is required of you", is the language of the return of a loan. This is one of the major, often hidden, truths of Scripture. Life is not a right but a gift – a loan.'[18]

Everything about this world is relativised in the light of what is to come: 'the appointed time has grown short; from now on, let [those] . . . who buy [be] as though they had no possessions, and those who deal with the world as though they had no dealings with it. For the present form of the world is passing away' (1 Cor. 7:29–31).

The world of sin and judgement

Outside of the Gospel and Letters of John, the majority of references to the group of words that convey the meaning of world are found in Paul's writings.[19] Many of the occurrences speak of *kosmos* as a place that is organised in opposition to the purposes of God. The world is now thoroughly contaminated by sin, which entered through the transgression of one man. The whole human race has inherited the consequences of Adam's act of defiance against his Creator, of which the most pronounced is death. The world, therefore, is marked by death, which has spread to all people, because all have sinned (Rom. 5:12). Death is the equivalent of losing the glory of God (Rom. 3:23); it is the state of being banished from God's presence and thus forfeiting that intimate relationship with the Creator that Adam and Eve enjoyed for a short time in Eden. The glory of God rested on Mount Sinai (Exod. 24:16), in the pillar of cloud (Exod. 16:10), in the temple (1 Kgs 8:11) and on the ark of the covenant (Exod. 25:22; Ps. 80:1; Rom. 9:4). God's glory was a token of his absolute goodness and purity, written into the creation itself. This has been lost because human beings refused to submit to God's rule.

---

[18] Kenneth E. Bailey, *Jesus through Middle Eastern Eyes: Cultural Studies in the Gospels* (London: SPCK, 2008), p. 306.

[19] *Kosmos* occurs 47 times and *aion* occurs 31 times.

The world is also the place of temptation, where human beings do not have the strength on their own to resist the deceptions of the devil, called the 'god of this world' (2 Cor. 4:4), 'the power of darkness' (Col. 1:13; Eph. 6:12), 'the tempter' (1 Thess. 3:5) and 'the evil one' (Eph. 6:16; Matt. 5:37; 13:38). The New Testament is redolent with language that speaks of the reality of two kingdoms that offer completely contrasting states of affairs: 'the Father . . . has rescued us from the power of darkness and transferred us into the kingdom of his beloved Son' (Col. 1:12–13; Acts 26:18); 'The kingdom of the world has become the kingdom of our Lord and of his Christ' (Rev. 11:15, NIV); 'The fifth angel poured out his bowl on the throne of the beast, and his kingdom was plunged into darkness' (Rev. 16:10, NIV). The relationship between the two kingdoms is one of permanent hostility, in which no truce and peaceful coexistence is possible (Rev. 17:12–14). The normal situation of human beings living in the world is to be dead to the life of God, seeking to gratify 'the passions of our flesh, following the desires of flesh and senses' (Eph. 2:3). The reality is that human beings follow 'the course of this world (age) . . . [and] the ruler of the power of the air' (Eph. 2:2). They are captive to 'the elemental spirits of the world' (Gal. 4:3; Col. 2:8,20):

> Notwithstanding the lack of attestation from writings earlier than the New Testament, *stoicheia* (elemental spirits) was already being used in the religious syncretism of the first century, in which astrology played so important a part, to denote the astral powers which were believed to influence the destiny of mankind . . . Thus *elemental spirits* is yet another designation for the heavenly powers enumerated in 1:16 and 2:15. The Colossian 'philosophy' required men to do homage to these powers and to accept their authority over at least some areas of human behaviour.[20]

Several times in different letters Paul spells out to his Christian readers how once they were held as prisoners to the spirits of this age (1 Cor. 6:9–11a; Eph. 4:17–19; Rom. 1:21–32). These were influential in shaping 'the wisdom of the world' (1 Cor. 1:20–25) noted for giving prominence to those who wielded influence (*dunatoi*) and who, through superior family origins, enjoyed high status in the community (*eugeneis*) (1 Cor. 1:26). In other words, according to the wisdom of this age, it is considered self-evident that people of wealth, who have the means of wielding social and political dominance, are fortunate. The spirits who control human affairs in this age are clearly smiling on them. The Christian community is to be careful not to yearn for the 'spirit of the world' once it has received 'the Spirit that is from God' (1 Cor. 2:12). It has to

---

[20] G.B. Caird, *Paul's Letters from Prison* (Oxford: OUP, 1976), p. 191.

be careful how it reacts to 'the affairs of the world' (1 Cor. 7:33–4). This may mean that Christians must not assume that they need to conform to the expectations of people who still belong to this age, but must carry out their responsibilities according to the pattern of the new world, shaped by the Spirit of Christ.

Not only is the world a place where human beings constantly fail to resist temptation and sin, it is also the place that exists under the unrelenting judgement of God (Rom. 1:18–32). The 'wrath of God' (Rom. 1:18) is manifest in the freedom that God has given to human beings to choose for themselves what they will believe and how they will act. Paul's account of the Gentile world emphasises the truth that degrading behaviour springs from a false view of what is true. A failure to recognise the reality of a world created and governed by God (ungodliness [*asebeia*]) has led to wickedness (*adikia*). The first step has been to deny what is obvious from observation, namely that the universe owes its existence to an eternal, divine being. There is no other rational explanation for the existence of life, for what is visible had to have a beginning, brought about by that which is invisible (Rom. 1:20). The second step has been to believe in the efficacy of intra-mundane realities to make sense of life and protect people from harm (Rom. 1:23). In other words, the truth about the ultimate reality of existence has been exchanged for a fabricated story.

God's judgement takes the form of allowing human beings the freedom to go on believing the falsehoods that humanity has constructed in the wake of rejecting the truth. In the passage in Romans 1 this is signified in the triple phrase 'God gave them up' (Rom. 1:24,26,28). One might say that God has so respected the liberty with which he endowed his creatures that he has handed them over (*paredoken*) to revel in the choices they have made. It is a judgement, because humanity is now constrained to live out the series of falsehoods about reality that it has created. The key word is exchange (*allasso*/*metallasso*): human beings have exchanged the truth about the world as God's creation, ruled by the laws he has set in place for human flourishing, for a world of their own creation.

The judgement follows a logical progression: human beings have been given the freedom to acknowledge and live by the reality of their status as creatures or to choose to deny their creaturehood by exchanging the real world for one of their own making. Having made the choice to exchange 'the truth about God for a lie' (Rom. 1:25), God says in effect, 'Now live in the world of your choice.' So, the handing over is the consequence of the exchange.[21] The outcome is the register of

---

[21] The connection is made in the use of the conjunctions 'therefore' (Rom. 1:24), 'for this reason' (Rom. 1:26), 'and since' (Rom. 1:28).

degrading passions listed in the rest of the chapter, beginning with 'the exchange' of 'natural intercourse for unnatural' between people of the same gender (Rom. 1:26–7).

Elsewhere, the New Testament uses the word 'futility' a number of times to describe the present condition of the world in its rebellion against its Creator: 'you must no longer live as the Gentiles live, in the futility (*mataiotes*) of their minds' (Eph. 4:17); 'The Lord knows the thoughts of the wise, that they are futile' (1 Cor. 3:20, quoting Ps. 94:11); 'the creation (*ktisis*) was subjected to futility, not of its own will but by the will of the one who subjected it' (Rom. 8:20). The word has a range of meanings, such as emptiness, purposelessness, frustration. There are echoes here of Ecclesiastes, where the Teacher (Qoheleth) attempted to discover through wisdom what could be the meaning of life – 'What do people gain from all the toil at which they toil under the sun?' (Eccl. 1:3). It is well known that he came to the conclusion that, apart from fearing God and keeping his commandments (Eccl. 12:13), 'all was vanity and a chasing after wind, and there was nothing to be gained under the sun' (Eccl. 2:11).

Thus, one could say that God's judgement on human sin takes the form of not constraining people from taking the path that they have willingly chosen. His wrath (or anger) is a settled attitude towards human folly, almost a kind of grief that human beings could be so foolish as to think that by abandoning the Creator's blueprint for their lives they will find fulfilment and contentment.

The world to come

However, the drama of the biblical narrative tells the story of a Creator who has not abandoned his creation, even though the creation has abandoned its Creator. Twice in his letter to the Romans, Paul emphasises, with the emphatic conjunction 'but now (*nuni de*)', the transformation that has occurred as a result of God's direct action: '*But now* . . . the righteousness of God has been disclosed' (Rom. 3:21); '*But now* we are discharged from the law, dead to that which held us captive, so that we are slaves not under the old written code but in the new life of the Spirit' (Rom. 7:6). This signals a point of transition from one reality to another. Through 'the sacrifice of atonement' (Rom. 3:25), God's judgement is turned into God's justification of the foolish sinner: his justice is satisfied and his mercy and forgiveness are available to restore the broken relationship that has occurred as a result of humans choosing to follow their own wisdom, rather than the wisdom of God.

A new reality has come into being: 'new life of the Spirit' (Rom. 7:6; 8:2–4,9,11). The gift of the Spirit is a foretaste of a whole new creation.

In many ways, Paul's understanding of the gift of the Spirit has this future-oriented focus. The Holy Spirit is 'the pledge (*arrabon*) of our inheritance towards redemption as God's own people' (Eph. 1:14). In other words, the possession of the Spirit of Christ is a guarantee that God 'who began a good work among you [believers] will bring it to completion by the day of Jesus Christ' (Phil. 1:6):

> In the present the Spirit is simultaneously a portion of the life and power of the future age, and a sign pointing beyond the present, telling believers that the fullness of the messianic age has not yet arrived . . . The Spirit is himself an in-breaking of the powers of the age to come and a guarantee of the reality of that age together with the believer's part in it.[22]

It is not surprising that the Spirit is the inspirer of hope (Rom. 15:13) in the final transformation of this present world into a world filled with the glory of God in the full presence of Jesus Christ (Titus 2:13–14). Hope is a distinctive Christian feature, for it speaks of what will be one day, in spite of the evidence that may point in another direction: 'we ourselves, who have the first fruits of the Spirit, groan inwardly while we wait for adoption, the redemption of our bodies. For in hope we were saved. Now hope that is seen is not hope . . . if we hope for what we do not see, we wait for it with patience' (Rom. 8:23–5): 'This hope is a confidence that believers will not be disappointed, that the down payment of the Spirit will indeed be one day confirmed by participation in God's glory and in the renewal of all creation.'[23]

When speaking of the world to come, the New Testament writers never use the word *kosmos*. They speak instead of new creation (*ktisis*) (Gal. 6:15–16; Eph. 2:14–16) and of the age to come (Eph. 1:21; 2:7; Matt. 12:32; Mark 10:30; Luke 20:34–5; Heb. 6:5). The use of both *ktisis* and *aion* underline the continuity between the first and second creations. God did not decide to demolish the universe and start again, but to 'purge, purify and renew the whole creation'.[24] There will be a process of destruction, likened to the perishing of the world through the flood (2 Pet. 3:6). However, this time the means of destruction will not be water, but fire (2 Pet. 3:7). The present heavens and earth will give way to a recreated universe; only this time it will not be *ex nihilo*, for all that has remained of the goodness of the original creation will be found in the recreated city of God (Rev. 21:26). The physical resurrection of Jesus guarantees a

---

[22] Gerald F. Hawthorne, Ralph P. Martin and Daniel G. Reid, eds. *Dictionary of Paul and His Letters* (Downers Grove, IL: IVP, 1993), p. 411.

[23] Hawthorne et al., *Dictionary of Paul*, p. 411.

[24] Christopher Wright, 'World in the Bible', p. 217.

transformed material existence in the new earth. The whole of human reality will be redeemed – spirit, mind and body. So the contrast between the old and the new is not between the material and the spiritual, or even between time and eternity, but between sin and holiness: 'nothing unclean will enter it' (Rev. 21:27); 'we wait for new heavens and a new earth, where righteousness is at home' (2 Pet. 3:13):

> 'The world to come' . . . will not be a blank sheet, with all that humanity has accomplished in fulfilment of the creation mandate simply crumpled up and tossed in a cosmic incinerator. Rather it will take that accomplishment, purged and disinfected of all the poison and corruption of our fallenness, as the starting point of an unimaginable future – an eternity of new creation and creativity.[25]

The world in the Johannine writings

Due to the fact that the use of the vocabulary for 'world' is so extensive and prominent in the Gospel and Letters of John, it is appropriate to consider them in a separate section. Undoubtedly there are aspects and nuances of the use of the concept that are peculiar to John, and therefore deserve to be treated separately.

A literal sense
As elsewhere in the Scriptures of both Testaments, the world comprises the whole created universe: 'all things came into being through him [the Word]' (John 1:2). More particularly it refers to the whole inhabited planet: 'The true light . . . was coming into the world. He was in the world' (John 1:9–10). It also is used of the human world, the world of social interaction: 'As you have sent me into the world, so I have sent them into the world' (John 17:18); 'that the world may know that you have sent me' (John 17:23); 'he is the atoning sacrifice for our sins, and not for ours only but also for the sins of the whole world' (1 John 2:2). Occasionally, John also uses the word earth (*ge*) as a synonym: 'I glorified you on earth' (John 17:4); 'when I am lifted up from the earth' (John 12:32). However, the occurrence of the world in this general sense is limited. The vast majority of instances of its use in John's writings is of a different order.

A metaphorical sense
So, almost universally, when John refers to the world he is depicting humanity in its opposition to the plans and purposes of God. It is a

---

25 Christopher Wright, 'World in the Bible', p. 218.

sphere of unbelief.[26] It is a worldly system opposed to God: 'The world is human society as it is structured in opposition to Christ and the followers of Christ.'[27]

The world opposes God and resists the redeeming work of God's Son. It not only does not believe in him, but actually hates him: 'The world . . . hates me because I testify against it that its works are evil' (John 7:7); 'If the world hates you, be aware that it hated me before it hated you' (John 15:18). The human world, in its resistance to the Father and hostility to the Son is actually ruled by the ruler of this *kosmos*: 'now the ruler (*arkon*) of this world will be driven out' (John 12:31); 'the ruler of this world has been condemned' (John 16:11); 'We know . . . that the whole world lies under the power of the evil one' (1 John 5:19).

In the Prologue to the Gospel of John, there is a dramatic shift of emphasis between verses 10a and 10b. In the beginning of all things, there was God and there was the Word. They belonged inseparably together. All matter throughout the universe owes its existence exclusively to the initiative and creative power of God through his Word. There is no other pre-existent being. He brought life into existence through his own life-giving power, and this life was the one and only means of interpreting the significance of the created order. 'The light [illumination] shines in the darkness [uncertainty], and the darkness did not overcome it' (John 1:5).

A prophetic word was made available through 'a man sent from God, whose name was John' (John 1:6). The lesser word testified to the greater Word (John 1:15) that this was indeed 'the true light, which enlightens everyone, [and he] was coming into the world' (John 1:9). In other words his nature and identity were in the process of being revealed.

Nevertheless, 'the world did not know him' (John 1:10b), even though he was the life and light of all people. Even more surprising, he was born as one of the people that God had chosen in a special way to represent him to the nations, and yet this people ('his own') did not accept him (John 1:11). In this respect, they behaved no differently from the non-Jewish world. His coming into the world, then, set up a new kind of division: not based on any ethnic or cultural distinctions (John 1:13), but on reception or rejection (John 1:11–12). This contrast remains constant throughout the Johannine writings.

---

[26]   Okure, *Johannine Approach to Mission*, p. 199.

[27]   Johannes Nissen, 'Mission in the Fourth Gospel: Historical and Hermeneutical Perspectives', in *New Readings in John: Literary and Theological Perspectives* (ed. Johannes Nissen and Sigfred Pedersen; Sheffield: Sheffield Academic Press, 1999), p. 217.

The world in defiance of God and the ones he has sent

The world is 'consistently characterised as a dark place, alienated from God . . . It is in bondage to sin'.[28] It is blind (John 9:39–41) and unregenerate (John 3:3,5), a world that resists God's life-giving purposes. This is because it has accepted another ruler to whom it gives allegiance. Its peace, then, is contrary to the peace or wholeness that God provides. It is a travesty of God's *shalom*: 'my peace I give to you. I do not give to you as the world gives' (John 14:27). Here there may be an implied criticism of the *pax romana*, seen as an unjust imperial order: 'The world, then, comprises the hierarchical, unjust society that the ruling authorities have established for their own benefit and defend with violence (John 18:36).'[29]

In John's first letter, there are twenty-two references to the world; all but three of them are negative:

> Do not love the world . . . The love of the Father is not in those who love the world; for all that is in the world – the desire of the flesh, the desire of the eyes, the pride in riches – comes not from the Father but from the world. And the world and its desires are passing away. (1 John 2:15–17)

Here there is a clear reference to a sphere of activity that absorbs the energies, motivates the activities and controls the desires of human life in ways which are inimical to the wholesome and worthy purposes of God. The world's problems stem from the fact that those who belong to the world do not know God (1 John 3:1), believe in false prophets that 'have gone out into the world' (1 John 4:1), who are controlled by the 'spirit of the antichrist . . . [which is] already in the world' (1 John 4:3). This world has to be conquered or overcome; otherwise it will draw the children of God away from God's life-enhancing gifts. The instrument with which the world may be rendered ineffective is faith in the reality of Jesus, the Son of God (1 John 5:4–5), sent to be the Saviour of the world (1 John 4:14) and to destroy the works of the devil (1 John 3:8).

So the world is a place where God, present in human affairs, is engaged in a contest with spiritual powers that enslave human beings: 'You are from (belong to – NIV) your father the devil, and you choose to do your father's desires. He was a murderer from the beginning and does not stand in the truth, because there is no truth in him. When he lies, he speaks according to his own nature, for he is a liar and the father of lies' (John 8:44–5).

---

[28] Andreas J. Kostenberger, *The Missions of Jesus and the Disciples According to the Fourth Gospel* (Grand Rapids, MI: Eerdmans, 1998), p. 187.

[29] Warren Carter, *John: Storyteller, Interpreter, Evangelist* (Peabody: Hendrickson Publishers, 2006), p. 91.

In this passage John refers to two families: the family of God, through faithful Abraham, and the family of the devil. They are divided from one another on the basis of whether they accept that Jesus is from God and his words are true, or not: 'Whoever is from God hears the words of God. The reason you do not hear them is that you are not from God' (John 8:47). So, the world is divided between those born of the Word and Spirit of God and those born of the devil (1 John 4:4–6): 'They who surrender themselves to the father of lies render themselves insensible to the truth, and so manifest their real paternity.'[30]

There is a clear demonology throughout the New Testament. It is also explicit in John's writings.

> This diagnosis of man's plight in the world cannot simply be dismissed as stemming out of the apocalyptic speculation that was common among the Jews of New Testament times. As Emil Stauffer says, 'In primitive Christianity there is no theology without demonology . . . ' We have lost sight of the demonic nature of the whole spiritual environment that conditions man's thought and conduct.[31]

When faced with the truth of Jesus Christ, the world as it were 'turns a blind eye'; it cannot see what is in front of it. The tragedy is that it believes that it understands well what is true and false, what is good and bad. Yet the world is blind, precisely because it claims to be able to see and yet fails to recognise God's Messiah in its midst (John 9:39–41). As long as the world holds to its own version of reality, it is in control. Sadly, however, it completely misses the true nature of things. Only by submitting to the truth transmitted from the Father by the Son, who is 'Lord and Teacher' (John 13:14) will its eyes be open again. This is the world for which Jesus does not pray (John 17:9), and to which he cannot reveal himself, because of its resistance to him and his Spirit (John 7:3–8; 8:23; 17:16).

It is not surprising that, as the world hates the Son, so it also will hate the one whom the Son sends in his name (John 15:18; 17:14; 1 John 3:13). Antagonism from the world is grounded in the disciples' non-alliance with the world. This is exacerbated by the fact that Jesus chooses them 'out of the world' (John 15:16a,19). Since the world persecuted Jesus, it will also persecute his followers (John 15:20b). Symbolic of this victimization is the act of being expelled from the synagogues (John 16:2a; 9:22,34; 12:42).[32] It is worth noting that 'in chapters 14–16 of the last discourse,

---

[30] George R. Beasley-Murray, *John* (Word Biblical Commentary 36) (Milton Keynes: Word Books, 1991), p. 136.

[31] Padilla, *Mission Between the Times*, pp. 6–7.

[32] For this section, see Tan Yak-Hwee, *Re-Presenting the Johannine Community: A Postcolonial Perspective* (New York: Peter Lang, 2008), pp. 144–7.

which foresees a time after Jesus' departure, the term *Ioudaioi* (Jews) does not occur'.[33] So, 'while the Johannine school reflects on the traditions of the narratives that it transmits, the question of Israel is no longer at the centre of its concern . . . the polemic front in relation to which it constructs the Christian identity'.[34]

The world as the object of God's love

In spite of the world's opposition to God's good purposes for its life and wellbeing, his constant, gratuitous love for what he has created has found a way of offering it a new beginning. In the most often quoted verse of the whole Gospel of John (3:16), the meaning and extent of this love is spelt out: God sends his Son into the world to offer to all humanity eternal life rather than death. He takes the initiative to save it from its self-selected destruction and transform it (John 3:17). Jesus is the agent of this salvation (John 4:42; 1 John 4:14), who has laid down his life (John 10:17–18; 1 John 3:16), in order to take away the world's sin (John 1:29). He is the bread and water of life, who alone can quench the hunger and thirst of those dissatisfied with mere religious observance (John 6:35; 7:37–8; 4:23–4,39–42).

So, God has done all that could possibly be expected, and all that is necessary, to rescue the world from its blindness and its inability to save itself. Although the world deserves judgement, for it has had plenty of opportunity to listen to the testimonies to the truth and see the signs that point to God's active involvement in the world, Jesus Christ has not come to condemn the world (John 3:17). His purpose has been to give the world every opportunity to believe and be saved.

However, the world is faced with a choice between life and death (see Deut. 30:15,19–20). If they choose to turn their back on God's offer of life (John 6:66–7), they condemn themselves (John 3:18). This is the way that God's judgement works on a world that continues to go its own way: 'And this is the judgement, that the light has come into the world, and people loved darkness rather than light because their deeds were evil. For all who do evil hate the light and do not come to the light, so that their deeds may not be exposed' (John 3:19–20).

The self-inflicted judgement is that the world remains in its sin, ignorant of the transforming new life that it could enjoy. Although it believes itself to be free, and not subservient to anyone (John 8:33), it remains a

---

[33] Raymond E. Brown, *An Introduction to the Gospel of John* (New York: Doubleday, 2003), p. 478.
[34] J. Zumstein, 'The Farewell Discourses (John 13.1–16.33) and the Problem of Anti-Judaism' in *Anti-Judaism in the Fourth Gospel* (ed. Reimund Bieringer; Assen: van Gorcum, 2001), p. 478.

slave to sin and in the grip of lies that it wishes to believe. Whereas, 'the
Son of God has come and has given us understanding so that we may
know him who is true . . . his Son Jesus Christ' (1 John 5:20), 'the whole
world lies under the power of the evil one' (1 John 5:19).

> The tragedy of so many in John's day (and in ours) is that they have been
> so wise in their own estimation that they have rejected the ways of God and
> have set up their own way as the way to life. Jesus pointed out that some of
> his hearers did not really 'seek the glory that is from the only God' (5:44); they
> did not 'have the love of God in themselves' (5:42).[35]

Jesus' kingship is not of this world

The clash between the loving and gracious purposes of God and the world,
in its refusal to hear and obey the truth as manifest in the coming of God's
Word into the world, comes to its climax in the events leading up to the crucifixion of Jesus. Immediately after the raising of Lazarus (John 11:43–7a), the
Jewish leaders in Jerusalem called a meeting of the Sanhedrin, 'the supreme
Jewish religious, political and legal council in Jerusalem'.[36] The agenda was
to find a convenient way of either silencing or getting rid of Jesus altogether.
The leaders saw themselves in danger of losing their power and authority
because of the popular following that Jesus was attracting: 'This man is
performing many signs. If we let him go on like this, everyone will believe
in him' (John 11:47–8). They were faced with an enormous dilemma: how
to do away with a person who posed a threat to their rule, and yet had
committed no crime worthy of the death penalty (John 8:46).The answer
had to be the trumped-up charge of presenting a danger to the Roman
forces of occupation (John 11:48). In any case, they needed the sanction of
the Roman procurator to have Jesus put to death (John 18:31).

So after Jesus' final entry into Jerusalem, six days before the Passover (John 12:1), and directly following the Passover meal, which Jesus
celebrated with his disciples, the chief priests and the Pharisees sent a
contingent of soldiers and police to arrest Jesus (John 18:3,12). It was late
at night (John 13:30). After a summary hearing before Annas (the high
priest's father-in-law) and Caiaphas (the high priest), Jesus was brought
to Pilate's headquarters (the praetorium). It was early in the morning
(John 18:28), at the time of the first cock-crow (John 18:27).

The so-called trial before Pontius Pilate (in reality a dialogue between
Pilate and Jesus, interspersed with the clamour of the Jerusalem leaders

---

[35] Leon Morris, *Jesus is the Christ: Studies in the Theology of John* (Grand Rapids,
MI: Eerdmans, 1989), p. 128.

[36] Craig A. Evans and Stanley E. Porter, *Dictionary of New Testament Background*
(Downers Grove, IL: IVP, 2000), p. 1061.

and the 'rent-a-mob' they had assembled for the purpose of calling for
his crucifixion) proved to be a remarkable piece of drama. Pilate began
proceedings by asking whether Jesus claimed to be the king of the Jews
(John 18:33). Presumably this title was used by the Sanhedrin to impress
Pilate with the reality that Jesus was a dangerous, subversive liability. In
point of fact, their real grievance was that Jesus claimed to be the Son of
God, thereby committing blasphemy and deserving to die (John 19:7).
Now, the title Son of God might also have been interpreted as a threat to
Roman hegemony, seeing that the emperor was regarded as *divi filius* (son
of the divine). Either way, whether king of the Jews or Son of God, they
were able to portray Jesus as an unacceptable risk to the authority of Rome.

It is in this context that Jesus uttered the famous words, 'My kingdom
is not from (*ek*) this world . . . my kingdom is not from here (*enteuthen*)'
(John 18:36). If taken on its own as an isolated saying, it could possibly be
interpreted as meaning that Jesus' kingdom has little or nothing to do with
this world but refers to an inner kingdom of the individual heart where
God reigns. This is not, however, what Jesus has in mind. Jews of the first
century would not have understood the *malkuth YHWH* in these terms.
In fact, Jesus clarifies exactly what he means in the conditional clause that
follows: 'If my kingdom were from (*ek*) this world, my followers would
be fighting to keep me from being handed over to the Jews.' There are
two kinds of logic at work: the logic of Barabbas, the Jewish leaders and
the Roman Empire that violence is a legitimate means of advancing one's
cause in the world, and the logic of Jesus that human-animated violence
is inimical to God's sovereign presence in the world:

> One can imagine what might have happened. Jesus sanctions a violent response
> to his arrest. There is a skirmish at the foot of the Mount of Olives. One or two
> of the disciples are killed. Jesus is arrested and tried for sedition. This time,
> however, it is for real. In terms of the political reality of the day, his crucifixion
> would have been the result of his own folly. There is little doubt that no more
> would have been heard of him. If the kingdom of God represents a new order of
> living it is inconceivable that it functions on the basis of the old order of forced
> compliance. Hence the sequence of commands, 'love your enemies, do good to
> those who hate you, bless those who curse you, pray for those who abuse you'
> (Luke. 6.27–28), is the only possible way of living in this kingdom.[37]

Now, some have interpreted Jesus' saying to imply that the early church
had a dualist understanding of the two kinds of kingship (that of Jesus

---

[37] J. Andrew Kirk, *Civilisations in Conflict? Islam, the West and Christian Faith*
(Oxford: Regnum International, 2010), pp. 69–70.

and that of Caesar), each with its proper sphere of authority (understood as heaven and earth or the inner life of the individual and the public world of the state). As neither overlaps the other, there is no conflict. So Johannine Christians are not rivals or enemies of Roman power, but faithful citizens of both worlds. The charges against Jesus are not genuinely political but are false accusations designed to manipulate Pilate. In truth, the Roman Empire has no good grounds for persecuting Christians.[38]

On the other hand, another reading of the passage, which still emphasises its political implications, maintains that the point of the passage is to distinguish between the rule of force by Rome and the peaceable kingdom of Jesus. In other words, the conflict between his kingdom and the kingdoms of this world is not carried out on the world's terms. Jesus' followers cannot establish his kingdom by coercion of any kind. Their weapon is to bear witness to the truth: 'You say that I am a king. For this I was born, and for this I came into the world, to testify to the truth' (John 18:37). To Pilate's question, 'What is truth?' the implied answer is Jesus' teaching (John 8:31–2).

There is not even a hint of dualism in this passage. Nowhere in John's Gospel does Jesus deny being a king; only that, given the misunderstandings surrounding the notion (John 6:15), he is very careful to distance himself from the normal interpretation. His kingdom is not established by any worldly power, but by the power of God. The authority and power of Caesar and his representatives are derivative, limited to the earthly sphere and intended to be used in the service of God: 'You would have no power over me unless it had been given you from above' (John 19:11).

'Jesus challenges Rome, not as a rival to Caesar on earth, nor as a ruler in heaven instead of on the earth, but instead as his superior, ruling both heaven *and* earth.'[39] It appears, therefore, that the contrast between the two kingdoms is intended also as a critique of the way in which the kingdom, which is from this world, operates: 'The Jerusalem leaders and their allies, committed to maintaining a social structure contrary to God's purposes, are "of this world" (John 8:23).'[40] This accounts for the fact that they did not understand the significance of his message (John 8:27).

---

[38] This argument is set out in Lance Byron Richey, *Roman Imperial Ideology and the Gospel of John* (Washington: Catholic Biblical Association of America, 2007), pp. 158–9.

[39] Richey, *Roman Imperial Ideology*, p. 164.

[40] Carter, *John: Storyteller*, p. 92.

2

'The Ends of the World': The Meaning and Scope of Mission in the Old Testament

On the Mission Calling of God's Chosen People

In a study of the relation of the church to the world, a high priority has to be given to the nature, meaning and scope of its mission in the world. This chapter and the next will focus on a survey of the most closely related biblical material. Such a task is not altogether straightforward. The notion of mission (in some circles articulated as missions) is contested. Many definitions have been attempted. I have suggested the following: 'The Church's self-understanding and sense of identity (its ecclesiology) is inherently bound up with its call to share and live out the Gospel of Jesus Christ to the ends of the earth and the end of time.'[1] 'By mission I mean the imperative laid upon the Christian community to communicate, through life and words, the transforming good news of Jesus Christ as set forth in the apostolic testimony of the New Testament.'[2]

Lesslie Newbigin understands mission in the following terms: 'Mission . . . is faith in action. It is the acting out by proclamation and by endurance, through all the events of history, of the faith that the kingdom of God has drawn near.'[3]

The World Council of Churches has set out its interpretation in the following words: 'The Church is sent into the world to call people and nations to repentance, to announce forgiveness of sin and a

---

[1] J. Andrew Kirk, *What is Mission? Theological Explorations* (London: Darton, Longman & Todd, 1999), p. 30.

[2] J. Andrew Kirk, 'Christian Mission in Multifaith Situations', in *Theology and the Religions: A Dialogue* (ed. Viggo Mortensen; Grand Rapids, MI: Eerdmans, 2003), p. 154.

[3] Lesslie Newbigin, *The Open Secret* (London: SPCK, 2nd edn, 1995), p. 39.

new beginning in relations with God and neighbours through Jesus Christ.'[4]

Mission possesses several indispensable elements. It means communicating a particular message to all who will hear. It implies a style of life that gives evidence for the truth of the message. It involves going to every corner of the globe, wherever people live, to share with them the good news that the conflict and confusion caused by human self-interest has been resolved by God in an act of astonishing self-sacrifice. It implies creating new communities of people who desire to live out together the demands of being a follower of Jesus Christ and to enjoy a new life under the control of God's rule.

Questions of Procedure

The subject matter of these two chapters is vast in scope.[5] An attempt to cover adequately the relevant biblical material and issues in such a short space may be foolhardy and is probably unachievable. Nevertheless, given the overall theme of the book, it would be inconceivable not to make an effort to cover as much of the ground as is feasible. Therefore, I will endeavour to make reference to the major features usually covered under the heading of the Bible and mission. Limited space means that some issues of historical reconstruction that are alleged to underlie the texts in their final canonical form cannot be pursued; nevertheless, one or two will have to be addressed, because they are so central to understanding the topic. By and large, I will take the Bible at face value and allow it to interpret itself.[6]

As many people writing on the subject have pointed out, the mission of the people of God cannot be made to depend on a number of isolated

---

[4] WCC, 'Preface' to *Mission and Evangelism: An Ecumenical Affirmation* (Geneva: WCC, 1983).

[5] Eckhard Schnabel, for example, has recently written three volumes on Christian mission in the church's earliest period. Each volume runs to 400 to 500 pages; see *Early Christian Mission* (2 vols; Downers Grove, IL: IVP, 2004); *Paul the Missionary: Realities, Strategies and Methods* (Nottingham: IVP, 2008).

[6] If anyone is interested in discovering in more detail the way I approach the interpretation of the Bible with reference to the theme of mission, they can read J. Andrew Kirk, *God's Word for a Complex World: Discovering how the Bible Speaks Today* (Basingstoke: Marshall Pickering, 1987) and the article J. Andrew Kirk, 'How a Missiologist Utilizes the Bible' in *Bible and Mission: A Conversation between Biblical Studies and Missiology* (ed. Rollin G. Grams, I. Howard Marshall, Peter F. Penner and Robin Routledge; Schwarzenfeld: Neufeld Verlag, 2008), pp. 246–68.

texts, however much influence they may have had on the church's missionary self-awareness. Of these texts, the so-called Great Commission in its various forms, found at the end of each of the gospels, is the most significant. These passages will be assessed further on for their contribution to a biblical perspective on mission. For the moment it is sufficient to emphasise that the whole Bible has to be taken into account in its portrayal of the missionary implications of God's activity in history for the salvation of the world: 'We consider it of great importance that a "theology of mission" be based not only on the narrow strip of some "missionary texts", but on the whole witness of both the Old and New Testament.'[7]

> To read only Luke-Acts, to discover procedures and criteria for planting churches, ignores other New Testament witnesses. To concentrate solely on the classical prophets as a means of buttressing strategies of social transformation and liberation precludes the complex witness of Jesus in the synoptic Gospels. And to direct one's motivation wholly to the Great Commission in Matthew 28 without looking into the complexity of experience attested to by Paul in Romans 9–11 makes for superficial missionary activity.[8]

The Scope of Mission

Among both biblical scholars and missiologists it is becoming increasingly recognised that the Bible is a missionary book through and through. At the risk of over-generalizing, at least in its New Testament section, it is a collection of treatises written by missionaries for missionaries about the missionary activity of God the Father through the Son and the Spirit: 'The Bible is a kind of project aimed at the kingdom of God, that is, towards the achievement of God's purposes for good in the whole of God's creation.'[9]

The kingdom of God is nothing else but the rightful exercise of God's dominion over everything that he has brought into being and is in the process of reshaping so that it reflects his just, compassionate and faithful character:

[7] Johannes Blauw, *The Missionary Nature of the Church: A Survey of the Biblical Theology of Mission* (Guildford: Lutterworth Press, 1974), p. 16.
[8] Robert J. Schreiter, 'Foreword', in *The Biblical Foundations for Mission* (Donald Senior and Carroll Stuhlmueller; London: SCM Press, 1983), p. xi.
[9] Richard Bauckham, *Bible and Mission: Christian Witness in a Postmodern World* (Carlisle: Paternoster Press, 2003), p. 11.

All your works shall give thanks to you, O LORD . . . They shall speak of the glory of your kingdom, and tell of your power . . . Your kingdom is an ever-lasting kingdom, and your dominion endures throughout all generations. (Ps. 145:10,11,13)

Then comes the end, when he [Christ] hands over the kingdom to God the Father, after he has destroyed every ruler and every authority and power. For he must reign until he has put all his enemies under his feet. (1 Cor. 15:24–5)

Thus, God's mission has to encompass the activities of creation, salvation and the consummation of the 'history of time'. It consists of God's project to restore creation to its original wholeness and excellence by eliminating all that has corrupted and deformed it, regenerating it and bringing it to perfection.[10] Because of the intricate unity of the whole biblical story, it is possible to begin at the beginning and read the narrative forwards, or to begin at the end and read the narrative backwards in the light of the final drama.[11] So, mission in the light of the biblical text is seen in the context of the whole created order, the unity and diversity of humanity (one stock, many peoples), the formation of a special community (given the task of listening to and transmitting God's revelation to all the other communities living on earth), the salvific life and work of God's anointed Son and Servant, and the ingathering of the nations into the new creation.

Mission Before the Coming of Jesus Christ

The covenant with creation

Creation itself is the first part of God's missionary activity; God begins by establishing a covenant with the entire universe, and especially with that minute portion of it that we refer to as the planet earth. The universe is the necessary context for life to have been able to come into existence. Unless events, since the original explosion that brought matter into being and flung it into the immense depths of space, had occurred in exactly the way it did, human beings would not be around to contemplate and

---

[10] For this reason, Howard Peskett and Vinoth Ramachandra in their book, *The Message of Mission* (Leicester: IVP, 2003), are right in beginning their study (ch. 1) with a contemplation of Christ's glory as co-creator, and reconciler of all things, as set out in Col. 1:15–23.

[11] Reading history backwards is an excellent way of understanding how contemporary events have been shaped in particular ways.

use to their benefit their living environment.[12] According to the story of creation in Genesis 1, each act of formation was preceded by a deliberate decision on the part of God, 'Let there be . . .'; the climax comes at the end of the passage, 'Let us make . . . ' (Gen. 1:26).

Although the creation narratives do not use the terminology of covenant, the terms of such an arrangement are implied in the various mandates given to the first human beings:

> Be fruitful and multiply, and fill the earth and subdue it; and have dominion over the fish of the sea and over the birds of the air and over every living thing that moves on the earth. (Gen. 1:28)

> The LORD God took the man and put him in the garden of Eden to till it and keep it . . . The LORD God formed every animal of the field and every bird of the air, and brought them to the man to see what he would call them; and whatever the man called each living creature, that was its name' (Gen. 2:15,19).[13]

After the disaster of humankind's rebellion against the purposes of God, and thus against its own nature and vocation, God renewed his covenant with the created order. The first reference to a covenant between God and the earth comes in the story of Noah: 'As for me, I am establishing my covenant with you and your descendants after you, and with every living creature' (Gen. 9:9; also 6:18).

The covenant has two main clauses: first, in spite of the evil inclination of the human heart, God promises never again to curse the ground (Gen. 8:21); second, God pledges never again to destroy every living creature by means of a flood (Gen. 8:21; 9:11). The features of this covenant were that it was established entirely by God's initiative; it was unconditional and unlimited, universal and eternal. So the covenant is made with all the living inhabitants of the earth.[14] The sign of its existence is the rainbow, which reminds God of his promise (Gen. 9:14–17); it can also be seen by human beings who are able to interpret its significance:

---

[12] On the amazing precision required, only one millionth of a second after the 'big bang', for the universe to persist and produce the necessary conditions for life (known as 'fine tuning' and 'the anthropic principle'), see Alister E. McGrath, *Surprised by Meaning: Science, Faith and How We Make Sense of Things* (Louisville: Westminster John Knox Press, 2011), pp. 58–65

[13] The man also gave a name to his special companion: woman (*ishshah*).

[14] Ps. 104 seems to reflect God's covenant to 'set the earth on its foundations, so that it shall never be shaken' (v. 5) and to 'renew the face of the ground' (v. 30).

Humankind sets out under the rainbow arch which is the sacrament of the primal covenant with all humankind and with the created world for humanity's sake. Noah is told to be fruitful and multiply and replenish the earth.[15]

Yahweh's covenant commitment to and redemptive purposes for creation, embodied in the Noahic covenant, provides the basis and pattern for all his redemptive dealings, including with Israel, whose religious life expresses, in microcosm, God's purpose for the whole created order.[16]

The episode of the flood is part of what many commentators call 'pre-history', meaning the events leading up to the call of Abraham to migrate to a new territory that would eventually belong to his descendants (Gen. 12:7). It is essential to read the Abraham story in the light of these prior events, as God's concern is with all that he has made. Thus immediately after the flood narrative, the reader is introduced to the 'table of the nations' (Gen. 10). And when Abraham is introduced, it is specifically stated that he will be a blessing (Gen. 12:2) to all the nations (Gen. 22:18). From then on, in all sorts of different ways, the nations accompany the history of Israel as a permanent backdrop.

The covenant through Abraham

The text does not tell us why God, in order to begin a new chapter in the saga of the human race, chose to reveal himself specifically to Abraham. It appears that Abraham's father, Terah, for undisclosed reasons, decided to emigrate from his home in Ur and settle in the land of Canaan (Gen. 11:31). However, he and his family never made it. They stopped on the way in Haran, a trading centre in North Mesopotamia. There Terah died, and from there Abraham was called to resume the journey to the land of Canaan (Gen. 12:4–5).

Undoubtedly the call of Abraham to leave his settled way of life and move to an altogether different land has great significance for the rest of the biblical narrative. The story is shot through with purpose. Thus, the threefold 'go from . . .' ('your country, your kindred and your father's house') is matched by a threefold 'so that . . .' ('I may make you a great nation', 'I may make your name great and be a blessing', and 'I may bless

---

[15] Newbigin, *Open Secret*, p. 31.

[16] Robin Routledge, 'Mission and Covenant in the Old Testament' in *Bible and Mission: Christian Witness in a Postmodern World* (ed. Richard Bauckham; Carlisle: Paternoster Press, 2003), p. 8.

those who bless you' [see Gen. 12:1–3]).[17] The repeated blessing formula (Gen. 12:2–3) is a reminder of the creation narrative: 'God blessed them [the male and the female]' (Gen. 1:28); 'God blessed the seventh day and hallowed it' (Gen. 2:3).

God's creative intention was to place human beings in an environment rich in resources. The blessings referred to the progeny that would be born, to the work that would be required to bring the earth into a good and fruitful shape and to the weekly rhythm of work and leisure. The blessings to Abraham signified his role in being an agent by whom God would reverse the curse that followed Adam and Eve's act of folly in thinking they could be free from the limits of self-will set by God's purpose for them. So, in Abraham 'all the families of the earth shall be blessed' (Gen. 12:3).

In the context of the nations, some of which inhabited the land to which Abraham and Sarah and their household had moved (Gen. 12:6), Abraham is to bear witness to the righteousness and justice that the Lord requires (Gen. 18:19). The people living in the twin towns of Sodom and Gomorrah, however, had excelled themselves in the corrupt and depraved way of life that they habitually followed. From now on Abraham is called to give an example of a completely different way of living, in which righteousness is to be distinguished absolutely from wickedness (Gen. 18:25). The Lord's response to his eloquent plea not to judge the cities, in order that Lot and his family may not be destroyed, shows God's mercy and the blessing that even ten righteous people may be amidst so much perversion (Gen. 18:32).

Although this new departure in God's dealings with his creation is marked by the choice of one particular person to be the father of a great nation, it is unequivocally set in the wider context of all the inhabitants of the world. God now sets his sights on reaching the nations through a people specially chosen to serve his purposes of justice and mercy to all.

The covenant through Moses

The covenant with the Hebrew people, which took place at Sinai at 'the third moon after the Israelites had gone out of the land of Egypt' (Exod. 19:1), consolidated the particular mission God was calling them to as an integrated community. It comes as the climax to the story of the people's great escape from the oppression they suffered at the hand of the Egyptians; it is followed by the giving of God's law and regulations for their life as a new nation in formation.

---

[17] See Peskett and Ramachandra, *Message of Mission*, p. 90. The purpose clauses are not indicated in the NRSV, NIV or Jerusalem Bible, so the reader of these translations does not receive the full force of the construction.

Having delivered the descendants of the patriarchs from a situation of abject (racial) subordination and victimization and revealed himself as the God of their forebears (Exod. 3:6), God now sets out his proposals for this new-found community. This is a new step signalled by a fresh revelation of God's name – 'I AM WHO I AM' and 'the LORD (YHWH)': 'This is my name for ever, and this is my title for all generations' (Exod. 3:14–15; 6:2–3). It is also placed in the context of the covenant made with Abraham 'to give them the land of Canaan, the land in which they [had] resided as aliens' (Exod. 6:4) and the decision to liberate them from the harsh cruelty they were undergoing as aliens among another people: 'I have also heard the groaning of the Israelites, whom the Egyptians are holding as slaves, and I have remembered my covenant . . . I am the LORD, and I will free you from . . . slavery to them. I will redeem you with an outstretched arm and with mighty acts of judgement' (Exod. 6:5–6).

The terms of the covenant are set out by the senior partner. On the one hand, the people's responsibility is to obey the voice of God and keep his covenant. On the other hand, God will treat the people as his 'treasured possession out of all the peoples' (Exod. 19:5). He then sets out the vocation to which he is calling them: 'You shall be for me a priestly kingdom and a holy nation' (Exod. 19:6).

As a result of God's decision to put an end to the suffering of a people descended from Abraham through Isaac and Jacob, in remembrance of a former covenant and in token of his mighty intervention to rescue them from a position of powerlessness, God sets them on the path of his mission.

The historical task assigned to them has three main dimensions: missiological, liturgical and ethical. As a kingdom of priests, the people are responsible for revealing to the nations the law of the Lord (Mal. 2:7); making known to the whole world the true nature of God and the conditions he has set down for a fruitful and abundant life. They are also responsible for interceding on behalf of the nations and, in the sacrificial system, for bearing witness to the truth that without atonement there is no release from the burden and guilt of sin:

> The dual movement in the priestly role (from God to people and from people to God) is reflected in prophetic visions concerning the nations . . . There would be a going out from God and a coming in to God . . . The priesthood of the people of God is thus a missional function that stands in continuity with their Abrahamic election, and it affects the nations.[18]

___

[18] Christopher J.H. Wright, *The Mission of God: Unlocking the Bible's Grand Narrative* (Nottingham: IVP, 2006), p. 331.

As well as being called to be a kingdom of priests, Israel is also assigned the task of being a holy nation, witnessing to God's holiness in the midst of the nations' corruption and decadence, for 'the whole earth is mine' (Exod. 19:5). The call to holiness is reflected in the struggle for a true concept of God in relation to the delusions by which the nations served images of gods that were no gods. Israel was to be a people that demonstrated a distinctive way of life that reflected God's intention in creating and redeeming humankind.

Some of the main elements of a holy way of living are set out in short commands in Leviticus 19, including 'economic generosity in agriculture' (vv. 9–10), 'economic justice in employment rights' (v. 13), 'social compassion to the disabled' (v. 14), 'judicial integrity in the legal system' (vv. 12,15), 'sexual integrity' (vv. 20–22,29), 'practical love for the alien' (vv. 33–4), and 'commercial honesty in all trading transactions' (vv. 35–6).[19]

And it is this chapter that includes 'the second command of the law': 'love your neighbour as yourself' (Lev. 19:18). The covenant nature of these statutes is highlighted by the oft-repeated refrain, 'I am the LORD' by the introductory instruction, 'You shall be holy, for I the LORD your God am holy' and by the warning against creating or turning to idols (Lev. 19:2,4).

The covenant through David

In the course of Israel's history, as the nation struggled to maintain its hold on the portion of land that it acquired at the end of its long migration from Egypt, and establish some kind of *modus vivendi* with those peoples who already inhabited the areas to the east and west of the river Jordan, the question arose about how it would be governed over the long term. For a time, after the death of Joshua, 'the LORD raised up judges, who delivered them out of the power of those who plundered them' (Judg. 2:16). However, there was little or no cohesion among the different tribes. They were threatened constantly by their neighbours who resented the appropriation of some of their land. They fought among themselves and they constantly adopted the idolatrous practices of the indigenous populations. The book of Judges ends with the verdict, 'In those days there was no king in Israel; all the people did what was right in their own eyes' (Judg. 21:25).

The situation improved under Samuel. For a time Israel's main enemy, the Philistines, was defeated, the towns they had taken from Israel were restored and there was a period of peace between Israel and the Amorites

---

[19] For the full list, see Christopher J.H. Wright, *Mission of God*, p. 374.

(1 Sam. 7:13–14). However, law and order broke down again under the leadership of Samuel's sons, Joel and Abijah. They did not follow their father's ways, but 'turned aside after gain; they took bribes and perverted justice' (1 Sam. 8:1–3). The elders of Israel had had enough and appealed to Samuel in his old age to appoint for them 'a king to govern us, like other nations' (1 Sam. 8:5).

Presumably the leaders in Israel were anxious to experience stability in the governance of the people. They wanted a leader who would combine several attributes, in particular the ability to administer justice and to be a good army commander in defence of the nation. The request was granted, but came with a severe warning of the way in which the resulting increased concentration of power would institutionalise oppression (1 Sam. 8:11–18). A whole new industry would be created to maintain and equip a standing army. The king would spawn a new civil service and establish all the trappings of monarchy. All this would have to be paid for by raising revenue on a permanent basis. In an agricultural economy the method of payment was both in land, that was appropriated, and in the fruit of the land. The people, therefore, would lose a portion of their livelihood. This was the price of demanding a king to rule over them, 'like other nations'.

The outlook did not seem very favourable for the covenant between God and his people. As long as God alone was recognised as the legitimate king over the people there would be equality among the different families, clans and tribes, for all the land belonged to God. However, when 'like other nations' a king was instituted he could lay claim to the freehold of all the territory, whilst his subjects would at best be tenant farmers and at worst slaves.[20]

In spite of the implications of kingship in Israel, God used the reality to portray an ideal image of what kingship could be, when exercised according to the original expectations of the Sinaitic covenant. Although the majority of kings, subsequent to Saul, turned their backs on the ways of the Lord, some kings (most notably Hezekiah and Josiah) ruled in righteousness. Josiah, on finding the 'book of the law' (2 Kgs 22:11; probably Deuteronomy) initiated political and religious reform (2 Kgs 23:4–14), renewing the covenant with the Lord (2 Kgs 23:1–3). However, David became the paramount pattern for the projection of a kingly prototype that God promised his people for the future.

The covenant made with David and his successors (2 Sam. 7:8–16) was intended to establish a dynasty in which the king would rule entirely at the

[20] See Christopher J.H. Wright, *Old Testament Ethics for the People of God* (Leicester: IVP, 2004), p. 94.

behest of God. The relationship envisaged is that of a father and son. The father loves the son and guides him into the right paths. If the son strays, the father disciplines him and brings him back. So, the Davidic kingship was to be a model on earth of how God wishes political, social and economic governance to be undertaken. This kingship was launched in the limited environs of one people; however, it was destined to have a universal significance. Psalm 72:8–11 envisages a universal reign for 'a king's son' (Ps. 72:1). The language, 'May all the nations be blessed in him' (Ps. 72:17), echoes the Abrahamic covenant. Psalm 2:7–9 speaks of the ultimate submission of the nations to the king, who is the son of God (Ps. 2:7). Their resistance and hostility towards the one true God will be ended. Psalm 89 'closely associated Yahweh's "steadfast love" (v.2) with David's "throne [built] for all generations" (v.4) . . . it implies God's intention to extend this covenantal assurance of steadfast love to the entire world' (vv. 9,11,13).[21]

The prophet Isaiah enlarges the vision of the reign of the coming Davidic king. It begins with Israel: 'His authority shall grow continually, and there shall be endless peace for the throne of David and his kingdom. He will establish and uphold it with justice (*tsedekah*) and with righteousness (*mishpat*) from this time onwards and for evermore' (Isa. 9:7). However, Gentiles will also be beneficiaries: 'in the latter time he will make glorious the way of the sea, the land beyond the Jordan, Galilee of the nations. The people who walked in darkness . . . on them light has shined' (Isa. 9:1–2).

The future Davidic king (from the stock of Jesse) will be endued with the sevenfold Spirit of the Lord. He will be commissioned to set right the injustices suffered by those who have no power to defend themselves – the 'poor' and 'the meek of the earth' (Isa. 11:4). He will gather out of all the nations God's people who have become exiles because of war (Isa. 11:11–16). These acts will proclaim to the nations the deeds of the Lord. Israel is called to proclaim the living reality of its God, who is the God of the whole world (Isa. 12:4–5). The transforming power of the coming king will extend to every living being. In a powerful eschatological vision of a new creation, old enmities will be done away with and violence will cease (Isa. 11:6–9). Where the kingdom of God is characterised by the fear of the Lord, fear among the Lord's creatures will cease to exist. The passages from the early part of Isaiah anticipate:

the worldwide benefits of a future fulfillment of the Davidic covenant . . . Coming at the climax of the whole section devoted to the encouragement of the exiles, this word ('I will make with you an everlasting covenant, my steadfast,

---

[21] Donald Senior and Carroll Stuhlmueller, *The Biblical Foundations for Mission* (London: SCM Press, 1983), p. 98.

sure love for David' [Isa. 55:3]) links the future of God's people not only to the hope of return from exile . . . but also to the restoration of the covenant with David . . . The future rule of the new David will not be limited to ethnic Israelites but will extend to peoples and nations.[22]

Israel and the nations

So the righteous king will not fail, as did the monarchy in Israel right from the beginning. He will bring to his people a true and lasting peace – a Sabbath rest (Ps. 95:11) – in which they will enjoy the rich provisions of God's abundant creation without fear of violent intervention from outside: 'nation shall not lift up sword against nation' (Isa. 2:4).

Therefore, 'they shall all sit under their own vines and under their own fig trees, and no one shall make them afraid' (Mic. 4:4). So 'they shall not plant and another eat . . . my chosen shall long enjoy the work of their hands. They shall not labour in vain' (Isa. 65:22–3). All this will happen (symbolically) in a regenerated Jerusalem in a new earth (Isa. 65:17,19). And it will happen because Israel's adversaries will be drawn to acknowledge and worship the one and only God of the universe.

In the time between the exodus and the emergence of a strong prophetic tradition within Israel (Nathan, Elijah and Elisha), the nations 'hovered at the fringes of Israel's existence, a sort of "people of the periphery"'.[23]

However, with the writing prophets and in some of the psalms they began to come into much clearer focus and to play a more central role in the unfolding of God's plans for the whole of the created order. Now, increasingly, the nations are drawn into the sphere of blessing promised to Abraham and his descendants:

> The call of Abraham, and the history of Israel which begins at this point, is the beginning of the restoration of the lost unity of mankind and of broken fellowship with God. Here it becomes clear *that the whole history of Israel is nothing but the continuation of God's dealings with the nations, and that therefore the history of Israel is only to be understood from the unsolved problem of the relation of God to the nations.*[24]

Psalm 87 'speaks of Zion as the destined metropolis of Jew and Gentile alike . . . Nothing is explained with any fullness, yet by the end there remains no doubt of the coming conversion of old enemies and their full incorporation in the city of God.'[25] It appears that the psalmist has chosen

---

[22] Christopher J.H. Wright, *Mission of God*, p. 346.
[23] Harry R. Boer, *Pentecost and Missions* (Grand Rapids, MI: Eerdmans, 1961), p. 138.
[24] Blauw, *Missionary Nature*, p. 19 (emphasis in the original).
[25] Derek Kidner, *Psalms 73–150: A Commentary on Books III, IV and V of the Psalms*

to mention a highly symbolic representative sample of the Gentile world as belonging to God's dwelling-place: they are those 'who know me;' they were 'born there' and their names are registered, as if by the giving of a birth certificate (Ps. 87: 4,6). Those included are:

- Egypt (Rahab) and Babylon – the two superpowers of the Middle East;
- Philistia – a permanent hostile presence;
- Tyre – a significant commercial and trading centre; and
- Ethiopia, symbolizing the outer limits of the known world.

Other passages confirm God's inclusion of the nations in his purposes:

> Are you not like the Ethiopians to me, O people of Israel? says the LORD. Did I not bring Israel up from the land of Egypt, and the Philistines from Caphor and the Arameans from Kir? (Amos 9:7)

> The LORD will make himself known to the Egyptians . . . The LORD will strike Egypt, striking and healing; they will return to the LORD, and he will listen to their supplications and heal them . . . On that day Israel will be the third with Egypt and Assyria, a blessing in the midst of the earth, whom the LORD of hosts has blessed, saying, 'Blessed be Egypt my people, and Assyria the work of my hands, and Israel my heritage.' (Isa. 19:21–5)

In these passages (and others), there is an anticipation of the time when the nations will finally recognise the existence and true nature of the God of Israel and submit to him, taking him as their God. They will have observed the special relationship that exists between God and Israel and how that people, albeit falteringly, attempted to organise a community around the revealed will of the Creator of all peoples. An incipient desire to reach out to the nations with a proclamation of God's blessing for all can be seen in Psalm 67: 'that your way may be known upon earth, your saving power among all nations . . . Let the nations be glad and sing for joy, for you judge the peoples with equity and guide the nations upon earth . . . May God continue to bless us; let all the ends of the earth revere him' (vv. 2,4,7).

Messianic expectations

The origins of the promise that God would send a special representative to the world may be traced to Genesis 49:10; here we find an anticipation of the (Davidic) king to come. Other figures are also used to describe this

(Leicester: IVP, 1975), p. 314.

unique agent, called to a special mission on behalf of God. Daniel has a vision of one 'like a human being [son of man] coming with the clouds of heaven' (Dan. 7:13), who will be appointed as the ruler of the nations: 'To him was given dominion and glory and kingship, that all peoples, nations, and languages should serve him. His dominion is an everlasting dominion that shall not pass away' (Dan. 7:14). Micah speaks of a shepherd who 'shall stand and feed his flock in the strength of the LORD' (Mic. 5:4; compare, Isa. 40:11; 49:9; Ezek. 34:11–16).

However, the most prominent character is the 'servant of the LORD'. This enigmatic figure is introduced in the second part of Isaiah. The figure's 'identity seems to oscillate between a corporate embodiment of Israel and its mission . . . and an individual figure who has a mission to Israel and beyond'.[26] The figure also progressively reduces from the many to the few to the remnant to the one. His mission is to establish justice among the nations. He will be given as a covenant for the people[27] and a light to the nations (Isa. 42:1,4,6). His ministry is undoubtedly universal: the reference to 'those who sit in darkness' (Isa. 42:7) suggests the Gentiles; the 'new song' comes 'from the end of the earth' (Isa. 42:10).

The global reach of his mission is made even clearer in the second servant song (Isa. 49:1–6), with the words,' I will give you as a light to the nations, that my salvation may reach to the end of the earth' (Isa. 49:6). The third and fourth songs (Isa. 50:4–9; 52:13 – 53:12) introduce the notion of suffering as central to the servant's mission. It now becomes evident that God's salvation is to be achieved through the vicarious sacrifice of the servant who bears 'the iniquity of us all' (Isa. 53:6), like 'a lamb that is led to the slaughter' (Isa. 53:7), and thus makes 'his life an offering for sin' (Isa. 53:10). The salvation is open to 'everyone who thirsts' (Isa. 55:1). They are exhorted to 'seek the LORD while he may be found, [and] call upon him while he is near' (Isa. 55:6). The mission of the servant to 'call nations that you do not know' means that 'nations that do not know you shall run to you' (Isa. 55:5).

Jonah

The story of this recalcitrant prophet has often in the past been taken as the clearest example of mission to the Gentiles on the part of a representative Israelite. God summoned Jonah to 'Go at once to Nineveh, that great city, and cry out against it; for their wickedness has come up before me' (Jonah 1:1). After many travails, due to Jonah's extreme reluctance to heed

---

[26] Christopher J.H. Wright, *Mission of God*, p. 520.
[27] The reference is probably to Israel. However, the wider notion of God's people as embracing other nations may be implied here.

God's command, Jonah eventually makes it to Nineveh and proclaims an extraordinarily short message (of precisely five Hebrew words) – 'Forty days more, Nineveh overthrown' (Jonah 3:4) – to a city renowned as one of the most deadly of Israel's enemies.

Jonah is unlike any of the other prophetic books, for it is not a collection of prophecies, but the story of one man, a great city and an exceptionally merciful God. Jonah's reluctance is understandable, given the aversion an Israelite would have had to the idea of walking down the streets of a non-Jewish city in the heart of enemy territory.

There are a number of strange features in this remarkable story. First, it required three days to traverse the city (Jonah 3:3). Taking account of high temperatures, the prophet might have done approximately 7 miles (11 kilometres) per day. That would imply that the city had a diameter of 21 miles (33 kilometres). There is no archaeological evidence for a city of that size at that time.[28] One might speculate, therefore, that it took three days to walk up and down all the streets and alleyways. Second, the abruptness of the message is surprising, given the 'oracles on the nations' proclaimed by other prophets. One could imagine Jonah wearing a sandwich board; on one side: 'The end is near'; on the other: 'Forty days and counting.' The message was one of unconditional judgement and disaster. Unlike all the other prophets, there was no warning, no call to repent and believe and no mention of mercy and forgiveness. Third, the nature of the reaction was astonishing. On the very first day the people collectively accepted that Jonah was speaking from God. They believed the message was true, and reacted in the only way they knew: 'they proclaimed a fast' and 'put on sackcloth,' as a sign of humility and penitence. This was a people's movement; it happened before their ruler even knew what was going on (Jonah 3:5–6). The king followed his people. The king's decree confirmed and extended the mood of contrition, all with a view to persuading God to change his mind: 'Who knows? God may relent and change his mind; he may turn from his fierce anger, so that we do not perish' (Jonah 3:9).

And God did change his mind: 'When God saw what they did, how they turned from their evil ways, God changed his mind about the calamity that he said he would bring upon them; and he did not do it' (Jonah 3:10).

Now, in two contrasting sentences, comes the story's punch line. First, God's forbearance was mightily displeasing to Jonah. He was infuriated and outraged (Jonah 4:1): 'Jonah had no problem accepting that judgement could be pronounced on Nineveh, but to offer grace was another

---

[28] If Jonah, son of Amittai, is the one mentioned in 2 Kgs 14:25, living during the reign of Jeroboam II, the date would be around 750 BC.

matter.'[29] 'Jonah goes to speak God's word to the pagan world, and his obedience is met by a stupendous miracle. There is universal repentance. The pagan world has been humbled. But Jonah is utterly disappointed. The heathen are not to be punished after all. What justice can there be in a world where God is so absurdly generous?'[30]

Second, the true nature of God is reluctantly admitted by the prophet: 'You are a gracious God and merciful, slow to anger, and abounding in steadfast love, and ready to relent from punishing' (Jonah 4:2). Robin Routledge has suggested that this is a deliberate repetition of a covenant formula, which is found several times in the Old Testament, 'where it generally related to God's gracious treatment of his people'.[31]

This is remarkable, for it raises the question: 'how can a formula so closely linked with Israel's covenant relationship with God be offered as a basis for God's forgiveness of a non-Israelite nation?'[32] The answer has to be that it indicates 'that significant elements that are demonstrated in Israel's covenant relationship may also find expression in God's historical dealings with other nations'.[33]

So, Jonah is not a story about mission in the conventional sense of making converts among those not yet aware of the nature and purposes of the one true God. It is more a treatise directed against Israel itself, 'not to be self-satisfied in their enjoyment of God's favour'.[34] It warns against Jewish religious and nationalistic exclusivism.[35] 'The sailors and the Ninevites seem to have grasped something about God which the orthodox Jonah has not reached.'[36]

Thus, even when Jonah was able to recite the covenant formula and admit in theory that it might apply beyond Israel, he still could not shed his ethnic prejudices. The book ends pedagogically with a rhetorical question: 'Should I not be concerned about Nineveh, that great city . . . ?' (Jonah 4:11).

In another sense, it *is* a book about mission, for it conveys the message that God's special people do have a responsibility to bring the knowledge

---

[29] Ken R. Gnanakan, *Kingdom Concerns: A Biblical Exploration towards a Theology of Mission* (Bangalore: Theological Book Trust, 1989), p. 52.

[30] Newbigin, *Open Secret*, p. 33.

[31] Routledge, 'Mission and Covenant', p. 10. The passages are Exod. 20:6, 36:6; Neh. 9:17; Joel 2:13; Ps. 103:8–10. The same formula is applied to the whole of creation in Ps. 145:8–9.

[32] Routledge, 'Mission and Covenant', p. 13.

[33] Routledge, 'Mission and Covenant', p. 20.

[34] Roger Bowen, *So I Send You: A Study Guide to Mission* (London: SPCK, 1996), p. 19.

[35] Blauw, *Missionary Nature*, p. 33.

[36] Peskett and Ramachandra, *Message of Mission*, p. 131.

of God to all peoples, and especially to their enemies. The lesson to be
learnt is that 'the redemption of Israel includes the re-creation of her world;
and because Israel does not live in isolation, God's re-creative activity also
extends to the surrounding nations'.[37]

The particular and the universal

Books that explore the biblical foundations for mission to the ends of the
world often begin with a discussion of the enduring tension throughout
the history of Israel between its election by God to be a specially chosen
people (e.g. Exod. 6:7; Lev. 26:12; Deut. 26:18; 1 Sam. 12:22; 1 Kgs 3:8; 2
Chr. 7:14; Pss 33:12; 144:15; Isa. 51:4; Jer. 2:32; Ezek. 37:13; Mic. 6:2) and
the vision of a universe where 'the [whole] earth will be filled with the
knowledge of the glory of the LORD, as the waters cover the sea' (Hab. 2:14;
Isa. 11:9; 45:22; 52:10; Ps. 98:2–3). Thus, for example, Richard Bauckham
states in the first sentence of his book that 'a major theme of this book is
going to be the relationship between the particular and the universal'.[38]
He says later, 'I have taken this route into the subject of this book because
the issue of universality and particularity is essential to what I shall say
about mission and what I shall say about the way the Bible invites us to
read it.'[39]

So, he begins an exploration of the Old Testament narrative (under
the heading 'From the One to the Many') with the singular calling of
Abraham. It is appropriate to make Abraham (particularity) the first
port of call in a discussion of mission, since God's ultimate intention in
choosing one family is universal in scope. However, in completing this
discussion, I should emphasise again that God's mission is accomplished
within the wide context of creation, redemption and the eschatological
promises of a renewed or recreated earth (universality). If we are right to
see the Abrahamic narrative as a natural step following the stories of creation, corruption, the flood and the scattering of the nations, then universality precedes particularity and is the spoken and unspoken context for
all God's dealings with Israel.

Both emphases are crucial to understanding how God shapes history
to fulfil his purposes to bring his justice and salvation to all he has
made. On the one hand, 'If God's universality is dealt with apart from
his particularity we allow room for the kind of error that removes all
uniqueness from . . . mission.'[40] If it is true that humankind in general

---

[37] Routledge, 'Mission and Covenant', p. 17.
[38] Bauckham, *Bible and Mission*, p. 1.
[39] Bauckham, *Bible and Mission*, p. 10.
[40] Gnanakan, *Kingdom Concerns*, p. 51.

has abandoned the purpose of its creation – to belong to God, to glorify him and to enjoy his benefits according to his laws – in order that God may re-enter into dialogue with people in general, he must choose one people in particular who will hear his voice and convey his message to the rest. There is no specific revelation of God that does not come through a specific channel that needs special provisions to be made so that the message is transmitted faithfully and accurately.

On the other hand, particularity by itself can very easily slide into arrogance, protectionism and exclusivism. There is a fine balance to be made, in order to avoid two equal and opposite dangers.

Alan Le Grys believes that Israel never properly overcame its propensity to think and act in terms of an exclusivist outlook.[41] He argues that 'Scripture contained two closely related but opposing views: the tendency to assert the universal sovereignty of God over all peoples, versus the tendency to assert the exclusive rights of the Jews as the chosen people of God.' For Le Grys these are but the two sides of the same coin: 'The only major difference was one of emphasis not of substance. Both views shared a common acceptance of the concept of election: Israel had been called to be a unique witness to the saving power of the one God.'

In other words, both these views express a similar exclusivist attitude when it comes to Israel seeking to express its identity within the concourse of the nations. Israel was a specially chosen people and its God, and only its God, had the right and the power to command the nations. Thus, although these seem to be conflicting tendencies, in reality 'they were both similarly rooted in the same idea of the primacy of Israel. Even the protests of Ruth and Jonah define Gentiles in terms of their relationship with the chosen people. Universalism and exclusivism are not as incompatible as is sometimes suggested.'

In the light of the material I have touched on in this chapter, I believe that Le Grys has made a prior assumption about the particularism of Israel and then selected the texts that most accord with that position. Or, put another way, he has chosen to interpret these texts within a dominant framework in which Israel sees itself as the centre of God's concerns for the whole of humanity. However, it is perfectly legitimate to view the matter from another perspective, as I have done here. God's major concern is not with Israel, but with the restoration of creation to the beauty and goodness it enjoyed at the beginning. As humanity, after the fall, was inclined continually to thinking and doing evil (Gen. 6:5) and to practising corruption and violence (Gen. 6:11), God chose one family

---

[41] See Alan Le Grys, *Preaching to the Nations: The Origins of Mission in the Early Church* (London: SPCK, 1998), pp. 17–19.

(and its descendants) to be the receptacle of his teaching about what makes a just and flourishing society. Moreover, this chosen people was called and mandated to be the kind of community defined by the revelation of God's own nature.

Thus, it is not Israel, but the revelation of the one, holy, Creator God, that is at the centre of the witness of the Old Testament Scriptures. If it is true that 'mission' is seen much more in centripetal than in centrifugal terms, nevertheless the nations are summoned to know the universal God and live under the liberating demands of his law:

> He who has *made* the nations (Ps. 86:9) and who has made them *His* nations (Ps. 87) is also the only one that can call them to Himself. That which will bring the world of nations to Him is *not* Israel's calling them, *nor* her going out to them, but exclusively the visible manifestation of the deeds of God in and with Israel; only so will they recognize Yahweh as *their* God, i.e. confess that Israel's God is *their* God, the God of the whole earth, the *only* God.[42] (emphasis in the original)

In the light of the servant songs and passages like Isaiah 66:19; 24:14–16 and Psalm 48:10, some going out to the nations is presupposed. Nevertheless, the vision of the 'Day of the Lord' is the ingathering of the nations, together with a repentant and restored Israel, into the fullness of the presence of the Lord.

---

[42] Blauw, *Missionary Nature*, p. 37.

3

'Go Into All the World': The Meaning and Scope of Mission in the New Testament

Where is the Beginning?

As we come to the dawn of a new era in the history of Israel, marked by John initiating baptisms of repentance for the forgiveness of sins in the river Jordan, we are confronted with a dilemma. If taking 'the good news of Jesus Christ, the Son of God' (Mark 1:1) to the nations was the supreme task of the early church, at what point should we start our review of the data? Do we follow the canonical order of the New Testament and begin with the gospels? Or should we refer first to the story of the birth of the Christian community in Jerusalem, following its baptism by the Holy Spirit on the day of Pentecost, and look at the early narratives recounted in Acts? Or would it be more appropriate to open the exploration with the earliest Christian writings, namely the first letters of Paul to young churches which he founded?

A natural inclination is to start chronologically with the fourfold account of the life and times of Jesus of Nazareth. After all, he is the centre-piece of the collection of books that we now know as the New Testament. It is because of the impact that he made initially on a disparate group of people during a teaching, preaching and healing ministry lasting approx-imately three years that we have any record of this remarkable phenom-enon known as church at all. One could give reasons why this may not be the most appropriate place to set out on our journey.

First, the gospel narratives were written following on from the early Christians' experience of discovering their identity and mission in the world. Many new communities had already been planted as far afield as Rome, North Africa and, maybe, to the east of the Euphrates. Some of the first generation of Christians, including some of the original followers of Jesus, had died. There is a suspicion that some of the material compiled as an account of the earthly life, death and resurrection of Jesus had been shaped to respond to events on the ground some thirty or more years after his earthly life ended.

Second, the coming of the Holy Spirit into the life of the new community (called the Way [Acts 9:2; 24:14]) seems to have been more decisive in fashioning the church's initial mission than the teaching of Jesus.[1]

Third, the first Christian to develop a 'theology of mission' was the apostle Paul. His letters to the young churches he founded are probably the earliest Christian writings that we have records of. We can assume, therefore, that they reflect a situation of Christian activity and expansion before the gospels and the Acts of the Apostles were written.

Nevertheless, the coming into being of a new 'sect', radically different from the various branches of Judaism of the time, presupposes some unprecedented historical event as its cause. It is proper, therefore, to attempt first to trace in outline the main features of this happening.

The actual sequence of events is relatively easy to reconstruct as long as we take more or less at face value the accounts that we have in their final form. Problems emerge, however, when it is assumed that the authors of some of the New Testament books (particularly the gospels and Acts) may have used written or oral sources creatively in order to give emphasis to a particular way of interpreting the impact of Jesus on his contemporaries or the relationship between the early Christian community and the Jewish and Roman authorities. For one thing, we do not have any certainty about the dates of any of the early Christian literature. We cannot be sure in what order they were written, and therefore which earlier writers might have influenced which later ones. For another thing, we do not have access to independent copies of sources that the authors may, or may not, have used. All we do have are the extant books that now appear as a collection of 'apostolic' writings in the Christian portion of the Bible, together with some interesting (and sometimes significant)[2] variant readings from the ancient manuscripts that have transmitted surprisingly accurately the original, autograph copies. Any attempt, therefore, to reconstruct a precise history of the compilation of the gospels and Acts is a matter of conjecture and

---

[1] We will return later to a discussion of the curious fact that the so-called 'Great Commission' was not invoked as a conclusive reason to include the Gentiles in the new 'Israel of God' (Matt. 28:19–20; Acts 10:28,34–5; Gal. 6:16).

[2] One example would be the expanded text of the book of Acts in the 'Western' manuscript tradition – 'the version of the text found in Codex Bezae and other manuscripts that come from the Western area of early Christendom'; see I. Howard Marshall, *Acts: An Introduction and Commentary* (Leicester: IVP, 1980), p. 46.

speculation, as the various 'quests' for the 'historical' Jesus have amply demonstrated.[3]

There is no space here even to begin to delve into the complexity of unravelling the connection between historical reality and theological intent. It may be useful to attempt a reconstruction, but only where there appear to be serious anomalies in the various accounts. The over-whelming weight of evidence points to the fact that some twenty years after the death of Jesus of Nazareth there were small communities meeting together regularly in his name, scattered throughout Judea, Syria, Asia Minor and into Northern Greece. These communities were distinct in all kinds of ways from other religious and political assemblies, both in the message they proclaimed and the beliefs that shaped their ethical behaviour. Such a phenomenon needs an adequate explanation: what plausible cause produced this effect? To be more precise: what event(s) turned this new body of people, who claimed to inherit specific promises from the God of Israel, into a centrifugal missionary force? The New Testament is unanimous in its answer: God sending his 'beloved Son' and the Son sending the Spirit of God into the world. In other words, it was the concrete manifestation of God in the world, present not just through prophetic utterances, but in person. The motivation for sharing their beliefs with all who would listen – Jew and Gentile, men and women, wise and foolish, the powerful and the weak, rich and poor, nobility and servants, the 'cultivated' and 'barbarians' (1 Cor. 1:26–8; Gal. 3:28; Col. 3:11) – was the fact that God had entered into the world in person in a singular way. I will attempt to trace both the cause and the effect in this chapter.

The Life and Work of Jesus, Called the Christ

We left the story of Israel, as recorded in the writings of the Hebrew Scriptures, with the expectation of a final renewal of God's people and an ingathering of those in the nations willing to abandon false gods and seek God's righteousness and justice as revealed through prophetic oracles. This expectation is summed up in terms of the restoration of God's perfect rule over the affairs of Israel in particular and humanity in general.

---

[3] One of the fullest explorations of the relationship between the original histor-ical Jesus, the testimony of eyewitnesses, the transmission of Jesus traditions and the Jesus of testimony is given in Richard Bauckham, *Jesus and the Eyewit-nesses: The Gospels as Eyewitness Testimony* (Grand Rapids, MI: Eerdmans, 2006).

It is not surprising, therefore, that the Christian Scriptures begin with an announcement that God's reign is exceedingly close, that this same reign was still the preoccupation of the disciples after the death and resurrection of Jesus, and that it occupied a central place in the message that the early Christians shared with those around them (Matt. 4:17; 9:35; 10:7; Mark 1:14–15; 12:34; Luke 4:43; 10:10–11; 12:32; Acts 1:3,6; 8:12; 19:8; 28:31). It is clear that the declaration that the reign of God is on the threshold of the lives of the Jewish people was no mere theoretical proposition, but a wake-up call to change direction. It was, in modern linguistic terminology, an *illocutionary*[4] act, i.e. a message that implied within it the performance of a deed.

The kingdom of God can be partially understood in terms of its antecedents in the Old Testament Scriptures and in the thinking and practice of various groups within Judaism prior to the preaching of John and Jesus. It is better understood in light of the portrayal of the public ministry and teaching of Jesus.

The kingdom of God

'God's kingdom, to the Jew-in-the-village in the first half of the first century, meant the coming vindication of Israel, victory over the pagans, the eventual gift of peace, justice and prosperity.'[5] The rule of God over the nations meant for most Jews a new exodus and a fresh return from exile. The one nation would be gathered together again in the promised land, free from the humiliation of conquest by heathen nations and able to live out obedience to the law of the Lord under their own governance. In that day the twin elements of Israel's core sense of identity would be re-established: *election* as a people called into a special relationship with God to manifest his holiness and justice, and *monotheism* to demonstrate that the God of Abraham, Isaac, Jacob, Moses and the prophets was supreme and in control of the events of history.

The early hints of God's concern for all that he had created, which increased towards the end of the prophetic period, and the resultant promises concerning the expansion of his people to include those who would listen to his voice (Isa. 55:1–11), had all but disappeared. Israel under Roman rule was almost as far from the ideal state as it was possible to be. The land was defiled and their religious practices sometimes mocked and despised. The presence of the Roman standing army,

---

[4] Illocution is defined as 'an act performed by a speaker by virtue of uttering certain words, as for example the acts of promising or of threatening'; see *Collins Dictionary of the English Language* (Glasgow: Collins, 1979), p. 730.

[5] N.T. Wright, *Jesus and the Victory of God* (London: SPCK, 1996), p. 204.

collaborators within their own people and the burden of heavy taxation reminded them that God did not yet reign.

For John the Baptist and Jesus to announce, within this context of hope and despair, the coming reign of God as the central platform of their teaching, raised great expectations that at last God was about to act decisively in favour of his people:

> In the light of the Jewish background . . . this cannot but have been heard as the announcement that the exile was at last drawing to a close, that Israel was about to be vindicated against her enemies, that her god was returning at last to deal with evil, to right wrongs, to bring justice . . . We are bound to say, I think, that Jesus could not have used the phrase 'the reign of God' if he were not *in some sense or other* claiming to fulfil, or at least to announce the fulfilment of, those deeply rooted Jewish aspirations. The phrase was not a *novum*, an invention of his own. It spoke of a covenant renewed, of creation restored, of Israel liberated, of YHWH returning.[6]

When Jesus, therefore, proclaimed 'the good news of the kingdom of God to the other cities also; for I was sent for this purpose', and continued 'proclaiming the message in the synagogues of Judea' (Luke 4:43–4), he embarked on a high-risk strategy. If, as becomes evident later, he reinterpreted the nature of the kingdom and redefined the significance of belonging to Israel, he was open to serious misunderstanding: 'Jesus made a regular practice of retelling the story of Israel in such a way as to subvert other tellings, and to invite his hearers to make his telling of the story their own . . . Jesus was articulating *a new way of understanding the fulfilment of Israel's hope*'[7] (emphasis in the original).

Both Jesus' teaching and his actions caused bewilderment and astonishment among the crowds who followed him. On numerous occasions his most intimate disciples did not understand what was going on. If his ministry was designed to act out the meaning of God's rule, it did not fit at all into the preconceived categories. Among the innermost circle of disciples were collaborators with Rome. He allowed himself to be 'defiled' by the company he kept at the meal-table and generally by his association with the excluded of society (Samaritans, tax-collectors, lepers, prostitutes) and by the special attention he gave to those who counted for little (women and children). His teaching on forgiveness (Matt. 18:21–35) and love for one's enemies (Luke 6:27–36) was amazing, given the general climate of opinion in Israel at the time. His indiscriminate healing of all

---

[6] N.T. Wright, *Jesus*, p. 172.

[7] N.T. Wright, *Jesus*, pp. 174, 176.

who came to him, especially the Roman centurion's servant (Matt. 8:5–13), was confusing, since many of those healed belonged to the class of the 'non-deserving'. His reconfiguring of the law of Moses in relationship to anger and reconciliation, adultery and sexual craving, taking oaths and the integrity of one's word, retaliation and generosity, the keeping of the Sabbath, honouring one's parents and the true meaning of defilement moved the meaning of holy and merciful living to the deepest possible level of action: 'Unless your righteousness exceeds that of the scribes and Pharisees, you will never enter the kingdom of heaven' (Matt. 5:20).

His understanding of the significance of the kingdom, in the light of God's desire to bring about the healing of the nations, comes out clearly in the episode of the sermon in the synagogue in Nazareth and in the healing of the centurion's servant. In proclaiming the fulfilment of the messianic prophecies in Isaiah in his own person (Luke 4:18–21), he stresses the fact that God's favour is clearly shown to those outside Israel: in the omission of the words 'the day of vengeance of our God' (Isa. 61:2b; Luke 4:19) – a reference to the coming judgement on Israel's enemies; in the 'gracious words', or words of grace (rather than condemnation), that were noted by the hearers (Luke 4:22), and in the references to the widow of Zarephath and Naaman the Syrian (Luke 4:25–7). In the case of the centurion's servant, it is symbolic that Matthew places this as the second particular healing that he mentions (after the cleansing of a leper). Also significant is the fact that Jesus was ready and willing to enter his house, that he commended the Roman's faith as greater than that of any Israelite he had encountered, and that many people will come from the Gentile nations into the kingdom, whilst the heirs of the kingdom will be excluded (Matt. 8:7,10,11–12).

'Although Jesus did not lead a social uprising against the Romans, his project of inclusion and radical forgiveness was deeply revolutionary. It constituted nothing less than a restructuring of human relations, both within Israel and between Jew and Gentile, so as to reflect God's gracious reign.'[8] Eventually, his representation of the meaning of the kingdom in his ministry led to his arrest and execution. In order to make plain that kingdom did not stand for armed rebellion as was currently being implied by the resistance movement within Israel, he defined its origin as being 'not from this world' (John 18:36).[9]

In a truly dramatic climax to Jesus' trial as told by John, the accusation of blasphemy – levelled against Jesus because he had claimed to be the

---

[8] Howard Peskett and Vinoth Ramachandra, *The Message of Mission* (Leicester: IVP, 2003), p. 165.

[9] On the meaning of this phrase, see pp. 27–29.

Messiah, the Son of God (John 5:18; 10:33; 19:7; see Matt. 26:63–6) – was reversed. The true meaning of the kingdom could be summed up in the short phrase, 'no king but God'; the Jewish leaders, in order to get their way with Pilate, were driven to confess, 'no king but the emperor' (John 19:15). In the subsequent mission of Jesus' disciples the clash between these two confessions marked out the boundary between the children of the kingdom and those that remained under the thrall of the principalities and powers of this world (Col. 1:13).

The 'Great Commission'

There is no doubt that the commands of the risen Jesus Christ to his disciples regarding their mission to the nations has played a large part in the missionary outreach of many Christians, since the beginning of the modern missionary movement. However, as we shall see, some misgivings have been expressed about how justifiable the use made of them is in motivating Christians to engage in mission.

Each of the gospels records a different version of Jesus' final directive to his disciples.[10] Matthew stresses that the goal of mission is the making of disciples, and that the means to this end is baptism and instruction (Matt. 28:19–20). Baptism is the definitive act of commitment, whereby new believers identify themselves with Jesus' salvific act of death and resurrection. This marks them out as belonging to a new community, distinguished from all other religious groups, bearing the name of God as Father, Son and Holy Spirit. The instruction is to follow 'everything that I have commanded you'. Matthew's Gospel is organised as a teaching text, divided into five didactic discourses: 'Mission, for Matthew, was *catechetical* mission . . . It is no less than the *evangelization of each generation*, learning together the way of the kingdom, in a community of disciples, at each stage in life . . . Disciples are not born, they are made, and it takes a whole lifetime'[11] (emphasis in the original).

The first piece of teaching is the 'Sermon on the Mount' (Matt. 5 – 7), which includes instruction on reconciliation, sexual morality, the integrity of one's word, non-retaliation, generosity, love for one's enemy, prayer and fasting and trust in the providence of God. The last piece of

---

[10] The book by Mortimer Arias and Alan Johnson, *The Great Commission: Biblical Models for Evangelism* (Nashville: Abingdon Press, 1992), explores each of the texts in some detail in the context of the gospel to which it corresponds, and supplies an extensive study section at the end.

[11] Arias and Johnson, *Great Commission*, pp. 19, 20.

teaching is the vision of the judgement of the nations (Matt. 25:31–46): 'In this parable, the historical, human, concrete character of the kingdom is revealed, and the universal meaning, scope, and test of mission are anticipated.'[12]

The Great Commission in Mark (Mark 16:15–16) is problematic, in that it does not occur in the oldest and most reliable manuscripts of the gospel. Nevertheless, most translations include it in the main text. We cannot know why and when it became added to the established text. Notwithstanding, in so far as it faithfully reflects the tenor of the whole gospel, it is possible to see it as a faithful transmission, if not of the actual words of Jesus, the words of Jesus spoken through the Spirit to the church. The theme of the Gospel of Mark is the 'good news of Jesus Christ, the Son of God' (Mark 1:1). Arias and Johnson start their discussion of Mark's version from the observation that the whole gospel is proclamation of the good news in the form of a story.[13] The commission itself speaks of the call to the nations (also Mark 13:27) to believe the good news, brought by Jesus, which refers to his fulfilment of the promises of the coming kingdom (Mark 13:10). Salvation is a gift given to those who believe in the truth and reality of the gospel and become part of the baptised community. Those who refuse to believe bring condemnation upon themselves.

Luke shares with Matthew and Mark an emphasis on the universal scope of mission; it is 'to all nations' (Luke 24:47). In other ways, however, it is quite distinct. There is no direct command. The commission is cast in the indicative rather than the imperative:[14] 'Thus it is written, that the Messiah is to suffer and to rise from the dead on the third day, and that repentance and forgiveness of sins is to be proclaimed in his name to all nations, beginning from Jerusalem. You are witnesses of these things' (Luke 24:46–7).

The same applies to a different form of the commission in Acts 1:8. Here Jesus speaks about what will happen, not what ought to happen: 'you will be (*esesthe*) my witnesses in Jerusalem, in all Judea and Samaria, and to the ends of the earth'.

So, the emphasis in Luke is on the gift of the Holy Spirit, enabling the disciples to be witnesses to the fulfilment of 'everything written about me in the law of Moses, the prophets, and the psalms', namely that 'the Messiah is to suffer and to rise from the dead on the third day' (Luke 24:44–6). In the book of Acts, the promise of the Holy Spirit comes first and the witness to Jesus follows. In Luke's Gospel the statement, 'you

---

[12] Arias and Johnson, *Great Commission*, p. 24.

[13] Arias and Johnson, *Great Commission*, pp. 37–8.

[14] This interpretation assumes that the infinitive *keruxthenai* is also governed by the words 'it is written'. Luke believes that the proclamation of repentance to all nations is foretold in the Scriptures (see Acts 10:43; 13:47, 26:22–3).

are witnesses of these things' is followed by the promise of being clothed with power from on high (Luke 24:48–9). In both cases the result of the Spirit's coming is assured.

The main object of witness is repentance (*metanoia*) and forgiveness (*aphesis*). The latter word is also emphasised in the quotation from Isaiah 61 as recorded in the episode of Jesus' sermon in the synagogue at Nazareth: 'he has sent me to proclaim release (*aphesin*) to the captives . . . to let the oppressed go free (*en aphesei*)' (Luke 4:18). This coincidence has led Arias and Johnson to conclude that probably the Year of the Jubilee ('the year of the Lord's favour' [Luke 4:19]) was in mind. They trace through the gospel the announcement of the kingdom in terms of the Jubilee: as good news to the poor; the restoration of life; healing; the forgiveness of sins; rectification and salvation.[15]

Again the form of the commission is quite different in John's Gospel (John 20:21). The wording is almost exactly the same as that pronounced in the 'high-priestly' prayer (John 17:18). In the latter case, Jesus states a fact: 'As you have sent me into the world, so I have sent them into the world.' In the second case, it comes more in the form of a direct mandate, 'As the Father has sent me, so I send you.' In both cases the emphasis falls on the 'as' and the 'so' (literally 'I also'): in the same way that the Father sends the Son, the Son sends the disciples. The sending was into the world (in all the senses that we explored in Chapter 1), thus reiterating the incarnational theme that runs throughout the gospel. It was also a sending evidenced both by the marks of crucifixion (John 20:20) and the gift of the Holy Spirit. The main content of the message (as in Luke) was forgiveness and repentance.[16]

The Great Commission and the Origin of the Church's Mission

The question concerning the decision of the early church to include the Gentiles as recipients of the good news of Jesus might seem quite straightforward. Jesus in his ministry of teaching and healing is recorded on some occasions as including non-Jews in the benefits of the kingdom of God. The healing of the centurion's personal attendant is a case in point (Matt. 8:5–13). There are a number of remarkable features in this story. Matthew places this as the second healing incident, after that of the leper. Thus, he begins a description of Jesus' public ministry with people from two excluded categories.

---

[15] Arias and Johnson, *Great Commission*, pp. 66–73; compare Acts 10:37–43 as a summary of the ministry of Jesus to which the disciples were witnesses.

[16] The 'retention of sins' (John 20:23) suggests a situation where people refuse to acknowledge their need for forgiveness.

The centurion, probably 'a junior officer in the auxiliary forces under the command of Herod Antipas, which were non-Jewish, drawn largely from Lebanon and Syria',[17] approached a Jewish rabbi who was becoming notorious as a healer, in desperate need. Jesus' immediate reaction was to go to his house to make him well. To have entered the house of a Gentile would have rendered him ritually unclean. The centurion saved him from such a compromise with an act of unparalleled faith (Matt. 8:8–9). This drew Jesus' exceptional praise: 'Truly I tell you, in no one in Israel have I found such faith' (Matt. 8:10). Here was a man with a more intense belief in the power of God than any member of God's people. Finally, Jesus declares, in line with prophetic oracles from the Scriptures, that Gentiles would be gathered into the coming kingdom to enjoy the fullness of its blessings, whilst those who were destined to be participants will be excluded for their unbelief (Matt. 8:11–12).

Then, as we have seen, each of the gospels finishes with what seem to be explicit instructions to the disciples to take the good news of forgiveness and reconciliation to the whole world without any prejudice. Therefore, one would assume, the disciples had a concrete and direct mandate to proclaim the gospel to all and sundry, irrespective of ethnic or religious considerations. However, curiously, the Great Commission is never mentioned as the conclusive argument that Gentiles too were to be included in all the blessings of the gospel. It was by means of coincidental dreams and the special manifestation of the Spirit that Peter was persuaded to overcome the taboo of ritual uncleanness and enter the house of another centurion to bring him the message of salvation in Jesus Christ and to baptise him and his whole household.

In an endeavour to explain this anomaly, Alan Le Grys has elaborated the theory that Christian mission began in the first tentative steps taken by Hellenist Jewish Christians in Jerusalem:

> The evidence suggests that the origins of mission lie buried in the incident behind the expulsion of Jewish Christian radicals from the Hellenist synagogue in Jerusalem. Disowned by their host community, these Jewish believers looked for new support around the existing fringes of first-century Judaism. They attracted Samaritans, Gentile sympathizers like the Ethiopian eunuch, and benefactors, like Cornelius. A trickle of these God-fearers was drawn into membership of the embryo movement, and enabled the Hellenist Jewish Christian community to survive.[18]

---

[17] R.T. France, *Matthew* (Leicester: IVP, 1985), p. 154.
[18] Alan Le Grys, *Preaching to the Nations: The Origins of Mission in the Early Church* (London: SPCK, 1998), p. 177.

This reconstruction makes a number of assumptions that run counter to the more traditional way of reading the missionary outlook of the Scriptures. First, on this reading, the universalism of the Old Testament and the scattered references to centripetal mission,[19] are minimised: 'It is difficult . . . to find any antecedent in Judaism for later Christian mission . . . the Christian concept of a universal mission was a shocking novelty in the ancient world.'[20]

Second, the references to a universal outreach to the nations recorded as coming from Jesus are either reinterpreted to discount their relevance or are assigned directly to the redactive hand of the evangelist:

> Matthew reports a specific instruction to limit mission to the people of Israel . . . (Matthew 10.5 and 10.23). This is locked into the tradition, and confirmed by the statement added by Matthew to the story of the Syrophoenician woman: Jesus is 'sent only to the lost sheep of the house of Israel' (Matthew 15.24). Further, it goes 'against the grain' of Matthean redaction and of later Christian activity, and so passes the authenticity test as an embarrassment to the gospel. It shows that Jesus had no interest in a Gentile mission.[21]

Third, the texts recording the Great Commission and the commissioning of the Twelve are identified as having arisen from the experience of the early church at a much later date, when mission had been accomplished through large tracts of the Roman Empire, and even further afield:

> Both traditions have been significantly reshaped by the evangelists, and reflect the theological priorities of the post-Easter church. The original basis for the Great Commission is too difficult to determine, but perhaps rests on the inspired word of an early Christian prophet. The Commissioning of the Twelve is probably rooted in an authentic Jesus tradition, but has been extensively modified in the light of later Christian experience. Stripped of these redactional elements, the underlying tradition does little to support the view that Jesus taught his followers to adopt a unique understanding of the Gentiles.[22]

> The Great Commission is evidence of the beliefs of the post-Easter church, not the historical Jesus.[23]

---

[19] Explored in Chapter 2.
[20] Le Grys, *Preaching to the Nations*, p. 37.
[21] Le Grys, *Preaching to the Nations*, pp. 59–60.
[22] Le Grys, *Preaching to the Nations*, p. 51.
[23] Le Grys, *Preaching to the Nations*, p. 46.

In response to these assumptions we may note certain other points of discussion. First, there is enough evidence from particular passages in the prophets and the Psalms to conclude that a later generation could legitimately read them as pointing in the direction of a centrifugal mission.

Second, it is a dubious methodology that sets up a theory of interpretation of what can be known about the historical Jesus and then assigns to the theological interests of the evangelists all evidence that does not fit the theory. There is nothing implicitly unlikely about Jesus having interpreted his mission in the light of the more universalistic traditions of the Old Testament Scriptures, even though his own ministry did not take on a geographical dimension beyond the confines of the territory of Israel and its immediate neighbours. The limiting of mission largely to his own people had a temporal rationale; one cannot conclude from this that he had little or no interest in the Gentiles.

Third, although it seems likely that in the case of each of the texts of the Great Commission, the evangelist has shaped it to bring out particular emphases, nevertheless 'it cannot be doubted . . . that common traditions underlie these accounts, the basic nucleus being that Jesus commanded his disciples to spread the good news widely and offer forgiveness of sins and that he promised them divine power for their task'.[24]

Even for those cautious about assigning too much of the gospel narratives directly to the original Jesus there is sufficient 'authentic' material to suggest that Jesus did envisage a continuing mission conducted by his disciples, which would have included the Gentiles. Christopher Rowland, for example, in a careful study of 'Jesus and the Future' believes there is sufficient evidence that 'Jesus looked forward to a time when the Gentiles would share in the glory of the age to come . . . some Gentiles would in due course be allowed to enter the kingdom of God and so fulfil the divine promises.'[25]

Moreover, he believes that the sayings about the church in Matthew 16 and 18 may 'in one form or another go back to Jesus and should not be lightly dismissed, therefore'.[26] However, they should be interpreted, not in terms of the church that developed at a later date, but of the eschatological community of Israel. He concludes: 'He [Jesus] may have prepared for the existence of an identifiable group as a necessary, if temporary, measure during the short period before the kingdom of God came, by delegating to his followers his authority to preach and act on God's

---

[24] I. Howard Marshall, *The Gospel of Luke; A Commentary on the Greek Text* (Exeter: Paternoster Press, 1978), p. 904.

[25] Christopher Rowland, *Christian Origins: The Setting and Character of the Most Important Messianic Sect of Judaism* (London: SPCK, 2nd edn, 2002), p. 147.

[26] Rowland, *Christian Origins*, p. 149.

behalf. Their task would be to continue to bear witness to the eschatological convictions, after his departure.'[27]

The Coming of the Holy Spirit

Bearing witness to Jesus is related directly to the gift of the Holy Spirit
who will 'come upon' the disciples and endue them with power. Then,
and only then, will they 'be my witnesses . . . to the ends of the earth'
(Acts 1:8; Luke 24:49). In the book of Acts, which is a continuation of all
that Jesus 'began (*erxato*) to do and teach from the beginning' (Acts 1:1),
the Holy Spirit is the key to mission:

> The missionary witness of the Church begins *at the precise moment* of the
> descent of the Spirit, and the place and power of the Spirit to that witness
> are repeatedly attested in the book to its very end . . . The preponderance of
> emphasis in Luke's account of the coming of the Spirit at Pentecost and in his
> description of the missionary expansion of the Church in the remainder of
> Acts, lies on the witnessing activity of the Spirit and of the recipients of the
> Spirit.[28] (emphasis in the original)

A new beginning in God's plan of salvation for the whole world is now
dawning: the Holy Spirit fell upon the disciples 'at the beginning (*en
arche*)' (Acts 11:15).[29]

Stephen Bevans and Roger Schroeder helpfully identify seven stages
in the story of the church emerging in mission: before Pentecost; Pentecost; the Stephen narrative; Samaria and the Ethiopian eunuch; Cornelius
and his household; Antioch; and the mission to the Gentiles.[30] They interpret the nature of the church in relation to its missionary witness in the
following way:

> a study of the Acts will confirm that the church only comes to be as it under-
> stands and accepts mission anywhere and everywhere in the world . . . Even
> though the word *church* is used to designate the community in Acts occasion-
> ally (for example 5:11; 8:1,4; 9:31), our contention is that the disciples really

---

[27] Rowland, *Christian Origins*, p. 150.
[28] Harry R. Boer, *Pentecost and Missions* (Grand Rapids, MI: Eerdmans, 1961), pp.
109–10.
[29] Compare *en arche epoiesen ho theos ton ouranon kai ten gen* (Gen. 1:1, LXX) and,
en arche en ho logos (John 1:1).
[30] Stephen B. Bevans and Roger P. Schroeder, *Constants in Context: A Theology of
Mission for Today* (Maryknoll: Orbis Books, 2005), pp. 14–30.

do not fully *recognize* themselves as church – a separate reality from Judaism – until they recognize that they are called to a mission that has its scope 'the ends of the earth' (Acts 1:8) . . . Pentecost was not, contrary to what is usually said, the 'birthday of the church'; rather, the church is born only as the disciples of Jesus gradually and painfully realize that they are called beyond themselves to all peoples.[31] (emphasis in the original)

It is not surprising then that the story of Cornelius (Acts 10:1 – 11:18) and the founding of the church in Antioch take on huge significance in the entire narrative of Acts. The coincidental visions given to Cornelius and Peter are repeated three times; whilst the descent of the Spirit on all who responded to Peter's proclamation of the good news of Jesus (Acts 10:36–43) is recited twice. It is the gift of the Spirit, confirmed by speaking in tongues (Acts 10:45–6), that persuades Peter to baptise them in the name of Jesus, just as the Jews on the day of Pentecost were similarly baptised (Acts 10:48; 2:41); it also persuades the Jewish believers in Jerusalem to accept that 'God has given even to the Gentiles the repentance that leads to life' (Acts 11:18): 'Even Gentiles can partake in the blessings of the messianic age, and Jews and Gentiles can live and work together in bringing the message to them.'[32]

Antioch is significant for a number of reasons. It was the scene for the first real encounter between the gospel and the pagan world. The missionaries who took the gospel to this important city are unnamed. Luke refers to them as men from Cyprus and Cyrene; otherwise, they are incidental to the story. Up to that point, Jesus had been proclaimed using the Jewish title Messiah; now he was given the title Lord, so that the Gentiles would better understand his significance.[33] On hearing the news, the church in Jerusalem chose Barnabas to investigate what was going on. He was probably chosen because he was a native of Cyprus and was 'full of the Holy Spirit' (Acts 11:24). The believers received the nickname *Cristianous* (Acts 11:26) for the first time in Antioch. Finally, it was from Antioch that the Holy Spirit 'set apart . . . Barnabas and Saul for the work to which I have called them' (Acts 13:2). So, for the first time the church becomes a community quite distinct from the synagogue; and the church's mission to the Gentiles is launched, so that 'all other peoples may seek the Lord – even the Gentiles over whom my name has been called' (Acts 15:17, quoting Amos 9:12). The Gentiles are now incorporated into the people (*laos/'am*) of God. The book of Acts closes with Paul's final words: 'this salvation of God has been sent to Gentiles' (Acts 28:28).

---

[31] Bevans and Schroeder, *Constants in Context*, p. 10.

[32] Bevans and Schroeder, *Constants in Context*, p. 25.

[33] See Andrew Walls, *The Missionary Movement in Christian History: Studies in the Transmission of Faith* (Maryknoll: Orbis Books, 1996), p. 34.

There is a sense in which, in Luke's narrative, the 'Great Commission' given by Christ as recorded in the gospels is taken over by the Holy Spirit. The motivation for mission is not so much an external command as an internal prompting. The disciples will be witnesses to all that Jesus began to do and teach (Acts 1:1), and now to all he continues to carry out through his appointed emissaries by the presence of the Spirit in their midst:

> It is thus by an action of the sovereign Spirit of God that the church is launched on its mission. And it remains the mission of the Spirit. He is central. It is he who brings about the meeting of Philip with the finance minister of Ethiopia (8:26–40). It is the Spirit who prepares Ananias to receive the archpersecutor Saul as a brother (9:10–19) and who prepares Peter to break his cherished principles and go to be the guest of a pagan army officer (10:1–20). It is the Spirit who initiates the first mission to the Gentiles (13:1–2) and guides the missionaries on their journeys (16:7).[34]

The enigma of the Great Commission remains, for 'we do not find in Acts many exhortations to obedience to the Lord's command . . . Rather, Luke's narrative portrays mission as the overflow of joy and energy, given by the Holy Spirit: what Jesus predicts actually comes to pass when his followers are filled with his Holy Presence'.[35] One can only assume that in the initial stages of the early church's sharing of the good news of Jesus and the kingdom (Acts 28:31), the Holy Spirit's powerful presence with the community was sufficient motivation to go (eventually) to the ends of the earth and be witnesses of Jesus (*martures mou*) (Acts 1:8). At a later stage, the internalised command was also remembered as an external command of the same risen Jesus who had baptised his disciples with the same Spirit with which he himself had been baptised (Acts 10:37–8; 11:16). At the beginning, the Great Commission faded into the background; the disciples were directed by the Spirit to go to the Gentiles. In different circumstances, it was also necessary to be reminded that the authority and presence of the Lord was with them as they were to make disciples of all nations.

Mission in the Life of Paul, the Apostle

The encounter between Saul of Tarsus and the risen Jesus Christ has been celebrated in the church's liturgical year as the 'conversion of St

---

[34] Lesslie Newbigin, *The Open Secret* (London: SPCK, 2nd edn, 1995), pp. 58–9.
[35] Peskett and Ramachandra, *Message of Mission*, p. 214.

Paul'. However, as portrayed not once but three times in the book of Acts, the story is more about his call to be a special messenger to the Gentiles.[36] The Lord commanded Ananias in a vision to go to Paul in Damascus to restore his sight. When Ananias demurred, he was told to 'Go, for he is an instrument whom I have chosen to bring my name before Gentiles and kings and before the people of Israel' (Acts 9:15), and to say, 'you will be his witness to all the world of what you have seen and heard' (Acts 22:15), and 'I will rescue you from your people and from the Gentiles – to whom I am sending you to open their eyes'(Acts 26:18).

Paul himself reiterates several times his consciousness of the privilege and responsibility of being 'a debtor both to Greeks and to barbarians' (Rom. 1:14): 'Inasmuch then as I am an apostle to the Gentiles, I glorify my ministry (Rom. 11:13); 'the grace God gave me to be a minister of Christ Jesus to the Gentiles' (Rom. 15:15–16, NIV); 'God . . . was pleased to reveal his Son to me, so that I might proclaim him among the Gentiles' (Gal. 1:15–16); 'he . . . also worked through me in sending me to the Gentiles' (Gal. 2:8).

The missionary task

Paul understands the work (*ho ergos* – Acts 13:2) of mission as communicating the message enshrined in the gospel to everyone he was able to speak to: in Jewish synagogues (Acts 17:1–3), in the open air (Acts 14:15–17; 16:13–14; 17:17), in a lecture theatre (Acts 19:9), under house-arrest (Acts 28:23) and in prison (Phil. 1:13).

Paul explains the logic of the missionary task. The message is about salvation through Jesus Christ. In order to receive the benefits of salvation it is necessary to believe in the truth of the message. In order to believe, it is necessary to hear what the message is about. For that to happen there have to be messengers who have themselves believed. The messengers have to be sent (Rom. 10:14–15):

> Paul's understanding of his own task as *preaching* is seen in the use of the verb *kerusso* in Romans 10:8 (cf. 1 Cor. 1:23; 9:27; 15:14; 2 Cor. 1:19; 4:5; 11:4; Gal. 2:2; 1 Thess. 2:9) . . . In the same way he uses the verb 'to preach the gospel' (*euaggelizomai*, Isa. 52:7; Nah. 1:15) of his own activity (Rom. 1:15; 15:20) . . . The language used thus confirms that the task of a missionary is to convey

---

[36] See P.F. Penner, 'The Use of the Book of Acts in Mission Theology and Praxis', in *Bible and Mission: A Conversation between Biblical Studies and Missiology* (ed. Rollin G. Grams, I. Howard Marshall, Peter F. Penner and Robin Routledge; Schwarzenfeld: Neufeld Verlag, 2008), p. 79.

what for want of better terms must be called a combination of information and invitation.[37] (emphasis in the original)

In so far as Paul believed his main mission was to bring the good news to the Gentiles, the message he proclaimed began with the folly of idolatry and the need, therefore, to turn from the deception of trusting in futile practices to the living God, who alone is active in the affairs of human beings (1 Thess. 1:9; Rom. 1:21–3). It is only when human beings recognise the folly of trying to live in God's world by substituting all manner of other objects for the living Creator, and thereby failing to honour the only One who 'gives to all mortals life and breath and all things' (Acts 17:25; Rom. 1:23), that the message of Jesus Christ can begin to make sense.

Paul was seeking to address two major problems of the pagan world. First, by failing to acknowledge the evidence of the eternal power of the one divine being in creation, pagans suppressed the truth about reality (Rom. 1:18–20). Second, in believing that human wisdom alone could search out the meaning of existence they displayed both an intellectual and moral arrogance and a depth of deception: 'Claiming to be wise, they became fools' (Rom. 1:22); 'in the wisdom of God, the world did not know God through wisdom' (1 Cor. 1:21). The consequence of relying entirely on human wisdom is that humans create a fantasy world by exchanging the real world for one of their own devising.[38] This is the fundamental problem of a world structured by sin. But, says Paul, there is no excuse (Rom. 1:20; 2:1), for the Gentile, who does not have access to the revealed law of God (Rom. 2:14), nevertheless possesses a conscience – an inner moral compass – that bears witness to what is good and what is evil (Rom. 2:1–3,15–16; 1:32).

So the gospel, which is 'the power of God for salvation to everyone who has faith' (Rom. 1:16), begins with the uncovering of the true nature of the human predicament. The 'righteousness of God is revealed as the answer to the 'ungodliness' (asebeia) and 'wickedness' (adikia) (Rom.

---

[37] I. Howard Marshall, 'Paul's Mission According to Romans,' in *Bible and Mission: Christian Witness in a Postmodern World* (ed. Richard Bauckham; Carlisle: Paternoster Press, 2003), p. 102.

[38] Three times, in as many verses, Paul uses the verb *allasso* (twice in a strengthened sense as *metallasso*) – meaning to change or exchange one reality for another: 'they exchanged the glory of the immortal God for images resembling a mortal human being' (Rom. 1:23); 'they exchanged the truth about God for a lie' (Rom. 1:25); 'women exchanged natural intercourse for unnatural, and in the same way also the men' (Rom. 1:26–7).

1:17–18),[39] which are both the cause and the consequence of suppressing
the truth about fallen human nature. From this beginning, the unveiling
of the meaning of God's righteousness as the remedy for human folly
(Rom. 3:21) makes perfect sense. In this way the Gospel turns human
achievements upside down: 'God decided through the foolishness of our
proclamation, to save those who believe' (1 Cor. 1:21):

> The Christian missionaries proclaimed convictions that Gentiles found very
> difficult to accept; the existence of only one God, the redemptive significance
> of a crucified Jew, the bodily resurrection from the dead, and the claim that
> salvation is tied exclusively to faith in Jesus Christ . . . To accept faith in a
> crucified Savior as necessary condition for salvation was rationally impos-
> sible, as was faith in a bodily resurrection.[40]

The missionary task of the early church was not just about proclaiming
a message of salvation, the like of which no one had ever heard before.
That was difficult enough! It also involved, and most importantly, the
creation of communities of people, prepared ultimately to give their lives
in following Jesus, the Messiah, as the Way, the Truth and the Life. The
ekklesiae (local churches), scattered across the Mediterranean world of the
first century, were the 'assemblies' of a 'third race' of human beings, a
society of 'twice born' people (2 Cor. 5:17; Rom. 6:4; Gal. 6:15; Col. 1:18):
'The purpose of the gathering of the followers of Jesus is formulated
by Paul in terms of "edification" or "upbuilding" (Gk *oikodome*) . . . The
process of edification is integrally linked with the ministry of the word
of the apostles and prophets (Eph. 2:20–22) and other preachers and
teachers (Eph. 4:11).'[41]

The teaching given to the new converts would have included theological and ethical[42] guidance, instruction concerning church life and training
for missionary outreach.[43] Much of the content of the letters collected

---

[39] In most translations, as in most Greek texts of the New Testament, a paragraph break has been inserted between Romans 1:17 and 1:18. This interrupts
the flow of Paul's argument, which emphasises the parallel nature of the two
occurrences of the verb *apokalupto* (revealed / disclosed), joined emphatically
by the conjunction *gar* (for / because), used in both a causal and explanatory
sense – 'for you see . . .'
[40] Eckhard Schnabel, *Paul the Missionary: Realities, Strategies and Methods*
(Nottingham: IVP, 2008), pp. 361–2, 371.
[41] Schnabel, *Paul the Missionary*, p. 235.
[42] We will examine the ethical patterns of behaviour expected of those 'in Christ'
in the next chapter.
[43] See Schnabel, *Paul the Missionary*, pp. 236–55.

together in the New Testament assumes that life in the 'new-style' assemblies of the Greco-Roman villages, towns and cities would be entirely different in many respects from that hitherto experienced.

The geography of mission

One of the remarkable features of early Christianity is just how quickly the message about Jesus was spread throughout the known world of the first century. By the time that the Letter to the Colossians was written,[44] barbarians and Scythians were included among those who belonged to Christ (Col. 3:11). It has been suggested that the *barbaros* refer to people who live at the southern extreme of the world, whilst the *Skuthes* could probably have been people of East Asian descent, who had emigrated westwards and settled on the northern extremes of the empire.[45] So Paul makes reference to peoples living at least as far south as Ethiopia (and, maybe, even into the 'Horn of Africa') and peoples living at least to the north of the Danube and around the Black Sea.

In a rather enigmatic note, in writing to the church in Rome, Paul mentions that 'from Jerusalem and as far around as Illyricum I have fully proclaimed the good news of Christ' (Rom. 15:19). Alan Le Grys believes that Paul meant that 'he has identified the nodal points in the regional network of cities, established missions in those places and relied on the normal communication system to spread the word to the dependent communities beyond'.[46] A case in point would have been the churches founded in the Lycus Valley, upstream from Ephesus. The church in Colossae, for example, was established by Epaphras (Col. 1:7; 4:12–13), a resident of Colossae, who had probably come to faith in Jesus through the ministry of Paul during his time in Ephesus (around AD 52–5). Schnabel is somewhat ambivalent about the thesis that Paul adopted a deliberate strategy of 'targeting' prominent cities. Thus, he questions Roland Allen's famous proposition that Paul's missionary practice was to establish centres of Christian life in important places from where knowledge of the gospel might be spread around.[47] On the other hand, he also states that there does appear to be a focus on strategic cities in the expectation that people coming from outlying areas, on turning to Christ, would

---

[44] If written by Paul (and the arguments against Pauline authorship are not particularly convincing), then it may be dated around AD 63.

[45] See Richard Bauckham, ed. *Bible and Mission: Christian Witness in a Postmodern World* (Carlisle: Paternoster Press, 2003), p. 69.

[46] Le Grys, *Preaching to the Nations*, p. 97.

[47] See Roland Allen, *Missionary Methods: St. Paul's or Ours?* (Grand Rapids, MI: Eerdmans, 2001 [original, 1912]).

take the message that Paul preached back to their towns and villages.[48] He summarises his discussion of Paul's missionary movements in the following way:

> The geographical scope of Paul's missionary work was not controlled by a 'grand strategy' that helped him decide in which cities to begin a new missionary initiative. The evidence indicates that Paul moved to geographically adjacent areas that were open for missionary work. This is true for provinces, regions and cities . . . As an apostle whose ministry focuses on Gentiles, he targets cities because they are the major population centers and centers of communication and of education where people certainly speak Greek.[49]

Paul tells the Christian community in Rome that he wishes to visit them en route to Spain (probably to be identified with the Tarshish of the book of Jonah; also, Isa. 66:19; Jer. 10:9; Ezek. 27:12). There is no information that Paul ever reached the western extremity of the Mediterranean. However, his desire to move a long way beyond the capital of the empire shows his vision for making Christ known as widely as was feasible: 'The Biblical eschatology certainly has a geographical component, to the extent that the whole world belongs to Christ and He must be preached to the whole world . . . Christ's dominion over the world presses to a proclamation across *all* boundaries'[50] (emphasis in the original).

Could it be that Paul interpreted his missionary calling in terms of the mission of the servant of the Lord in Isaiah, who was sent to 'the ends of the earth' (Isa. 49:6)? Although he does not quote from this particular Servant Song, in Romans 15:21 he does interpret his missionary vocation in terms of the final Servant Song: 'Those who have never been told of him shall see, and those who have never heard of him shall understand' (quoting Isa. 52:15). He uses Old Testament passages freely to show that his mission to the Gentiles is part of the fulfilment of God's promises that the Gentiles will also form part of his chosen people (Rom. 15:9–12).

Harry Boer captures the witnessing dynamic and commitment of the church of the first generation of Christians:

> The New Testament witness knows no boundaries, acknowledges neither limits not exceptions . . . When we discuss the relationship of Pentecost to the witnessing Church we must qualify the Church in the sharpest possible manner as being *in her nature* a witnessing community and that she is this

---

[48] Schnabel, *Paul the Missionary*, pp. 282–5.
[49] Schnabel, *Paul the Missionary*, p. 287.
[50] Johannes Blauw, *The Missionary Nature of the Church: A Survey of the Biblical Theology of Mission* (Guildford: Lutterworth Press, 1974), pp. 112, 118.

precisely because she derives her life from the Pentecost event. Witnessing is not one among many functions or activities of the Church; it is of her essence to witness, and it is out of this witness that all her other activities take their rise . . . The Church is both a living and a life-communicating body, and the manner in which her life is manifested, sustained, and transmitted is the proclamation of the gospel.[51] (emphasis in the original)

---

[51] Boer, *Pentecost and Missions*, pp. 101, 102.

4

'The Light of the World': The Ethical Witness of the Christian Community

In his longest and most systematic piece of teaching, Jesus declares that his disciples are the 'salt of the earth' and 'the light of the world' (Matt. 5:13–14). Salt is used both to preserve food and to enhance its flavour. If it has degraded, it no longer serves its primary purpose and, therefore, might as well be thrown out and disposed of. Likewise, the function of light is to dispel darkness and enable people to see clearly the path ahead. In order to fulfil its purpose, a lamp is placed in a position where it can shed the maximum amount of light.

Jesus uses these two metaphors to indicate the role that his followers, as those blessed by God (Matt. 5:1–12), will have in the world. They will bring about so much good that societies will be sustained, enriched and illuminated by the truth. Jesus does not cast this task in the form of a command; he states it as a fact. His disciples are salt and light, just because their lives have been transformed dramatically by their encounter with him. The disciples' responsibility is to maintain their ability to influence for good the communities in which they live. Thus, Jesus closes this section of his teaching by exhorting his followers to ensure that the light of their lives brings brightness and clarity to the lives of others.

The light to which Jesus refers are the good works (*ta kala erga*) which will be visible to the entire world. This phrase may be open to misunderstanding. The notion of good works may conjure up a vision of people meddling in the lives of others by telling them how they should behave. This, emphatically, is not what is intended by Jesus' teaching. Rather, as he goes on to explain, it is the way they conduct themselves, as those who 'strive first for the kingdom of God and his righteousness' (Matt. 6:33), that will provide light in dark places:

If it be asked what the 'saltiness' and 'brightness' of Christian holiness are, the rest of the Sermon on the Mount gives us the answer. For in it Jesus tells us not to be like others around us: 'Do not be like them' (Matt. 6:8). Instead he calls us to a greater righteousness (of the heart), a wider love (even of enemies), a deeper devotion (of children coming to their Father) and a nobler ambition (seeking first God's rule and righteousness). It is only as we choose and follow his way, that . . . our light will shine, we shall be his effective witnesses and servants, and exert a wholesome influence on society.[1]

In this chapter I am using light as an image for good and right ethical behaviour. I will explore the ethical witness of the Christian community, as a response to its reading and application of the biblical text. So we will need to discover how it is possible to perceive and implement the moral teaching of the Bible in the changed circumstances of the world some two thousand and more years after it was written.

What is Meant by Ethics?

The idea and substance of ethics might seem fairly obvious. Much is made, for example in the teaching of young children, of *values* as standards of behaviour that have generally come to be accepted in society. Many of these, such as kindness and fairness, are generally extolled by society as laying down norms for civilised conduct between people and communities. Less common, but still articulated in discussions about how we would like people to act, are the *virtues*. Classically these have been summed up in seven approved attributes: charity, faith, fortitude, hope, justice, love, prudence and temperance. The influence of the Christian faith can be seen in the choice. Today, in societies that no longer pay much attention to the Christian tradition, the list might be compiled differently.

So, for most people, ethics or morality is a meaningful concept. Only small minorities would confess themselves baffled by talk of ethical values and virtues; perhaps they do not recognise the existence of any objective norms or standards of behaviour beyond what is chosen individually as working guidelines. For the majority, ethics can be defined as 'the craft of right living'[2], a set of principles or rules which has to be learnt; or, it might be 'the organization of moral convictions'[3] by means

[1] John Stott, *Issues Facing Christians Today* (Basingstoke: Marshall, Morgan & Scott, 1984), p. 67.
[2] Wayne A. Meeks, *The Moral World of the First Christians* (Philadelphia: Westminster Press, 1987), p. 61.
[3] Glen Stassen and David P. Gushee, *Kingdom Ethics: Following Jesus in Contemporary Context* (Downers Grove, IL: IVP, 2003), pp. 99–107.

of particular judgements and basic convictions. For the humanist, Anthony Grayling, ethics poses the general question, which has to lead to particular answers, 'How shall I live, in order to live a good life?'[4] The sub-title of his book implies the existence of a hierarchy of values that drives forward a comparison of different responses to the question about what is good. Ethics, then, is about discerning which alternatives should be embraced, and which rejected.

For Christians, ethics clearly has to do with what God requires of those he has created to bear his image: 'Do not be conformed to this world [or age], but be transformed by the renewing of your minds, so that you may discern what is the will of God – what is good (*agathos*) and acceptable (*euarestos*) and perfect (*teleios*)' (Rom. 12:2).[5]

As Philippians 4:8–9 suggests, there is 'an objective world of value grounded in the God of truth to which we are invited to attend with all our mind'.[6]

My purpose in this chapter is to lay out as clearly as possible some of the main matters that have to be considered in discovering for ourselves 'what does the LORD require' (Mic. 6:8). It is not my intention to engage in a general debate about the nature of ethics, or the many different theories that have been advanced to account for our sense, as human beings, of a moral order. In keeping with the overall aim of the book, I propose to reflect on moral behaviour as recounted in the Old and New Testaments and interpreted and embodied in the approved practices of the Christian community. A discussion with non-Christian versions of the moral life is for another time.[7] Such a discussion would have to look closely at the different alternatives and argue for those that appeared to give the best explanation of how the real world operates for good or ill. In this context, a Christian would begin by seeking to demonstrate that there are ways of being human that conform to the way human beings have been created, and there are ways that deform and destroy their humanity.

---

[4] Anthony Grayling, *What is Good? The Search for the Best Way to Live* (London: Wiedenfeld & Nicolson, 2003), p. 1.

[5] The translation in the NRSV margin is: 'what is the good and acceptable and perfect will of God.'

[6] David Clyne Jones, *Biblical Christian Ethics* (Grand Rapids: Baker Books, 1994), p. 16.

[7] I have attempted to initiate such a debate in my book, *The Future of Reason, Science and Faith: Following Modernity and Post-modernity* (Aldershot: Ashgate Publishing, 2007), pp. 174–87, 220–222, also in my book, *Christian Mission as Dialogue: Engaging the Current Epistemological Predicament of the West* (Nijmegen: Nijmegen Institute for Mission Studies, 2011), pp. 117–22.

Questions of Interpretation and Application

Although the content of the Bible includes much more than ethical commands and prohibitions, nevetheless information, warnings, guidance, and instructions about the good life and the right way to live are prominent throughout its pages. However, for those living some two thousand years after the last book was written, it is natural to ask how this particular text could possibly be relevant to ethical topics that confront humanity at such a distance:

> It deals with situations, customs and beliefs which are bound to seem remote to a culture built on a belief in progress and the superiority of the latest ideas . . . We might read it as an interesting account of the history and religious convictions of a small tribe from the Fertile Crescent. There seems, however, so little in it which actually touches the complexities of our way of life and so much in our world which is not even hinted at in the text. Even if one were able to make some direct connections between two such foreign worlds, why should the Bible be granted any privileged status?"[8]

The problem is not so difficult for Christians as they have, by definition, committed themselves to believing in the truth of the central message contained in its pages, namely that God, the Creator of all that exists, has himself entered the world of human beings to rescue them from the folly of turning their back on their Creator and getting lost in the process. Teaching on the kind of life that God has put forward to enable human flourishing, and that which thwarts and destroys such an achievement, is intimately linked to the message.

There are many passages which connect God's actions to liberate humans from sin and its consequences and a right moral life. Thus, for example, Paul directs the Christians in Ephesus to 'be imitators of God, as beloved children, and live in love, as Christ loved us and gave himself up for us, a fragrant offering and sacrifice to God. But fornication and impurity of any kind, or greed, must not even be mentioned among you, as is proper among saints' (Eph. 5:1–3). He continues by pointing out the kind of lifestyle which expresses, and is incompatible with, their new-found status as children adopted into God's family.

The principal message of the Bible may be likened to the most exquisitely beautiful painting, hanging in a gallery, but which has been severely damaged by someone throwing acid at it. A master-craftsman

---

[8] J. Andrew Kirk, *God's Word for a Complex World: Discovering How the Bible Speaks Today* (Basingstoke: Marshall Pickering, 1987), p. 4.

then spends a lengthy period of time and much effort in restoring the painting to its original glory. The ethical sections of the Bible describe both the nature of the acid which defaces the painting and the glory of the original as the artist created it.

This image may help to answer the question whether the moral standards set out in the Bible are universally valid. The short answer is that human life in the world comes as a gift and a given. There is a prior order to human life which is written into the very nature of human existence. We experience life in a certain way, because we encounter the particular reality of being human. No amount of denial can alter the essence of our species-being: 'Man does not encounter reality as an undifferentiated raw material upon which he may impose any shape that pleases him.'[9]

Whether humans agree with the proposition, or not, they inherit a certain constitution as created beings. A choice either to resist their intrinsic nature or to accept it and promote its wellbeing, under instruction from the one who has made it, is part of being human. This is probably the most basic life choice that any human being has to make.

These affirmations about the innate complexion of human reality are not mere arbitrary dogmas or unverifiable religious claims; they have been shown to be valid by numerous empirical studies regarding the optimum conditions for human thriving. Thus, even in a highly secular culture, not disposed to accept any belief, which has not been subject to intense critical examination, the second section of the Ten Commandments is still considered a basic moral standard, applicable at all times and in all places: so, one day of rest a week is a necessary part of the rhythm of life; it is right to respect and cherish one's parents; murder is a crime against our own humanity; coveting another person's property and then stealing it is a violation of the trust necessary for communities to flourish; and deliberately fabricating untruths about others undermines confidence in a person's integrity, creates doubt, confusion and suspicion, all of which leads to the breakdown of relationships.

This discussion points to an acceptance of the fact that at least certain ethical norms, which are prominent throughout the different strands of the biblical story, are right whatever the circumstances. However, at the same time, there are elements of the story and certain teachings which have been deemed by contemporary society to be unacceptable. The most notorious are the reputed divine injunctions to destroy whole social groups, which can be found in certain Old Testament passages (most notably in Joshua and Deuteronomy).

---

[9] Oliver O'Donovan, *Resurrection and Moral Order: An Outline for Evangelical Ethics* (Leicester: IVP, 1986), p. 25.

In a book designed to investigate the strategies that have been used by biblical commentators to understand and respond to these latter injunctions, Eryl Davies concludes that none of them explain adequately how the religious literature of Israel and the Christian church can include what appear to be such morally decadent commands.[10] Among the strategies, he outlines the evolutionary approach – namely that the people of God only gradually comprehended God's nature, moving from an inadequate concept of a tribal God to one whose purposes included all peoples equally.[11] In other words, the imprecatory passages reflect the underdeveloped moral consciousness of the people of Israel at the time. He also mentions a variety of strategies which argue that the injunctions are relative to time and place, being culturally conditioned; clearly, at a later stage of Israel's history, they have been abrogated.

There is also the paradigmatic approach which attempts to rescue what could be morally appropriate in the injunctions by looking for underlying moral principles. Thus, for example, Christopher Wright[12] argues that judgement upon wickedness has to be part of the action of a God of justice. He also points out that the particular commands, which appear to be so morally objectionable, have nothing to do with a supposed act of genocide or 'ethnic cleansing', seeing that other nations are equally used, as God's agents, to punish Israel (Lev. 18:28; Deut. 28:25–68). The punishment may seem ruthless and excessive. However, it remains in the canon of Scripture to remind all generations just how corrosive the 'acid' of corruption and perversion is of the wellbeing of human societies. In the New Testament, the Christian community is forbidden to take vengeance on those who have declared themselves to be its enemies and enemies of God (Rom. 12:14–21). Judgement is wholly God's prerogative and will take place in his way and at a time of his appointment. Christians may not presume to exercise it on God's part.

In attempting to deal with morally problematical texts, I have demonstrated something of the complexity of the task of interpretation and application of the ethical demands of an ancient script. I will now address some of the ways and means that are utilised to ensure that communities that take the Bible seriously do justice to its ethical teaching in their practices.

In the first instance, it is important to recognise the nature and character of the Bible, so that we do not expect it to be able to perform tasks for

---

[10] Eryl Davies, *The Immoral Bible: Approaches to Biblical Ethics* (London: T & T Clark, 2010).

[11] See for example, Gerd Thiessen, *Biblical Faith: An Evolutionary Approach* (London: SCM Press, 1984).

[12] Christopher Wright, in the Appendix, 'What about the Canaanites?' in *Old Testament Ethics for the People of God* (Leicester: IVP, 2004).

which it was not devised. The Bible is not a textbook on ethics;[13] it does not provide a series of ethical codes fit for all situations in life, nor does it outline a set of case studies to illuminate particular moral dilemmas. Moreover, the Bible does not engage in theoretical ethical debate. It does not, for example, engage critically or creatively with the general ethical sentiments of the communities surrounding Israel, although in its wisdom literature (such as the book of Job and Proverbs) there are clear echoes of moral precepts found in non-biblical sources of the times. In many ways, the demand to 'walk in the way of the LORD' is presented as unproblematic, for the various writings present themselves as a direct word from the Creator of the universe and the redeemer of his people Israel: 'He has told you . . . what is good; and what does the LORD require of you' (Mic. 6:8).

Nevertheless, what the Lord has showed does not come invariably in the form of precise commands, but is also woven into narratives, prophecies, meditations (such as Ecclesiastes) and liturgical passages (the Psalms). This poses the question of determining how each type of literature is to be understood. There is the added challenge of working out the appropriateness of certain injunctions or models of behaviour to situations encountered two or three millennia later. First, readers of the text have to be able to immerse themselves imaginatively in the original situation to discover, as far as possible, what was being implied in that context. Second, they need to have a clear view of the contemporary circumstances that require an ethical response; this latter may be vitiated by conflicting versions of a particular state of affairs, influenced by prior commitments. Third – the trickiest part – they need to establish a method of moving from one situation to another that does not appear anachronistic or inconsistent. When people appeal to the Bible to shape and support ethical decisions, they are making a case for a proposal about how the Bible informs and stipulates particular courses of action.[14]

This triple (hermeneutical) process will be explored in more detail at a later stage in the discussion. For the moment, I may postulate that the task involves discovering the ethical principles underlying the exhortations in the text and extrapolating from Scripture the most appropriate teaching by uncovering the common factors in both situations, which bring them together.[15]

---

[13] See I. Howard Marshall, 'Using the Bible in Ethics', in *Essays in Evangelical Social Ethics* (ed. David F. Wright; Exeter: Paternoster Press, 1979), p. 41.

[14] See Gareth Jones, 'The Authority of Scripture and Christian Ethics', in *The Cambridge Companion to Christian Ethics* (ed. Robin Gill; Cambridge: CUP, 2001), p. 18.

[15] Marshall, 'Using the Bible in Ethics', pp. 50–51.

The Historical Context

Although, as we have considered, the Bible does not engage directly with the ethical beliefs of those not belonging to God's people, to know something of the content of these beliefs and how they were practised at the time of the compilation of the various writings throws light on the assorted directives that are presented. Thus, for example, in understanding Paul's admonitions to the Christians living in Corinth, it is helpful to know that the guiding principles of conduct in Greco-Roman societies of the time were shaped by an honour–shame culture.[16] Honour referred not to one's personal integrity, but to the social recognition of one's worth and value as determined by one's status in the community.[17] Also in this milieu, economic and political life was built on an accepted pattern of patron–client relations. Rome in the first century exploited this arrangement to great effect by delegating power to local subordinates, who paid for the privileges they received.

It is suggested that in the world of the first Christians two kinds of approach to ethical matters predominated: that of Jewish scribes who based the search for justice and holiness on the strict observation of codified laws, and that of the Greeks characterised by wisdom and the pursuit of the classical virtues with a view to attaining perfection and happiness.[18] For Judaism there is a strong ethic of reward for obedience to clearly identified precepts: 'The main lesson to be learnt from this history, by any who cares to peruse it, is that men who conform to the will of God, and do not venture to transgress laws that have been excellently laid down, prosper in all things beyond belief, and for their reward are offered by God felicity.'[19] The Jew who performs specific commandments shows that he is a child of the covenant.[20]

For Aristotle, in his influential *Nicomachean Ethics*, the chief end of human existence is the achievement of *eudaimonia* – often incorrectly translated happiness – which is to be understood as flourishing by doing

---

[16] See Lisa Sowle Cahill, 'The Bible and Christian Moral Practices' in *Christian Ethics: Problems and Prospects* (ed. Lisa Sowle Cahill and James F. Childress; Cleveland: Pilgrim Press, 1996), p. 7.

[17] Cahill, 'Bible and Christian Moral Practices', p. 10.

[18] See Servais Pinckaers, *The Sources of Christian Ethics* (Edinburgh: T & T Clark, 1995), pp. 110–11.

[19] Josephus, *The Jewish Antiquities*, 1.14.

[20] See Robert J. Daly, *The Moral World of the First Christians: From Biblical Revelation to Contemporary Christian Praxis: Method and Content* (Ramsey, NJ: Paulist Press, 1984), pp. 95–6.

good and faring well:[21] 'It consists . . . in "living well or doing well", in certain deliberative activities (*praxeis*), and not in any psychological state which results from these.'[22]

Eudaimonia is achieved as people realise the functions for which they exist. One might interpret Aristotle's teaching as a kind of teleological natural ethic. It is possible to discover the chief purpose of life by rational reflection on actual living and deduce from this the chief virtues which ennoble human character. The rational and contented life is one in accord with nature.

The historical context also has a contemporary dimension:

> Western moral thought since the Enlightenment has been predominantly 'voluntarist' in its assumptions. That is to say, it has understood morality as the creation of man's will, by which he imposes order on his life, both individually and socially . . . Any ethic, however 'reasonable' it may be in terms of its prac-ticality or internal consistency, is originally a posit of the will, a choice to which either individual or society has, in free self-determination, committed itself.'[23]

It might be argued that modern moral consciousness in Western societies is encapsulated in thinking about human rights. In common parlance, human rights are understood to imply that human beings in certain instances possess justified claims that entitle them, either as individuals or as a well-defined group, to require certain behaviour from others.[24] Rights are assumed to be inherent somehow in the nature of things.

As the concept of rights began to develop, it lost its original founda-tion in the notion that individual conscience has to be free to refuse the arbitrary interpretation of civic duties by unrepresentative authorities of the state. Conscience had appealed to the higher authority of the will of God as manifested in his written word and interpreted by a community consciously indwelt by the Spirit of the incarnate Word. With the coming of the Enlightenment, divine law was transmuted into natural law built upon an assumed innate constitution or essence inhering in human beings as such. So it has come to be taken for granted that rights are a given fact of nature that do not have to be authorised or sanctioned by some temporal power but discovered in the very reality of being human.

In other words, rights are justified by virtue of human nature. They can be known by the light of human reason, independently of belief in

---

[21] David Clyne Jones, *Biblical Christian Ethics*, p. 17.
[22] David E. Cooper, *World Philosophies: An Historical Introduction* (Oxford: Black-well, 1996), p. 123.
[23] O'Donovan, *Resurrection and Moral Order*, p. 16.
[24] See Neil Messer, *Christian Ethics* (London: SCM Press, 2006), p. 62.

God: 'The notion of universal, inviolable human rights – now enshrined in many international treaties, declarations and legal frameworks – owes much to the kind of natural rights theory that stems from Grotius.'[25] This presumption might be called 'the *intuitive* theory': repeated cognitive insight in all ages and across cultures simply tells us that human rights are to be inferred from the reality of human nature.

Rights, however, comprise an abstraction; they constitute a theoretical entity. They do not exist simply by virtue of a dogmatic statement that they exist. Moreover, it is not self-evident that they exist. For large periods of human history it has not been at all obvious that all human beings possess innate rights to life and liberty. Up to the beginning of the nineteenth century (a mere 200 years ago), slavery was considered a natural condition, and therefore justifiable. Many societies in the past (and some still today) have queried whether women are endowed with reason, at least to the same capacity as men. The claim to an inviolable, individual conscience is of recent historical appearance, and has been disputed (for example in the case of conscientious objection to military service) until well into the twentieth century, even in so-called liberal societies.

Alasdair MacIntyre points out the inherent difficulty of the notion of human rights within a purely secular and humanistic perspective. He maintains that there are no such things as self-evident truths. The recognition of a truth depends upon a prior commitment to a tradition of discourse in which the idea of truth makes sense. In the case of human rights no such tradition exists:

> The concept of rights was generated to serve one set of purposes as part of the social invention of the autonomous moral agent . . . When claims invoking rights are matched . . . against claims based on some traditional concept of justice, it is not surprising that there is no rational way of deciding which type of claim is to be given priority or how one is to be weighed against the other.[26]

He refers to the claims as substitute artefacts for concepts of an older and more traditional morality. One such tradition, of course, is the Christian, which argues, precisely from a belief in the creation of the universe by

---

[25] Messer, *Christian Ethics*, p. 63. If space allowed, it would be possible to expound the contribution that John Locke has made to the theory of natural rights; for a short explanation see e.g. Garrett Thomson, *On Locke* (Belmont, CA: Wadsworth, 2001), pp. 68–73. It should be noted that Locke, although he believed in the light of reason, never divorced it wholly from the revelation of God's will revealed in the Bible.

[26] Alasdair MacIntyre, *After Virtue: A Study in Moral Theology* (Notre Dame: University of Notre Dame Press, 1981), p. 68.

a personal divine being, that there is a given reality made known not by some kind of universal intuition but by the One who has created it. However, such a ground for a meaningful conversation about rights is not open to a non-theist, be he or she an evolutionary naturalist or a religious monist.

Those who wish to use the Bible to determine what is good and right and which virtues should be practised have to come to terms with the prevalent modern opinion that human beings are entirely self-sufficient in their ability to perceive, by the light of reason alone, how we should conduct our lives in every dimension of existence. The contemporary historical context is often one of disdain and hostility towards the basic Christian claim that moral rectitude depends on the will of the One who has brought everything into existence, has ordered it in a particular way and has made known to chosen messengers how that way is to be followed. The call to disciples of Jesus to let their light shine before others is the occasion for demonstrating, both in theory and practice, that the way of Jesus is both a condition for ethical reflection and the best way of living. I turn, therefore, to a review of some of the principal elements that go to make up the biblical witness to what the Lord requires, beginning with the Old Testament.

Ethics in the Old Testament

The Old Testament is a library of books that reflect the relationship between the Lord and his people using a variety of literary modes. Here we find historical records, legends, ceremonial and moral law codes, songs of praise and lament, 'philosophical' reflections, a love poem, advice about everyday living, prophetic warnings about the present and anticipations of the future. What the Lord requires may be deduced, in differing ways, from each one of these forms of literature. Ethical expectations, therefore, are derived from a number of sources. Because the Ten Commandments have become so prominent in the history of Christian moral discourse, it is natural to jump to the conclusion that ethics are based primordially on direct orders – 'You shall' or 'You shall not'. The Old Testament is full of such orders. However, there are a number of other foundations for considering a true ethical life: the examples, both good and bad, of key actors in the history recounted; the character of the Lord as shown forth in liturgical and prophetic writings; the implied ethical demands contained in the warnings of judgement and in the announcement of a future new creation, and the sayings of the wise.

Many commentators have pointed out that ethical requirements flow from two basic suppositions: the nature of God and his actions in the life of the nations. The two flow together. A classic case can be found in Leviticus 19. The various moral injunctions spring from the obligation laid upon God's people to be holy, for the Lord is holy (Lev. 19:2). Many of the requirements in this passage are based on the iniquity of exploiting another person. They are based on the fact that Israel exists as a people delivered from exploitation in Egypt: 'you shall love the alien as yourself, for you were aliens in the land of Egypt. I am the LORD your God' (Lev. 19:34).

The oft-repeated refrain, 'I am the LORD', or 'I am the LORD your God' in the chapter (fourteen times) refers to both the nature and the deeds of the Lord:

> For Israel to be holy . . . meant that they were to be a distinctive community among the nations . . . Or to be more precise, Israel was to be YHWH-like rather than like the nations . . . Holiness for Israel is a practical down-to-earth reflection of the transcendent holiness of YHWH himself . . . Israel was to respond to their redemption by reflecting their Redeemer.[27]

John Rogerson, in reflecting on the way ethical injunctions depend on the prior nature and activity of God, talks about the 'imperatives of redemption' and 'structures of grace'. The first, he says, are the motive clauses which give the reasons why God commands certain things. The second are administrative and practical arrangements designed to introduce graciousness and compassion into the details of everyday life.[28]

The law, therefore, is a matter of God's gracious acts of deliverance; it is not to be experienced as a mere duty or burden. The righteousness created and shared by God is the presupposition not the goal of obedience. We are to walk in the ways of the Lord out of gratitude and love and in loyalty to the One who has taken a special interest in preparing a people who will reflect his compassion and justice.[29]

So God's people should act on the basis of interpreting their story as the story of God with them. Their ethical conduct will originate in their beliefs about the meaning and purpose of their history: 'It was in the remembering and retelling of their past, and in the hope that this generated for the

---

[27] Christopher J.H. Wright, *The Mission of God: Unlocking the Bible's Grand Narrative* (Nottingham: IVP, 2006), pp. 373, 374, 375.

[28] John Rogerson, 'The Old Testament and Christian Ethics', in *The Cambridge Companion to Christian Ethics* (ed. Robin Gill; Cambridge: CUP, 2001), p. 37.

[29] See Stephen Charles Mott, *Biblical Ethics and Social Change* (Oxford: OUP, 1982), pp. 25–6.

future, that Israel most learned the shape of its own identity and mission and the ethical quality of life appropriate to both.'[30]

The foundational story, from which the law derived, was the liberation from oppression in Egypt and the covenant that the Lord made with the people at Sinai: '[God] delivered them and made them his people and *then* called them to keep his law. Ethical obedience is a response to God's grace, not a means of achieving it.'[31] 'Nearly all the laws in the Pentateuch appear within a covenant framework. Law is therefore integral to God's saving plan which is worked out through covenants.'[32]

In light of the discussion so far, we can turn to consider legitimate ways of appropriating the ethical precepts that are manifest throughout the Old Testament. Once we have established the general dictum that many (but not all) ethical proposals have relevance across time,[33] probably the most fruitful recommendation is to work at discovering intermediate principles as the bridge between the ancient texts and modern contexts. Otherwise, the specific nature of many commands could lead one to assume that the laws of the Old Testament have little to do with the complexities of living in the twenty-first century.

These principles are known technically as *middle axioms*: 'A middle axiom is a specific principle which stands either between a universal proposition and a concrete situation or between concrete applications in different situations.'[34]

Thus, for example, in order to find a way from the general command, 'Open your hand to the poor and needy neighbour in your land' (Deut. 15:11) to the intricacies of contemporary economic life, one might use a middle axiom like the redistribution of wealth across a particular community through progressive taxation. In the case of Israelite society, redistribution was never an end in itself; its purpose was to give the person who had fallen on hard times an opportunity to re-establish himself as a viable economic unit, able to provide for his extended family and participate fully in the life of the covenant community.

Closely related to middle axioms is the notion of *dynamic equivalents*. Borrowed from the work of translation, 'the intention is to convey to contemporary readers, using appropriate forms, meanings *equivalent* to

---

[30] Christopher J.H. Wright, *Old Testament Ethics*, p. 26.

[31] Christopher J.H. Wright, *Old Testament Ethics*, p. 28 (emphasis original).

[32] Gordon Wenham, 'Grace and Law in the Old Testament', in *Law, Morality and the Bible* (ed. Bruce Kaye and Gordon Wenham; Downers Grove, IL: IVP, 1978), p. 9

[33] See Walter Kaiser, *Toward Rediscovering the Old Testament* (Grand Rapids, MI: Zondervan, 1987), pp. 155–66.

[34] Kirk, *God's Word for a Complex World*, p. 101.

those understood by the original readers'.[35] 'A dynamic equivalent works on the basis of being able to distinguish between form and content. In searching for God's revealed will, the content remains the same across the ages. The outward form, however, may change dramatically both in terms of social development from simple to complex societies and of culture, from what is appropriate in one community's set of traditions to another.'[36]

Thus, the equivalent of the remission of debts in the legislation for the Year of Jubilee (Lev. 25:25–8) might be the setting of interest rates according to a person's, a business's or nation's ability to repay. The purpose of the original legislation was to avoid situations of perpetual impoverishment. The dynamic equivalent is flexibility in dealing with debt, to save businesses and thus avoid the human tragedy of the loss of jobs.

Some consider the use of *models* as an imaginative way of applying the Old Testament to modern situations. A model is a pattern to be copied. For example, events and institutions in the life of Israel could be prototypes to be adapted and followed centuries later. The confederation of tribes at the time of the judges might point to the desirability of a decentralised government, whilst the advent of a king (1 Sam. 8:4–18) might serve as a warning against both a centralised power and a hereditary dynasty (Judg. 8:22–3).[37]

Without being able to exhaust all hermeneutical possibilities, I would suggest the use of *precedents* as a final example of appropriation. A precedent is a legal judgement which serves as an authoritative case in making later judicial decisions. It works by way of analogy from one case to another. If in one set of circumstances, one particular course of action was followed, what is suggested (recommended or expected) in similar situations at another time? In the contemporary practice of detaining people without charge or trial for lengthy periods of time, the biblical precedents might be the near-total absence in Israel of punishment by imprisonment and the demand that legal hearings should happen swiftly.

Ethics in the Ministry of Jesus

Today Christians, in attempting to discover appropriate ways of living from the revelation of God's will and purposes, would always try to survey the whole of the Bible. Thus, it would be most unusual to seek to

---

[35] Kirk, *God's Word for a Complex World*, p. 103.
[36] Kirk, *God's Word for a Complex World*, pp. 103–4.
[37] Kirk, *God's Word for a Complex World*, p. 100.

apply ethical norms from the Old Testament without first seeing whether and how the New Testament (the fullness of revelation) deals with the material. In particular, the recorded words and actions of Jesus in the four gospels come with an especially weighty authority.

It is quite beyond the scope of this book to explore the complexities of recovering the actual teaching of Jesus. If it is admitted that the gospel narratives contain, along with reliable historical data, a certain interpretation of events by the respective authors in the interests of shedding light on later contexts in which the early church found itself, it also has to be admitted that finding reliable criteria to distinguish between the one and the other is well-nigh impossible. The long debate between scholars concerning the various 'quests for the historical Jesus' has engendered more heat than light. It is my intention to proceed, therefore, on the basis that the canonical text provides its own authority for matters of ethical conduct, irrespective of whether anyone can be sure that we are listening to the actual words that Jesus spoke.

One of the first principles in deducing appropriate ethical stances from Jesus' ministry is to set it in the historical context in which it was exercised. It was the constant hope of the most pious among the Jews that God would free the nation from the dominance of foreign powers, so that the people might be able to live according to the laws and statutes of the Lord and thus bring closer the promised kingdom of God. As one might expect, however, there was disagreement about what the law required among different groups, all of whom claimed to be most faithful in their respective interpretations. Josephus identifies four main groups: the Pharisees, the Sadducees, the Essenes and the Zealots.[38] Although Josephus himself is probably not wholly accurate in his portrayal of the groups, owing to his own interests,[39] other historical sources confirm the prominence of these groups in the religious and political life of the times. Of the four groups, the Pharisees and Sadducees feature most prominently in the gospel narratives. There are also hints here and there of the other two groups.

What links all the groups together is the hope that one day the Lord would be acknowledged throughout the nation as the only sovereign ruler of the people. The Lord would be the true king who would re-establish the nation's former glory, as in the days of David and

---

[38] Detailed accounts of each group can be found in Craig A. Evans and Stanley E. Porter, *Dictionary of New Testament Background* (Downers Grove, IL: IVP, 2000).

[39] See for example, Alan Storkey, *Jesus and Politics: Confronting the Powers* (Grand Rapids, MI: Baker Academic, 2005), pp. 52–3.

Solomon, giving peace and prosperity.[40] In other words his kingdom will be restored to his people as prophesied in Daniel: 'The kingship and dominion and the greatness of the kingdoms under the whole heaven shall be given to the people of the holy ones of the Most High; their kingdom shall be an everlasting kingdom, and all dominions shall serve and obey them' (Dan. 7:27).[41]

This hope is echoed in the disciples' question to Jesus after the resurrection: 'Lord, is this the time when you will restore the kingdom to Israel?' (Acts 1:6)[42]

It is not surprising, therefore, that a new prophetic era seemed to be dawning when both John the Baptist and Jesus are reported as proclaiming that the kingdom has come near (*engiken he basileia ton ouranon*) (Matt. 3:2; 4:17). Both, for different reasons, raised enormous expectations among the people – John, because of his ministry of baptism and his announcement of the advent of the Messiah; Jesus, because of his teaching and healing ministry. Now Jesus' ethical teaching has to be seen as intimately related to his interpretation of the meaning of God's reign. Thus, in answer to the disciples' question about status in the coming kingdom, Jesus points to a child and proclaims that the only way of becoming part of the kingdom is to turn away from such notions and accept the humble position of a child, who counted for little in the social observances of the time (Matt. 18:1–4).

The imminent arrival of the reign of God would betoken a reversal of normal worldly values, including the standard religious and social criteria of worthiness. Jesus' inclusive practices demonstrated a rejection of the entire world of power, prestige and rank, and a call to an unassuming service to the community.[43] The restoration of marginalised people to mainstream society, as exemplified supremely in the woman who had 'been suffering from haemorrhages for twelve years' (Mark 5:25–34), dramatises the meaning of God's rule. Jesus did not interpret her action in touching him as a violation of social norms, which undoubtedly it was, but as an act of faith that brought restoration to that wholeness of life that the kingdom promised.[44]

Jesus taught quite explicitly that right and just behaviour springs from the heart. It cannot, therefore, be directed by a set of external rules

---

[40] In the first century, hope in God's rule would have emphasised: i) deliverance from national enemies; ii) the faithful worship of God, and iii) living in justice (e.g. *Pss. Sol.* 17:26,28; *Jub.* 1:15–19); see Mott, *Biblical Ethics*, p. 87.

[41] See also Isa. 14:2; 2 Sam. 7:13; Pss 145:13; 22:27–8; 72:11.

[42] See also Matt. 17:11.

[43] See Sowle, 'The Bible and Christian Moral Practices', pp. 8, 11.

[44] See Robert L. Brawley, ed. *Character Ethics and the New Testament: Moral Dimensions of Scripture* (Louisville: Westminster John Knox Press, 2007), p. 63.

(Mark 7:1–23). This is because sin is a function of the whole person; reason, volition, emotions and bodily sensations are all disordered.[45] A person, therefore, needs to be reordered from the inside out. So the first approach to an ethical life under God's rule, demonstrated in the life of Jesus, is repentance and the desire to have one's sins forgiven, not hidden from view by extra efforts to fulfil the established pattern of a devout life. John refers to the need for a new birth of water and the Spirit (John 3:5) in order to enter into God's kingdom. This stress on the new inner being echoes Jeremiah's promise that God would make a new covenant with his people, writing his law on their hearts, forgiving their iniquity and remembering their sins no more (Jer. 31:33–4).

On different occasions, and in relation to separate incidents, Jesus clearly distinguishes between strict observances of the law and the principles that lie behind them. The first occasion is related to keeping the Sabbath and the second to divorce (Matt. 12:1–8; 19:3–12). In both cases, Jesus showed his reverence for the authority of the Scriptures, but also showed that he was not bound by the casuistic interpretations found in the oral traditions of the scribes.[46] In the cases of paying the temple tax (Matt. 17:24–7) or taxes to the Roman Empire (Matt. 22:15–22) he showed that he distinguished between the principle behind his response and its application. In all these episodes, the religious authorities were trying to trap Jesus into advocating a compromise that would demonstrate his infidelity to the written text or tradition.

The Sermon on the Mount

Jesus' teaching recorded at length in Matthew's Gospel (Matt. 5 – 7) and in a shorter version by Luke (Luke 6:20–49) has rightly been called the charter of Christian discipleship and the ethics of the kingdom. The block of teaching begins with a reference to the kingdom by stressing the type of people that will be part of God's new world order: they will be poor in spirit, humble, merciful, pure in heart, and peacemakers. They will hunger and thirst for justice. They will be persecuted, because those outside the kingdom will not be able to tolerate either the way they live or the One for whom they live ('persecuted for righteousness sake', 'people revile you and persecute you . . . on my account').

---

[45] See Timothy P. Jackson, 'The Gospels and Christian Ethics' in *The Cambridge Companion to Christian Ethics* (ed. Robin Gill; Cambridge: CUP, 2001), p. 52.

[46] See Robin Nixon, 'Fulfilling the Law: The Gospel and Acts' in *Law, Morality and the Bible* (ed. Bruce Kaye and Gordon Wenham; Downers Grove, IL: IVP, 1978), p. 60.

To belong to the kingdom is to be blessed (*makarios*). The meaning of the Beatitudes is not that Jesus is invoking a blessing upon them, nor is it part of a wish. Rather, 'they affirm *a quality of spirituality that is already present*.'[47] Thus, 'As a group, the Beatitudes do *not* mean "Blessed are the people who do X because they will receive Y." The point is not exhortation for a certain type of behavior. Instead they should be read with the sense, "Look at the essential spirituality and joy of these people who have or will be given X." '[48]

In other words, the ethic of the Sermon on the Mount is underpinned by God's sheer grace. It is notable that Luke uses the classic word for grace (*charis*) in his version of the teaching: 'If you love those who love you, what *grace* is that to you? . . . If you do good to those who do good to you, what *grace* is that to you?' The usual translations (credit, reward) miss the point. Jesus is emphasizing that this type of behaviour is only possible because of the gracious action of God. We should, therefore, translate the phrases: 'If you do X, how are you demonstrating the gift of grace? For even sinners do the same; but, if you do Y – "love your enemies, do good and lend, expecting nothing in return" – you will know you *are* already children of God, and that will be your reward.' Surely this is why Jesus can tell his disciples that their righteousness should exceed that of the scribes and the Pharisees (Matt. 5:20), just as it should exceed that of the tax-collectors (Matt. 5:46) and Gentiles (Matt. 5:47; 6:7). So, living according to the normal behaviour expected of those who have tasted the grace of God is the outworking of a state of affairs; it is not a reward for great ethical strivings.

It is a failure to appreciate the source of ethical conduct that has led many to misunderstand the nature and purpose of the Sermon on the Mount. People as eminent as Tolstoy and Gandhi have extolled the ideals of the sermon because, if only they could be reached by ordinary mortal humans, social relationships would be transformed. However, others have judged the ideals unattainable. Therefore, some have concluded that the ethical norms being promulgated are for a future age – the end times, when the disciples are awaiting the imminent return of Jesus to claim his sovereign rule over the whole of creation. Others think they are intended only for a select group of disciples called to a heroic effort on behalf of the majority; the latter are merely expected to live by less exacting standards.

---

[47] See the discussion in Kenneth E. Bailey, *Jesus Through Middle Eastern Eyes: Cultural Studies in the Gospels* (London: SPCK, 2008), p. 68 (emphasis in the original).

[48] Bailey, *Jesus Through Middle Eastern Eyes*, p. 68 (emphasis in the original).

However, Jesus' teaching should not be interpreted as a general ethical guide given to humanity as a whole. It is not intended to form the kind of moral imperative that the philosopher Kant made the foundation of his practical reason. In the popular imagination the mission of Jesus is often summed up in terms of a law-giver, or teacher of wisdom, who has instructed us how to live. However, a moment's thought demonstrates that this kind of understanding is not possible. Jesus' intention cannot be that of providing a general code of moral excellence. The Sermon on the Mount teaches a liberating ethic. Mere obedience to an external standard of teaching enslaves.

The teaching is not intended either to give an ethic for another world; an ethic, so it is supposed, that was meant to guide the first disciples as they eagerly awaited the imminent return of their Lord in a temporary situation of extreme persecution: 'Do not worry about tomorrow, for tomorrow will bring worries of its own. Today's trouble is enough for today' (Matt. 6:34). The troubles are said to refer to the exceptional trials that will come upon the disciples signalling that the last days are already here. 'Today' (also occurring in the Lord's Prayer), it is suggested, refers to this interim moment of waiting. However, this cannot be the intention of the sermon either, for elsewhere a period of church growth is implied. In this context it takes its place as a rule of life to be taught to the disciples as part of their obedience to the preaching of the word: 'Everyone therefore who hears these words of mine and acts on them will be like a wise man who built his house on the rock' (Matt. 7:24).

The ethic of the sermon cannot be limited to a particular historical or temporal situation. There is no evidence that the disciples held to one particular set of ethical norms, whilst they waited expectantly the coming of their Master, and then changed to another when their hope was apparently not fulfilled. On the contrary, there is plenty of evidence, for example in the ethical sections of the epistles, to suggest that the sermon deeply influenced the teaching of the apostles a generation or two after it was delivered.[49]

We are not dealing here either with an ethic for a minority. During its history the church has proposed that the teaching of the Sermon on the Mount is applicable only to a small group of Christians specially called to a life of exceptional dedication to the kingdom of God. It has been called a 'heroic' ethic.[50] The minority has been entrusted with a

---

[49] See the discussion in David Wenham, *Paul: Follower of Jesus or Founder of Christianity?* (Grand Rapids, MI: Eerdmans, 1995), pp. 250–52, 265–6, 271–4.

[50] By Juan Luis Segundo, *Masas y Minorias: en la dialectica divina de la liberacion* (Buenos Aires: La Aurora, 1973).

special calling to uphold the strictest interpretation of Jesus' teaching on behalf of the baptised Christian masses. According to the argument, it is quite impracticable for the latter in ordinary life to fulfil such high moral precepts.

This belief led to the practice of monasticism. The monks and nuns could consecrate themselves to the challenge of living an exemplary life, untrammelled by the normal cares, ambiguities and contradictions of secular living. It also led to the idea of the merits of the 'saints'. Outstanding lives of ethical integrity, beyond what it was thought God normally required of average believers, could earn excess merit. Together these constituted the church's 'treasury of merits' to be applied, where necessary, for the benefit of all those who had fallen short of the exacting standards of the kingdom.

Apart from the false notion that pleasing God and following Christ is based on a kind of moral transaction that compensates for the failure to attain a sufficient standard of righteousness to fit a person for heaven, there is no suggestion in the sermon that Christ is only addressing a small minority of his disciples. In the Great Commission at the end of the gospel, Christ commands his followers to 'make disciples of all nations . . . teaching them to obey everything that I have commanded you' (Matt. 28:19–20). The command refers to all who become disciples. The obvious conclusion can be drawn that discipleship entails obedience to Jesus' teaching in its entirety, to which there are no exceptions. There is no hint either in the sermon or in the rest of the New Testament of two different standards of ethical requirement.

There appears to be left only one possible alternative interpretation. The clue to the proper understanding of the sermon is given in the command of Jesus to teach all nations (Matt. 28:20). The highest priority for the new community after Jesus' resurrection was to go throughout the world to make disciples. These disciples were to be taught to live on the basis of Jesus' teaching.

The Sermon on the Mount can, therefore, be called the ethic of the kingdom or new order of life made possible by Jesus' death and resurrection. It is the new *torah* for the new community of God's people. Although, like the kingdom, it will never be fully realised in human history, it cannot demand anything less than absolute perfection. There is no such thing as an interim ethic of apocalyptic expectation. Nor is there an ethic intended only for those who are called to a particularly heroic life of self-sacrifice. Just as the kingdom is open to all, so the ethic of the kingdom is a possibility for all who would sincerely follow in the way of Jesus the Messiah. It is realizable not just for those who may have internalised a high moral ideal and integrity but for all who have taken upon themselves the yoke of the kingdom, which is the yoke of the servant king: 'Take my yoke upon you, and learn from me . . . For my yoke is easy, and my burden is light' (Matt. 11:29).[51]

When Jesus says, 'Take my yoke upon you, and learn from me', he is saying, in effect, acknowledge my sovereignty and be my disciple. The ethic of the kingdom goes a long way beyond a generally accepted morality. The corollary of this is that people will not be judged on the basis of a shallow profession of faith in Jesus or by the external manifestation in their lives of the standards of the kingdom, but by whether they have truly centred their lives on obedience to the king (Matt. 7:21–3).

The revolutionary nature of Jesus' attitude to the law is very simple. It lies in the fact that the law, now interpreted in terms of the ethic of the kingdom, and the kingdom itself are completed in his person and are subordinate to him. It is not surprising, then, that the crowds, accustomed as they were to the ever-increasingly minute regulations of the law given by the scribes for their obedience, should recognise something completely novel in Jesus' teaching (Matt. 7:28–9).

Stassen and Gushee find in the sermon not so much a set of twofold antitheses – 'You have heard that it was said . . . but I say to you' – but a threefold pattern of transforming initiatives. The climactic parts are where the imperatives are situated (e.g. 'be reconciled to your brother or sister' [Matt. 5:24]). They invite deliverance from the vicious cycles of anger, insult, hate, etc. So the emphasis is not on the negative prohibitions, but on transforming practices as signs of grace. They do not refer merely to inner attitudes, vague intentions or moral convictions, but real, practical actions:[52] 'The Sermon on the Mount . . . points to the practices of deliverance in the midst of a world of sinful bondage to vicious cycles of despair and destruction.'[53]

Wayne Meeks sums up the ethical teaching that Jesus sets before his disciples in the following way: 'The sectarian character of the ethic consists in the demand that prudential and publicly enforceable rules be set aside altogether.'[54]

---

[51] In rabbinic literature the recitation of the divine name, the *shema* (Deut. 6.4), to which there is reference in the Lord's Prayer, 'hallowed be your name', was often referred to as taking upon oneself 'the yoke of the kingdom'. This meant recognizing God as a personal Lord and King and rejecting all other gods. In the context of Jesus' teaching the subsequent prayers, 'your kingdom come, your will be done on earth as it is in heaven', would be a natural sequence to this commitment.

[52] See Stassen and Gushee, *Kingdom Ethics*, pp. 123–45.

[53] Stassen and Gushee, *Kingdom Ethics*, p. 144.

[54] Meeks, *Moral World*, p. 139.

The only valid standard is 'the will of the Father'. This is not an abstract perfection, for the rules belong to the realm of the everyday: marriage; truth-telling; facing foreign soldiers and other enemies; giving alms; praying; forgiving. The rules are exemplary, not comprehensive. They are not philosophical principles from which guidelines for behaviour could be rationally derived. The teaching does not add up to an ethical 'system'. It points to the kind of life expected in the new community that was coming into being.[55]

Ethics in the Ministry of Paul

Paul adopts a similar approach to his ethical teaching. Naturally, he couches it in language that reflects the events of the death and resurrection of Jesus, as he had come to understand their meaning. He emphasises the communal dimension of Christian living. Thus, for example, reconciliation takes place within a community created for that purpose. The church is a new reality, which brings together antagonistic parties (Eph. 2:12–19; 3:5–6) to follow a calling of mutual care and consideration (e.g. Gal. 6:1–10; Rom. 12:1–2,9–21; Col. 3:9–15).

This new community was called to an ethical lifestyle often in contrast to the social traditions of the surrounding Hellenistic and Roman cultures. Thus, for example, the so-called 'household rules' (e.g. Eph. 5:21 – 6:9; Col. 3:18 – 4:1) speak about reciprocal duties that were non-existent in the Roman household. In the household of faith, the mutual relationship to Jesus Christ was the controlling criterion of all relationships.[56] Even if the rules are intended to ensure a proper order, in order to guard against an unbridled liberty that might turn into anarchy (1 Cor. 6:12; 10:23), the structures of social and personal existence are being transformed by the reality that Christians have a new identity in the body of Christ. In Christ things can never be the same again. All relationships in the family and in civic society are to be measured by what it means to be 'in the Lord' (Col. 3:18).[57]

Paul's ethical instructions might well be called 'counter-cultural.' Obviously, as someone trained in the strict rabbinic traditions of the Pharisees (Phil. 3:5; Acts 23:6), Paul condemns the lax morality of pagan cultures without a knowledge of the law of the Lord (Rom. 1:24–31; 1 Cor. 6:9–10;

---

[55] Meeks, *Moral World*, pp. 139–40.
[56] See Pinckaers, *Sources of Christian Ethics*, pp. 129, 133.
[57] See Stephen C. Barton, 'The Epistles and Christian Ethics', in *The Cambridge Companion to Christian Ethics* (ed. Robin Gill; Cambridge: CUP, 2001), p. 71.

Eph. 4:19; 5:3–5,11–12,18; Col. 3:5–9). He does not allow them any excuses on the grounds that they have not received a direct revelation from God, for the natural order of things is a guide to right conduct (Rom. 1:26–7; 2:14). So, through reflection and the dictates of conscience (Rom. 2:15), they can come to the correct conclusion as to what the law requires (Rom. 1:32; 2:15). His instructions with regard to the generally accepted moral standards of the pervading culture are unequivocal: 'Now this I affirm and insist on in the Lord: you must no longer live as the Gentiles live' (Eph. 4:17); 'Take no part in the unfruitful works of darkness' (Eph. 5:11); 'Let us then lay aside the works of darkness' (Rom. 13:12).

More importantly, when the Gentiles turn to Jesus Christ in repentance and faith they receive a new status and a new position in life. This new creation (*kaine ktisis*) (2 Cor. 6:17; Gal. 6:15) is the key to Paul's teaching on ethics. He uses a number of different images to express the dawning of a new state of affairs. One of the most fundamental is that of baptism. Entering the waters of baptism and surfacing again are symbols of death and resurrection. Through faith believers in Jesus have been united in Jesus' death and resurrection. They have renounced one way of life and entered on another: 'We have been buried with him by baptism into death, so that, just as Christ was raised from the dead by the glory of the Father, so we too might walk in newness of life' (Rom. 6:4).

For believers it is as though a momentous change has taken place. Being united with Christ in his death means that the sinful nature with which we were born has been crucified (put to death), 'so that the body of sin might be destroyed' (Rom. 6:6). Likewise, 'when you were buried with him in baptism, you were also raised with him through faith in the power of God, who raised him from the dead' (Col. 2:12). The consequences of this act of death, burial and resurrection are significant for right ethical conduct for a number of reasons. First, Christians are free from the condemnation of the moral law (Rom. 8:1), because Jesus has taken the document that lists all our transgressions and nailed it to the cross, where it has been left (Col. 2:14). Second, Christians are no longer enslaved to sin, i.e. they are freed from the habit of sinning, for 'sin will have no dominion over you' (Rom. 6:14). Therefore, third, 'having been set free from sin, [they] have become slaves of righteousness' (Rom. 6:18). Doing what is good springs naturally from the event of death and resurrection through which they have passed. The passions they used to follow and the wickedness they used to indulge in, probably without an awareness of its destructive nature, have been buried with Christ. Christians are now free to be obedient to the form of teaching (*tupos didaches*) (Rom. 6:17), which indicates the path of true goodness and purity.

Another image that Paul uses is that of circumcision. This is used in a similar way to that of baptism. In Christ believers 'were circumcised with a spiritual circumcision [one not made with hands]' (Col. 2:11). Christ's death is likened to an act of circumcision in the sense that all the power of sin and evil, which he bore in his body on the cross, has been cut away, disarmed and discarded (Col. 2:15). The consequence is that the 'body of flesh' (*ho soma tes sarkos*) has been taken off (Col. 2:11), as though it were a worn-out piece of clothing. The believer is no longer subject to rules, regulations and rituals (Col. 2:16–23; Gal. 4:8–10). These cannot penetrate to the heart of righteousness. They are powerless to effect change, for 'they are of no value in checking self-indulgence' (Col. 2:23). They are superfluous, given the new garment of Christ's righteousness that has now been donned.

A third image that Paul uses is that of 'the ages'. This age, in which the world is enmeshed, is passing away and is doomed to perish (1 Cor. 1:20; 2:6,8). A 'new age' has broken into the world, into which believers have been relocated (1 Cor. 10:11; Eph. 2:7). The present age is dominated by the wisdom of the philosophers and the teachers of morality. They may have reached a certain level of understanding of the difference between vices and virtues, through observation, reason or meditation on holy books, but are ignorant of the wisdom of the gospel. Through the preaching of the gospel Christ's wisdom is made known. He is the wisdom of God in the sense that he is the source of redemption from sin and the means of growing in holiness (1 Cor. 1:30–31; 6:11).

Allied to the image of the two ages is that of the kingdom. The word does not occur frequently in Paul's writings. Nevertheless, he uses it at key moments in his teaching about how Christians should live. Those who, despite all they have received in Christ, have not put to death the passions of the flesh, but allowed them to creep back into their lives, will not inherit the kingdom (1 Cor. 6:9,10; Gal. 5:21; Eph. 5:5). However, Paul does not believe that Christians will turn back to their old ways of life, because they have experienced what Christ has done for them (1 Cor. 6:11), encountered the working of the Spirit in their lives (Gal. 5:17–18,22,25), and have now been enlightened (Eph. 5:8,14).

Nevertheless, as the correspondence to the Corinthian and Galatian churches shows, some Christians entertained a serious misconception about the nature of liberty in Christ; one which led to a certain ethical libertarianism. Paul argued strongly against this delusion: 'do not use your freedom as an opportunity for self-indulgence [literally, the flesh]' (Gal. 5:13). On the contrary, the Christian life is quite compatible with a certain level of self-discipline (1 Cor. 9:24–7), for, as in the case of athletes, there is a prize to be won – entry into the eternal reign of God. Therefore, it is advisable to be careful that all we do is governed by a vision of the final goal, the coming dominion of God, marked by the end of the reign of all opposing powers (1 Cor. 15:24–6). We are to behave as those who are already citizens of this coming kingdom (Phil. 3:20). We are never to submit to evil, whether in our own lives, the life of the church or in the structures, policies and governance of the world.

A final image is the contrast between flesh and spirit. In Paul's ethical teaching this is decidedly not a form of Hellenistic dualism, in which the physical is considered inferior and an obstacle to the spiritual part of human life. Flesh (*sarx*) has a particular meaning. It is the old nature, which is permeated by desires and attachments to a way of life that brings disorder and destruction. It issues in 'works of the flesh' (*ta erga tes sarkos*) (Gal. 5:19). These may be expressed through the physical body, but the body is not the cause. The origin is a nature governed by noxious passions. Those who have died to these passions and been raised with Christ receive, as he promised, the gift of the Holy Spirit (Gal. 3:5; Rom. 8:9). It is by the power of the Spirit, who indwells the believer, that the residual desires and deeds of the old nature may be neutralised and destroyed (Rom. 8:6; Gal. 5:16–17). As a consequence, the believer may now live an ethical life guided and empowered by the Spirit.

So these five images reveal the crux of Paul's teaching on the moral life. He himself, on more than one occasion, sums up the ethical life as love.

> The one who loves another has fulfilled the law. The commandments . . . are summed up in this word, 'Love your neighbour as yourself.' Love does no wrong to a neighbour; therefore, love is the fulfilling of the law. (Rom. 13:8–10)

> The whole law is summed up in a single commandment, 'You shall love your neighbour as yourself.' (Gal. 5:14)

> Above all clothe yourselves with love, which binds everything together in perfect harmony. (Col. 3:14)

Having said that, one has said everything, yet also conveyed little. Love is a magnificent, inspiring concept; yet, in modern parlance, it has been trivialised and degraded. The meaning of love needs to be filled out with substance. Paul does precisely this in what have been considered the more explicitly didactic (rather than kerygmatic) sections of his letters. The most obvious example comes in Romans 12 towards the end of his exposition of the gospel. As a result of their new status in Christ, having received mercy and grace, Christians are to present their whole lives as a holy and acceptable sacrifice to God. Here, ethics becomes worship (*logike latreia*) (Rom. 12:1–2).

Following on from this, he then speaks of a person's own personal self-assessment as a member of Christ's community. Love requires each person to exercise his or her gifts of grace for the benefit of all (Rom. 12:3–7). Love must be without dissimulation, i.e. all our actions must be done not to enhance our own sense of self-worth (1 Cor. 13:3–5), but to honour others (Rom. 12:10). The chapter ends with specific exhortations: 'Contribute to the needs of the saints; extend hospitality to strangers. Bless those who persecute you . . . associate with the lowly . . . Do not repay anyone evil for evil . . . never avenge yourselves . . . if your enemies are hungry, feed them' (Rom. 12:13–21).

Similar precepts are scattered about in his other writings:

Do not seek your own advantage, but that of others. (1 Cor. 10:24)

Take care that this liberty of yours does not somehow become a stumbling-block to the weak. (1 Cor. 8:9)

Bear one another's burdens, and in this way you will fulfil the law of Christ. (Gal. 6:2)

Do nothing from selfish ambition or conceit, but in humility regard others as better than yourselves. Let each of you look not to your own interests, but to the interests of others. (Phil. 2:3–4)[58]

Paul speaks about 'testing the genuineness of love' (2 Cor. 8:8) by means of the way that the new converts to Christ conduct themselves within the community and towards outsiders. Love means the giving of oneself to the utmost on behalf of others for the sake of their attaining the best which God wills for them. It is measured, of course, by the example of Christ (Eph. 5:1–2). In an extended study of parallels between Jesus' ethical teaching and practice and the Pauline ethical directives,[59] David Wenham comes to the conclusion:

We have noticed how there seem to be a considerable number of possible echoes of the sermon on the mount (e.g., salt, light, fulfilling the law, cutting off offending limbs, prohibition of oaths, love of enemies, not judging), of sayings about relationships in the church attested in Matthew 18/Mark 9/

---

[58] Also, Col. 3:12–13; 1 Thess. 4:9–12; 5:14–15.
[59] David Wenham, *Paul*.

Luke 9 (e.g., receiving, stumbling blocks, cutting off limbs, peacefulness, salt, forgiveness), and of the sayings about marriage, divorce, and celibacy that are found in Matthew 19.[60]

It is highly likely that Paul is exhorting the new believers in Jesus to show the reality of their new creation by seeking to re-orientate their lives by following the teaching and example of Jesus. Paul's ethics are not controlled by law-like regulations, but take the form of examples. The mind of Christ directs them; this mind has already expressed itself in Jesus' (in whom they now believe) concrete teaching and practice.[61] Therefore, as the Holy Spirit moulds the individual and community into the image of Christ, they are to imitate Christ (Phil. 2:5; 1 Thess. 1:6–7; Eph. 5:1).In this way, they too can become models.

Conclusion: the Biblical Grounding of Christian Ethics

To be the light of the world, Jesus' disciples are called to show forth the kind of life that is made possible by the working of God's grace. The standard for this life is the will of the Father as demonstrated in the life and ministry of Jesus, the Son of God. By the power of God, believers in Jesus have been 'rescued from the power of darkness and transferred into the kingdom of his beloved Son' (Col. 1:14).

To settle matters of conduct, Jesus himself appealed to the word of God as communicated through the Scriptures of Israel. The law was designed to make explicit and uphold the order written implicitly into the pattern of creation. Therefore, 'the way the universe *is*, determines how man *ought* to behave himself in it.'[62] This is true, for example, in the case of marriage and divorce. However, the law also reflects the disorder created by humans' rejection of God's order ('hard-heartedness', see Matt. 19:8). The given order of creation is demonstrated by the partial recognition by human societies everywhere of true moral ideals. At the same time, the disorder is also blatantly exposed by ways of life that contradict the will of the Creator. Knowledge of God's mind is only possible if God reveals his thoughts: 'Any certainty we may have about the order which God has made depends upon God's own disclosure of himself and of his works.'[63]

---

[60] David Wenham, *Paul*, pp. 281–2.

[61] See Bruce Kaye, 'Law and Morality in the Epistles of the New Testament' in *Law, Morality and the Bible* (ed. Bruce Kaye and Gordon Wenham; Downers Grove, IL: IVP, 1978), p. 79.

[62] O'Donovan, *Resurrection and Moral Order*, p. 17 (emphasis in the original).

[63] O'Donovan, *Resurrection and Moral Order*, p. 19.

Jesus' own teaching is part of this revelation, as he deepened the meaning of authentic observation of the law.

Under the new covenant, God's law is written on the hearts of those who belong to Christ. The law as an external demand brings knowledge of failure. The result, therefore, is either despair for conscientious practitioners, because they cannot meet the expectations, or the creation of lower standards. Rightly understood, the law is not an arbitrary code of practice imposed by a capricious fiat. On the contrary it reflects the nature of the One who has established it. The law, as it manifests the absolute goodness of God, has to be distinguished from human traditions[64] that often obscure its original intention ('I desire mercy and not sacrifice' [Matt. 12:7]): 'God can command or will only what conforms to his nature. As, by definition, God is absolute goodness, justice and loving-kindness, he could only desire human beings to follow whatever those supreme ethical virtues demand.'[65]

So, right living is defined by the character of God, the order of the creation he has devised, the law he has set forth, and the teaching and example of Jesus. These external realities help believers to discern what God is about. They are to be taken together as an interpretative bundle, each throwing light on the others. God's Spirit takes all these and inscribes them in the living being of those who are united in baptism with Christ in his death and resurrection. In the complexity of situations not necessarily envisaged in biblical times, the Spirit will guide the disciples into a true understanding of how they should live (John 14:26; 16:13): 'The Spirit forms and brings to expression the appropriate pattern of free response to objective reality.'[66]

Having, as far as possible, laid out the crucial elements that have to be taken into consideration when using the Bible to make ethical choices, the practical work of seeing them in action in real-life situations still has to be done. The skills of biblical interpretation and application are honed by having to decide what practices are required of the followers of Jesus in specific situations. Case studies are a good way of discovering how the different aspects of biblically grounded ethics work out in practice. I have attempted elsewhere to move from the context to the text in two cases: those of race relations and the use of violence.[67]

---

[64] 'Scripture is *norma normans* ("the norming norm"), while tradition is *norma normata* ("the normed norm")'; see Richard B. Hays, *The Moral Vision of the New Testament: A Contemporary Introduction to New Testament Ethics* (New York: Harper Collins), p. 210.

[65] Kirk, *Christian Mission as Dialogue*, p. 121.

[66] O'Donovan, *Resurrection and Moral Order*, p. 25.

[67] See J. Andrew Kirk, 'How a Missiologist Utilises the Bible' in *Bible and Mission: A Conversation between Biblical Studies and Missiology* (ed. Rollin G. Grams,

We do not have, of course, the luxury of being able to wait until all the hermeneutical axioms are properly in place before attempting to utilize the Bible . . . in
fitting ways. We have to do it, as Latin Americans have a habit of saying, 'on the
way.' However, before we set out, it is good to be as prepared for the journey as
possible.[68]

This chapter has endeavoured to create a map and point out some of
the significant landmarks that will help to guide disciples in their ethical
response to the world surrounding them. They are, however, no substitute for the journey itself.

(cont.) I. Howard Marshall, Peter F. Penner and Robin Routledge; Schwarzenfeld: Neufeld Verlag, 2008), pp. 262–6.
[68] Kirk, *Bible and Mission*, p. 267.

Part Two

Patterns from History

5

The 'New' World: Church and Mission in Sixteenth-Century Latin America

The Christianizing mission carried out in the lands 'discovered' and later colonised by Spanish adventurers in the late fifteenth century has had a deep impact on a whole continent, shaping in many ways its subsequent political, social, economic and religious history. The reasons for the colonization of Central and South America and the means used to carry it out set these regions apart from the colonization processes of the continent to the north.

Within the parameters of one chapter, I will attempt to trace briefly the significant historical events of the *conquista* and the impact that it made on the indigenous populations, describe something of the pre-Spanish civilizations, outline the justifications given for the occupation of foreign lands and the subjugation of their inhabitants, assess the attempts made by notable individuals to defend the 'Indians' from brutality and exploitation, explain the processes and methods of evangelization and consider the ways in which the Christian faith became indigenised in its new environment. The survey will conclude with a discussion of the church and the world in relation to this particular experience of the first major missionary movement beyond Christendom. I will limit myself to an approximate seventy-year period following Christopher Columbus's first voyage to the 'Indies'.

Lands to the West

The year 1492 was memorable for two interrelated reasons. First, the Spanish, under the leadership of their majesties, Ferdinand and Isabella, overcame, at Grenada, the last Muslim stronghold on the peninsula. Thereby, they ended an occupation by the Moors that had lasted several centuries. Second, Christopher Columbus (born in 1451) set sail from Palos de la Frontera with three ships, the *Santa Maria*, the *Pinta*, and the

Santa Clara, headed, so he supposed, for Japan by a route to the west.
Disregarding the scholarly opinion of his day, he had estimated that
Japan lay considerably further east than it does.[1] He believed, therefore,
that a westward route to Asia would be feasible and shorter.

After much lobbying at the royal court, Columbus persuaded Ferdinand
and Isabella to back his expedition. They paid for half the costs; the rest
came from private investors. A contract was drawn up between the royal
house and the explorer. He was given the rank of Admiral of the Ocean Sea
and appointed viceroy and governor of any new lands that he might find.
He also secured for himself a good stake in any profits that might be made
from new opportunities for trade.

On 12 October 1492, Columbus landed on the island of Guanahani (the
indigenous name for an island now part of the Bahamas). There he found
native people who were peaceful and friendly, but without the means
to defend themselves from attack and enslavement. On 28 October he
arrived off the northeast coast of Cuba and on Christmas Day the *Santa
Maria* ran aground on the northern coast of Haiti (part of the island,
together with the Dominican Republic, the adventurers named Hispaniola). He kidnapped around a dozen natives and took them back to Spain,
where he arrived in March 1493.

He completed three further voyages to the western isles. In September
1493 he set sail with seventeen ships and about twelve hundred men
with the purpose of colonizing the lands they came upon. The contingent
included soldiers, farmers and priests: the first to subdue any resistance
from the inhabitants; the second to settle on the lands, and the third
to convert the natives to the Catholic Christian faith. He encountered
several of the islands on the eastern extremity of the Caribbean before
moving on to Puerto Rico, Hispaniola – where he found the corpses of
eleven of the thirty-nine people he had left behind on his first voyage
– the southern coast of Cuba and Jamaica. He returned to Spain late in
1494.

The third voyage to the 'New World' began on 30 May 1498. This time he
sailed with six ships, reaching Trinidad on 31 July. From there he explored
the mainland of South America, including the mouth of the Orinoco River.
He returned again to Hispaniola to find that the settlers left there after the
second voyage were disaffected, complaining that the land was not as rich
as they had been led to suppose. Some of them returned with him to Spain.

---

[1] He believed the Eurasian land mass extended for a longitudinal span of 225
degrees, rather than the actual 130, and that Japan was considerably further
to the east of the mainland, with other inhabited islands even further east. He
also underestimated the length of the earth's circumference by some 10,000
kilometres.

The final voyage took place in 1502. This time he reached the coast of Central America, off present-day Honduras. From there he explored south as far as Panama, where he established a small garrison, before leaving again for Hispaniola. However, owing to tropical storms, he became stranded in Jamaica, where he and the crew remained for a whole year. He was eventually rescued from Hispaniola, in spite of the efforts of the then governor, Nicolas de Ovando y Caceras, to thwart his progress. He arrived back in Spain for the last time on 7 November 1504, some twelve years after first encountering a new continent. He died of a heart attack, provoked by acute arthritis, in Valladolid on 20 May 1506 at the age of fifty-five.

The Conquest and Colonization

Cortes and the subjugation of the Aztecs

The appropriation of properties and peoples had already begun as a result of the expeditions of Columbus. Acquiring further sovereignty over foreign lands was achieved through the military campaigns of Hernan Cortes in Mexico and Francisco Pizarro in Peru between 1519 and 1533.

Cortes (born 1485) chose to pursue a living in the new lands across the Atlantic being opened up to the Spanish invaders at the turn of the sixteenth century. He arrived in Santo Domingo, the capital of Hispaniola, in 1504 (still only eighteen years old). He was given land to farm and an allocation of Indians to do the work. In 1511 he took part in the conquest of Cuba, where he received a large estate, and Indian slaves to go with it, from the military commander in recognition of his role in the war. He rapidly rose to a position of considerable power and influence in the new colony.

Meanwhile, a new colony in Mexico was established under the leadership of Juan de Grijalva. The governor of Cuba, Diego Velazquez, decided to send Cortes to support the new enterprise on the mainland and secure the interior for settlement. Eventually, defying the orders of the governor, who had revoked his permission for the expedition, Cortes left Cuba in February 1519 with eleven ships, about five hundred soldiers, horses and artillery. He landed on the Yucatán Peninsula in the territory of the Mayan people. The rest, as is said, is history.

Cortes travelled north and took over leadership of the colony at Veracruz, placing himself under the direct orders of the Spanish king, Charles V. From there, in mid-August he marched towards the Aztec capital Tenochtitlan, where, on 8 November 1519, he was received in peace by the Emperor Moctezuma. On his way to the heart of the Aztec Empire he formed treaties with indigenous tribes, who had been in conflict with the Aztecs. After a series of misadventures, Cortes, reinforced with additional troops from Cuba, managed to subdue the city of Tenochtitlan on 13 August 1521. He renamed the place Ciudad de Mexico and became its governor until 1524.

Pizarro and the subjugation of the Incas

Pizarro was around thirty years old when he sailed in 1502 to the New World in a fleet of thirty ships carrying approximately two and a half thousand colonists. He settled later in Panama, where he became the first European to view the Pacific coast of the New World. Hearing stories of immense riches in a country along the western coast of South America (the legendary *El Dorado*), Pizarro began to prepare an exploratory expedition to the south, with the intention eventually of conquering the land and seizing its treasures.

The first expedition (1524) ended off the coast of Colombia in adversity, owing to bad weather, a hostile reception from indigenous peoples and lack of provisions. A second trip was organised in 1526. After a number of travails, a remnant got as far as northwestern Peru, where they were received hospitably. There, the explorers did get a sight of some of the natural resources that awaited them, if they could prevail over the local inhabitants by force. In order to mount a proper military campaign, they needed to return to Panama for reinforcements and substantial provisions.

Owing to the decision by the new governor of Panama to refuse Pizarro permission for a third expedition, he was obliged to return to Spain to appeal directly to the king for authorization to extend his empire along the western coast of the continent. A document giving permission to annex the lands of Peru to the Spanish crown was issued by the royal court. Pizarro was named as governor of the new territory for a distance of two hundred leagues along the coast.

Returning to Panama, he organised the third and final voyage to the south. The fleet of ships set sail on 27 December 1530. They arrived off the northwest coast of Peru, which they had visited before, and set up a settlement in the interior. From there, a small group was sent to explore the surrounding area. After some days they returned with an envoy from the Inca Emperor Atahualpa; he had sent an invitation to meet the Spaniards at Cajamarca in the high Andes of north Peru.

Pizarro took just over one hundred foot-soldiers and sixty horsemen, arriving in Cajamarca after a two-month march. On being refused an immediate audience with the emperor, Pizarro attacked the Inca army. Despite his greatly inferior forces, he defeated it and took Atahualpa prisoner (16 November 1532). Nine months later, on the pretext that

Atahualpa had killed his own brother and was plotting against the Spaniards, and against the wishes of his (Pizarro's) own brother Hernando
and lieutenant, Hernando de Soto, he had the emperor executed. The
following year (1534), Pizarro invaded and captured the Inca stronghold
of Cuzco and thus virtually ended the resistance of the Inca Empire to the
intruders. In 1535 he founded the city of Lima on the coast, making it the
capital of the newly acquired territory.

Six years later (1541), as an act of revenge for having had his most
trustworthy former companion Diego de Almagro executed, following
the latter's defeat in the battle of Las Salinas (1538), Pizarro was assassinated in his palace. In military terms the conquest was astonishing,
although it was carried out with the help of deceit and broken promises. The Spaniards were now in control of a vast empire with its stores
of precious metals, jewels and other natural resources. Colonisers came,
settled and made their fortune. Members of religious orders and priests
also came to begin the work of Christianizing the population.

The Spanish World in the Late Fifteenth Century

To be able to explain the mentality of the explorers in setting in motion
the vast enterprise of colonizing newly 'discovered' lands beyond
Europe, it is necessary to understand something of the historical circumstances of the Iberian peninsula at this period. By the time of the reign
of Ferdinand and Isabella, the myth of the *reconquista* (re-conquest) was
firmly embedded in the psyche of the Spanish people. After centuries
of struggle against the Muslim Moors, the Spanish finally drove them
beyond their borders. They interpreted this as a victory of the Catholic
God over false-believers, using the sword legitimately to do God's work.
Less than three months after the fall of Grenada in 1492, all practising
Jews in Spain were to be converted to Christianity by royal decree or face
expulsion from the country. Some 150,000 left Spain. A century later, all
remaining Muslims in the country were forced to leave.[2]

The contest against the Muslims inspired a strong nationalism within
the nation. It also produced a militant form of Christianity, strengthened
later by the need to counteract the teaching and progress of the Protestant
Reformation, which threatened to destabilise the hegemony of the Catholic
Church. As far as the church and the rulers were concerned, to be Spanish
was also to be Catholic. There was an indissoluble, almost mystical, link

---

[2] See Ondina E. Gonzalez and Justo L. Gonzalez, *Christianity in Latin America: A
History* (Cambridge: CUP, 2008), pp. 21–5.

between the land and the faith. The goal of maintaining the unity of the nation was so urgent that, if necessary, excessively violent means were justified to secure it, as the Spanish Inquisition eloquently testified.[3]

In many ways the Spanish attitude to peoples who did not share the same faith was like that of the Muslim caliphates. First a region had to be occupied militarily. Then it had to be pacified and a government organised. Only after that process would the indigenous population be ready for an introduction to the faith of their conquerors. The Spaniards saw the new lands to the west as an extension of Spanish Catholic territory, whose subjugation was rationalised by reference to the supreme good of believing in the salvation of Christ through the ministry of the church.[4]

The Pre-Spanish New World

The Aztec, Mayan and Inca civilizations had well-established religious beliefs and rituals. It is true that, in the case of the Aztecs, sacrifices to the gods took the horrific form of offering up human beings, whose hearts had been extracted from the victims. Basic to their view of life was the belief, characteristic of primal societies, that divine beings controlled the affairs of human beings for good or ill. The aim of rituals, therefore, was to ensure that the gods acted favourably towards mortal beings through the maintenance of harmonious relations between the two parties. As the gods, according to their beliefs, had sacrificed themselves on behalf of humans to bring life back to earth after violent destructions, so humans had to recompense the gods with their own sacrifices. The offering up in death of the most precious commodity which they possessed – life itself – was necessary to sustain a peaceful relationship with those who ultimately controlled their fate: 'From the Aztec perspective, a good life still had to be earned through a lifelong series of acts of penance and sacrifice, precisely because the gods had done likewise to bring humanity back to earth.'[5]

The sacrificial victims were taken as trophies of war from surrounding tribes. The Aztecs, therefore, were on a constant war-footing, partly to ensure the required supply of sacrificial victims. The number of people sacrificed every year is disputed.[6] However, in one sense, such a calculation is immaterial. In terms of the conquest, the system enabled Cortes

[3] See Enrique Dussel, *Historia de la Iglesia en America Latina* (Barcelona: Nova Terra, 2nd edn, 1972), pp. 54, 59.
[4] Dussel, *Historia de la Iglesia*, p. 60.
[5] Gonzalez and Gonzalez, *Christianity in Latin America*, p. 16.
[6] See Gustavo Gutierrez, *Las Casas: In Search of the Poor of Jesus Christ* (Maryknoll: Orbis Books, 1992), p. 524, note 63.

to secure allies among the surrounding tribes in his bid to subdue this warlike nation.[7]

The Incas believed in a creator god – Viracocha. He created a first world. He then destroyed it because of human sin, and made a second one. This faired little better; so Viracocha abandoned the human community to its own devices, promising to return only at a time of extreme emergency. The Incas also worshipped Ilyapa, the god of thunder, Quilla, goddess of the moon and Inti, the sun god. It was through Inti that the Inca emperor derived his semi-divine nature. The Emperor Yupanki (given the title of *Pachacuti* – 'the renewer') had the Inca capital city, Cuzco, rebuilt in the mid-fifteenth century 'as a ceremonial center with its great temple to Inti'.[8] Pizarro was evidently much impressed, for in a letter he wrote to the king of Spain, he said, 'This city is the greatest and finest ever seen in this country or anywhere in the Indies . . . We can assure your majesty that it is so beautiful and has such fine buildings that it would be remarkable even in Spain.' Such an opinion confirms the view that the Incas, like the Aztecs and Mayas, had created an advanced civilization.

The Incas also inculcated an official pattern of ancestor worship, centred on the deceased Inca emperors, whilst the people gave reverence to many common objects that they believed were indwelt by the spirits of gods (*wakas* or *huacas*):

> All of these gods and ancestors required worship and praise, often in the form of public ritual, sometimes in the form of offerings, and occasionally in the form of human sacrifice . . . Unlike the Aztec gods, who required human blood in order to keep the world going, Inca gods viewed sacrifice and offerings as forms of thanksgiving . . . The Inca world was structured much like a pyramid, with the Sapa Inca as the principal contact with the world of the gods. Then came the priests, whose main responsibility was to ensure that rituals were carried out correctly and the desires of the gods were made known to the people. And supporting this pyramid were the people who believed that everything they had, from their children to the harvests, belonged to the gods.[9]

The Impact of Conquest on the Indigenous Peoples

The contact between Europeans and the original inhabitants of the lands to the west brought devastation to the latter. Three separate elements

---

[7] We return later to the question of whether war against the Aztecs was justified as a means to end this barbaric practice.

[8] Gonzalez and Gonzalez, *Christianity in Latin America*, p. 18.

[9] Gonzalez and Gonzalez, *Christianity in Latin America*, pp. 19, 21.

caused the destruction of populations and the annihilation of their liveli-
hoods, living conditions and cultures: war, disease and slavery.

Although Columbus met a generally peaceable and friendly people,
forced subjection of them to Spanish purposes seemed uppermost in his
mind from the beginning of the encounter. In his journal entry for 12
October 1492 he wrote: 'They ought to make good and skilled servants, for
they repeat very quickly whatever we say to them . . . I could conquer the
whole of them with 50 men, and govern them as I please.'[10] 'Once they had
landed . . . the newcomers unfurled before the astonished eyes of the Lucay
Indians the banners of the Spanish king and queen, claiming possession of
the islands (in the presence of a notary, naturally) without their indigenous
inhabitants so much as grasping what was taking place.'[11]

Apparently it never occurred to the Spanish adventurers that there
was any other way of treating the native inhabitants of the new lands
they had found than by ruling over them. The Pope, as the presumed
supreme representative on earth of Jesus Christ, to whom all authority
on earth had been given, claimed the right to concede to the Catholic
monarchs the title of the lands which had recently been discovered. In
the Treaty of Tordesillas (1494), Spain and Portugal negotiated a line of
demarcation between the two nations, dividing the Americas between
them 370 leagues west of the Cape Verde Islands. Clearly, the Pope's
assertion concerning his authority to grant such a prerogative to European powers begs the question: by what authority could the papal office
claim a temporal power over the whole world?

The legality and justice of this decision was not seriously challenged
at that particular moment although, as we shall see, it was seriously
disputed some years later. It was taken by wave after wave of newcomers
as permission to expropriate both lands and people and take them into
their possession. When, as was to be expected, they resisted by force of
arms, they were ruthlessly suppressed.[12]

The populations of the Caribbean islands in particular were decimated,
not only by war, but also by new diseases (such as smallpox) against
which the Indians had no natural immunization. Some twenty-five years
after Columbus ended his first voyage to Hispaniola, around 80 per cent
of the population had died. In Cuba, when the Spaniards first arrived,
the population numbered around 100,000; forty years later it had fallen
to some 14,000, a drop of around 90 per cent: 'The conquest of Cuba

---

[10] Robert H. Fuson, ed., *The Log of Christopher Columbus* (London: Tab Books, 1992).

[11] Gutierrez, *Las Casas*, p. 23.

[12] It has been said derisively that the European colonialists' only show of superiority over the people they subdued lay in their possession of gunpowder.

was effected under the command of Diego Velazquez, who reached the island with some three hundred men . . . After a bloody campaign, many Indians were taken prisoner and many more killed, Indian resistance being unable to stand up to the superior military prowess of the Spaniards.'[13]

The Spaniards practised in the *encomienda* system what, in all but name, was slavery. The early settlers, for their military feats, were rewarded by the Spanish crown a grant of the free labour of the defeated peoples.

> Indians were to work for the encomendero in whatever capacity he chose. In the Caribbean, Indians were parcelled out to settlers who could demonstrate a need for laborers in mining, farming, or any other effort they might undertake. In theory the Indians were considered free and allowed to exercise that freedom within limits; in reality, the encomienda was slavery . . . As a result of this forced labor system, and the accompanying disruption of family and community structures, diet and their way of life, thousands of people died[14] . . . Certainly, perhaps even more than the devastation wrought by disease, the introduction of the encomienda signalled the beginning of the destruction of indigenous civilizations in the Caribbean.[15]

Processes of Evangelization

The efforts of the Roman Catholic Church to bring the message of Christ to the indigenous peoples of the Americas were contradictory. On the one hand, the evangelists used what today would be recognised as the enlightened methods of inculturation and indigenization. On the other hand, procedures were employed, quite contrary to a gospel of love, justice and reconciliation: 'What we see in all these efforts to impose Roman Catholicism and Catholic institutions and the responses to them is the ambivalence of the church – both benevolent and brutal, gentle and cruel . . . The two faces of the church remained throughout the middle colonial years.'[16]

On the more positive side, for the most part the missionary orders – Franciscans, Dominicans, Augustinians and Jesuits – were committed

---

[13] Enrique Dussel, ed. *The Church in Latin America: 1492-1992* (Tunbridge Wells / Maryknoll, NY: Burns & Oates / Orbis Books, 1992), p. 46.

[14] For example, the birth rate of the native population declined rapidly, as men were forcefully separated from their spouses for long periods of time.

[15] Gonzalez and Gonzalez, *Christianity in Latin America*, pp. 29–30.

[16] Gonzalez and Gonzalez, *Christianity in Latin America*, p. 63.

to proclaiming the Christian faith in the languages of the peoples. To this end, dictionaries were published to aid the preachers. The Franciscans, who first arrived in New Spain (Mexico) in 1524, opened a school in Tlatelolco, with the intention of creating a group of Indian leaders, educated according to European ideals, who would become intermediaries between the two cultures. They also hoped to train indigenous men for the priesthood. However, these enterprises were strongly resisted by the colonists, and after twenty years they were closed.

The Dominicans also sought to communicate in the Indian languages and understand the underlying meaning of their religions:

> The community produced its own material for evangelization, in the form of the first catechism written in America, Fray Pedro de Cordoba's *Doctrina cristiana*. This was a methodically organized treatise of pastoral and catechetical practice. Armed with this, the members of the first religious community in the Caribbean went out to preach the Kingdom of God and its justice . . . and put into effect a programme of evangelization based on the actual situation in which the Indians were living.[17]

From an early period in the history of the conquest, the Dominicans, as we shall see, took a strong stance against the brutal conditions of servitude and exploitation to which the Indians were subjected. They made attempts in Central America to secure areas of land free from the machinations of the colonialists, so that the work of evangelization could be conducted in an atmosphere of respect and trust. The attempt by a small group, led by Fray Bartolome de las Casas, to establish an ideal type of settlement on the Venezuelan coast (called the Cumana project), that would treat the Indians with the full dignity their humanity demanded, did not last long. The Indians turned against the missionaries when Spanish slave-raiders attacked their villages. Las Casas's vision was to activate a model of peaceful evangelization and colonization, in which Indians and Spanish peasants would share a common life.[18] This would be an outworking of the kingdom of God as it was meant to be.

On the negative side, the 'black legend' persists:

> Those who support the *Black Legend* denigrate (and) criticise the work of Spain and Portugal, calling them . . . intolerant – because of the *tabula rasa* approach –, exploiters – because of the extraction of gold and silver –, with a slave mentality – because of the attitude towards the Indian –, and in the last

---

[17] Dussel, *Church in Latin America*, p. 45.
[18] See Gutierrez, *Las Casas*, pp. 54–5.

resort, superficial – because the new Christianity planted in America would be merely superficial and quasi-pagan.[19]

The Franciscans, who began the work of evangelization in the Americas, justified their programme of mass baptisms on two considerations. The first was a strong millenarian conviction that the second coming of Christ was very near. The second was a response to the appalling death rate that was being suffered by the Indians. Both these factors – one a belief, the other a reality – drove them to implement a plan of baptizing as many Indians as was feasible, given the small number of priests available to administer the sacrament: 'For them [the friars], baptism was the first and foremost duty of the day, and mass ceremonies were common with thousands of Indians baptised at one time. By 1533 the sixty or so Franciscans who were in Mexico claimed to have performed the sacrament for 1.2 million Indians. By 1536 another 3.8 million had been brought into the family of Christ through this method.'[20]

The lack of an initial understanding on the part of the Indians as to the meaning of baptism, the frequent use of force to compel them to join the faith of their masters, and the almost complete lack of subsequent teaching of the faith led to an inevitable mix of the ancient and the new religious cultures. In spite of the attempts, particularly in the Andean region, to eradicate the Indians' former religious beliefs and practices, often by torture,[21] the old traditions persisted. The outcome of the process was a syncretistic mixture of Roman Catholic beliefs, particularly around the veneration of Mary and the saints, and indigenous religious practices related to the preservation of the rhythm of the seasons and social stability.

Defence of the Indians

The most interesting and important aspect of the Spanish mission to the 'New World' is the struggle between two opposing forces, both of which claimed to represent the mind and will of the Spanish authorities. The settlers justified armed intervention to take possession of the lands they had found. A small group of missionaries, theologians and lawyers disputed the claims of conquest and championed the rights of the indigenous peoples to be free of every kind of external coercion. In the middle, we find the Spanish court, anxious to follow the right path but under immense pressure to accede to the wishes of the colonialists. To this protracted debate I now turn.

[19] Dussel, *Historia de la Iglesia*, pp. 61–2.
[20] Dussel, *Church in Latin America*, p. 51.
[21] Gonzalez and Gonzalez, *Christianity in Latin America*, pp. 60–61.

Montesino

In recounting this particular history, a fitting place to begin is with a sermon that has become famous down the years and across the continents. Friar Anton Montesino was a Dominican priest, who had arrived in Hispaniola in 1510. He and the other members of the order were appalled by the conditions being suffered by the Indians. They decided collectively to confront the governor of the island, other authorities, the military and the settlers with the true nature of their cruel oppression. Montesino was detailed to preach a sermon highlighting their atrocities and warning them of God's judgement upon them.

The Sunday chosen was the fourth in Advent; the year, 1511. Invoking the example of John the Baptist, he claims that he is also 'a voice crying in the wilderness', the wilderness of the hardened consciences of the Spanish invaders. He then launches into a series of accusations against them:

> You are all in mortal sin and in it you live and die, because of the cruelty and tyranny which you use among these innocent peoples. Tell me, by what right and with what justice do you hold these Indians in such cruel and horrible servitude? With what authority have you embarked on such detestable wars against these peoples, who were living in their gentle and peaceful lands, where you have devoured infinite numbers of them, with unheard of killings and devastations? . . . Are these not human beings? Do they not possess rational souls? Are you not bound to love them as you love yourselves? . . . Be absolutely certain, that in the state in which you find yourselves you can no more be saved than the Moors or Turks who do not have nor wish to have the faith of Jesus Christ.[22]

The sermon sums up the essence of the case against the conquistadors. They have no defence when required to state on what lawful or moral grounds they have pursued their terrible acts of aggression and violation of the dignity of fellow human beings. Each one of these charges was taken up and debated over the next half-century in law courts, theological classrooms and royal palaces: the nature of right and rights, the meaning of justice, the criteria for justified war, the essence of human nature, the conditions for salvation and the content of the gospel of Jesus Christ.

---

[22] This is my translation of parts of the original that was reproduced by Bartolome de las Casas in his treatise, 'Historia de los Indios' (in *Obras Escogidas*) (Madrid: BAE, 1957–8), bk 3, ch. 4.

As a result of the Dominicans' bold move and following a conference to deal with the question of right and authority, the king of Spain passed the Laws of Burgos in 1512. Whilst these alleviated some of the harsh treatment meted out to the Indians and allowed a minimum of basic rights, they did nothing to scrap once and for all the evil practice of the *encomienda*.[23] In practice the Laws of Burgos were largely ignored and the subjugation of the Indians carried on as before. At a later date, Antonio de Valdivieso, the Bishop of Leon, became embroiled in a bitter dispute with the landowners, who refused to comply with the latest attempts by the Spanish crown to mitigate the harsh treatment of the indigenous population, namely the passing of the New Laws in 1542 that condemned slavery and the *encomienda* system. As a result he suffered martyrdom, being assassinated in February 1550 by a gang of supporters of the governor of Nicaragua , Rodrigo de Contreras. Nevertheless, those who believed that they had a prophetic calling to protect the incontrovertible human sanctity of the Indian continued their mission. Among them was Friar Bartolome de las Casas, who became the main protagonist in the efforts to have the whole colonial apparatus dismantled.

Las Casas

The one who was to become the most renowned 'Defender of the Indians' was eight years old when Columbus arrived in the Caribbean. Ten years after the initial voyage to the 'Indies', Bartolome emigrated to Hispaniola with his father. He gained all the privileges of the recently arrived Spanish colonialists, becoming a landowner and possessor of slaves. Like them he participated in slave raids and wars against the native Taino population. He saw no incongruity between these actions and a vocation to the priesthood. In 1510 he was ordained priest in Hispaniola.

For a time he remained unmoved by the preaching and arguments of the Dominicans on the island. He defended the legitimacy of the *encomienda* system. In 1513, as part of his duties as a priest, he was involved in the conquest of Cuba. Later, however, commenting on the massacre of Canonao, he wrote: 'I saw here cruelty on a scale no living being has ever seen or expects to see.'[24] By 1514 Las Casas was beginning to have doubts about the Spanish attitude towards the native populations. His celebrated 'conversion' happened as he was preparing to celebrate and preach on the day of Pentecost. He chose a passage from the Apocrypha: Ecclesiasticus 34:24–7. There he read these words:

---

[23] A full account of the events surrounding the sermon and the subsequent reactions can be found in Gutierrez, *Las Casas*, pp. 30–37 and 280–91.

[24] Las Casas, 'Historia de los Indios', bk 3, ch. 29.

Like the man who slays his son in his father's presence
is he who offers sacrifice from the possessions of the poor.
The bread of charity is life itself for the needy,
he who withholds it is a person of blood.
He slays his neighbour who deprives him of his living;
he sheds blood who denies the labourer his wages.

Gustavo Gutierrez comments on the impact that this passage made on the preacher:

> Las Casas allows himself to be challenged by the biblical passage, which calls in question his position in the nascent colonial system. This rereading was the occasion for him to 'consider the misery and servitude that those people suffer' owing to a greed for gold on the part of others . . . Scripture and reality are mutually illuminating. They reinforce one another, and this relationship produces Las Casas's transformation.[25]

The combination of the prophetic message from the word of God and direct experience of the daily afflictions of the natives was a powerful motivation to work tirelessly for change. It sustained him for the rest of his life, as he never gave up on the task of reversing the fortunes of the people for whom Christ died. Las Casas breathed his last on 18 July 1566 in Madrid.

The Justification for Conquest

As I have recounted, the fundamental questions posed by Montesino, just before the feast of the Nativity in 1511, echoed down the century: 'By what right . . . with what justice . . . with what authority?' Their Catholic majesties in Spain wished to have a clear conscience that the processes of conquest were in accordance with the best Catholic teaching and did not break generally accepted legal codes of practice at the time. Gutierrez has pointed out that Spain alone had the courage to hold a comprehensive debate on the morality of armed intervention in foreign lands. Other European nations accepted that the right to occupy other people's territories was too self-evident to be questioned.[26]

One immediate reaction to the Dominicans' challenge to the authorities in Hispaniola came from the Dominican provincial in Spain, Alonso de Loaysa: 'These Islands have been acquired by his Highness (King Ferdinand) *jure belli* (by right of war), and his Holiness (Pope Alexander VI) has

---

[25] Gutierrez, *Las Casas*, pp. 47–8.

[26] Gutierrez, *Las Casas*, p. 3.

made our Lord King a donation of the same, wherefore the servitude of the Indians is meet and just.'[27]

We might call this double justification for conquest – through a just war and by the supreme authority of Christ's emissary on earth – the external reasons, designed to provide legitimation. Clearly, both of them beg the question: were the wars against the Indians just? Did the Pope have a supreme jurisdiction throughout the world over temporal matters?

Interestingly, neither king nor pope was comfortable with such a simplistic solution to a matter of enormous controversy. In the light of the stern opposition of a group of theologians and jurists based at the University of Salamanca (of whom the most well known were Francisco de Vitoria[28] and Domingo de Soto[29]), both of them clarified what was and was not acceptable practice in the treatment of the indigenous peoples.

In 1537, Pope Paul III issued the Bull, *Sublimis Deus*, which has been called the Indians' 'Magna Carta'.[30] The two most significant statements refer to the humanity of the indigenous peoples and to their inherent freedoms in virtue of their humanity:

> Inasmuch, furthermore, as the human being has been created for a share in eternal life and happiness and can attain to this everlasting life and happiness only by way of faith in the Lord Jesus Christ, as Sacred Scripture attests, it necessarily follows that the human being is of such condition and nature as to be capable of receiving the faith of Christ, and that anyone endowed with human nature is capable of receiving that faith.[31]

The implication of this papal pronouncement is that the full humanity of the Indians is confirmed by their ability to receive the grace of salvation. Further,

---

[27] Quoted in Roger Ruston, *Human Rights and the Image of God* (London: SCM Press, 2004), p. 67.

[28] His most influential works were written in 1539 as summaries of his lectures to his students for that year: *De Indis* (On the Indians) and *De Jure Belli* (On the Right of War). They are now published as *Relectio de Indias o libertad de los indios* (Madrid: CSIC, 1967) and *Relectio de Iure Belli* (Madrid: CSIC, 1981); an English translation can be found in *Political Writings* (ed. Anthony Pagden and Jeremy Lawrance; Cambridge: CUP, 1991). For the wider significance of his thought, see Thomas Woods, *How the Catholic Church Built Western Civilization* (Washington: Regnery Publishing, 2005).

[29] See Domingo de Soto, *De justitia et jure* (5 vols, Madrid: Instituto de Estudios Politicos , 1967–8), and *Deliberacion en la causa de los pobres* (Madrid: Instituto de Estudios Politicos, 1965).

[30] Ruston, *Human Rights*, p. 130.

[31] Quoted in Gutierrez, *Las Casas*, p. 304.

because they are fully human, 'Although they be outside the faith of Christ, they neither are nor ought to be deprived of their freedom or dominion over their goods. Indeed, they may freely and licitly use, possess, and enjoy freedom and such dominion and must not be reduced to slavery.'[32]

In 1542, Charles V passed the 'New Laws', which succeeded in halting temporally the most oppressive activities of the colonists towards the Indians. They condemned slavery and the *encomienda* system, 'allowing the establishment of Indian townships, whose inhabitants were to be considered as subjects of the crown and therefore not obliged to work for the colonialists. Their work was to be free.'[33]

Tragically, the New Laws were swiftly revoked under immense pressure from the *encomenderos* of the Indies. In particular, prohibition of the practice of passing on the inheritance of the *encomienda* from one generation to another was cancelled. Charles V also believed that the Bull, *Sublimis Deus*, had been revoked by the Pope's Brief, *Non Indecens Videtur* (1538). He acted on this assumption; however, it is likely that the Pope only intended to annul an official pastoral instruction to the Archbishop of Toledo, Juan de Tavera.[34] In this latter, the Pope threatens with excommunication all those who mistreat the Indians. Whatever the case, the emperor had shown his ability to counteract even the teaching of the Supreme Pontiff, in order to maintain intact his own supreme authority over the Indies. The outcome of both these incidents is that both pope and king remained ambivalent about the status and situation of the Indians under Spanish rule.

The matter did not rest there. In 1550, Charles V convoked a disputation in Valladolid to 'inquire into and constitute the manner and laws whereby our holy Catholic faith may be preached and promulgated in the new world that God has revealed to us', and 'to seek a suitable manner of subjecting those people to the Emperor's majesty'. The debate was conducted between Las Casas and Juan Gines de Sepulveda. The latter was a chaplain to the royal court. He was a noted humanist in the tradition of the Italian city-states, which espoused the elitism of urban, civilised aristocrats over illiterate, uncultured artisans and agriculturalists.[35] For him the language of natural rights was quite foreign.

However incongruous it may seem to us today, the Spaniards believed they had a divine duty to bring the Indians into subjection in order that

---

[32] Text reproduced in Gutierrez, *Las Casas*, p. 305.

[33] Rodolfo Cardenal, 'The Church in Central America', in *The Church in Latin America: 1492–1992*, p. 243.

[34] The complex historical question of the revocation is discussed by Gutierrez in *Las Casas*, pp. 308–10.

[35] See Ruston, *Human Rights*, p. 143.

they might the more easily deliver the message of the Christian gospel to them. Various arguments were used to defend the right to make war and subject the defeated antagonists to the rule of the 'most excellent Christian monarchs'.

Sepulveda gave the following reasons for making war before preaching the gospel. They encapsulate the weightiest arguments used to justify conquest, suppression and enslavement. First, the Indians must be punished for their sin of idolatry in worshipping false deities. Second, they must be prevented from continuing the abominable practice of killing people in order to offer them as sacrifices. War was justified as intervention on behalf of innocent victims: 'By claiming they were removing tyrants and stopping evil practices such as human sacrifice the Spaniards could claim a moral superiority and a right of conquest.'[36]

Third, the faith could only be proclaimed once all physical resistance to the Christian evangelists had been ended. This measure was not considered an advocacy of forced conversion, but of the removal of as many hindrances to believing in the truth of salvation as possible.[37] Finally, following Aristotle's division of humanity into natural masters and slaves, the Spanish were justified in ruling over a people, who had demonstrated the primitiveness of their wits, for their own good.[38] This latter view of Sepulveda is expressed in his own words in the treatise *Democrates alter*: 'The Spaniards rule with perfect right over the barbarians, who, in prudence, talent, virtue and humanity are as inferior to the Spaniards as children to adults, women to men, the savage and cruel to the mild and gentle, the grossly intemperate to the continent.'[39]

One final reason was given to justify the right of possession. It is set out in a document called the *Anonimo de Yucay* (*The Yucay Opinion*),[40] which has all the hallmarks of being a self-serving vindication of what was entirely agreeable to the colonists:

> In an effort to explain the reasons for the existence of the mines in Peru, the author of that text will declare this wealth to have been a gift of divine providence itself: after all, it is thanks to it that the Spaniards, with the encouragement of their sovereigns, have been inspired to come to these lands. And in coming here, they have brought the Christian faith.[41]

---

[36] Ruston, *Human Rights*, p. 185.

[37] See Gutierrez, *Las Casas*, pp. 133–5.

[38] See Ruston, *Human Rights*, p. 145.

[39] Ruston, *Human Rights*, p. 144.

[40] The authorship of the document is contested; see Gutierrez, *Las Casas*, p. 598–9, note 2.

[41] Gutierrez, *Las Casas*, p. 361.

Amazingly, the doctrine of providence is also used to sustain the argument that the wealth of Peru is meant to be exploited to pay for the war in Europe against the Ottoman Empire:

> The need for resources for the defense of the Catholic faith (and European Society) against its enemies, as well as for 'the great riches of God's glory and the souls that with these riches are sure to be led to the Kingdom of Christ our Lord' justify, our author says . . . the exploitation of the mines of Peru.[42]

> I believe and hold it for a certainty that it has justified the labour of these mines and treasures.[43]

Although given a veneer of respectability, this kind of justification amply confirms the suspicion of Las Casas and other champions of the cause of the Indians that the prime motive for conquest had little to do with evangelization and everything to do with greed for gold. This supposition I will explore further when I come to the defence of the Indians.

The invalidity of conquest

The principal argument against the enforced colonization of the 'New World' hinged on the question of the human status of the Indian. The indigenous peoples had given plenty of evidence of their humanity in their ability to organise themselves in communities, create artefacts and make objects of design. Even their religious beliefs and practices, though repugnant to a Christian conscience, displayed the capacity for rational, logical thought. Vitoria and the School of Salamanca asserted that they were by nature fully human, bearing the image of God. He argued that, if they were human, then, according to the creation narrative of Genesis 1, they had been given full dominion over the lands where they lived and the possessions for which they had worked. The possessor, having dominion, could do what he pleased with his possession, as long as he did not destroy the common good. As the Indians were clearly masters of their own acts, they were entitled to enjoy the fruit of their labour.

Vitoria was the first person to develop a case for affirming that certain rights belonged to human beings as such: 'This was the doctrinal starting-point that enabled Vitoria and his colleagues to challenge all those theories thrown up to justify the domination and enslavement of indigenous peoples . . . The foundation of dominion is the fact that we are

---

[42] Gutierrez, *Las Casas*, p. 423.
[43] For the full text of the Yucay Opinion, see Isacio Pérez Fernández, *El anónimo de Yucay frente Bartolomé de las Casas* (Cusco: Centro Bartolomé de las Casa, 1995).

formed in the image of God; and the child is already formed in the image of God.'[44]

This being so, a supposed limited mental capacity or lack of cultural refinement (according to the standards of European culture of the time) was a matter, not of nature, but of education. He further argued that unwillingness to accept the Christian faith, and even savage crimes against fellow humans, did not remove the capacity and right of dominion, since this was a gift of nature rather than grace. This was a universal law built into the created constitution of the human world.

Vitoria also established a notion of rights that moved beyond Aquinas's notion of right as what is just in a law-governed community. In a hierarchically ordered society, what is right may be aligned to certain concepts of human dignity in which some are born to a superior position and others to an inferior. This would make it right for some to govern and others to be governed: 'Person and dignity refer in Aquinas's writings to special individuals with special roles.'[45] At the same time, those with the special right to direct others also had the moral obligation to act according to what is right and to uphold justice.

Vitoria, and others, following the early lead of Jean Gerson (1363–1429), moved the notion of the right from the objective moral world of duty to the subjective world of entitlements, equality and liberty. As the image-bearer of God, the individual was entitled to exercise dominion, meaning the right to participate in and control the world as a gift made equally to all human beings. The obvious corollary to this state of affairs is that other human beings (in this case, invaders from across the sea) had no right to deprive the Indians of their livelihood or of their natural liberty.

The conquistadors used another set of arguments to legitimise their seizure of other people's possessions. It referred to the three 'donations' that the Popes Alexander VI and Julius II granted the Spanish (and Portuguese) monarchy. In the Bull *Inter Caetera*, the king was granted the right of dominion over the new lands in exchange for the responsibility of bringing into the Christian religion any peoples living there. Subsequently, the crown was given permission to collect tithes in the Americas to pay for the activities of the missionaries. Finally, the crown was assigned the *patronato real*, permission to nominate all ecclesiastical posts in the Americas, both priests and bishops.[46]

The right of dominion was interpreted as a gift of territory, as if the Pope had a universal jurisdiction over the whole globe and was able to

---

[44] Ruston, *Human Rights*, p. 86.
[45] Ruston, *Human Rights*, p. 100.
[46] See Gonzalez and Gonzalez, *Christianity in Latin America*, p. 28.

'franchise' this jurisdiction to whom he pleased. So the donation was used as the sanction for grabbing lands, exploiting natural resources and making war. All this was done in the alleged, and highly dubious, interest of spreading Christ's rule on earth. It was implemented through the quite farcical *requerimiento* (notification). This was a document that was to be read to the Indians, whenever encountered, inviting them to submit to the Spanish sovereigns and to become Christians – the first call was obligatory, the second supposedly a matter of free choice. The document also contained a severe warning:

> Unless you comply, or if you postpone your compliance in bad faith, I certify to you that, with God's help, we shall mightily invade you, and make war on you . . . shall subject you to the yoke and obedience of the Church and Their Highnesses; shall take your persons and those of your women and children, make them slaves and, as such, sell them and dispose of them as Their Highnesses may order; shall take from you your goods; and shall do you all the harm and evil we can.[47]

This is without doubt the document that the friar, Vivente Valverde, read to the Inca Emperor Atahualpa in Cajamarca.

Now, the Dominicans of Salamanca fiercely disputed the official version of the donation. They proclaimed boldly that the Pope did not possess any universal jurisdiction in temporal matters. His only prerogative was to authorise the Spanish king to spread the Catholic faith to the newly discovered territories in fulfilment of Christ's commission to his followers to make disciples of all nations. So, the king of Spain had a 'dominion of jurisdiction' (*dominium iurisdictionis*) as far as the preaching of the gospel was concerned, but he had no 'dominion of ownership' (*dominium rerum*) to take away the lands from the Indians and make them into slaves.[48] One might say that the Genesis account of the creation of humans trumps all papal claims to have the authority to delegate dominion to whom he chooses. The rights of the Indians arise from their intrinsic liberty as fully human beings and from the necessity of having control of their environment in order to live a dignified existence.

The Salamanca School also developed a theory of the just war that made the aggressive invasion of the Indian communities illegitimate. The opinion of Vitoria is summed up in a letter written on the occasion of hearing about the conquest of the Inca Empire:

---

[47] Text in Gutierrez, *Las Casas*, p. 115.
[48] Ruston, *Human Rights*, p. 68.

I must tell you, after a lifetime of studies and long experience, that no business shocks me or embarrasses me more than the corrupt profits and affairs of the Indies. Their very mention freezes the blood in my veins . . . Here, since the property belonged to someone else, they can allege no title other than the law of war . . . During the recent battle with Atahualpa, neither he nor any of his peoples had ever done the slightest injury (*iniuria*) to the Christians, nor given them the least grounds for making war on them . . . If they are men and our neighbours . . . I do not see how to excuse these conquistadors of utter impiety and tyranny.

Systematically, the arguments of the Dominicans removed all the specious reasons that were given by the conquistadors and their supporters in the 'Old World' for plundering the Indians' goods and forcefully subjecting them to their will. Domingo de Soto, a younger colleague of Vitoria, in his treatise *De Dominio*, wrote: 'To go beyond this (the right to defend ourselves against anyone who obstructs the preaching) and take their goods and to subject them to our empire, I do not see where such a right comes from.'[49]

War could be justified only on the grounds of self-defence. Such a condition would have to preclude a provocation on the part of those defending themselves. In other words, wars of offence or pre-emptive attack were ruled out. However, one exception might be made to this general rule: that of defending the physical integrity of the victims of others' brutality. In the case of the Indies, this pointed to the victims of the Aztec sacrificial system. If the victims had the right to defend themselves, but were unable to do so, the Christian king, through his deputies, had the duty to defend them, since the victim's right to life was paramount. The right to attack, in this one case, was given because human sacrifice manifestly involves *iniuria* being committed against people with a prior right to life. Nevertheless, defence of others could not justify expanding the goals to include the seizure of territory or property. Only in this case, on the grounds of humanitarian intervention, would war be justified.[50]

It is intriguing to note that Las Casas would not sanction war, even in the circumstances of defending others from what amounted to murder. He argued that, according to their own lights, because that was the way they interpreted the meaning of worship, the Aztecs were duty bound to offer human sacrifice: 'Nature itself dictates that in offering God the most precious thing they have they may show themselves especially grateful for so many benefits received.'[51]

---

[49] Both quotes are taken from Ruston, *Human Rights*, pp. 70 and 71.
[50] See Ruston, *Human Rights*, pp. 93–4.
[51] Quote in Ruston, *Human Rights*, p. 150.

Naturally, he believed that human sacrifice and cannibalism were utterly repugnant and a total distortion of what true worship should be. Nevertheless, attempting to bring it to an end by violent means was counterproductive. In the first place, killing the perpetrators of violence, before they had a chance to hear the gospel, repent and believe, defeats the principal object of the Spanish presence. In the second place, deaths caused by attacking the Indians inevitably will vastly outnumber deaths due to ritual killings. So, war would be the greater of two evils.[52] In this discussion, Las Casas takes the theory of natural rights to an extreme. It could even be said that he contradicts it, for even by the natural light of reason, human beings ought to be able to judge that the right to life of other humans outweighs any other consideration. Murder has often been justified on the grounds that the victim is in some way sub-human.

Perhaps Las Casas's extravagant defence of the Indians' justification for killing other humans, in the interests of maintaining harmony with the gods, has to be set within the context of his polemic against the conquistadors' fallacious vindication of the right to wage war. Las Casas was not attempting to find plausibly just reasons for fighting the Indians, but erecting the strongest possible theological, juridical and moral barriers in the way of all forms of physical coercion. Moreover, using the same argument employed by those who justified war against them, he raised the issue of who, then, should protect the innocent victims of Spanish atrocities. It was plain, to anyone who had been in the Indies, that the conquest had caused infinitely more deaths than the system of religious sacrifices. It could also be condemned as idolatry: 'In all truth, it would be far more accurate to say that the Spaniards have sacrificed more to their beloved goddess Codicia ["greed", "covetousness"] every single year that they have been in the Indies . . . than the Indians have sacrificed to their gods throughout the Indies in a hundred years.'[53]

The most characteristic reasoning employed by Las Casas in defence of the Indians was based on his understanding of the duty and means of bringing the message of Christ to these people, who had never before had the opportunity to hear his name proclaimed. All use of force under the pretence of evangelizing was a disgrace. To imagine that it was necessary to subjugate the peoples before they were in a fit condition to hear about Christ was to deny that the message proclaimed was good news. Only dialogue and persuasion were valid means of presenting the Saviour of the world. Either evangelism was peaceful or it was not evangelism.[54]

---

[52] Ruston, *Human Rights*, pp. 147–51.

[53] Las Casas, *Obras Escogidas*, vol. 5:333b.

[54] See Gustavo Gutierrez, ' "If you were Indios . . ." Bartolome de Las Casas'. *Concilium* 5 (2009), pp. 27–8.

Las Casas's line of reasoning followed a long tradition of thinking. Wherever conversion to Christianity is, even remotely, the result of some exterior force or inducement, the proper exercise of faith is absent. Moreover, force makes God appear as a cruel tyrant and Christ as a conqueror who wishes to bring about submission and obedience, whatever the cost. Las Casas was considerably out of step with his time. He argued that the same freedom necessary for authentic belief was also a legitimate cause for rejecting belief. Many other people, however, thought that it was dishonouring to God for anyone to refuse the gospel, and therefore sinful; and, because sinful, the protagonists of the message could exercise God's punishment on his behalf. Las Casas, needless to say, fundamentally disagreed.

Conclusion: the Impact of the New on the Old (World)

The spirit of adventure and exploration that drove generations of Spaniards to leave their homes on the peninsula, cross a large expanse of water and settle in strange environments had immense repercussions for all concerned: 'The "discovery" and conquest of the "New World" forever changed the "Old" . . . The Americas would never be the same after that fateful 12th of October 1492, when Columbus first set foot on these lands. But Europe as well would never be the same after Columbus returned on the equally fateful but less known March 15, 1493.'[55]

The arrival of quantities of silver and gold from the colonies distorted the economy of the colonial power: '[It provided] capital for the rapidly developing industrialization in other European nations from which Spain found it easy and convenient to purchase goods rather than producing them itself.'[56]

Much of the wealth was also wasted on innumerable wars that the emperor, Charles V, waged across Europe. The abundant source of easy riches had the effect of delaying Spain's own sustainable process of wealth creation through innovation, industrialization and capital accumulation.

The impact of the encounter with new races of people, unlike any familiar to the Europeans hitherto, was keenly felt by the church. Up to 1492, the only people known outside Christendom were Jews and Muslims. Now the church had to recognise and deal with people whose religious way of life was not remotely comparable to its own. It became engaged, then, in a highly significant debate about the human status of the

---

[55] Gonzalez and Gonzalez, *Christianity in Latin America*, p. 1.
[56] Gonzalez and Gonzalez, *Christianity in Latin America*, p. 2.

indigenous peoples of the Americas, the legitimacy of slavery, the nature of salvation, the means of evangelization, freedom of religion, self-determination and human rights. It is largely to the credit of the Dominicans of Salamanca and the tireless efforts of the Dominican, Fray Bartolome de las Casas, that new theological ground was broken in response to this novel situation.

As Gutierrez has manifested in his extensive study of the life and witness of Las Casas, he was inspired, from the time of his 'conversion' in 1514 to his death in 1565, by his reading and understanding of the Scriptures. In 1531, writing to the Council of the Indies, he told its members that 'God has a very present and lively memory of the littlest and most forgotten'.[57] Here he picked up the gospel motif of the evangelization of the poor. He reversed the general attitude to the Indians: the conquistadors saw them as people to be exploited for what could be extracted from them; Las Casas saw them as people, created by God as equals, to be the privileged recipients of the good news of a salvation which would enhance their humanity. In his thinking, the only justification for the presence of the Spanish in the Americas was the divine commission to share the good news of Jesus Christ. It could not be treated as an excuse for other sordid ends: 'The proclamation of God's love and not conquering lands for the king of Spain, still less desire for gold, should be the guiding star for the Christian presence in the Indies. He uses the Gospel preference for the least in history to affirm the equality of all human beings.'[58]

In many ways the Spanish who came with notions of superiority and self-righteousness were in more need of the gospel than the inhabitants of the lands they encountered. The real idolaters, in danger of eternal condemnation, were the people who lived and died for the sake of Mammon; more so than those who followed their own religions.

In his magisterial *Apologetica Historia* (Apologetic History), Las Casas expounds reasons for accepting the ability of the Indians to exercise rational judgement, comparing their laws and customs favourably with those of the Greeks and Romans and 'even our own Spaniards of Cantabria'. He further disputes, at some length, the use of the epithet 'barbarian' to describe the original inhabitants of the Americas. He sets out the four characteristics of the meaning of the word and concludes that, although the Indians qualify as barbarians in two senses – lack of a written language and lack of belief in the one, true God – the Spaniards are barbarians in a more serious sense, namely they have 'deserted and forgotten the rules and order of reason and the gentleness and peacefulness which man should naturally possess;

---

[57] Las Casas, *Obras Escogidas*, vol. 5:44b.
[58] Las Casas, 'If you were Indios . . .', p. 26.

blind with passion, they change in some way, or are ferocious, harsh, cruel, and are precipitated into acts so inhuman that fierce and wild beasts of the mountains would not commit them'.[59] He concludes that, if it is legitimate to refer to the Indians as barbarians in the sense of having no proper government or laws of their own, it is because the Spaniards have made them so.

As a result of the Spaniards' encounter with the Indies, it may be said that some of their theologians and experts in law became the first to elaborate a theoretical basis for human rights, derived from the Scriptures and the writings of previous divines, pointing to equality and liberty, freedom of religion[60] and a democratic society.[61] It is regrettable that in many discourses on the origin of these beliefs[62] due acknowledgement is not given to these first pioneers. They were ahead of their times. Had their voices been listened to and acted on, the whole history of colonialism would surely have been vastly different and, perhaps, the world a more peaceable place in which to live.

---

[59] Bartolome de las Casas, *Obras Completas*, vols 6–8 (Madrid: Alianza Editorial, 1992), ch. 264.

[60] It has to be recognised that Las Casas asserted freedom of religion for those who had not yet converted to the faith of the church. Such freedom was a prerequisite for an authentic act of faith. However, he probably would not have defended the right of European peoples to abandon the Catholic faith for a different version of Christianity: 'It was unclear to anyone in the 16th century, Catholic or Protestant, that toleration of religious diversity could be anything other than a source of danger to the community'; see Ruston, *Human Rights*, p. 113.

[61] The first principal of a democratic society was enunciated in the concept of 'consent to be governed' summed up in the Latin tag *quod omnes tangit debet ab omnibus approbari* (what touches all must be approved by all); see Ruston, *Human Rights*, ch. 9, for a full discussion of this important ideal.

[62] For example, neither Vitoria, de Soto nor Las Casas is cited in Max L. Stackhouse, *Creeds, Society and Human Rights: A Study in Three Cultures* (Grand Rapids: Eerdmans, 1984).

6

The 'Old' World: Church and Mission in the Radical Reformation

Introduction

The subject of this study needs some justification. In the massive political and religious upheavals witnessed within Europe in the sixteenth century, to touch on the movement that has come to be known as 'Anabaptist' might seem to be disproportionate. The Anabaptist communities appeared to be small, marginal and insignificant in comparison with either the dominant Catholic Church or the reforming efforts associated with Luther, Zwingli and Calvin. However, it is precisely the lack of space generally accorded to the early Anabaptist views on the church and the world that offers a good reason for including this group's thinking and practice in relation to its own identity as a missionary body.

By and large, the history of the two main protagonists of the period – Catholicism and mainstream Protestantism – is well known. The thinking behind the various conflicts that erupted as a result of a strong reforming impulse, linked to the desire on the part of city-states and provinces for greater independence from the Holy Roman Empire, has been rehearsed countless times; the same cannot be said for the Anabaptist Reformation. Moreover, the latter has often been misrepresented by historians who have tended to identify it with some of its more extreme elements, rather than considering seriously its strengths, as well as its weaknesses.

I will attempt to highlight some of the more significant elements of the Anabaptist event during its earliest formative years. Inevitably, this study will be limited. In accordance with the theme of the book, I will concentrate on Anabaptist understandings of the nature of the church and its relationship with the world in which it found itself. Several important issues occupied the minds of the early leaders, and about which they wrote both short and long treatises. Naturally, one of the most crucial was the nature of faith in relation to baptism and entry into the Christian community. Others included the sharing of goods, evangelistic preaching, persecution and suffering, engagement with political power and the use of physical coercion in matters to do with both the church and the state.

All of these concerns arose out of the circumstances of the time. They should be interpreted, therefore, in the light of a particular historical situation. The leaders, some of whom had received a good theological education, and some of whom had little formal training, had to wrestle with conditions of life not encountered before. In order to help guide newly formed communities, which were put under great pressure by the civil authorities, they had to formulate responses in the midst of tough hostile events. Their theological thinking and practical action was unavoidably contextual. For this reason, it is appropriate to look first at an outline of the main historical episodes. Much interesting detail will, unfortunately, have to be omitted.

A brief history

The beginnings

Although the Anabaptists had a number of characteristics (which will be explored later) that set them apart from the mainstream Reformation, the most telling (literally a matter of life and death) was their insistence on reserving baptism only for those who freely professed faith for themselves in Jesus Christ's work of salvation. Their insistence on the need of conscious faith preceding baptism implied that those who had been baptised in infancy should be 'rebaptised'. It is not surprising, therefore, that the beginning of the Anabaptist movement is generally traced back to an event that took place in Zurich on 21 January 1525 in the house of one Felix Mantz: there, for the first time, one of the group at the meeting, Conrad Grebel, baptised another for a second time. As far as these people were concerned, since they had repudiated infant baptism as invalid, this was the one true Christian baptism. The Anabaptists never used the title for themselves, as they did not consider this a second baptism; nevertheless, the designation, used by their opponents, has remained.[1]

It would be well-nigh impossible to trace all the preceding events that brought to pass this dramatic break with past custom. A number of the first leaders of the new movement were already engaged with Ulrich Zwingli in working for reform in Zurich and the surrounding

---

[1] See Ian M. Randall, *Communities of Conviction: Baptist Beginnings in Europe* (Schwarzenfeld: Neufeld Verlag, 2009), p. 1.

district.[2] Encouraged at first by his reforming zeal, they soon became disillusioned with the slow pace of reform and the seeming compromises with what they considered to be plain biblical teaching that the Swiss leader was prepared to countenance.

In October 1523, a disputation was held in Zurich on the meaning and observance of the Lord's Supper. There was a sharp disagreement between Zwingli and his disciples on the question of the abolition of the mass. The latter believed that Scripture was so plain about the matter that nothing should thwart its authority; in their opinion, a radical reinterpretation of the sacrament was essential. Zwingli agreed in theory. However, in practice, he allowed the city council to decide. It took a much more conservative stance: 'By December 19, Zwingli had completely capitulated to the judgement and authority of the council . . . In the eyes of the Brethren he had compromised revealed truth in deference to constituted political authority. The authority of the Word of God had been sacrificed on the altar of human expediency.'[3]

This dispute symbolised one of the main areas of contention between the mainstream and radical reformers: 'The decision of Conrad Grebel to refuse to accept the jurisdiction of the Zurich council over the Zurich church is one of the high moments of history, for however obscure it was, it marked the beginning of the modern "free church" movement.'[4] This decision signalled the initiation of a struggle to eliminate the power of the state to decide on matters pertaining to Christian doctrine and practice.

Gradually in Zurich, then, a group of people who had studied with Zwingli began to find considerable points of divergence with the master. Apart from dissent over the Lord's Supper and civil authority, the question of infant baptism came to the fore on 17 January 1524 at a disputation on baptism held in Zurich. The outcome was a ruling that infant baptism accorded with biblical teaching. As a result, the city council required the baptism of all infants within eight days, forbade meetings organised by the circle of radicals and expelled from the city all non-residents who opposed the baptism of infants.[5]

Underlying these disputes about authority and church order was the question of who was authorised to give a definitive interpretation

<hr>

[2] See J. Denny Weaver, *Becoming Anabaptist: The Origin and Significance of Sixteenth Century Anabaptism* (Scottdale, PA: Herald Press, 2nd edn, 2005), p. 17.
[3] William R. Estep, *The Anabaptist Story: An Introduction to Sixteenth-Century Anabaptism* (Grand Rapids, MI: Eerdmans, 3rd edn, 1996), p. 18.
[4] Harold Bender, *Conrad Grebel* (Goshen: Mennonite Historical Society, 1950), pp. 99–100.
[5] See Weaver, *Becoming Anabaptist*, p. 46.

of the word of God. Whereas the radicals, following the logic of the reformers' emphasis on the 'priesthood of all believers', came to believe in a community interpretation under the direct guidance of the Holy Spirit, the mainstream reformers fell back on the authority of the accredited preachers of the state churches. The renowned doctrine of *sola scriptura* was reinterpreted to mean that correct teaching from Scripture was decided by whoever could persuade the magistrates of their views.[6]

The Spread of Anabaptism from Zurich

It appears that this more radical desire for change began as a grass-roots alternative movement for reform of both the church and state. People were catching a vision (somewhat utopian no doubt) of a society of much greater social equality and economic fairness. The early promise of a substantial break with the past that seemed to be part of the Zwinglian agenda appeared, in their eyes, to have stalled. The movement for change was going neither fast nor far enough.[7]

The Peasants' War

One of the outcomes of dissatisfaction with the pace of change was the German Peasants' War (*Deutscher Bauernkrieg*) of 1525–6. It originated as a revolt against feudal oppression. A petition, known as the 'Twelve Articles of the Black Forest', was delivered to the Holy Roman Emperor petitioning for substantial changes in both the ecclesial and social orders. Among other matters, the Twelve Articles demanded the right of communities to elect and depose clergymen, substantial revisions of the tax system assessed against the peasants' agricultural labour, and the abolition of serfdom and death tolls. The nobility were no longer to have exclusive fishing and hunting rights. The full use of forests, pastures and other privileges, which the nobility had withdrawn from communities and individuals, were to be restored and excessive rents reduced.[8] The Twelve Articles sought to ground their demands on the teaching of Scripture.

The articles represented a condensation of grievances that had been smouldering among peasant communities in Southern Germany and

---

6   This precept applied, not only in the city-states controlled by the Protestant Reformation, but also in the few cases, Munster being the most notorious, where the radicals gained dominance.

7   See C. Arnold Snyder, *Anabaptist History and Theology: Revised Student Edition* (Kitchener, Ontario: Pandora Press, 1997), pp. 107–9.

8   See Weaver, *Becoming Anabaptist*, p. 52.

Austria for a few years previously. They were presented to the emperor
in 1524. On being ignored, the peasants, supported by the leadership of
some cities, rose up against the clergy and nobles in an attempt to force
their demands. Ultimately they were defeated in the Battles of Frank-
enhausen and Sindelfingen (in May and June 1525) and the cities of
Wurtemberg and Wurzberg had to surrender.

Although the causes of the war may have been largely economic and
political, religious factors undoubtedly contributed a strong motivating
force under the leadership of people like Thomas Muntzer. Initially
Zwingli supported the grievances of the common people and Luther
showed some sympathy by listening at first to the complaints. After the
uprisings turned especially violent, Luther turned against the rebels and
urged the authorities to suppress 'the murdering hoards'. Nevertheless,

> The overwhelming majority of commoners in the movement of 1525 thought
> of it as part of the Reformation and took for granted that it was appropriate
> to apply God's law to economic, political, and social abuses . . . Their polit-
> ical programmes sought to remove the clergy, but not the aristocracy, from
> positions of worldly authority. They sought greater autonomy for village
> self-government and greater power for all urban and rural commoners in the
> representative assemblies of the territorial states.[9]

Some individuals, who later became prominent in the Anabaptist movement, were involved in the uprisings. Balthasar Hubmeier, the pastor of
the church in Waldshut near Zurich (a parish in transition – from Catholic
to Protestant to Anabaptist), has been suggested as one of the possible
authors of the Twelve Articles. The town sent an armed contingent to join
the peasant army in the siege of Radolfzell. Wilhelm Reublin in Hallau,
Hans Hut and Melchior Rinck also took part in the disturbances. Hut's
participation was linked to certain apocalyptic expectations. He believed
that as the end times approached and Christ's second coming was imminent, it was legitimate to take the sword to overthrow godless rulers.
Later, however, he modified his views, teaching that the armed rebellion had been premature, as the final judgement and day of vengeance
had not yet arrived.[10] The peasants had acted too early in the apocalyptic
scheme of things.[11] On the other hand, Conrad Grebel famously wrote a

---

[9]   *The Global Anabaptist Mennonite Encyclopedia Online*, see also Snyder, *Anabap-
      tist History*, pp. 68–78.
[10] See Weaver, *Becoming Anabaptist*, pp. 70–71.
[11] Meic Pearse, *The Great Restoration: The Religious Radicals of the 16th and 17th
      Centuries* (Carlisle: Paternoster Press, 1998), pp. 67, 71.

letter to Muntzer condemning the use of the sword: 'They (the true disciples of Christ) employ neither worldly sword nor war, since with them killing is absolutely renounced.'[12]

One of the results of the aborted attempts to introduce substantial reforms to the existing established social order was the growth of groups that advocated a more radical programme of transformation than that envisaged by the mainstream reformers such as Luther, Melanchthon, Zwingli and Bucer. Many of the rebels now responded positively to the fresh preaching of the word of God as interpreted by those becoming known as rebaptisers. So, the message spread north and east through South Germany, the Tyrol and into Moravia. It also spread north and west into central Germany and the Netherlands. Along with Switzerland these were the main areas of Anabaptist activity up to the early 1540s.

Moravia

Following the disturbances unleashed by the grievances of the common people against church institutions and privileged classes throughout central Europe, the newly constituted groups of believers, who did not offer allegiance to the old structures of church and state, became the object of severe persecution by both Catholic and Protestant authorities. They were accused of having associated themselves with the revolutionaries,[13] and of being schismatics and dangerous subversives, who would ultimately destroy the existing order if allowed to continue.

So, the Zurich council introduced the penalty of death by drowning[14] in 1526 for all those engaged in the practice of rebaptism.[15] Felix Mantz was the first Anabaptist leader to suffer martyrdom for his convictions about baptism. In 1529, at the Diet of Speyer, both Catholic and Protestant authorities came together to promulgate the most severe punishments against the new communities. These were harassed, pursued, imprisoned, tortured

---

[12] See Leland Harder, ed., *The Sources of Swiss Anabaptism: The Grebel Letters and Related Documents* (Classics of the Radical Reformation, Vol. 4) (Scottdale, PA: Herald Press, 1985), p. 293. Differences of opinion among early Anabaptist leaders about the legitimate use of violence in certain circumstances will be discussed later in the chapter.

[13] See Estep, *Anabaptist Story*, p. 4.

[14] This form of death was a mocking commentary on the practice of adult baptism, even though the early Anabaptists generally did not baptise by total immersion.

[15] James Stayer, 'The Anabaptist Revolt and Political and Religious Powers' in Benjamin W. Redekop and Calvin W. Redekop, *Power, Authority and the Anabaptist Tradition* (Baltimore: John Hopkins University Press, 2001), p. 54.

and executed in their thousands because they refused to conform to the existing church–state *modus vivendi*, captured in the celebrated maxim, *cuius regio, eius religio* (roughly translated as, 'whoever the ruler, that will be the religion').

The unleashing of persecution on a massive scale resulted in considerable migrations to places where the authorities were deemed to be more tolerant of dissent. One such area was Moravia, where the rulers came to sympathise with the exiles and even adopt their beliefs. So, the first communal Anabaptist settlements were established at Austerlitz[16] on the estates of the lords of Kaunitz. These defended both their own semi-independent status and that of the Anabaptists against the encroachments of the Austrian authorities.[17] A number of Anabaptist leaders (for example, Jacob Wiedemann, Balthasar Hubmaier, Hans Hut, Wilhelm Reublin, Pilgram Marpeck and Jacob Hutter) either sent or accompanied communities into this area.

There, divisions occurred among the different groups. Those influenced by Hubmaier continued to insist on the legitimacy of the use of the sword by Christians to execute justice in society; those who followed the teaching of the Schleitheim Articles (1527)[18] believed that such action was not permitted to true followers of Christ. Other disputes arose over authoritarian leadership and community of goods, leading to split communities and further migrations within Moravia. Eventually, between 1533 and 1535, some order and stability was restored to the communities by Hutter. Although he was burnt at the stake in 1536, the *Bruderhof* in Auspitz took his name for their community. After a year in exile, they returned to Moravia in 1537 under the leadership of John Amon and established many new communities.[19]

North Germany and the Netherlands

Meanwhile to the west, in the Low Countries and Northern Germany, a different brand of Anabaptism developed. Its origin is associated with Melchior Hoffmann. He broke with Lutheranism in 1529, accepted

---

[16] At this time there were already other separatist groups of believers living in the region: the survivors of the *Unitas Fratrum*, the Gabrielites (followers of Gabriel Ascherham) and the Philippites (followers of Philip Plener).

[17] Estep, *Anabaptist Story*, p. 129.

[18] See below, pp. 137–138.

[19] On the migration to Moravia and the subsequent history of the settlements, see George Hunston Williams, *The Radical Reformation* (Philadelphia: Westminster Press, 1962), pp. 417–33.

believers' baptism under the influence of Karlstadt and, in contrast to the Swiss Brethren,[20] held a more positive view of the role of Christians in government. He envisioned the birth of a new society, beginning on earth as the work of God.[21] Pious political rulers would operate as instruments of God in bringing about the final victory of God's people over their enemies. He believed in and encouraged prophetic revelations, like those spoken by Barbara Rebstock.[22]

The combination of his teaching on the righteous use of the sword, eschatological expectations of the imminent birth of a redeemed society and contemporary prophetic utterances inspired others to take extreme measures in forcing through social changes in anticipation of the new world order. The city of Strasbourg was first nominated as the New Jerusalem on account of its more tolerant attitude to contentious voices. When the city failed to grasp what some saw as its divine destiny, hope passed to the German city of Munster: 'With the idea that extermination of the godless must precede the day of final judgement, and with the conception of the earthly reign of the saints in a theocratic intermediate kingdom until the return of Christ, Hoffman had created the most important ideological presupposition for the Anabaptist kingdom of Munster.'[23]

At that time, a struggle was going on within Munster to gain independence from the prince–bishop in whose jurisdiction the city lay. The leaders of the revolt believed that an alignment with the Anabaptists in the city would best further their cause. They did not, perhaps, reckon with the aggressive crusading mentality brought into the city by Jan Matthijs of Haarlem, who quickly took over the reigns of leadership and began to convert the city into a militant theocracy after his image.[24] When he was killed outside the city in a skirmish with the besieging forces of the prince–bishop, his colleague Jan Beukels (John of Leiden) took over leadership of the city. Eventually the uprising was crushed and the leaders executed.[25]

Melchior Hoffman had been incarcerated in Strasbourg in 1531, where he remained until his death in 1543. He was not directly responsible for the fiasco that played itself out in the supposedly elect city. Nevertheless, Anabaptism was considered by ecclesiastical and civil authorities throughout the empire to have been directly linked to the uprising. It was

---

[20] Those communities of Anabaptists who grew out of the first wave of missionary work following the first baptisms in Zurich.

[21] Weaver, *Becoming Anabaptist*, p. 120.

[22] Snyder, *Anabaptist History*, pp. 209–12.

[23] K. Deppermann, 'Melchior Hoffman' in H.G. Goertz (ed.), *Profiles of Radical Reformers* (Scottdale, PA: Herald Press, 1982), p. 187.

[24] Snyder, *Anabaptist History*, pp. 215–19.

[25] Snyder, *Anabaptist History*, pp. 362–71.

assumed, therefore, that any rejection of the current church-state status quo would lead to another Munster.[26]

In the aftermath of the Munster rebellion, Anabaptism throughout the region was in some disarray. Fortunately for the movement, about this time a person of considerable ability in the role of a peacemaker arose within the Anabaptist ranks. Menno Simons (a former Catholic priest), rebaptised in early 1536, began the difficult task of rallying and unifying the scattered groups of believers from the Low Countries to the Vistula Delta. In his treatise, *The Blasphemy of John of Leiden* (1535), he repudiated the thinking and the events behind the Munster debacle. In a further work, *Foundation of Christian Doctrine*, Menno set forth his case for the establishment of peaceful associations which would not cause any physical threat to the stability of the existing society. His unremitting work preserved the movement from fanaticism and disintegration.[27] It is significant that, for different reasons, the two groups which adopted the main Anabaptist teachings[28] were the ones who survived the turmoil and persecutions of the following years and centuries, namely the Hutterites and the Mennonites.

The main characteristics

Baptism

The most clearly visible mark that distinguished the Anabaptist communities from both Catholic and mainstream Protestant churches was the practice of baptism on profession of faith in Christ and the willingness to follow him as a conscious disciple. It was a symbol of commitment that set people apart from the mixed congregations made up of everyone born in a particular parish.[29] It challenged, therefore, the whole notion of a territorial church, coextensive with a particular population living in a specific location. At its heart was the conviction that salvation through Christ was not a mere formality that could be accomplished by a ritual in infancy. Salvation was a gift granted to those who consciously responded to the message of God's word by repentance and who gave evidence of the desire to live a life worthy of Christ's kingdom. Belonging to the church was a voluntary act; when it became an enforced obligation, faith lost its true nature.

---

[26] See Weaver, *Becoming Anabaptist*, p. 131.
[27] Williams, *Radical Reformation*, pp. 393–4.
[28] These I will attempt to summarise in the rest of the chapter.
[29] See Estep, *Anabaptist Story*, p. 20.

The earliest written evidence of the Anabaptist position on baptism was contained in a letter written to Thomas Muntzer by Conrad Grebel and his companions.[30] William Estep calls it 'probably, the most revolutionary act of the Reformation'.[31] It implied a repudiation of all the established churches, which in the eyes of these radical reformers had not had the courage to take reform as far as the Scriptures demanded. Believers' baptism, therefore, was an emblem of being part of a community which was forging a new identity in seeking first the kingdom of God. It also, therefore, symbolised the willingness of the baptised to submit themselves to the discipline of the congregation. It was simultaneously a theological confession, a witness to an inner transformation, a political statement and an act of dissent.

In the circumstances of persecution, some Anabaptists spoke of a threefold baptism: by the Spirit, in water and through blood – the order is important. The baptism of blood was understood as both the mortification of the flesh and martyrdom: 'The flesh must daily be killed since it only wants to live and reign according to its own lusts . . . By this the old Adam is martyred, killed and carried to the grave.'[32] The acceptance of physical death is closely linked to the death of the old nature.

Believer's baptism, therefore, indicated a new understanding of the church, a new relationship to the state, a new approach to the world and a new vision of the call of discipleship. Melchior Hoffman, in his *The Ordinance of God*, exhorted all those 'who have surrendered themselves to the Lord' to 'lead themselves out of the realm of Satan . . . into the spiritual wilderness and also wed and bind themselves to the Lord Jesus Christ, publicly through the true sign of the Covenant, the water bath and baptism'.[33]

Separation

In the first ten years of its existence as an independent movement (from early in 1525 until the catastrophe of Munster in 1535), opinion remained quite divided between different leaders on the question of Christian involvement in the political affairs of this present world. As far as their attitude towards the mainstream churches was concerned, there was little discussion. The

---

[30] See 'Letters to Thomas Muntzer by Conrad Grebel and Friends', in *Spiritual and Anabaptist Writers* (George Hunston Williams and Angel M. Mergal; Philadelphia: Westminster Press, 1957).

[31] Estep, *Anabaptist Story*, p. 201.

[32] H. Wayne Pipkin and John H. Yoder, eds, *Balthasar Hubmaier: Theologian of Anabaptism* (Scottdale, PA: Herald Press, 1989), quoted in Snyder, *Anabaptist History*, p. 161.

[33] Quoted in Williams, *Radical Reformation*, p. 308.

group that had begun as disciples of Zwingli in Zurich became quickly disillusioned with the reformer. Even by the time of the second disputation in
Zurich in October 1523, when Zwingli bowed to the authority of the city
council, Grebel signalled that the Reformation was failing.[34] George Blaurock called Zwingli and the city fathers of Zurich 'false prophets'.

In effect these intrepid pioneers were calling into question the whole
long tradition of the Constantine succession, with its attempt to Chris-
tianise an essentially pagan society. Beginning with the Edict of Innocent
I in 407, when infant baptism was made compulsory, the church ceased to
be the fellowship of the regenerate;[35] it reneged on its original calling to
witness by its words and deeds to the kingdom of Christ. In a parody of
the end times, when 'the kingdom of the world [will] become the kingdom
of our Lord and of his Messiah' (Rev. 11:15), the kingdom of the Lord had
coalesced with the kingdom of the world: 'With the union of church and
state and the accompanying use of force to compel conformity to the state
church, the fall was complete.'[36]

Baptism, as practised in the mainstream churches, both Catholic
and Protestant, had become a tool to require conformity to a political
settlement, engineered by those in power. It denied people freedom of
conscience and of action to interpret and live by the Scriptures as they
were being rediscovered in the new vernacular translations:

> Anabaptists believed the church was fallen beyond reform. Thorough
> restoration of New Testament Christianity was necessary, which required
> freedom from state control and ecclesiastical traditions . . . Anabaptist ideas
> resonated with earlier movements, such as the Unitas Fratrum, Walden-
> sians and Lollards. Anabaptists were heirs of the 'old evangelical broth-
> erhoods', an alternative tradition that had reappeared throughout the
> centuries, advocating beliefs and practices the established church ignored
> or marginalised.[37]

It is not surprising that their interpretation of what was happening, or
failing to happen, in the Reformation led them to part company with the
established churches, were they Catholic or Protestant.

The issue of a complete separation from the affairs of the state was not,
apparently, quite so clear-cut. According to Arnold Snyder, the question of

[34] See Estep, *Anabaptist Story*, p. 38.
[35] See Franklin Hamlin Littell, *The Anabaptist View of the Church* (Boston: Starr King Press, 1958), p. 63.
[36] Estep, *Anabaptist Story*, p. 243.
[37] Stuart Murray, *Post-Christendom Church and Mission in a Strange New World* (Milton Keynes: Paternoster Press, 2004), p. 335.

the separation from the world was still being worked out in the movements in South and North Germany and the Netherlands until well into the last half of the sixteenth century.[38] The position of the Swiss Brethren in 1527 was clarified in the brief statement of belief known as the Schleitheim Articles.[39] They advocated a sharp separation between two kingdoms. Christians, who belonged to the kingdom of heaven, could not participate in the affairs of the earthly kingdom, because their membership of the former implied an exclusive loyalty that made compromise with official duties in the latter impossible.[40]

The relevant sections of Article VI (concerning the sword) summarise the argument:

> The sword is ordained of God outside the perfection of Christ. It punishes and puts to death the wicked, and guards and protects the good. In the Law the sword was ordained for the punishment of the wicked and for their death, and the same (sword) is (now) ordained to be used by the worldly magistrates . . .
>
> It will be asked concerning the sword, whether a Christian shall pass sentence in worldly disputes and strife such as unbelievers have with one another. This is our united answer. Christ did not wish to decide or pass judgment between brother and brother in the case of the inheritance, but refused to do so. Therefore we should do likewise.
>
> It will be asked concerning the sword, Shall one be a magistrate if one should be chosen as such? The answer is as follows: They wished to make Christ king, but He fled and did not view it as the arrangement of His Father. Thus shall we do as He did, and follow Him, and so shall we not walk in darkness. For He Himself says, He who wishes to come after Me, let him deny himself and take up his cross and follow Me. Also, He Himself forbids the (employment of) the force of the sword saying, The worldly princes lord it over them, etc., but not so shall it be with you. Further, Paul says, Whom God did foreknow He also did predestinate to be conformed to the image of His Son, etc. Also Peter says, Christ has suffered (not ruled) and left us an example, that ye should follow His steps . . .
>
> It will be observed that it is not appropriate for a Christian to serve as a magistrate because of these points: The government magistracy is according to the flesh, but the Christian's is according to the Spirit; their houses and dwelling remain in this world, but the Christian's are in heaven; their citizenship is in this world, but the Christian's citizenship is in heaven; the weapons of their conflict

---

[38] Snyder, *Anabaptist History*, p. 164.
[39] Probably drawn up by Michael Sattler.
[40] See Snyder, *Anabaptist History*, pp. 271–2.

and war are carnal and against the flesh only, but the Christian's weapons are spiritual, against the fortification of the devil. The worldlings are armed with steel and iron, but the Christians are armed with the armour of God, with truth, righteousness, peace, faith, salvation and the Word of God. In brief, as in the mind of God toward us, so shall the mind of the members of the body of Christ be through Him in all things, that there may be no schism in the body through which it would be destroyed. For every kingdom divided against itself will be destroyed. Now since Christ is as it is written of Him, His members must also be the same, that His body may remain complete and united to its own advancement and upbuilding.[41]

Others, however, most notably Balthasar Hubmeier, believed that Christians could bear the sword and act as magistrates to protect civic society.[42] In his treatise, 'On the Sword' (*Von dem Schwert*) he argued for the legitimacy of governments and of Christians' participation as magistrates, when called upon to do so.[43] He reasoned that Christ's disciples for the time being are stuck in this world 'right up to our ears'. Therefore, they cannot escape to an alternative citisenship in heaven, completely removed from the kingdom of this world. As Christians are fundamentally incapable of living as Christ lived, an appeal to the *imitatio* is not so convincing. Moreover, the example of Christ's life is not universally binding, as his disciples cannot follow him in everything. Everyone (as Paul taught in 1 Cor. 7) should remain in the condition in which they were called. If it is God's will that the sword (the use of force and punishment) be used for upholding justice, then failure to defend the innocent is equivalent to being guilty of their death. It is, therefore, consistent with this line of reasoning that Christians, by using the sword in a righteous cause, are doing the will of God.[44]

Following the Munster episode, Anabaptists generally opted for a position that forbade Christians from engaging in any actions which required the use of lethal force. This meant not only that they would not defend themselves physically from violence or seek to take revenge for acts of violence committed against them, but they would not participate in the civil authorities' use of the sword. George Williams identifies four main reasons for a commitment to non-violence: war is wanton and futile, and a just war is extremely rare and usually avoidable; it is the way of Jesus Christ and, therefore, has to be followed by his disciples; to suffer persecution and

[41] *The Schleitheim Confession* (Crockett, KY: Rod & Staff Publishers, 1985).
[42] See Randall, *Communities of Conviction*, p. 6.
[43] Estep, *Anabaptist Story*, p. 100.
[44] The argument is outlined in Snyder, *Anabaptist History*, pp. 273–4, and in Pearse, *Great Restoration*, p. 72.

martyrdom, without retaliation, is a confirmation of the true faith of the elect; it is the provisional way of life for this dispensation.[45]

Nevertheless, Menno Simons, writing after the tragedy of Munster, and specifically against the perversions of the faith practised by Jan Matthijs and Jan van Leiden, took for granted the possibility of Christian rulership.[46] Gerald Biesecker-Mast[47] calls this a Mennonite dualistic toleration, which proclaims a certain separation from the world, but not withdrawal. Indeed, he argues that separation is necessary, in order that engagement with the world can be carried out on the terms of the gospel, not the world. So, he argues, we find in early Anabaptism two rhetorical practices of separation: the antagonistic (complete withdrawal) and the dualistic (partial separation). It is interesting to observe how the tension between these two approaches to a hostile environment continues to be worked out over the coming centuries and into the second millennium.

Community of Goods

As in the case of separation, different groups of Anabaptists inaugurated a variety of practices regarding the common ownership of possessions. Two distinct communities in Moravia observed a complete sharing of all property in common, after the pattern of the earliest Christian communities in Jerusalem and Judea (Acts 2:44–5; 4:32,34–5). For them this represented one aspect of the needed restoration of the church to its original high calling.

Jakob Wiedemann headed a group in Nikolsburg, and later in Austerlitz, that believed that Christian discipleship was best expressed by a complete surrender of all personal goods and a common purse:[48]

In 1528 Wideman separated from the Schwertler . . . rallying, together with Philipp Jager (or Weber), the nonresistant Stäbler around him. When this group was no longer permitted to live on the Liechtenstein territory at Nikolsburg, the Brethren moved away in great poverty, not knowing where to turn. It was a group of about 200 adults and many children. In this predicament several men laid a cloak on the ground upon which everyone voluntarily put whatever he possessed of money or goods, in order to support

---

[45] Williams, *Radical Reformation*, p. 226.

[46] Stayer, 'Anabaptist Revolt', p. 69.

[47] Gerald Biesecker-Mast, *Separation and the Sword in Anabaptist Persuasion: Radical Confessional Rhetoric from Schleitheim to Dordrecht* (Scottdale, PA: Herald Press, 2006), p. 23.

[48] See Williams, *Radical Reformation*, p. 432; Pearse, *Great Restoration*, p. 72.

the needy according to the teachings of the Book of Acts. Fortunately the manorial lords of Austerlitz viz., the four Kaunitz brothers, were willing to accept this group on their estates. Thus began the first fully communal Anabaptist settlement.[49]

For Wiedemann and the Stabler (people of the staff) community of goods became an indispensable mark of the true church.[50]

This way of life became characteristic of the Hutterite form of Anabaptism. Jakob Hutter spent much of the last few years of his life travelling between Moravia and the Tyrol. In August 1533 he returned to Moravia for the fourth and last time to try to sort out a dispute that had taken place within the community now resident in Auspitz. He set out to reorganise the group that wished to remain faithful to his leadership by building up an 'economically durable and socially cohesive organisation'[51] and by implementing a strict community of goods. He led the group there until April 1535.

At that time the group was expelled from Moravia by order of the Archduke Ferdinand I of Austria at the Diet of Znaim. They set out from their homes, but without anywhere to go: 'Nowhere were they permitted to camp until they reached the village of Tracht in the possessions of the lord of Liechtenstein. There they lay down on the wide heath under the open sky with many wretched widows and children, sick and infants.'[52]

Hutter himself was persuaded to return to the Tyrol, where he was captured and burnt at the stake in 1536. Leadership of the group passed to John Amon who was able to bring the group back to Auspitz after one year of exile and to consolidate the organization of the communities.

It may well be that originally commitment to having all possessions in common was the result of economic necessity among beleaguered communities of persecuted Christians. Hutter, however, gave the practice a more theological nuance, insisting that it was one of the marks of the true church in its demonstration of Christ-like love and unity of belief and purpose:

[49] Robert Friedmann, 'Wideman, Jakob (d. 1535/6)'. *Global Anabaptist Mennonite Encyclopedia Online* (1959) http://www.gameo.org/encyclopedia/contents/wideman_jakob_d._1535_6
[50] Estep, *Anabaptist Story*, p. 128.
[51] Williams, *Radical Reformation*, p. 422.
[52] Johann Loserth, 'Hutter, Jakob (d. 1536)', *Global Anabaptist Mennonite Encyclopedia Online* (1959) http://www.gameo.org/encyclopedia/contents/H887.html

It would be misleading to assume that the Hutterite way of community living started as a measure only of mere emergency and situational need . . . Perhaps this was true in the earliest years (1528 ff.) prior to the coming of Jakob Hutter (1533), but when this truly charismatic leader took up the reins and established a *Gemeinschaft* on strictly Christian spiritual foundations it became much more than an emergency experiment. It was a holy beginning, a radical actualization of the Christian commandment of love as Hutter and his fellow workers understood it. Here was *Nachfolge*, the practice of brotherly love by overcoming selfishness (*Eigennutz*) and the entering into complete brotherhood and unity of the spirit. Without giving up private and personal possessions, the leaders claimed, such a unity could never be achieved. To the Hutterite this way of life was his religion proper.[53]

Other Anabaptist communities (the Swiss Brethren and the Mennonites), whilst strongly advocating the sharing of possessions, deliberately did not adopt a full community of goods; they practised a redistribution of goods, but without extending this to a full common ownership of the means of production.

Set apart from normal civic communities by the twin decisions to refuse the baptism of their children and to rebaptise those who came to follow Christ according to their beliefs, Anabaptists cultivated an intense sense of belonging to a new family of believers. This awareness of being part of a distinctive fellowship was intensified by the frequent harassment and persecution that they suffered. It is not at all surprising, therefore, that they inculcated a deep commitment to looking after one another. Their community practice in this respect is summed up by Menno Simons:

> Those who are truly reborn of the Holy Spirit show mercy and love as much as they can. No one among them is allowed to beg. They take to heart the need of the saints. They entertain those in distress. They take the stranger into their houses. They comfort the afflicted; assist the needy; clothe the naked; feed the hungry; do not turn their face from the poor; do not despise their own flesh, Isa. 58:7–8. Behold such a community we teach.[54]

The crucial issue between these two different branches of Anabaptism referred to ownership: was the sharing of possessions to be left as a voluntary exercise on the part of the members of the communities (on

---

[53] Robert Friedmann, 'Community of Goods', *Global Anabaptist Mennonite Encyclopedia Online* (1953) http://www.gameo.org/encyclopedia/contents/C6593ME.html

[54] Menno Simons, *Complete Writings of Menno Simons* (trans. Leonard Verduin; Scottdale, PA: Herald Press, 1958), p. 316.

the basis of 2 Cor. 9:7 – 'Each of you must give as you have made up your mind, not reluctantly or under compulsion, for God loves a cheerful giver'), or was it to be legislated for as part of church discipline?[55] In the first case, the Anabaptists would have argued that as membership of the church was entirely voluntary, so should be the disposal of goods. The new community was to be non-coercive, not only in matters of belief, but also in matters of practice. After all, they were attempting to set up a radical alternative to the obligatory nature of church allegiance under both Catholic and Protestant rulers. In the second case, the Hutterites, and others, would have argued that survival as separate minority communities, despised and attacked by the majority, indicated strict regulation and control of all the community's assets: 'Community of goods became a rule against exploitation and about sharing in the congregation.'[56]

There was no disagreement about the necessity of as equal a distribution of resources as possible; nor did they dispute the fact that true Christian faith must show visible results in the whole of life, including economic matters. The difference centred on whether this should be made compulsory or left to the generous nature of each individual or family.

In sociological terms, one of the attractions of the Anabaptist movement was its ability to give support and hope to social classes that were going through harsh times. Gary Waite, for example, argues that:

> The early Anabaptist movement in Holland and particularly in Amsterdam was in part an attempt by a segment of the artisanal estate to cope with the social, economic, political and religious problems of the third and fourth decades of the sixteenth century, which affected them far more severely than any other social stratum. Their large numbers, their acceptance of apocalypticism, their almost complete lack of an intellectual leadership, and the desperate nature of their hope and migrations all attest to the fact that most of those who joined the Anabaptist movement in the Netherlands did so out of a profound sense of crisis.[57]

Mission

'Facing great obstacles and persecution from all sides, Anabaptists sought to engage in evangelism, to found new congregations, and to foster

---

[55] See Snyder, *Anabaptist History*, p. 316.
[56] Weaver, *Becoming Anabaptist*, p. 59.
[57] Gary Waite, 'The Anabaptist Movement in Amsterdam and the Netherlands, 1531–1535: An Initial Investigation into its Genesis and Social Dynamics', in *The Reformation: Critical Concepts in Historical Studies*, Vol. II (ed. Andrew Pettegree; London: Routledge, 2004), pp. 140–55.

Christian discipleship based on a distinctive ecclesiology and missiological practice . . . These convictions were to produce not only a different
kind of church, but a different vision for mission.'[58]

In accordance with a contemporary consensus about the meaning and
scope of mission,[59] I understand the mission of the church, following
God's call and commissioning, to include evangelistic, prophetic and
diaconal ministries. These incorporate church planting, discipling, political engagement, concern for the environment, reconciliation and peace-
building, community aid and development. Not all these are entirely
relevant in the sixteenth-century context. Nevertheless, the consensus
indicates that we should try to understand the missionary movement of
the Anabaptists in a wide framework.

The evangelistic practice of the Anabaptists was predicated on the
belief that much of the population of Europe, although Christianised,
was still semi-pagan, without a distinctive awareness and experience of
the saving work of Jesus Christ. Ignoring the conventional parish boundaries, and moving across national frontiers, Europe (the then known
world) was their parish. They called people to turn from superstition and
a moribund religion to the living Jesus Christ and experience his gift of
a new spiritual birth by the Holy Spirit: 'Rather than assuming that the
countries of Europe were Christian, they were committed to preaching
the evangel, calling people to turn to Christ, be baptised and become part
of gatherings in which corporate discipleship was practised.'[60]

Immediately after the first baptisms of adult believers in January 1525,
Grebel and Mantz conducted house-to-house visits, witnessing to the
people and, where the response was positive, baptizing and conducting
the Lord's Supper among them.[61] Although he was not to live for long (he
died of the plague in August 1526), Grebel carried on a prolific ministry
of preaching, baptizing and community formation. On one occasion, in St
Gall, he baptised a huge throng of people in the local river. Hans Hut was
known as 'the apostle to Austria', through whose preaching thousands came
to Christ and were gathered into the new communities.[62] George Blaurock,
towards the end of his life (he was burned at the stake in September 1529),
formed congregations up and down the Inn and Etsch river valleys in the
Tyrol. Later, Giles of Aachen became a widely known Anabaptist itinerant

---

[58] Colin Godwin, *Baptizing, Gathering, Sending: The Significance of Anabaptist
Approaches to Mission in the Sixteenth-Century Context* (University of Wales,
unpublished PhD dissertation, 2010), p. 64.
[59] See Introduction, note 1.
[60] Randall, *Communities of Conviction*, p.11.
[61] Estep, *Anabaptist Story*, p. 38.
[62] Randall, *Communities of Conviction*, p. 7.

preacher in the south of the Netherlands. He addressed small gatherings in concealed areas and larger groups in remote places.[63]

Evangelism was carried out often by people whose occupation took them travelling across Europe (Hut, for example, was a travelling book salesman). Before and after the missionary conference held in Augsburg in 1527, different strategic methods of witnessing were being employed. Hans Kasdorf notes the following means that were used to reach people with the gospel: meetings in people's houses, where whole families could be introduced to the meaning of real faith; readings of the newly trans-lated Bible by lay evangelists to illiterates in homes, barns and village churches; personal testimony of ordinary Christians among family, neighbours, acquaintances and fellow workers. Occupational contacts proved a fruitful opportunity for spreading the word.[64]

After 1527 more formal arrangements were made for commissioning missionaries to travel to different parts of the empire, sent out by local congregations. The emigrants to Moravia, deprived – by the circum-stances of unfamiliar surroundings and lack of ability to speak the local language – of much opportunity to evangelise, sent out missionaries to the places from which they had come, and beyond.[65] These missionaries, referred to as apostles, before being sent out had to undergo rigorous tests as to their ethical character.[66]

What has now come to be known as the 'Great Commission' (Matt. 28:19–20; Mark 16:15–16), namely Christ's command to his disciples to preach the good news of salvation and make disciples, was one of the chief motivating factors in the missionary zeal of the first generation of Anabaptists. These passages were linked to the actual practice of baptism by the early church as recorded in the book of Acts. Abraham Friesen argues that the Anabaptists who came out of the Zwinglian circle were influenced by the new preface that Erasmus wrote to the third edition of his Greek New Testament (1522). In this he hinted at the appropriateness of the rebaptism of children, that baptism should only follow a personal commitment of faith and that baptism was not enough for salvation, as believers had to be taught the 'perfection of evangelical godliness'.[67]

---

[63] See Williams, *Radical Reformation*, p. 400.

[64] Hans Kasdorf, 'The Anabaptist Approach to Mission', in *Anabaptism and Mission* (ed. Wilbert R. Shenk; Scottdale, PA: Herald Press, 1984), pp. 55–62.

[65] See Wolfgang Schaufele, 'The Missionary Vision and Activity of the Anabap-tist Laity' in *Anabaptism and Mission* (ed. Wilbert R. Shenk; Scottdale, PA: Herald Press, 1984), pp. 82–6.

[66] Shenk, *Anabaptism and Mission*, pp. 64, 69.

[67] Abraham Friesen, *Erasmus, the Anabaptists and the Great Commission* (Grand Rapids, MI: Eerdmans, 1998), pp. 44–5, 50–51.

Erasmus had already had a considerable influence on Zwingli's understanding of the interpretation of the New Testament, drawing him back
to the primary sources of Christianity and thus helping him to question
the teachers approved by the church.[68]

Erasmus made much of the order of events in Christ's command – that
baptism comes before teaching – implying the necessity of instruction in
the way of Christ as an integral part of Christian initiation. Felix Mantz in
his *A Declaration of Faith and Defense* (December 1524) links the Matthew
passage with that of Cornelius in Acts 10. Peter Walpot in his *Artikel-
buch* (1577) cited Erasmus's paraphrase of Matthew 28 as an authoritative
argument in favour of believer's baptism:[69]

> The necessity of Anabaptist mission to unconverted Europeans was gener-
> ated by the baptismal command of Matthew 28:18–20 and Mark 16:14–16,
> combined with the Anabaptist call to personal discipleship and obedience.
> This emphasis on the divine command to preach, convert, baptise, and teach,
> *in that order*, worked in synergy with a renewed appeal to human initiative
> both in accepting the divine message and convincing others of its import.[70]

Colin Godwin in his extensive research into Anabaptist mission in the
sixteenth century argues that baptism was seen 'as establishing the necessity of the Anabaptist mission'.[71] In the minds of the radical reformers,
the futility of infant baptism and the excessively porous boundaries of
the state churches led to a superficial commitment to Christian teaching,
and therefore, to a lax lifestyle. This was the result of an accumulated
tradition of belonging to the church, which, by dividing members into
the elite and the ordinary, had established a two-tier system of commitment to Christ's commands and the obligation to give witness.

The centrality of the issue of baptism has, perhaps, been overstressed.
There were certainly other motives that impelled the Anabaptist converts
to risk their wellbeing and their lives for the sake of testifying to the gospel
of Jesus Christ in the way they understood it. For them the churches of the
mainstream Reformation remained 'fallen'. They were still compromised
by the 'Constantinian settlement' that effectively united state power
and the church. The Christian faith still needed to be delivered from its
subservience to political interference and intrigue, in order that it might

---

[68] See Gottfried W. Locher, 'Zwingli and Erasmus' in *Zwingli's Thought: New
Perspectives* (Leiden: E.V. Brill, 1981), pp. 233–55.

[69] Friesen, *Erasmus*, p. 58.

[70] Godwin, *Baptizing, Gathering, Sending*, p. 192 (emphasis added).

[71] Godwin, *Baptizing, Gathering, Sending*, p. 128.

be holy, blameless and acceptable to God. The 'real' apostolic church had to be restored. For some Anabaptists, though not for the majority, this meant a turning inwards to a deep spiritual renewal, which minimised, or even did away with, the external symbols of water and the breaking of bread.[72]

Although the Anabaptists endorsed the Reformation catch phrase, *sola fide, sola gratia, sola Scriptura, solo Christi*, they did not believe that this encapsulated sufficiently the meaning and means of salvation. The Reformation emphasis on justification as a forensic expression neglected, in their opinion, the New Testament emphasis on new life and growth into holiness through following the way of Christ. Believers were to be transformed not only in their inner, formal relationships to God through faith in the finished work of Christ, but also in their external life of obedience to the teaching of Christ in fulfilling the love commands, which implied renouncing all forms of violence.

Baptism was certainly the act that signalled entry into the church as God's new created order; it expressed a baptism in the Spirit that had already taken place. However, it was more a vision of the church in its relationship to a world that was perishing and about to be recreated by the direct intervention of God that empowered their witness across a continent that had the trappings of religion but denied its authentic spiritual life.

This vision of the church was eminently practical. Where the Anabaptists were able to form settled communities for any length of time, their social concerns and community projects were remarkable. Within their communities, when a total reform of society seemed unattainable, they sought to put into practice wide-ranging social improvements, such as those inspired by Michael Gaismair, a representative of the Communal Reformation:[73] 'They became known for their many products and skills – their restoration of agricultural life, fine pottery, water systems, mills and the practice of medicine.'[74]

In the latter case, physicians like George Zobel, Balthasar Goller, and Hans Zwickelberger were well known throughout central Europe: Zobel was even called to attend the emperor, Rudolph II, in Prague, when he became sick.[75] The Hutterite communities established a system of primary schools at a time when most Europeans were still illiterate. Here their children learnt to read and to practise a trade, as well as being instructed in

---

[72] See Godwin, *Baptizing, Gathering, Sending*, p. 333, note 33.
[73] See Weaver, *Becoming Anabaptist*, p. 92.
[74] Randall, *Communities of Conviction*, p. 6.
[75] Estep, *Anabaptist Story*, p. 144.

the law of the Lord.[76] It is not surprising, therefore, that more enlightened rulers, like the lords of Liechtenstein, welcomed communities that had proved their peaceful intentions, hard work and innovative practices.

Conclusion

In this short study of some of the main issues concerning the church and the world in early Anabaptism, I have attempted to do justice to the reasons why these people went to such lengths to break with the mainstream understanding of the place of religion in society. They represented a decisive split from an order in society that had prevailed for centuries, and which suited the old aristocracy. They were also heirs of a new awakening to the contradictions of the old order that were being exposed by the Reformation insistence on personal faith, the priesthood of all believers and the unmediated authority of the word of God. Other groups in the past had raised their voices, and sometimes their armies, against the blatant corruption of state and church. Most of them were eventually suppressed. This time, however, the upheaval unleashed by the Reformation could not be so easily contained.

It is unfortunate that the excessively apocalyptic teachings of some Anabaptist leaders, with their highly negative attitude towards life in this world, together with the revolutionary excesses of the Peasants' War and the Munster revolt, became associated in the mind of some civil and church leaders with the Anabaptist cause. On the other hand, perhaps such an association became a devious excuse for intolerance and persecution; whilst the real issue between the radicals and the rest was the break-up of the unity of throne and altar, the hegemony of state control over religious belief and practice, and the threatened loss of power and privilege put at risk by communities who no longer accepted the old order.

Another factor that contributed to the formation of new communities and the disruption that they represented was the desire for new freedoms in political and economic matters associated with the rise of a mercantile class in the growing, wealth-creating city-states throughout Europe. It is beyond the scope of this chapter to enter the controversial discussion raised first by Friedrich Engels, and later by other Marxists, about the link between the Anabaptist movement, in some of its manifestations, and the yearning for political freedoms and economic opportunities signalled by newly arrived technological innovations and commercial arrangements:

---

[76] Estep, *Anabaptist Story*, pp. 142–3.

In his [Engels'] work on the Peasant War of 1524–25 he treated it as a first attempt at a national revolution, bourgeois or anti-feudal, frustrated by lack of combination between burghers and peasants, while the lowest strata, the disinherited, standing outside society, could only indulge in unrealizable dreams of an ideal world of the future, in the spirit of the millenarian element in early Christianity; their Anabaptism was the first faint gleam of modern socialism.[77]

Whilst Engels and others have justifiably been accused of a partial rewriting of history in the interests of demonstrating a grand theory of the 'class struggle', the relationship between religious innovation and social revolution is a legitimate area of study, which requires further investigation.[78]

The notion of the gathered church – no longer coextensive with civil society, but constituted only by those who, having responded personally to the word of the gospel, submitted to baptism and the discipline of the community, in anticipation of the remaking of human society by the direct intervention of Jesus Christ – has utopian overtones. Whereas for Marxist interpreters of human history the supreme impulse for social transformation is a complete change in the material relations of the means of production, for the Anabaptists a new world was only possible ultimately by action from outside human history. It was the work of the Spirit of God among those who pledged their allegiance to Jesus Christ and his kingdom of justice, mercy and peace. Here are two completely different visions of 'eschatology' and 'revolution'.

It is fitting to end this chapter on the Radical Reformation with a quote that summarises the thinking of Pilgram Marpeck. His perception concerning the place of the people of God in the midst of the world encapsulates core beliefs of the whole Anabaptist movement:

Marpeck's Anabaptism was grounded in ecclesiology. He sought to build congregations whose goal was to live out of the Sermon on the Mount on a day-to-day basis. This church was an extension of the incarnation of Christ. Marpeck saw the church as an advance party of the reign of God . . . The

---

[77] Tom Bottomore, ed., *A Dictionary of Marxist Thought* (Oxford: Blackwell, 2nd edn, 1991), p. 77; 'The Peasant War in Germany' is contained in the *Collected Works of Karl Marx and Friedrich Engels*: Volume 10 (New York: International Publishers, 1988), pp. 397–482.

[78] Some years ago, I attempted a preliminary study of the topic in *Theology Encounters Revolution* (Leicester: IVP, 1980). Since the demise of communism as a practical political option, the matter seems to have been quietly put on the back burner.

incarnation showed that God had used the ordinary things of the earth –
including the coming of Christ as a natural man – to witness to the presence
of God's reign. Since Christ had conquered the devil and restored the potential of creation with his death, the physical world as well as the human body
and mind could transcend the fleshly nature and take on a spiritual nature
. . . With Christ, then, there is a restoration of right order both among people
and within each individual. In Marpeck's church, the physical gathering was
indwelled by the Spirit, and inner and outer had become one reality.[79]

---

[79] Weaver, *Becoming Anabaptist*, p. 85.

7

'All the Non-Christian World': Church, Mission and the Edinburgh 1910 Conference

Introduction

On the 14 June 1910, some twelve hundred leaders of Western mission societies and mission boards from a variety of churches gathered together in the assembly hall of the United Free Church of Scotland, located just beneath the famous castle in Edinburgh. Their meeting on that day launched the inaugural session of a 'World Missionary Conference'. Subsequently, it has come to be known simply as 'Edinburgh 1910'.

This third chapter of Part II, looking at historical examples of the Christian church's engagement with the world, is of a different order from the other two. In the latter cases, we have explored the development of a church in mission over a period of time: in the case of Latin America during a period of approximately seventy years and in the case of the Anabaptists in Europe of some twenty years. Now, I will be examining one conference that lasted just ten days. The justification for switching from actual mission on the ground to an intense discussion about the reality and future of mission, as seen from the perspective of mainly Protestant churches at the beginning of the twentieth century, is that Edinburgh 1910 had far-reaching repercussions for the church in its mission in the world, stretching far into the century ahead.

This review of the conference will begin by considering first its historical context, and then the background, purpose and organization that brought it into being. It will briefly survey four of the eight commissions that were set up to gather information and engage in reflection in preparation for the main event. It will conclude by considering the assumptions that guided the conference and by looking at its significance, outcomes and legacy.

Historical Context

The mood of the nations of the North Atlantic at the beginning of the twentieth century can, perhaps, be well summed up in a message that the conference received just prior to its opening: 'The German Colonial Office recognises with satisfaction and gratitude that the endeavours for the spread of the Gospel are followed by the blessings of civilisation and culture in all countries.'[1]

The first decade of the twentieth century marked a high point in 'the optimistic self-confidence of a rapidly expanding Anglo-Saxon empire'.[2] The notion of an inevitable progress towards high civilization[3] was prominent in the thinking of politicians and church people alike. Missionaries believed that 'the practice of occupying other people's lands and educating their occupants was driven by a moral imperative to modernise primitive economies and to civilise barbarians . . . To meet these objectives the educational missionaries employed Western science to uproot superstition from the native mind and to develop in them a scientific consciousness.'[4]

'The gospel was viewed as an *instrument* for producing a vital transformation in the total human situation, a "weapon" that alleviated woes, a "divine medicament" and "antidote", a "remedy" and "appointed means of civilizing the heathen".'[5]

'The Gospel was a "tool", along with all the many new tools and implements Western technology was beginning to invent. It joined the three great gods of the modern era – science, technology, and industrialization – and was harnessed with them to serve the spread of the gospel and of Christian values.'[6]

The unbounded confidence in the powers of science to deliver a better world was epitomised by the building and naming of the largest ship in the world at the time. The RMS *Titanic*, named after the Titans who, in

---

[1] John R. Mott, *Addresses and Papers*, Vol. V (New York: Association Press, 1947), p. 13.

[2] Timothy Yates, *Christian Mission in the Twentieth Century* (Cambridge: CUP, 1996), p. 20.

[3] For an understanding of the meaning of civilization see J. Andrew Kirk, *Civilisations in Conflict?* pp. 14–18.

[4] M. P. Joseph, 'Missionary Education: An Ambiguous Legacy' in David A. Kerr and Kenneth R. Ross (eds.), *Edinburgh 2010: Mission Then and Now* (Oxford: Regnum Books International, 2009), p. 113.

[5] Charles L. Chaney, *The Birth of Missions in America* (Pasadena, CA: William Carey Library, 1976), pp. 240–42.

[6] David J. Bosch, *Transforming Mission: Paradigm Shifts in Theology of Mission* (Maryknoll, NY: Orbis Books, 1991), p. 336.

Greek mythology, were of enormous size and strength and challenged the supremacy of the god Zeus, struck an iceberg on 15 April 1912 on its maiden voyage to New York. Considered unsinkable, it went down swiftly with the loss of 1,515 lives.

The conference met at a time when the great European migration to foreign lands was at its climax.[7] There existed among European peoples a huge sense of duty towards peoples subjected to the European powers in the colonial enterprise. They were carrying forward, in their own eyes, the three great emphases that the explorer David Livingstone had so notably put before his Cambridge audience in 1857, 'Christianity, commerce and civilization': 'Livingstone . . . represents a sturdy, confident evangelicalism, secure in its place in national life, sure of its right and duty to influence public and government opinion, and, for all its emphasis on personal regeneration and personal religion, looking to the transformation of society as a normal fruit of Christian activity.'[8] He sincerely believed that these three great enterprises working together 'would pave the way for a prosperous, free and non-violent life for Africans'.[9]

The optimism engendered by the 'successes' of the imperial adventures overseas, coupled with rapid advances in scientific knowledge and technological innovation created a super-confident mood for the conference. In introducing the report of Commission I ('Carrying the Gospel to all the Non-Christian World'), John Mott spoke these stirring words:

> In our judgement the present is the time of all times with reference to the evangelization of the non-Christian world. It is so because of the awakening of these nations and the desirability of bringing Christianity in its full strength to bear upon these nations while they are *plastic*; it is so because of the critical movements and tendencies which are manifesting themselves in almost all the non-Christian nations, for example, the spread of corrupt influences of our western civilization, the expansion of the great systems of secular education, the growing racial pride and antagonism, the increasing activity and enterprise and aggressiveness of some of the non-Christian religions.[10] It is

---

[7] See Andrew Walls, 'Commission One and the Church's Transforming Century' in *Edinburgh 2010: Mission Then and Now*, p. 37.

[8] Andrew Walls, 'David Livingstone, 1813–1873: Awakening the Western World to Africa' in Gerald Anderson et al. (eds.) *Mission Legacies: Biographical Studies of Leaders of the Modern Missionary Movement* (Maryknoll, NY: Orbis Books, 1994), p. 141.

[9] Stephen B. Bevans and Roger P. Schroeder, *Constants in Context: A Theology of Mission for Today* (Maryknoll, NY: Orbis Books, 2004), p. 214.

[10] This was stimulated in part, it has to be said, by 'the activity and enterprise and aggressiveness' of some Christian mission work.

so because of the rising spiritual tide in almost all parts of the non-Christian world.

So, the commission spoke of 'open doors', 'world-wide opportunities', 'the yielding of other faiths to the gospel'. The mood was encapsulated in the watchword[11] that acted as the horizon towards which the whole missionary undertaking was moving: 'the evangelization of the world in this generation': 'The watchword both reflected and gave birth to the scintillating missionary optimism of the period. More than anything else, it epitomised the Protestant missionary mood of the period: pragmatic, purposeful, activist, impatient, self-confident, single-minded, triumphant.'[12]

Background to the Conference

As the watchword suggests, towards the end of the nineteenth century many Christian leaders were beginning to promote the idea of the evangelization of the whole world as the task of the whole church. The assumptions of the time, concerning the evolutionary progress of the whole of humanity towards a level of civilization made possible only by conversion to Christian faith, indicated the need for a significant forward movement in proclaiming the gospel to the non-Christian world. This project would be achieved by establishing communities of Christians in every nation, who would continue the work and prove to be leaven throughout society for Christian civilizing impulses and values.

With this need in mind, several other missionary conferences preceded Edinburgh 1910. The first of these was held in New York in 1854, occasioned by the visit of the Scotsman Dr Alexander Duff, a renowned mission leader of the time, to America. It was followed in the same year by a consultation held in London, at which representatives of all the main mission societies were present. These two gatherings gave an opportunity for a helpful sharing of opinion on a number of points related to the missionary enterprise. Further conferences were held in Liverpool in 1860 and London in 1878. In 1888, a conference was organised in London to celebrate the first centenary of the modern Protestant missionary movement. This represented an attempt to include participants from North America and the European continent; however, the overwhelming majority of those who attended came from the United Kingdom: 'The

---

[11]   According to R.P. Wilder, the watchword was first used at the Shanghai missionary conference of 1877; see Yates, *Christian Mission in the Twentieth Century*, p. 19.

[12]   Bosch, *Transforming Mission*, p. 336.

object of this conference, which was designated the "Centenary" Conference, was to diffuse information regarding the missionary enterprise throughout the world, to promote fellowship and cooperation among those engaged in it, and to impress on the mind of the Church a sense of its importance and fruitfulness.'[13]

A similar conference was held in 1900 in the Carnegie Hall in New York, convened by American and Canadian societies, and attended also by delegates from British, Continental and other foreign societies. In all, some forty-eight different nations were represented. Some fifty thousand tickets were issued to members of the general public for the open meetings. A further missionary conference ten years later was entertained, although no specific provision for its organization was made.[14]

As the result of a letter written (early in 1906) by Fairley Daly, honorary secretary of the Livingstonia Mission of the United Free Church of Scotland, to Robert Speer, secretary of the Presbyterian Board of Foreign Missions in New York, a conference of thirty-seven delegates from twenty missionary societies in Scotland was held at the beginning of 1907 to consider a proposal to hold a major missionary conference in Great Britain as soon as was feasible. The outcome of this deliberation was the decision to organise a conference in Edinburgh in June 1910 and to request the various foreign mission societies in Britain and Ireland to form a General Committee with the power to make all the necessary arrangements.[15]

This committee met twice in 1907 and decided that the nature of the conference, which was beginning to take shape in the minds of both this committee and a parallel Committee of Reference and Counsel set up on the other side of the Atlantic, demanded the appointment of a joint international committee with representatives from North America, Britain and the European continent. Its first meeting took place in Oxford in June 1908, just two years before the assigned date for the major gathering. As much as anything, the significance of this latter meeting resided in the fact that a person by the name of J.H. Oldham was appointed as the convening committee's honorary secretary.[16]

There were a number of good reasons for holding the conference in Scotland. First, 'Scotland had an importance in worldwide mission out of all proportion to its size. It had produced some of the most celebrated figures in

---

[13] Mott, *Addresses and Papers*, p. 2.

[14] Mott, *Addresses and Papers*, p. 3.

[15] Mott, *Addresses and Papers*, p. 3.

[16] For a brief profile of Joe Oldham, see Yates, *Christian Mission in the Twentieth Century*, pp. 22–4. Along with John Mott, he became the driving force behind the organization of the conference, the subsequent continuation committee and the formation of the permanent International Missionary Council.

the modern missionary movement'[17] (people like Robert Moffat, Alexander Duff, David Livingstone and Mary Slessor). Second, 'it had established some of the most highly regarded centres of mission work' (such as Livingstonia in Malawi and educational institutions in India). Third, 'no country has in proportion to its size contributed to the evangelization of the world during the last century so large a number of distinguished and devoted missionaries.'[18] Fourth, mission circles in Scotland offered a strong operational structure well able to organise and support a large international conference. It is not surprising, therefore, that a Scotsman took the initiative in enquiring about the possibility of a conference to follow the one in New York in 1900.

The main protagonists of the conference came from a background formed in an evangelical, pietistic and reformed tradition, greatly influenced by the spiritual awakenings of the nineteenth century and missionary conventions like those held at Keswick in England and Northfield in the USA. Of special importance was the creation and growth of the Student Volunteer Movement, which by 1910 had mobilised some four thousand students for cross-cultural mission.[19] The Student Volunteer Movement for Foreign Missions was an organization founded in 1886 that aimed to enlist North American students for overseas missionary service. It adopted the watchword in 1889. John Mott used the latter as the title for a book (published in 1900, with a revised edition in 1902). In this he succeeded in showing how 'the marvelous orderings of Providence during the nineteenth century'[20] were providing the church with a favourable context and enormous resources to complete the work of evangelization throughout the world. Already there were nearly eighty thousand native evangelists, pastors, teachers, catechists, medical workers and others working full-time in the cause of the gospel.[21]

The Purpose of the Conference

'The conferences of 1888 and 1900 had been chiefly great missionary demonstrations fitted to inform, educate, and impress. It was felt, however, that the time had now come for a more earnest study of the

---

[17] *Edinburgh 2010: Mission Then and Now,* p. 5.

[18] World Missionary Conference, *The History and Records of the Conference* (Edinburgh and London: Oliphant, Anderson & Ferrier, 1910), p. 18.

[19] Samuel Escobar, 'Mission from Everywhere to Everyone: The Home Base in a New Century,' in *Edinburgh 2010: Mission Then and Now,* p. 185.

[20] John R. Mott, *The Evangelization of the World in This Generation* (London: Student Volunteer Movement, 1902), p. 106.

[21] Bosch, *Transforming Mission,* p. 337.

missionary enterprise, and that . . . the first aim should be to make the conference as far as possible a consultative assembly.'[22]

Conscious of the danger of entering controversial terrain, and desirous of securing the widest possible participation of mission organizations in the gathering, it was decided early on that the subject matter would not be the theology of mission. Doctrinal matters would not be discussed, and in particular issues to do with church structures and polity would not be allowed on the agenda: 'No expression of opinion should be sought from the conference on any matter involving any ecclesiastical or doctrinal question on which those taking part in the conference differed among themselves.'[23]

Later, this decision was expanded to include an embargo on any resolution being put before the conference and voted on.[24] The topics to be debated, therefore, had to do with all aspects of mission work on which the various missionary societies represented were in agreement, i.e. missionary work among non-Christian peoples. In this way, Mott and Oldham were able to secure the participation of the Anglo-Catholic society, the Society for the Propagation of the Gospel, and the presence of high-church Anglican leaders such as Bishop Gore.[25]

The subject matter of the conference was designed, therefore, to deal with strategic issues: how to combine all available forces in one mighty united effort to complete 'the unfinished task'.[26] It was intended to be a study conference, in the sense of analysing what mission agencies had already achieved and investigating what still remained to be done.

The world was conceived as being divided into two parts: the Christian and non-Christian worlds. Mission (or missions) took place in one direction only: from Christian territories to those as yet 'unoccupied' (by the gospel). Edinburgh did much to perpetuate the deeply embedded view that mission is something that happens beyond the borders of Christian nations; mission can only happen by crossing geographical frontiers: 'The major challenge for missions and missionaries, therefore, was one of how to expand the Christian sphere at the expense of the non-Christian sphere in the world.'[27]

---

[22] Mott, *Addresses and Papers*, p. 5.

[23] Mott, *Addresses and Papers*, p. 5.

[24] Brian Stanley, *The World Missionary Conference, Edinburgh 1910* (Grand Rapids, MI: Eerdmans, 2009), p. 40.

[25] He was appointed chairman of Commission III: 'Education in Relation to the Christianisation of National Life.'

[26] See James A. Scherer, *Gospel, Church and Kingdom: Comparative Studies in World Mission Theology* (Minneapolis: Augsburg, 1987), p. 15.

[27] Tinyiko Sam Maluleke, 'Christian Mission and Political Power: Commission Seven revisited' in *Edinburgh 2010: Mission Then and Now*, p. 205.

Mission was, consequently, viewed mainly as the responsibility of churches in the Western world, sending out workers into the rest of the world to gather into Christ's kingdom the harvest of the ignorant and the lost.

The principal aim of the conference was summed up in the official document as that of promoting 'co-operative study of the common outstanding problems in the common missionary enterprise, with a view to helping (the participating societies and boards) to solve them, and achieve together the evangelization of the world':[28] 'The first duty of a World Mission Conference meeting at such an auspicious time is to consider the present world situation from the point of view of making the Gospel known to all men, and to determine what should be done to accomplish this Christ-given purpose.'[29]

Further aims will be reviewed, when I explore the findings of some of the commissions.

Organization of the Conference

When the organizing committee met for the first time in July 1908, the date of the conference had already been set for June 1910. The committee had, therefore, precisely two years to put together a major international study conference. Given the slow means of communication of those days, it did a truly remarkable job.

The decision was taken that eight commissions would be set up to gather information from across the world about the state of national and international affairs, the condition of religious observance in various localities, the opportunities and hindrances to evangelistic work, the preparation of men and women for cross-cultural mission, the strengths and weaknesses of the home mission base, the degree of cooperation and unity in mission between different churches and agencies, the place of education in mission and the relationship of mission work to local political authorities.[30] The findings of these commissions would become the basis for the major addresses at the conference. These would be given

---

[28] *Edinburgh 2010: Mission Then and Now*, p. 4.

[29] World Missionary Conference, *History and Records of the Conference*, p. 1.

[30] The actual title of the Commissions were as follows: I – Carrying the Gospel to All the Non-Christian World; II – The Church in the Mission Field; III – Education in Relation to the Christianisation of National Life; IV – The Missionary Message in Relation to Non-Christian Religions; V – The Preparation of Missionaries; VI – The Home Base of Missions; VII – Missions and Governments; VIII – Co-operation and the Promotion of Unity.

in the mornings to the registered delegates. The afternoons were to be allocated to sectional meetings, and the evenings would be dedicated to open meetings to which the general public were invited. The latter were held in the Assembly Hall of the Church of Scotland:

> In order to secure the attendance for those for whom this (part of the) confer-
> ence was planned, the tickets of admission were allocated to the various
> missionary societies in proportion to the number of their official delegates,
> and the societies were asked to place them in the hands of such local leaders
> and workers as were likely to be educated and inspired, through the meet-
> ings, to more effective service in the home field.[31]

The criteria applied to those eligible to attend the conference effectively excluded representation by churches in Africa, Asia and the Pacific region, since, according to the international committee's understanding, they did not have missionary societies that supported foreign missions.[32] Latin America was completely left out; in order to attract delegates to the confer-ence from the Catholic wing of the church, it was considered an already Christianised continent, and therefore not a legitimate location for evangeli-zation.[33] According to the historian Gonzalo Baez-Camargo, this condemned the evangelical missionaries who had been working there for more than half a century and the hundreds of thousands of Latin American Protestants who existed in 1910 to be pariahs excluded from the ecumenical movement.[34] In fact, in all some fifteen non-Westerners, from China, Japan, India, Korea and Burma, joined the conference (1.25 per cent of the total official delegates).

Each commission decided on its line of enquiry. It then drew up a comprehensive questionnaire addressed to those missionaries who had been recommended by various societies. These were sent out in February 1909 to different parts of the world. About one thousand replies were sent back, many gave lengthy answers to some of the questions. These then became the raw data, together with the thinking of the commissions' members, out of which the reports of the commissions were constructed. Each of the commissions also submitted some recommendations.[35]

---

[31] Mott, *Addresses and Papers*, p. 9.
[32] 'On this basis 176 missionary societies and boards sent delegations – 59 from
      North America, 58 from the Continent, 47 from the United Kingdom, and 12
      from South Africa and Australia', *Edinburgh 2010: Mission Then and Now*, p.7.
[33] See Samuel Escobar, *Tiempo de Mision: America Latina y la mision cristiana hoy*
      (Bogota, Ciudad de Guatemala: Ediciones Clara-Semilla, 1999), p. 36.
[34] Gonzalo Baez-Camargo, 'The Place of Latin America in the Ecumenical Move-
      ment,' *The Ecumenical Review*, Vol. 1, 1948–9, p. 311.
[35] *Edinburgh 2010: Mission Then and Now*, p. 8.

Reports of the Commissions

For the purposes of this study, I will consider only those reports which bear a particular relevance to the theme of the church and the world. To consider all eight commissions would be tedious. Although, in the nature of the case, they will all have something to say to the subject in hand, some will be more and some less appropriate. I have chosen, therefore, to concentrate on Commissions I, IV, VII and VIII.

Commission I – Carrying the Gospel to all the Non-Christian World

The intention of the report was to be largely descriptive. In considering each 'mission field' the plan was to indicate the number, distribution and character of the people to be reached, the extent to which the gospel had already been carried to them, the agencies for evangelization already working in the areas described and new agencies that might be recruited, the task of evangelization still to be undertaken and those circumstances that both favoured and obstructed the task.[36] This semi-statistical survey was aided by the publication in the USA of the *Statistical Atlas of Christian Mission*, that 'included a directory of Protestant missionary societies, statistics on the history of the missionary movement, maps of the distribution of Protestant mission throughout the world, and an index of mission stations "occupied" by foreign missionaries'.[37]

As already mentioned, the conference gathered at a time still of great optimism with regard to the proclamation of the gospel to every living human being. This first report begins, therefore, with an account of the unique opportunity for carrying the gospel to the ends of the world. 1910 was an opportune time (a *kairos* moment): 'In [God's] hands is the government of the world. He has entrusted enormous powers to Christian nations. His providence has opened the approach to the non-Christian countries, determined the order of their occupation, and developed agencies and influences which facilitate the spread of Christianity.'[38]

In the foreword, the commissioners set the scene by stressing that the time was critical, because the ancient faiths, ethical restraints and social orders were being weakened, and the spirit of national independence and patriotism was growing. It was also a testing time for the church: the commission considered that the adequacy of Christianity as a world

---

[36] Mott, *Addresses and Papers*, p. 25.
[37] *Edinburgh 2010: Mission Then and Now*, p. 24.
[38] Mott, *Addresses and Papers*, p. 26.

religion was on trial as to whether it met successfully the present world crisis. The hour was also decisive for Christian missions, for the present missionary force was inadequate to discharge the responsibility of world-wide evangelization.[39]

The commission directed attention to certain fields as being of special urgency in the task of mission work. First, there was a unique opportunity in China; the future of China and the whole East hung on the churches' ability to seize it. Second, the threatening advance of Islam in Equatorial Africa asked the question whether Africa would become Muslim or Christian. Third, nationalistic and spiritual movements in India presented a strong challenge to Christian missions to increase and intensify their outreach. Fourth, changes in Turkey and Persia (Iran) had given prominence to significant problems that required the urgent consideration of the churches. The commission also dealt with numerous other situations across Asia and Africa. It predicted that Muslims would yield to the gospel if Christians did their duty.

Counter to the impression often given of the Edinburgh 1910 Conference, that it was essentially about the Western missionary thrust into the non-Western world, this commission stated clearly that 'the Church on the mission field must be the chief evangelistic agency if the gospel is to be preached to all men in our day. The evangelization of the non-Christian world is not alone a European, an American, and Australasian enterprise; it is equally an Asiatic and an African enterprise.'[40] Therefore, right from the beginning, the church needed to capture an evangelistic spirit and to develop a strong indigenous leadership for evangelistic outreach.

In his deliverance of the findings of the report to the conference itself, John Mott spelt out six outstanding impressions and convictions.[41] First, there was 'the vastness of the task of evangelising the world'. This led the commission to begin to look at the world as a whole. This, in turn, implied a wide focus, incorporating the experiences of people working in many nations and from a variety of ecclesial backgrounds. Such a task presupposed a common task and goal, to be achieved through a much greater degree of cooperation than had hitherto been displayed.

Second, 'the present is the time of all times with reference to the evangelisation of the non-Christian world . . . there never has been a time when in *all* the non-Christian countries the conditions confronting Christianity were so favourable for a great and well-considered advance as

---

[39] Mott, *Addresses and Papers*, pp. 33–4.
[40] Mott, *Addresses and Papers*, p. 38.
[41] The quotations that follow come from Dr Mott's presentation to the conference's plenary meeting; Mott, *Addresses and Papers*, pp. 39–43.

at the present time.' The Western churches, therefore, should grasp the moment, giving themselves 'with promptness and thoroughness to the task'. Thoroughness implies well-considered plans, a careful assessment of the message to be proclaimed, and a thorough knowledge of the context into which it is to be inserted.

Third, 'the time is also at hand when the Church should enter the so-called unoccupied fields of the world'. 'What is needed is a large and comprehensive view on the part of present-day leaders and an agreement among them on some plan which actually embraces the whole non-Christian world. Let our high resolve be that before another world conference is held, these unoccupied fields shall be entered.'

Fourth, 'if this world situation is to be met there must be united planning and concerted effort on the part of the missionary forces of the Church.' The report gives an impassioned plea for the unity of the churches and agencies: 'we approach the task with calmness and confidence if the true disciples of Jesus Christ stand together as members of a common family.' It is not surprising that this commission called, therefore, for 'the formation of some simple representative international committee which will grapple with the problem of entering the unoccupied fields'.

Fifth, 'the great task of making Christ known to all mankind will not be achieved without a great enlargement of the evangelistic forces of the churches on the mission fields themselves.' This undoubtedly meant that the younger churches would have to become the main missionary force in the future. The older churches of the West, in spite of their enthusiasm, dedication, financial strength, and the technological assistance open to them, were not capable of finishing the task.

Sixth, 'the most crucial problem in relation to evangelizing the world is the state of the Church in the Christian countries.' 'It is futile to talk about making Christ known to the world in this generation or any generation unless there be a great expansion of vitality in the members of the churches of Christendom.' Spiritual renewal on an unprecedented scale would be necessary: 'if this conflict is to be waged with triumphant success there must be this expansion.' John Mott finished his presentation with stirring words about 'the sublime hope . . . that before the eyes of some of us shall close in death the opportunity at least may be given to all people throughout the non-Christian world to know and to accept, if they will, the living Christ.'

Reading all these words on a page hardly makes the kind of impact that the spoken word must have produced when first delivered. Befitting a major speech by the chairman of the conference towards the beginning of proceedings, there is more than a little rhetoric. This is designed for effect: to stir the hearts, minds, wills and affections and channel them towards the noble task of mobilizing Christians to be faithful witnesses to Christ to the ends of the earth. One can imagine a stunned silence, followed by prolonged applause, followed by prayerful meditation.

Commission IV – The Missionary Message in Relation to the Non-Christian Religions

From the non-Christian world (all inhabited lands outside of the West) I move on to the non-Christian religions. This report is based on the replies to an extensive questionnaire submitted by 125 missionaries working in lands dominated by different religious beliefs. It was divided into sections, according to the major religions represented in the areas: the 'animistic religions' of the African peoples; the religions of China – Confucianism, Buddhism and Taoism; of Japan – Shinto and Buddhism; the nations that had largely embraced Islam; the Hinduism of India and the Indian diaspora; and a final excursus on the Baha'i faith.[42] The missionaries were asked to report on points of contact with non-Christian religions, on the elements of the Christian faith that attracted and that repulsed non-Christians and 'the chief moral and intellectual and social hindrances to Christian belief'.[43] Submissions were also received from indigenous Christians, among them people who had recently left one or another faith to follow Christ.

On the whole, the report eschewed a polemical approach to other faiths. Christians should be courteous towards them. They should recognise that there are a number of aspects to admire and value. The commission used a number of analogies, mined from the Christian Scriptures. Other religions acted like a 'schoolmaster' (*paidagogos*) to lead their believers to put their trust in Christ (Gal. 3:24). Christ was the fulfilment of all that is good and true in other faiths, for he came not 'to abolish the law or the prophets . . . but to fulfil' (Matt. 5:17). Christ is the universal *Logos*, the Word of the Father made known to humans' spirit and conscience, whatever religion they professed, by the universal Spirit.

The report tended, therefore, to dwell on the positive aspects at least of some of the religions under scrutiny. At the same time, it opened up a commentary on both the deficiencies inherent in their beliefs and the deep aspirations of adherents to know God in a more personal way. An English missionary in India, Thomas Slater, is quoted as saying, 'The Gospel of Christ enlightens the conscience [of Hinduism] to its great need, and is a message of salvation [that] reveals the hidden craving of the human heart to possess a humanised God, which can only be satisfied in Christ.'[44]

---

[42] *Edinburgh 2010: Mission Then and Now*, p. 121.

[43] See Yates, *Christian Mission in the Twentieth Century*, p. 24.

[44] Quoted in *Edinburgh 2010: Mission Then and Now*, p. 123. In a recent study, Ivan Satyavrata has revisited 'fulfilment theology' in Farquahar's, *The Crown of*

A basic problem with the attempt to apply a 'fulfilment theology' universally was recognised in the case of Islam, for of all the world faiths surveyed it was the only one that chronologically post-dated Christianity: 'Islam had not appeared before Christianity and, as a later revelation, knowingly rejected Christian truths, claiming a higher place for Mohammad than Jesus. It could not therefore be regarded as a nascent tradition with potential for fulfilment through Christian transformation.'[45]

So the report had to conclude that 'in the case of Islam . . . similarities [in points of contact] were seen as a deformation of earlier Christian ideals, thus becoming "a hindrance to, rather than a preparation for, the acceptance of Christianity"'.[46] It is not surprising, perhaps, that the report talks about the widespread 'divorce between morality and religion' in Islam, a 'total lack of appreciation of the nature of sin' and the moral life of Muhammad being 'no inspiration to holiness'.[47] Nevertheless, in order, as far as possible, to maintain an irenic approach to all faiths, the report did acknowledge that Islam bears an uncompromising witness to the unity and sovereignty of God, and that Muhammad did not reject the biblical Christ, because the Christian church of the time had not made him known (there was no Arabic translation of the Bible available to Muhammad and his followers).

The report could be self-critical of the failings of the Christianity embedded in the moral outlook of the Western nations – for example, in the case of their treatment of China and even of the poor in their own midst.[48] Therefore, it recognised that through study of and personal contact with other faith traditions, it was possible to learn new truths about Christ.

With hindsight, and in the context of an extended debate within Christian circles worldwide over the next century about inter-religious relations, it is easy to see how the general attitude, presupposed in the idea of fulfilment, could be understood as patronizing. Other faiths have some

---

(cont.) of Hinduism, in Krishna Mohan Banerjea's 'Vedic Theology' and Sundar Singh's 'Bhakti Spirituality'; see God Has Not Left Himself Without a Witness (Oxford: Regnum Books International, 2011).

[45] Guli E. Francis-Dehqani, 'Adventures in Christian-Muslim Encounters since 1910' in Edinburgh 2010: Mission Then and Now, p. 127.

[46] Francis-Dehqani, 'Adventures', p. 127.

[47] See The Missionary Message in Relation to Non-Christian Religions, report of Commission IV (Edinburgh and London: Oliphant, Anderson & Ferrer, 1910), pp. 133–4.

[48] Vinoth Ramachandra, 'A World of Religions and a Gospel of Transformation' in Edinburgh 2010: Mission Then and Now, p. 141.

insights into the reality of life, but the Christian faith has the fullness of truth. Other faiths have fleeting perceptions of absolute moral values, but these are fully displayed only in the biblical teaching on the kingdom of Christ. Certainly the report included, on the basis of the general under- standing of the time, that there was a direct link between false religion and moral degradation; therefore, because Christianity spoke the truth about God, humanity and salvation from sin, the consequence of believing its message would be moral uplift.

Fulfilment theology may be likened to a kind of 'social Darwinism' applied to the history of religions.[49] Indeed the parallel with Darwinism, although not drawn out by the reports, is present in the notion of the 'survival of the fittest': the conference saw the real possibility of the universal triumph of Christianity because of its superior adaptation to the circumstances of the dawning twentieth century; other religions, because of inadequate mechanisms of mutation in response to their changing environments, were likely to die out gradually.

Commission VII – Missions and Governments

The subject matter of this commission had the potential to be the most controversial and explosive. It dealt with the relationship between missionary work, the newly established Christian communities and civil government. The commission had the incredibly difficult task of establishing guidelines for missionaries working in societies with quite different forms of political power and at different stages in what might be called political and social maturity. Moreover, it had the tricky assign- ment of sorting out the relation between the loyalty of missionaries to their own countries and to the nations in which they worked, and their higher loyalty to the truth of the gospel.

The commission, probably wisely, chose the option of treating the job it was allocated by beginning with an empirical survey. It described the range of governments that held sway in different parts of the globe: national governments (such as Japan), colonial governments (the sun, at that time, never set on the British Empire) and native chieftainships. It also classified these according to how they were perceived in relation to 'civilization', as understood by the measurement of Western criteria, and the task of mission: 'Thus, Japan was deemed the most civilised of "mission fields", since its government had established "such internal

---

[49] So, Kenneth Ross and David Kerr in the postscript to Edinburgh 1910, 'The Commissions after a Century', in *Edinburgh 2010: Mission Then and Now*, p. 310.

order and toleration that problems of missionary policy, *in relation to government* . . . , have ceased to exist in any acute form".'[50]

The commission listed the existing governments in terms of their administration on a sliding scale from higher to lower. Presumably the purpose of this classification was to produce a workable typology of how power was functioning in different regions, with a view to helping missionaries in the sensitive task of carrying out evangelistic work in the jurisdiction of a foreign power.

Having completed the empirical survey, albeit with analytical criteria that would be challenged in our post-colonial era, the commission moved on to articulate working principles applicable to a wide range of issues in mission-to-government affairs that kept recurring across all the regions. Here it encountered the problematic task of arriving at arrangements that sprang from a considered biblical-theological position, but without raising questions that might have proved controversial and divisive between the various theological traditions represented at the conference.

It chose to develop a notion of the two spheres of authority as indicated in the famous dominical saying, 'Give . . . to the emperor the things that are the emperor's, and to God the things that are God's' (Matt. 22:21; Mark 12:16). In other words, civil authority has a certain autonomy and should be respected and obeyed, provided that it practises justice and is solicitous for the welfare of its people. This principle was particularly important in the case of newly formed Christian communities, as they might be objects of discrimination on the basis of representing a 'foreign' religion.

Although the general advice to missions was to cooperate wherever possible with governments, and to take a conciliatory attitude wherever conflicts, actual or potential, threatened, there were at least three wrongs where confrontation could not be avoided: the traffic of opium and of alcohol and enforced labour.[51] The last of these wrongs (particularly identified with the Belgian colonial authority's working of rubber plantations in the Congo) also takes us back to the controversies of the Spanish conquest of the Americas.[52]

---

[50] *Edinburgh 2010: Mission Then and Now*, pp. 201–2, quoting 'Missions and Governments', Report of Commission VII, p. 89. This reference to civilization echoes, in a striking way, the debate that we encountered in Chapter 5 about the status of the Aztec, Mayan and Incan peoples. There we recorded how Bartolome de las Casas compared the level of life and organization of these empires favourably with the ancient civilizations of Egypt, Persia, Greece and Rome, and indeed of his native Spain.

[51] See Maluleke, 'Christian Mission and Political Power', p. 207.

[52] See Maluleke, 'Christian Mission and Political Power', p. 209.

In yet another echo of the situation of exploitation under the Spanish, the commission 'speaks with approval of situations where missionaries become "the champion of the people" among whom they live. This may be in missionary support of local cultures and languages, or advocacy of social change, or criticism of civil governments that are responsible for gross oppression and injustice, or sympathy with the awakened social and political aspirations of the people.'[53]

In light of the fact that many missionaries were working in colonially administered territories, the commission does not tackle the red-hot question of whether these social and political aspirations might have included legitimately the desire for independence and self-government: 'Even those missionaries who tried to see matters from the perspective of the indigenous populations among whom they worked ... were ... given short shrift by the Commission report . . . The Commission's decision to omit such material resulted in a document which can easily mislead historians who have not consulted the sources that lie behind it.'[54]

On the whole missionaries are counselled to be cautious in undertaking any interference in the affairs of the state in which they are operating. They are to bear in mind that their presence in other lands is as 'resident aliens' with limited rights. Nevertheless, the commission made some bold statements about certain contentious issues, such as the excessive deference to Islam made by successive British governments, the latter's placing of excessive restrictions upon missionary work in Muslim nations such as Egypt, the Sudan and Northern Nigeria, and the related question of 'freedom of action in religious profession' in the case of evangelism among Muslims. These issues continue to be disputed more than a century later.

Commission VIII – Cooperation and the Promotion of Unity

Although probably tackling the most controversial issue of the entire conference, the commission's report produced by far the most significant and far-reaching outcome of Edinburgh 1910: 'It is . . . the case that the work of Commission VIII had a far greater impact on subsequent ecumenical history than that of all the other Commissions put together.'[55]

Prior to and during the conference itself, the various bodies involved in the planning, the commissions themselves and the delegates were caught in an almost irresolvable tension. On the one hand, there was plenty of

---

[53] *Edinburgh 2010: Mission Then and Now*, p. 202.
[54] Stanley, *World Missionary Conference*, p. 271.
[55] Stanley, *World Missionary Conference*, p. 278.

evidence, not least coming from the younger churches of Asia, that the missionary task demanded a much greater degree of cooperation at all levels, both at home and overseas, than had hitherto been forthcoming. There were already in existence well-established patterns of collaboration among evangelical denominational and interdenominational agencies, without which Edinburgh 1910 probably would never have happened.[56] Associations of mission societies, regular conferences and even committees had been formed in England, the United States, Germany, Sweden and the Netherlands: 'A considerable momentum in favour of new forms of Protestant missionary co-operation had thus been generated before the World Missionary Conference or the publication of any of its reports.'[57]

The Centenary Missionary Conference held in Shanghai in 1907 went much further than collaborative efforts and partnerships by advocating that the ultimate goal of Christian missions must be to plant one undivided church of Christ in any nation. This was a call, however idealistic and remote the possibility of its implementation, for full organic unity.

Of the reports themselves, Commission I called for the promotion of unity if the work of carrying the gospel to all the non-Christian world and the goal of missionary work envisaged by the Shanghai Conference was ever to be achieved. Commission II ('The Church in the Mission Field') proposed 'closer unity [of churches in the mission field] within larger denominational lines [than those represented by Western churches].'[58] Some successful, although still limited, unions had already taken place, such as those in Japan and South India. Commission III ('Education in Relation to the Christianisation of National Life) urged much greater working together in common strategies related to education in Africa (for example, the joint training of teachers and efforts to promote the education of girls).[59]

On the other hand, to secure the widest possible ecclesial participation in the Conference itself, particularly that of the Anglo-Catholic wing of the Church of England, no disputed theological or doctrinal issues were allowed to be raised through the medium of the Conference. Questions of ecclesial order between churches, often built on profoundly different theological assumptions, were not to be touched. There were intense disagreements between the evangelical majority and the Anglo-Catholic minority on the nature and place of the church in the salvific purposes of God. Such were the sensitivities and fears of straying into unwelcome territory that the Anglican

---

[56] See Rose Dowsett, 'Cooperation and the Promotion of Unity: An Evangelical Perspective' in *Edinburgh 2010: Mission Then and Now*.

[57] Stanley, *World Missionary Conference*, p. 282.

[58] *Edinburgh 2010: Mission Then and Now*, p. 56.

[59] Ogbu U. Kalu, 'To Hang a Ladder in the Air: An African Assessment' in *Edinburgh 2010: Mission Then and Now*, p. 102.

high-church Society for the Propagation of the Gospel only consented to participate in the conference two months before its beginning.

Nevertheless, despite the misgivings of some within the worldwide church and the warning of its representatives that, unless an undertaking was given by the conference's international committee that such matters would not be addressed, they would withdraw, prior to the conference influential leaders called for the formation of a permanent international committee to consider international missionary questions.[60] The final result of the lobbying on both sides was that the conference, on the recommendation of Commission VIII, unanimously approved the resolution that a 'Continuing Committee' should be authorised 'to confer with the Societies and Boards as to the best method of working towards the formation of a permanent International Missionary Committee.'[61] The commission's report had stated unequivocally that:

> It appears to us that the adoption in some form of the proposal to create an international committee that would serve as a medium of communication between all the missionary societies is absolutely necessary for the carrying out of any statesmanlike and concerted plan for the evangelization of the world . . . It is in the interest of mission work in all its departments, and it is in the highest interests of the Church in all her branches, that the powerful influences, which the experience and necessities of work in land not yet Christian are creating, should freely operate in helping to heal her divisions and restore her broken unity.[62]

The rest, as the saying goes, is history. In 1921, a delay due to the First World War, the International Missionary Council was formed, and the modern ecumenical movement was conceived, if not yet born.

The Assumptions of the Conference

Already a number of suppositions, which underlay the beliefs of those who initiated and carried through the organization of the conference, have

---

[60] Space is too limited to present the details of the negotiations that took place, mainly between Joe Oldham and various Anglican leaders, leading up to the conference. However, a full account is given in Chapter 10 ('Missionary Co-operation: Its Limits and Implications') in Stanley, *World Missionary Conference*, pp. 277–302.

[61] The vote was made verbally. When asked whether there was anyone against the motion, a complete silence descended on the gathering. This was then followed a moment later by the spontaneous singing of the doxology!

[62] *World Missionary Conference*, Vol. VIII, p. 144.

been mentioned. Foremost among them was the conviction that the world that still needed evangelizing existed beyond the nations of Europe and the Americas. This was the non-Christian world, which in the frequently used military language of the documents and speeches had not yet been 'occupied'. (Today, the word 'reached' is commonly used as an equivalent.) Lands populated largely by white people were considered to be already fully evangelised.[63] Mission, therefore, was understood in terms of what happened beyond the frontiers of the Western world: 'It appears that mission was understood mainly in terms of foreign missions so that the "Church at home" was only conceived of as "the home base of missions" and not a site of missions in its own right and in its own context.'[64]

The mentality of Christendom, with its notion of sacred territory, was tacitly accepted. The belief, for which the Anabaptists had lived and died four centuries earlier, that what counted before God was a personal, living faith and not the sacramental ritual of infant baptism, was still not generally accepted with regard to the continent of Europe. Hence those areas of the world filled by nominal believers, 'Christianised' as babies, were not deemed to be part of the mission field; whereas, 'the Church in the Mission Field' [the title of Commission II] . . . is surrounded by a non-Christian community whom it is its function to subdue for the King-dom'.[65] Consequently, 'Converts are those who have been "taken", "gath-ered" or "rescued" from heathenism, darkness and superstition.'[66]

Due to the moratorium imposed by the organizing committee on the discussion of disputed theological and doctrinal issues, the conference had to proceed by accepting that the tasks of mission were self-evident: 'The *modus operandi* of missions remained unexamined . . . Difficult ques-tions were not asked, and the only things perceived as lacking were human and financial resources.'[67]

Deliberately the Conference was not designed to grapple with the theology of mission: 'It was a conference to design the "strategy" for a final campaign by the concerted forces of the kingdom of God as they assayed what was needed to complete the "unfinished task".'[68]

---

[63] See Anne-Marie Kool, 'Changing Images in the Formation for Mission: Commission Five in Light of Current Challenges – A World Perspective', in *Edinburgh 2010: Mission Then and Now*, p. 160.

[64] Maluleke, 'Christian Mission and Political Power', p. 204.

[65] World Missionary Conference, *The Church in the Mission Field*, Report of Commis-sion II, (Edinburgh and London: Oliphant, Anderson & Ferrier, 1910), p. 5.

[66] Teresa Okure, 'The Church in the Mission Field: A Nigerian / African Response, in *Edinburgh 2010: Mission Then and Now*, p. 60.

[67] Kool, 'Changing Images', p. 161.

[68] Escobar, 'Mission from Everywhere to Everyone,' pp. 189–90.

A third assumption seemed to be that conversion to Christian faith would be the best possible solution to social problems. Two further premises undergirded this belief. First, Western civilization had been brought to a high point of moral and juridical rectitude by the influence of the gospel upon the mentality of its inhabitants and the social and political structures that, as a result, were put in place. Second, social problems and moral degeneracy were largely due in non-Christian lands to false religion.[69] Logically, then, promotion of the message that Christ was the one true light of the world would ensure a wholly new presence in society of his followers, who would act as light, salt and leaven to bring in the marks of God's kingdom.

Significance of the Conference

The documents of Edinburgh 1910 abound in hyperbolic statements about its unparalleled importance in the history of Christian missions. Not surprisingly, given the enormous time and energy that he invested in its success, John R. Mott described the occasion as 'the most creative event of modern world missions': 'Never has there been such a gathering in the history of the Kingdom of God on earth . . . Until now in the memory of the conference, according to the testimony of not a few, it [the daily act of intercession] stands out as the most sacred experience in the great succession of sacred days.'[70] It was 'the most notable gathering in the interest of the worldwide expansion of Christianity ever held, not only in missionary annals, but in all Christian annals'.[71]

In an article for the *Scotsman*,[72] one of the participants, Dr Arthur J. Brown of New York, was reported as having described Edinburgh 1910 as 'a gathering that would be considered by future historians as the most remarkable assemblage of the people of God that the world had yet seen'. In terms of its representation, in the drawing together of people from across conflicting theological positions and ecclesial traditions normally suspicious of one another, the conference was a substantial achievement.

In terms of the reflection of the missionary correspondents, the findings of the reports, and the information gathered together on the present state of missionary outreach, the conference provided well-informed, often judicious comment on the nature and state of mission at the time.

---

[69] See Francis-Dehqani, 'Adventures', p. 129.
[70] Mott, *Addresses and Papers*, pp. xvii, 17.
[71] Quoted in *Edinburgh 2010: Mission Then and Now*, p. 3.
[72] Written by an anonymous contributor for its edition of 24 June 1946.

It provided a highly condensed microcosm of the prevalent thinking on mission at the end of one century and the beginning of another. As William Richey Hogg expressed the matter, 'it is the keystone through which developments in mission and unity in the one century relate to those in the other and apart from which the full meaning of neither can be assayed.'[73] 'J.H. Oldham had an almost uncanny prescience that Edinburgh was poised "between the times" and that very great issues hung in the balance.'[74]

In their conclusion to a series of commentaries on the eight commissions, Kenneth Ross and David Kerr say,

> Edinburgh 1910, more than any other occasion, gave expression to a concentrated distillation of the wisdom and experience of the modern missionary movement. Despite that movement's many limitations, it proved effective in re-shaping the religious demography of the world, with many of its most cherished dreams being fulfilled. Hence the concerted attempt to enunciate its leading principles and to strengthen its methodology . . . is one which continues to repay careful study and reflection, both by those concerned with the missionary task today and by those who, from a variety of perspectives, seek to understand the dynamics at play in the drama of human history.[75]

It is an extraordinary testimony to the vitality and enduring value of the conference that, in spite of numerous criticisms that have been laid against its assumptions, motivations, content and strategies, the centenary in 2010 was marked by such an enthusiasm to celebrate its huge symbolic merit. Not only churches and agencies that are the descendants of those that were represented one hundred years previously, but also those who were excluded, or excluded themselves, or were still in the infancy of their expansion (like the Pentecostal churches), were eager to participate in the commemorative events around the world.

Outcomes and Legacy

Most commentators on the World Missionary Conference conclude that by far and away the most significant result of the meeting was the formation of a continuation committee:

---

[73] William Richey Hogg, 'Edinburgh 1910 – Ecumenical Keystone'. *Religion in Life* 29 (1959–60): pp. 339–51.
[74] Yates, *Christian Mission in the Twentieth Century*, p. 22.
[75] *Edinburgh 2010: Mission Then and Now*, p. 307.

Commission VIII put the whole question [of further and permanent cooperation
in the missionary enterprise] formally before the conference by its proposal for
the appointment of a continuation committee to perpetuate the idea and spirit of
the conference and embody it in such further practical action as should be found
advisable. The proposal was welcomed on every side. It was felt that it would
stamp an aspect of unreality upon the conference if it simply dissolved without
an act of patient obedience to the heavenly vision it had seen.[76]

The committee was formed immediately and had its first meeting for
three days subsequent to the ending of the conference. It elected John
Mott as chairman and Joe Oldham as secretary. It then met several times,
on both sides of the Atlantic, up to the beginning of the First World War.
In January 1912 it instigated the launch of a new journal, *The International
Review of Missions*, under the editorship of Oldham. From October 1912
to May 1913, John Mott made an extensive tour of Asia, attending no less
than eighteen area conferences and three national conferences to which
both missionaries and national leaders were invited.[77]

Obviously the war interrupted the work of the committee, from which
the German members had withdrawn in 1917, due to their objection to
Dr Mott's adverse comments on the German nation. However, another
significant missionary congress was held in Panama in February 1916
to consider Christian work in the Latin American continent, which had
been excluded from consideration at Edinburgh 1910.[78]

Eventually, the continuation committee was turned into an international council (the IMC). It held its first meeting at Lake Mohonk, New
York, in October 1921.[79] It led, along with other events, to the formation of
the ecumenical movement in 1948, when the World Council of Churches
was established at an assembly in Amsterdam.[80] John Mott was invited
to give the inaugural speech. After much heart-searching, and not a little
opposition, the IMC became part of the WCC at its assembly in New
Delhi in 1961 and, under the new umbrella, became the Conference for
World Mission and Evangelism.[81]

---

[76] Mott, *Addresses and Papers*, p. 18.
[77] Full details of the effects of these conferences and the inauguration of the *IRM*
can be found in Mott, *Addresses and Papers*, pp. 60–178.
[78] Again, full details can be found in Mott, *Addresses and Papers*, pp. 179–217.
[79] Mott, *Addresses and Papers*, pp. 218–41.
[80] For an account of the influence of Edinburgh 1910 on Amsterdam 1948, see
Brian Stanley, 'The World Missionary Conference (1910: Edinburgh, Scotland)'. *Expository Times* 121 (2009), pp. 325–31.
[81] See Yates, *Christian Mission in the Twentieth Century*, pp. 155–8. Developments
within its work will be picked up in subsequent chapters of this book.

This was the main institutional outcome of the 1910 conference. However, there were other less obvious but perhaps not less significant results of Edinburgh 1910. The position and vital role of women in mission was picked up by some of the reports. Teresa Okure notes that, 'strikingly, the Report [Commission II] gives a laudable attention to the ministry and mission of women'.[82] 'In the training of both character and mind the Report [Commission III] emphasised the vital role of women, both as educators and as meriting education. In both respects they were considered equal with men.'[83] It may be that this emphasis on equality helped to accelerate the decline in women's missionary societies.[84] Although the intention was good, the consequence was an increased lack of opportunity, at least for a considerable time into the twentieth century, for women to exercise leadership in missionary work.

The promotion of universal education through the Report of Commission III was, according to M.P. Joseph, highly subversive:

Social harmony was dependent upon the adherence of the members of the community to the rules of hierarchy. The concept of individual freedom that missionary education introduced favoured social equality over social hierarchy . . . In India, where the right to education was mediated by the caste system and its rigid rules, promotion of the universal right to education was a subversive act. Caste rules prohibited the lower caste people from acquiring knowledge . . . Missionary efforts to educate Dalits, women, tribal peoples and other marginalized communities demonstrated its potential to initiate a social revolution.[85]

Three further consequences of the 1910 conference are more negative. First, the insistence on dividing the world into Christian and non-Christian lands, the logical conclusion of a territorial definition of Christendom, eliminated the importance of mission 'from everywhere to everyone' from the agenda of the mainline churches for decades to come: 'Mission was an "appendix" to the church, and missiology could be no more than that in the theological curriculum.'[86]

Mission, as Andrew Walls never tires in pointing out, was believed to be something that happened on the margins of Christendom.[87] It was

---

[82] Okure, 'The Church in the Mission Field', p. 64.

[83] *Edinburgh 2010: Mission Then and Now*, p. 89.

[84] Stanley, *World Missionary Conference*, p. 315.

[85] M.P. Joseph, 'Missionary Education: An Ambiguous Legacy' in *Edinburgh 2010: Mission Then and Now*, p. 106.

[86] Kool, 'Changing Images' p. 165.

[87] See Andrew Walls, 'Afterword: Christian Mission in a Five-Hundred-Year Context', in *Mission in the 21st Century: Exploring the Five Marks of Global*

an undertaking for specially trained missionary enthusiasts. The home churches' financial and prayer support was their contribution to the 'mission field'. The accommodation made to the Anglo-Catholic wing of the Anglican Church (mainly the Church of England) to ensure its participation was, in retrospect, a heavy price to pay.

Second, it also contributed, from the 1920s onwards, to a parting of the ways between those who remained passionate about world evangelization and those who began to interpret mission much more in terms of social action, inter-religious dialogue and ecumenical cooperation and the search for unity. The effects of splitting mission into two separate emphases are still being felt within the global church in the twenty-first century. There are still few, if any, theologies of mission that have successfully managed to integrate the different aspects of mission into a coherent theological unity, in such a way that they have been able to influence a missionary practice that takes seriously all the implications of being sent into the world.[88]

Third, the emphasis on the 'west' to the 'rest' in mission hindered the realization that 'mission [is] at the core of the DNA of the church wherever it may be. This almost certainly delayed the development of the mission movement from the global south by decades, and also hindered the churches from the global south from taking responsibility for the ongoing evangelization of their own people.'[89] The awakening of the 'slumbering giant' of the massively expanded churches of Africa, Asia, Latin America and Oceania to their missionary calling has only come about in the last thirty years. The direction of mission that dominated the thinking of the great mission conference of 1910 has now been reversed; the West is one of the most needy and most resistant of current locations for Christian mission. To use the admittedly outdated terminology of Edinburgh 1910, it is very far from being 'occupied' by the gospel. Some of the reasons for this will be explored in the final chapter of the book.

(cont.) *Mission* (ed. Andrew Walls and Cathy Ross; London: Darton, Longman & Todd, 2008), pp. 193–204.

[88] However, within the last twenty years, a number of mission theologians have attempted to produce a coherent pattern of reflection on mission that seeks to integrate its various features; see for example, Samuel Escobar, *The New Global Mission: The Gospel from Everywhere to Everyone* (Downers Grove, IL: InterVarsity Press, 2003); Michael Nazir-Ali, *From Everywhere to Everywhere: A World View of Christian Mission* (London: Collins, 1991); Stephen B. Bevans and Roger P. Schroeder, *Constants in Context: A Theology of Mission for Today* (Maryknoll, NY: Orbis Books, 2004); J. Andrew Kirk, *What is Mission? Theological Explorations* (London: Darton, Longman & Todd, 1999); Melba Maggay, *Transforming Society* (Oxford: Regnum/Lynx, 1994).

[89] Dowsett, 'Cooperation,' p. 255.

Part Three

Contemporary Concerns

8

God, the World and the Church

Setting the Scene

The World Mission Conference held in June 1910 took place four years before the war that supposedly was going to end all wars. My attention in this chapter will be focused on thinking about the church in relation to the world that began approximately four years after the Second World War.

The sombre realities of the Third Reich in Germany in the 1930s led a minority of outstanding church leaders in that nation – theologians, pastors and laity – to formulate a response to the claims being made by the Nazi party. It led to the famous Declaration of Barmen (1934), a statement of faith that upheld the independence of the church from the state. The statement was made as a rejoinder to the attempt by so-called 'German Christians', sympathetic to Hitler's political philosophy, to blend Protestant theology with Nazi ideology and allow the decisions of the German Evangelical Church to be accountable ultimately to the German chancellor.[1]

By the end of the decade, the so-called 'crisis theology', associated particularly with the Swiss theologian Karl Barth, with its central catch-phrase, *Jesus Christus ist das eine Wort Gottes* (Jesus Christ is God's only Word), was quite dominant in mission circles. An air of crisis pervaded the preparations for and deliberations of the International Missionary Council (IMC) Conference held in Tambaram, a suburb of Chennai (Madras) in 1938.[2] Barth's dialectical theology, although criticised in part by Hendrik Kraemer in his preparatory study for the conference,[3] had

---

[1] The full text may be found in Arthur C. Cochrane, *The Church's Confession Under Hitler* (Philadelphia: Westminster Press, 1962), pp. 237–42; see also David E. Roberts, 'Barmen Declaration (1934)' in *The Dictionary of Historical Theology* (ed. Trevor A. Hart; Carlisle: Paternoster Press, 2000), pp. 52–3.

[2] See Evert Jansen Schoonhoven, 'Tambaram 1938'. *International Review of Mission*, 67 (1978): p. 299.

[3] Hendrik Kraemer, *The Christian Message in a Non-Christian World* (London: Edinburgh House Press, 1938).

the effect of hastening the end of the distinction between the so-called
'Christian and non-Christian nations'. Henceforth, in light of the extreme
nationalist ideologies arising in Europe (Germany, Spain, Italy and
Portugal), mission leaders recognised that paganism knew no geographical boundaries. Not only did it pervade 'secular' society, but could be
found, tragically, in the heart of the church itself. Events in Europe and
Japan at that time, and later in China (the communist revolution), caused
a rethinking of the relation between the church, the state and society.

The rebuilding of Europe, the construction of a new world economic
order (Bretton Woods, July 1944) and the beginning of the end of colonial rule (India and Pakistan gained independence in August 1947) set
the context and mood for a fresh look at the missionary obligation of
the church. In this chapter, I wish to explore one particular focus on the
church and the world, which could be said to have originated in the
deliberations that took place at the Willingen Conference of the IMC held
in 1952.

The Willingen meeting witnessed a decisive shift from mission seen
from the perspective of the church to a God-centred vision.[4] Tambaram
had to some extent reinforced a church-centred focus, inherited from
Edinburgh 1910, although with much greater emphasis on the autonomy
and initiative of the former mission churches of the non-Western world.
John Mott reiterated this approach in his opening address: 'It is the church
which is to be at the centre of our thinking . . . the Divine Society founded
by Christ and his apostles to accomplish His will in the world.'[5]

The theme that was chosen had the title, 'The Upbuilding of the
Younger Churches as a Part of the Historic Universal Christian Community.' As Wolfgang Gunther says, 'This benefited from favourable winds
after the World Conference on Life and Work in Oxford in 1937 and the
World Conference on Faith and Order in Edinburgh in 1938, both of
which made the church central.'[6]

The Tambaram Conference took place in the context of the expansionist
policies of the German, Italian and Japanese regimes. War between Japan
and China was already being waged. Willingen was convened shortly
after the expulsion of all foreign missionaries from China following the
success of Mao Tse-Tung's internal revolution in 1948–9. If the forces of

---

[4] See David J. Bosch, *Transforming Mission: Paradigm Shifts in Theology of Mission*
     (Maryknoll, NY: Orbis Books, 1991), p. 370.
[5] The quote is taken from Timothy Yates, *Christian Mission in the Twentieth
     Century* (Cambridge: CUP, 1996), p. 120. A good survey of this conference is
     found in the same volume.
[6] Wolfgang Gunther, 'The History and Significance of World Mission Confer-
     ences in the 20th Century', *International Review of Mission* 92 (2003): p. 526.

fascism had been defeated in the military struggle of 1939–45, the new power of Communism in the most densely populated nation on earth proved a different challenge (or threat).

The most significant preparatory input into the conference came from a group of North American missiologists who produced a report on 'The Missionary Obligation of the Church'.[7] Although apparently focused on the mission of the church, in fact the report began and ended with God's action in the world in fulfilment of his purposes:

> The missionary obligation of the Church is grounded in the outgoing activity of God, whereby as Creator, Redeemer, Governor, and Guide, God establishes and includes the world and men within his fulfilling purposes and fellowship.[8]

> Missionary obligation, grounded in the reconciling action of the triune God, is . . . the sensitive and total response of the Church to what the triune God has done and is doing in the world.[9]

The final statement from Willingen endorsed this emphasis on the primacy of the mission of the Trinity:

> The missionary movement of which we are a part has its source in the Triune God Himself. Out of the depths of His love for us, the Father has sent forth His own beloved Son to reconcile all things to Himself . . . On the foundation of this accomplished work God has sent forth His Spirit, the Spirit of Jesus . . . We who have been chosen in Christ, reconciled to God through Him, made members of His Body, sharers in His Spirit, and heirs through hope of His Kingdom, are by these very facts committed to full participation in His redeeming mission to the world. That by which the Church receives its existence is that by which it is also given its world-mission. 'As the Father hath sent Me, even so send I you.'[10]

Missio Dei

So the Trinitarian foundation for and nature of Christian mission began to find a substantial expression in the discussions that took place at Willingen.

---

[7] The full text can be found in *Theology Today* 9 (1952): pp. 20–38.
[8] Lehmann, 'Missionary Obligation', p. 20.
[9] Lehmann, 'Missionary Obligation', p. 22.
[10] In N. Goodall, ed., *Missions under the Cross* (London: Edinburgh House Press, 1952), pp. 189ff.

Subsequently, this focus dominated theological reflection on mission within circles related to the IMC and the incipient ecumenical movement. However, the actual catch-phrase, *missio Dei*, did not appear in the documents. As far as can be ascertained, it was the German theologian and director of the Basle Mission, Hartenstein, who first introduced the actual phrase into missiological reflection in 1934: 'He calls missions towards a critical self-examination of whether she is what she is called to be, namely *missio dei*, God's own sending, expressed in Christ's command to the apostles.'[11]

He may well have been influenced by the address that Karl Barth gave to the Brandenberg Missionary Conference in 1932, which ended with these words, which summed up his rejection of the notion of mission as basically a human activity aimed at the betterment of human lives:

> Must not even the most faithful missionary, the most convinced friend of missions, have reason to reflect that the term *missio* was in the ancient Church an expression of the doctrine of the Trinity – namely the expression of the divine sending forth of the self, the sending of the Son and the Holy Spirit to the world? Can we indeed claim that we can do it any other way?'[12]

After Willingen, the emphasis on God's initiative in mission, the belief that the *missio ecclesiae* followed on the Father's sending of the Son and Spirit, came to be interpreted in two quite distinct and somewhat mutually exclusive ways. One continued to stress that God worked preferentially through the unique witness of the church, which alone was entrusted with the task of carrying the hope of the gospel to the ends of the earth. The other emphasised the free, providential action of God in the world by the Spirit, with little reference to the church.[13]

Both interpretations agreed that God's salvific work precedes both church and mission.[14] However, they were divided on the sequence to be followed in mission. Whereas hitherto mission was conceived firmly as the action of God through the church to the world, now there developed a conviction that the order of the last two elements should be reversed. Henceforth, then, mission should be understood as God's action directly in the world, with the church a kind of simultaneous interpreter of what

---

[11] Jurgen Schuster, 'Karl Hartenstein: Mission with a Focus on the End', *Mission Studies*, Vol XIX, 1, 37, 2002, p. 65.

[12] Part of the text is found in Norman E. Thomas, ed., *Classic Texts in Mission and World Christianity* (Maryknoll, NY: Orbis Books, 1995), pp. 104–6.

[13] See Michael Goheen, 'The Future of Mission in the World Council of Churches: The Dialogue between Lesslie Newbigin and Konrad Reiser', *Mission Studies* 21 (2004), p. 100.

[14] Bosch, *Transforming Mission*, p. 370.

God was doing. It is this second interpretation of *missio Dei*, in its many facets, that is the main focus of this chapter. At the same time, we will listen to critical assessments of this prevalent mood, in many respects characteristic of missiological debate in the 1960s.

According to Jacque Matthey, one of the main achievements of the fresh emphasis on the mission of God was to overcome an unhealthy ecclesio-centric approach to mission, highlighted since Tambaram. The *missio Dei* emphasis is a constant reminder that the church is not the ultimate goal of mission. It helps to open up the realm of political and economic life to become an integral part of the mission agenda, since God is also active outside the church. At the same time, he states, the *missio Dei* concept became linked with a theology that gave mostly positive appreciation of secularization and even secularism. Consequently, evangelism prac-tically disappeared from the mission agenda of the mainline churches in the West. These time-bound contextual interpretations of *missio Dei* aggravated the split within Protestant missionary organizations and led to the formation of two competing movements from 1974 onwards.[15] I will explore further some of the consequences, both positive and nega-tive, of this second interpretation of missio Dei in the rest of this chapter.

God–world–church

One of the most influential documents published by the WCC during the 1960s was the study, *The Church for Others: Two Reports on the Missionary Structure of the Congregation*.[16] It was the result of two working groups – one from Western Europe and the other from North America. The orig-inal title of each report is significant in showing the direction in which the participants were taking the debate about church and world. The first is called 'The Church for Others: A Quest for Structures for Missionary Congregations'. The second was entitled, 'The Church for the World'. Although working separately, the two groups exchanged the results of their thinking and came up with remarkably matching convictions.

The first report affirms that the primary context of mission is history. The God of the Bible is a sending God. He works out his purposes in the midst of the world and historical processes. God is leading 'history out of the old into the new, he creates hope, in the sense of an active expectation of good

---

[15] Jacque Matthey, 'God's Mission Today: Summary and Conclusions'. *Interna-tional Review of Mission* 92 (2004), pp. 580–81.

[16] World Council of Churches, *The Church for Others: Two Reports on the Missionary Structure of the Congregation* (Geneva: WCC, 1967).

in the transformation of the world for Christ's sake'.[17] The goal towards which God is working, i.e. the ultimate end of his mission, is the establishment of *shalom*,[18] and this involves 'the realization of the full potentialities of all creation and its ultimate reconciliation and unity in creation'.[19]

So, 'God's primary relationship is to the world, and it is the world and not the Church that is the focus of God's plan:'[20] 'If mission is basically understood as God working out his purpose for his creation, the church does not have a separate mission of its own.'[21]

So the role of the church is expressed entirely in terms of God's redemptive activity in the world in creating signs of *shalom* in anticipation of the creation of a new heaven and new earth in which justice will be the hallmark: 'It is the church's task to recognise and point to the signs of this [the establishment of *shalom*] taking place.'

The report identifies the kind of signs it is talking about:

> Each time a man is a true neighbour, each time men live for others, the life giving action of God is to be discerned. These are signs of the Kingdom of God and of the setting up of *shalom*. One may consider examples like this: the emancipation of coloured races, the concern for the humanization of industrial relations, various attempts at rural development, the quest for business and professional ethics, the concern for intellectual honesty and integrity. So God, as he moves towards his final goal, is using men and women, both inside and outside the churches, to bring signs of *shalom*.[22]

The second report unequivocally sets the church in its place as a self-effacing witness to evidences of God's redemptive activity in the world, not only among individuals, but more importantly in making structures serve truly human ends: 'In terms of God's concern for the world, the church is a segment of the world, a *postscript*, that is added to the world for the purpose of pointing to and celebrating both Christ's presence and God's ultimate redemption of the whole world.'[23]

---

[17] WCC, *Church for Others*, p. 14.
[18] 'This word is used to indicate all aspects of human life in its full and God-given maturity: righteousness, truth, fellowship, peace, etc. This single word summarises all the gifts of the messianic age . . . Shalom is a social happening, an event in interpersonal relations . . . It has to be discovered as God's gift in actual situations', WCC, *Church for Others*, p. 14.
[19] WCC, *Church for Others*, p. 15.
[20] WCC, *Church for Others*, pp. 16–17.
[21] WCC, *Church for Others*, p. 75.
[22] WCC, *Church for Others*, p. 15.
[23] WCC, *Church for Others*, p. 70 (emphasis in the original).

Humanization

One of the notable interpretations of God's activity in the world, especially prominent in all kinds of documents in the 1960s, was that of humanization. In a time marked both by a growing confidence in the power of technology and human planning to deliver great strides in the elimination of poverty and also an existential angst exemplified by philosopher novelists like Camus, Sartre and Marcel, the question of human meaning came to the fore.

The WCC World Conference on Church and Society held in Geneva in 1966 picked up the ways in which economic and political questions, dominated by issues such as decolonization and the deployment of nuclear weapons of mutual mass destruction, challenged the project of sustainable human development for all. Thus, for example, H.E. Todt, the then professor of Christian social ethics at the University of Heidelberg, declared that:

> the *humanum* remains a pressing question in our radically revolutionary world. Theological statements pose the question of man's humanity within a particular perspective but do not tell us how the *humanum* is to be understood in the modern world organization, in the process of revolution and emancipation, of nation building, and the change of social structures . . . Thus the Christian understanding of the *humanum* is always dependent on dialogue with the sciences.[24]

Professor Todt was clearly presenting the view that the church could not fulfil its mission of contributing to the healing of a wounded human race without listening to and taking on board the best wisdom coming from the worldly sciences. If the Christian faith has answers at one level of understanding, namely the drawing out of the implications of what it means to be *imago Dei*, at another level (what it means to be *imago Dei* in the concrete realities of particular historical moments) it is dependent on other disciplines of analysis for a more thoroughly comprehensive view.

The report, 'Renewal in Mission', adopted by the Fourth Assembly of the WCC, held in Uppsala in 1968, continued the theme. It begins with these words: 'We belong to a humanity that cries passionately and articulately for a fully human life. Yet the very humanity of man and of his societies is threatened by a greater variety of destructive forces than ever. *And the acutest moral problems all hinge upon the question: What is man?'*[25]

---

[24] See Paul Abrecht, 'Responses to the World Conference on Church and Society 1966', *Ecumenical Review* 20 (Oct. 1968), p. 450.

[25] WCC Fourth Assembly, 'Renewal in Mission: the Report as Adopted by the Assembly', *International Review of Mission* (April 1969), pp. 145–7, 354–60 (emphasis added).

It then goes on to describe the church's mission as being involved in 'this worldwide struggle for meaning, dignity, freedom and love'. The mission of God is given a theological gloss in terms of 'the gift of a new creation which is a radical renewal of the old and an invitation to men to grow up into their full humanity in the new man, Jesus Christ'. The main theological assumption behind this statement sets the scene for the rest of the report, namely that human beings, by virtue of their creation and the incarnation and atonement of Jesus Christ, are already implicitly redeemed in Christ.

Thus, the report enunciates the common religious view (although not one shared by the New Testament)[26] that 'men can know their true nature only if they see themselves as sons of God'. It continues in the same vein: 'through that death on the Cross, man's alienation is overcome by the forgiveness of God and the way is opened up for *the restoration of all men to their sonship*. In the resurrection of Jesus a new creation was born, and the final goal of history was assured, when Christ as *the head of that new humanity* will sum up all things.'[27]

Here we see the development of a new theology of the *missio Dei* that came to dominate WCC discourse for at least another two decades. The language of the new humanity takes precedence over that of church. The new humanity is both a goal and a gift that needs to be accepted by a response of faith. The Holy Spirit takes the word of God and makes it a living word that brings about a change of heart and mind.

> Often the turning point does not appear as a religious choice at all. Yet it is a new birth. It sets a pattern of dying and rising which will continually be repeated. For we have to be torn out of the restricted and perverted life of 'the old man'. We have to 'put on the new man' and this change is always embodied in some actual change of attitude and relationship.[28]

---

[26] At least according to Paul, the status of being children of God is by adoption into God's family through explicit faith in Jesus Christ: 'for in Christ Jesus you are all children of God through faith' (Gal. 3:26). As a result of trusting in the redemptive work of the Son of God 'we receive adoption as children' (Gal. 4:5). In Johannine thought, 'those who receive Christ, who believe on his name are given power to become the children of God' (John 1:12). John goes on to say explicitly that this is not the automatic heritage of being born into the world, for those who receive Christ 'were born, not of blood or of the will of the flesh or of the will of man, but of God' (John 1:13). By the God-given gift of faith and the transforming presence of the Holy Spirit, we are born again: 'what is born of the flesh is flesh, and what is born of the Spirit is spirit. Do not be astonished that I said to you, "You must be born from above." ' (John 3:6–7).

[27] WCC Fourth Assembly, 'Renewal in Mission', p. 145 (emphasis added).

[28] WCC Fourth Assembly, 'Renewal in Mission', p. 146.

Nevertheless, the church is not irrelevant. For signs of the new humanity are experienced 'as people find their true life . . . in the Church's life of Word and Sacrament, fellowship in the Spirit and existence for others'.[29] However, the report gives a clear impression that the new humanity can also come into being outside of institutional ecclesial bodies: 'We must see achievements of greater justice, freedom and dignity as a part of the restoration of true manhood in Christ.'[30]

This view is made explicit in the report, 'The Church for Others':

God's redemptive mission culminates in the coming of Christ, the true man, the head of the new humanity . . . In his earthly life as well as in his new existence as the risen Lord, Christ is providing signs of the fullness of humanity, *wherever men and women are led to restored relationships in love of neighbour, in service and suffering for the sake of greater justice and freedom.*[31]

Humanization as the goal of mission has good biblical warrant, for the New Testament speaks about people in community coming to 'maturity, to the measure of the full stature of Christ' (Eph. 4:13). It uses the metaphor of clothing oneself 'with the new self, created according to the likeness of God in true righteousness and holiness' (Eph. 4:24). This new self 'is being renewed in knowledge according to the image of its creator' (Col. 3:10). Jesus Christ is creating 'in himself one new humanity' (Eph. 2:15). It is God's purpose to restore to his special creatures the fullness of his image, which has become disfigured by human beings choosing, for themselves and others, paths of destruction. The process may be likened to a masterpiece severely damaged by someone throwing paint all over it, which then has to be painstakingly restored by a master craftsman to its original glory. According to this view, God's purpose is to create communities in which people are reconciled to one another from across every imaginable barrier; one in which they share their lives in free service to others. In the New Testament, the title given to this new community is *ekklesia*. It comes into being not by human effort, however this may be inspired by God's Spirit, but by human response in repentance and faith to God's calling to receive his salvation through Jesus Christ.

Looking back at the concern for humanization in the 1960s, we can see that a number of false theological assumptions were made. Hendrikus Berkhof, reflecting sympathetically on the Uppsala

29 WCC Fourth Assembly, 'Renewal in Mission', p. 146.
30 WCC Fourth Assembly, 'Renewal in Mission', p. 147.
31 WCC, *Church for Others*, pp. 77–8 (emphasis added).

Assembly not long after it had finished, said that the churches represented there had shown themselves ready and eager 'to share the great
movement for the development of human lives and societies towards
a fuller humanity'. At the same time, he highlighted the fact that 'the
Assembly was hesitant and divided so far as the relation between this
development and the message of the Gospel was concerned'.[32]

Berkhof, although clear that 'development' is 'part of the total salvation which God wills for his human creatures',[33] and that 'the present
concern for structural renewal is an essential element in Christian sancti-
fication',[34] nevertheless reaffirmed the conviction that 'the primary task
of the Christian Church is to call men to the source of God's grace and
promises'.[35] This will entail warning 'against the present overestimation
of the role of structures' and reminding 'modern man of both the centre
and the wide circumference of full humanity: the conversion to God, the
following of Jesus, the self-sacrifice towards our neighbour, and last not
least: the promise of eternal life in which God will fulfil all our longing
for a true humanity'.[36]

In this article a leading ecumenical theologian seeks to strike the right
relationship between mission as bringing people to realise and act on
their need of God's free gift of salvation through Christ, and mission as
a prophetic witness against dehumanizing structures and attitudes that
perpetuate injustice and abuse. This relationship has proved surprisingly
hard to articulate theologically and act out practically.

It would appear that this particular way of articulating the catchword,
'humanization', confuses creation and salvation. Whereas the two cannot
be separated, for salvation leads to a new creation; they are distinct. Creation is a *given* reality for all human beings, whether they recognise the fact
or not. Their humanity is irrevocably shaped by the mode of their existence in the world as created beings. Salvation is a *gift* that can be rejected,
as well as received; people are not involuntarily 'saved in Christ', so that
they can enjoy the fruits of salvation simply by recognizing their already
accomplished status. It is a change of relationship with the Creator that
has to be initiated by an act of the mind and the will in response to God's
gracious initiative and in thanksgiving for the sacrifice of Jesus Christ
that has made it possible.

[32] Hendrikus Berkhof, 'Re-Opening the Dialogue with the "Horizontalists"'.
   Ecumenical Review 21 (Oct. 1969), p. 289.
[33] Berkhof, 'Re-Opening the Dialogue', p. 289.
[34] Berkhof, 'Re-Opening the Dialogue', p. 292.
[35] Berkhof, 'Re-Opening the Dialogue', p. 295.
[36] Berkhof, 'Re-Opening the Dialogue', p. 298.

Mission as Presence

In 1943 an epoch-making book was published in France, *La France: pays du mission?*[37] Recognizing the alienation of the masses from the life of the church, the authors wrote about the church's urgent need to find new ways of identifying with and being present among these peoples. Taking their inspiration from the Little Brothers and Sisters of Jesus, communities set up by Charles de Foucauld to offer Christian service through being immersed in strange environments,[38] the thinking in the book led to the well-known 'worker–priest' movement, where members of the clergy took on jobs in the French industrial sector.[39]

In the 1950s, Max Warren, the General Secretary of the Anglican Church Missionary Society, became the general editor of a series of books, published under the title of 'Christian Presence'.[40] In his introduction to the series, Warren 'encouraged an expectation of finding Christ already present in alternative traditions'. The missionary task, he was to write later, was to 'unveil the Lord who is already there'. So, mission did not consist in taking 'Christ to some place from which he is absent but to go into all the world and discover Christ there . . . to uncover the unknown Christ'.[41]

Walter Hollenweger in his Introduction to the report, *The Church for Others*, points to the question asked by the North American Working Group: 'How can we recognise – in the flower shop, at the street-car stop, in the slums of the big cities, in the cinema, in the picket-line – that same Christ, whose body we have shared at the Lord's table'.[42]

The European Working Group acknowledged that if one speaks about God's action in the world, it raises the question of *Christus extra muros ecclesiae* – of Christ outside the walls of the church. Hence, 'when the Church is aware that the presence and activity of God are not only manifest in itself, it will be constantly vigilant to discern any signs whereby God makes himself known to the world.'[43]

---

[37] Godin, H. and Daniel, Y., *France, pays du mission?* (Paris: Editions du Cerf, 1943).

[38] See R. Voillaume, *Seeds of the Desert: the Legacy of Charles de Foucauld* (London: Burns and Oates, 1955).

[39] See Yates, *Christian Mission in the Twentieth Century*, pp. 136–7.

[40] The series included the notable books by Kenneth Cragg, *Sandals at the Mosque: Christian Presence and Islam* (London: SCM Press, 1959) and J.V. Taylor, *The Primal Vision* (London: SCM Press, 1965).

[41] Quoted in Yates, *Christian Mission in the Twentieth Century*, pp. 141–2.

[42] WCC, *Church for Others*, p. 4.

[43] WCC, *Church for Others*, pp. 11–12.

Speaking about the legacy of J.C. Hoekendijk, Bert Hoedemaker says that 'mission is the vicarious existence of the people of God for the whole world in presence and service, wherever the divine initiative in the world manifests itself in history.'[44] In the report, 'The Missionary Obligation of the Church', it is stated that Jesus Christ 'is not only the Head of the Church but ahead of the Church and the world, "making all things new." The problem is to keep abreast of Jesus Christ.'[45]

There are a number of theological rationales for this model of mission. The primary one, no doubt, is that of incarnation. This implies stepping outside of one's own world, in order to be immersed in the world of others by sharing their lives. It is predicated on listening, so as to understand the world of other people from their perspective, before speaking. According to this view, the aim of mission is not fundamentally that of conversion, but building understanding and working together for the common good. It seeks to redress and correct distorted images of Christian faith as imperialist, sanctimonious and patronizing.

A secondary motivation would be to stress the sheer grace of God in any move of individuals towards faith in Christ. Strongly evangelistic models of mission, with an emphasis on church-planting and church growth, seem to emphasise human initiatives in planning, programmes, strategies and organization. The presence model relies on the work of the Holy Spirit, who cannot be controlled and works in unknown ways. Conversion is a mystery which cannot be planned for. At most, advocates of the presence model will witness to their faith when invited to do so, but not in a way that necessarily implies that it is superior to other beliefs. The presence model may also be interpreted as an act of repentance for the way in which Christians have often acted aggressively towards peoples with different beliefs, particularly the Jewish community.

A third reason, one that is particularly significant in the context of the debate about the *missio Dei*, is the notion that the world is already redeemed in Christ, even if 'the redeemed' do not know and understand the meaning of salvation. The authors of the report, *The Church for Others*, believe that the growing secularization of Western societies and cultures is one among many signs of this salvation: 'Secularization can also be understood as a liberation from the control of metaphysics and theology.'[46]

By this they mean that the world has its own identity and integrity as the world. It is not part of a divine being: 'The possibility of letting the world be

---

[44] Bert Hoedemaker, 'The Legacy of J.C. Hoekendijk'. *International Bulletin of Missionary Research* (1 Oct. 1995), p. 169.
[45] Lehman, 'Missionary Obligation', p. 21.
[46] WCC, *Church for Others*, p. 10.

the world, of letting matter be matter and not divine, to use therefore nature and to subject it to human service, is inherent in the biblical teaching . . . The world, in the bible, is entirely secular and is placed under the mandate of men who are responsible to God for their stewardship.'[47]

So the world is freed from a false sacralization by being a created and contingent entity outside of the eternal God. It is also liberated from what the report calls 'a slavery under false authorities': 'The gospel of Christ's death and resurrection means that Christ has freed men from slavery to false powers and authorities and has restored them to the freedom of the children of God.'[48]

The implication of this way of looking at Christ's sacrifice for the sins of the whole world (1 John 2: 2) seems to be that the church's mission is to declare to the world its new status. Confident in the knowledge that 'the event of Christ has irreversibly changed the world', Christians are called to help people in the world live out a freedom, which is potentially theirs, from fear, superstition, taboos and every form of idolatrous power that lead to their dehumanization.

The consequence of this way of looking at the world is that the world as the object of God's love and transforming presence is to be embraced by Christians:

The historicity of the world implies its secularity, for in his history with the world God is moving to bring the world to its destiny, to make it truly worldly . . . The church is part of world history. Its history is no more a particular, sacred history than was the history of Jesus . . . He had been totally committed to this world, and he lived in it as the suffering servant. The world did not have to receive him; still, he was available and the world could receive him.[49]

From this way of reflecting theologically on the nature of the world in the purposes of God has come the notion of solidarity. Thus the main goal of the World Conference on Church and Society was to 'advise the churches and the World Council "in formulating policies which will give expression to a Christian concern for human solidarity, justice and freedom in a world of revolutionary change"'.[50] The solidarity in question concerns the victims of all forms of idolatrous power that hinder their development into their full humanity in Christ. The mission of the church is clear:

---

[47] WCC, *Church for Others*, p. 10.
[48] WCC, *Church for Others*, p. 11.
[49] WCC, *Church for Others*, p. 72.
[50] Abrecht, 'Responses', p. 446.

[*diakonia*] is this word that we find at the heart of the Gospel. The whole story of the New Testament . . . revolves round this one theme . . . The Christian life is assigned its place among people who need to be 'served' (the Bible calls them the 'poor' or 'the least'). It cannot be lived elsewhere. Outside this concrete sphere of service it would wither and choke; it would become ordinary, just a pious self-seeking.[51]

The Church-for-Others

The German pastor-theologian, Dietrich Bonhoeffer, executed in 1945 for his opposition to the Nazi regime, was the first to coin this memorable phrase. In his celebrated *Letters and Papers from Prison*, he wrote: 'The church is the church only when it exists for others . . . The church must share in the secular problems of ordinary human life, not dominating, but helping and serving.'[52]

This certainly became a watchword in some circles in the 1960s. The title of the report, to which we have already alluded several times, sets the tone. Its first paragraph ends with the words, 'the missionary church is not concerned with itself – it is a Church for others'.[53]

Hoekendijk takes up the theme: 'The church must prove her legitimacy . . . by being there for the other. She does not exist in herself and certainly not for herself either . . . Nor does the church live in co-existence with the world, but . . . in *pro-existence* – for that world.' He then goes on to ask what this *pro-existence* might mean in very practical terms. He takes as an example the budget of any local congregation and inquires how much of it is designated purely for people and projects outside the church. He wonders whether even 51 per cent would represent a true self-emptying.[54]

Some have criticised this notion of '*for* others', on the grounds that it conceals the reality of a typical, liberal-humanist, bourgeois church that see its function in terms of providing for the needs of others out of the riches of its bounty. Churches, whose members intrinsically know 'what is best for others', 'tend to proclaim themselves the guardians of others'.[55] Thus *pro-existence* may well stifle the church's deeper role of *coexistence*, being '*with* others'. Although this interpretation may alert to a potential danger, the original concept ('for others') was designed to counteract the

---

[51] J.C. Hoekendijk, *The Church Inside Out* (London: SCM Press, 1967), pp. 142–3.
[52] Dietrich Bonhoeffer, *Letters and Papers from Prison* (London: SCM Press, 1971), pp. 382ff.
[53] WCC, *Church for Others*, p. 7.
[54] Hoekendijk, *Church Inside Out*, p. 70.
[55] See Bosch, *Transforming Mission*, p. 375.

tendency of the church to spend much time and energy on ensuring its own security and survival. The context in which Bonhoeffer penned his famous words was that of the German church during the Third Reich.

The World Sets the Agenda

In thinking about new forms of Christian missionary presence within the world, the authors of the first part of the report, *The Church for Others*, considered that these must come 'from the interplay of the Gospel and the contemporary situation'. In elaborating this conviction, it soon becomes evident that the gospel rather fades from view and contemporary life becomes the given reality which plays the major role in shaping the church's mission. The emphasis was captured in what became at the time a notable, if ambiguous, catch-phrase: 'The message and structures of the churches can only be formulated with respect to the immense variety of actual realities amidst which we live. Hence it is the world that must be allowed to provide the agenda for the churches.'[56]

It could be that this phrase is understood to mean that the churches must wait to see what kind of challenges contemporary living throws up and then respond as best they may in the light of their fundamental faith convictions. The discussion that follows the announcement of this mission orientation certainly gives this impression. Over two pages the report identifies fifteen different characteristics of the contemporary world and immediately after each one makes a proposal as to how the churches need to act in response.

Taken at face value, this approach is unfortunate for a variety of reasons. First, the characteristics chosen are arbitrary. Who is to decide what the most important features of any given situation are? Might it not be that the elements picked out are actually symptoms of a deeper malaise, which is not properly analysed and addressed?

Second, the responses suggested offer only generalised and vague strategies. Here is one by way of example: 'The contemporary world is one in which people are continually forced to be crowded together, thus making privacy difficult to achieve. The churches because they are concerned to foster fellowship which only grows in freedom, must also ensure that men are given the opportunity to be themselves as private individuals.'[57] It is difficult to see what this might mean in practice, or even whether 'being themselves as private individuals' is ever a proper Christian calling.

---

[56] WCC, *Church for Others*, p. 20.
[57] WCC, *Church for Others*, p. 22.

Third, it may be too easily assumed that 'the world' would welcome Christian interaction of the kind that is recommended in these fifteen clauses. When, for example, the report says that 'the churches should encourage individuals to participate critically in this process of decision-making (about matters that can affect the whole of life) and the churches themselves must be prepared to challenge the process if necessary', it does not seem to have considered the reality that the intervention of Christians in the public square is often largely ignored or even greatly resented by the political elite.

This report was written at the same time that abortion became legalised across many parts of the Western world. The efforts of generations of Christians to argue that abortion on social, lifestyle grounds is an action that strikes at the heart of the sacredness of human life have been met by ridicule and abuse. The 1960s was the decade that began to see an accelerating decoupling of Christian faith from the moral convictions of an increasingly secularised generation. The report does not seem to have considered the missionary role of the churches to be a counter-cultural witness in faithfulness to the gospel. Charles Taylor, author of a massive study of the secularization process, *A Secular Age*,[58] brings a warning to those who hope for too much in their engagement with the world: 'the attempted remakings of the world to conform to the Gospel, stand themselves in perpetual danger of being or becoming also remakings of the Gospel to fit the world.'[59]

So, fourthly, the report does not do justice to what one might call God's agenda (or *missio Dei*). The message of the good news of Jesus and the kingdom of God is *sui generis*; it is incomparable. It penetrates to the heart of the reasons for the various forms of alienation, which the report rightly identifies, and proposes long-lasting solutions. However, by and large the world does not wish to hear, because to listen attentively to the gospel and respond positively to its message would mean a radical change of direction (*metanoia*), entering into a new relationship with the king of the universe. In the case of any disease, it is the diagnosis that sets the agenda for the most appropriate treatment. In the case of the church's missionary obligation, it is the divine diagnosis of humanity's manifold infirmities that sets the agenda for applying the 'medicine' of healing, salvation and liberation provided by the sacrificial ministry of Jesus.

Having made these points about the inadequacy of the notion of the world setting the agenda for mission, it is also necessary to recognise

---

[58] Charles Taylor, *A Secular Age* (Cambridge, MA: Harvard University Press, 2007).
[59] Charles Taylor, 'Foreword' to David Martin, *On Secularization: Towards a Revised General Theory* (Aldershot: Ashgate Publishing, 2005), p. x.

what the report is intending to achieve. It begins with the assumption
that God is concerned about the entire creation that he has brought into
being. This is to set the church's mission in an eschatological perspective
– the eventual creation of a new material order (a new earth). It wishes to
find a way of burying once-for-all the ever-persistent dichotomy between
the sacred and the secular, the spiritual and the material, the individual
and the corporate, which has so distorted the Christian world-view.

So, the report sets its sights on a missionary strategy which releases the
laity to fulfil their calling in the midst of the working world. The laity is
an indispensable part of reflection on what it means for Christ's disciples
to be witnesses to him to the ends of the earth, where the boundaries are
not just geographical, but social, cultural, ideological and religious. So the
report emphasises that it is the laity who possess the specialised knowledge and experience of grappling with the challenges of secular working
life. They are already on the frontiers of missionary encounter with the
world. Unfortunately, this is not sufficiently recognised by churches that
concentrate on their own life and structures. The report is right to make
this point forthrightly:

> Laymen are not non-clergy or non-experts but the members of the *laos*, the people
> whom God has chosen for a particular assignment in his mission . . . Speaking
> of the church in terms of laymen means speaking of the church in the world, the
> church in mission; it means thinking of laymen in terms of their secular compe-
> tence – in their occupations, their families, their involvement in community affairs
> and politics. They are to be the bearers of mission in these worldly contexts.[60]

The report then goes on to point out that the servant character of the
church is compromised by the dichotomy between clergy and laity which
tears apart the unitary nature of service, dividing it into the vertical and
the horizontal, one performed by the clergy and the other by the laity.
It concludes: 'The integration of the two aspects of ministry centred in
the laity as the reference group for mission will allow the missionary
congregation to bear clear testimony to the authority for, as well as to,
the authenticity of its ministry.'[61]

If this is the direction in which one might interpret the notion of the
world setting the agenda, it becomes more understandable, less ambiguous and less controversial. Even then, unhappily, it does not mean that
the church's hierarchy necessarily has a good grasp yet of the mission of
the whole *laos* of God.

---

[60] WCC, *Church for Others*, p. 80.
[61] WCC, *Church for Others*, p. 81.

Doing Theology in a Secular Age

Numerous studies have pointed to the decade of the 1960s as a period of transition between two societies: one that still largely accepted the moral, civil and ritual traditions inherited from a millennium and a half of Christian influence and the other that began seriously to question that inheritance and influence.[62] Germane to our discussion in this chapter is the fact that an influential group of theological thinkers heralded the process of secularization as a mark of God's activity in the world in bringing in his new order of freedom and justice.[63]

Looking back at his remarkably popular, but also highly controversial volume, *The Secular City*, Harvey Cox seeks to put the central thesis in perspective: 'I argued then that secularization – if it is not permitted to calcify into an ideology (which I called "secular-*ism*") – is not everywhere and always an evil. It prevents powerful religions from acting on their theocratic pretensions. It allows people to choose among a wider range of worldviews.'

> The thesis of *The Secular City* was that God is first the Lord of history and only then the Head of the Church. This means that God can be just as present in the secular as in the religious realms of life, and we unduly cramp the divine presence by confining it to some specially delineated spiritual or ecclesial sector. This idea has two implications. First, it suggests that people of faith need not flee from the allegedly godless contemporary world. God came *into* this world, and that is where we belong as well. But second, it also means that not all that is 'spiritual' is good for the spirit. These ideas were not particularly new. Indeed, the presence of the holy within the profane is suggested by the doctrine of the incarnation – not a recent innovation. As for suspicion toward religion, both Jesus and the Hebrew prophets lashed out at much of the religion they saw around them.[64]

---

[62] For example, Callum Brown, *The Death of Christian Britain* (London: Routledge, 2001); Alan D. Gilbert, *The Making of Post-Christian Britain: A History of the Secularization of Modern Society* (London: Longman, 1980). I will leave a discussion of the nature and impact of the secular on the social fabric of Western nations for the final chapter.

[63] For example, Harvey Cox, *The Secular City: Secularization and Urbanization in Theological Perspective* (1965) (Collier Books, 25th anniversary edn, 1990); Arendt Van Leeuwen, *Christianity in World History: The Meeting of the Faiths of East and West* (London: Edinburgh House Press, 1964).

[64] Harvey Cox, 'The Secular City 25 Years Later', *Christian Century* (7 Nov. 1990): pp. 1025–9.

He argues that secularization (the process of allowing the ordinary, mundane world to be freed from the control of religious or ideological hegemonies) is a movement in contemporary history that bears the marks of a world created by God to have its own integrity as the material order. As he says above, the world is not special because it is part of a divine being, but because the divine being chose to live in it; in Paul's words, 'he descended into the lower parts of the earth' (Eph. 4:9). Similarly, the place of his disciples is also in the daily dealings of human existence.

Secularization implies that religion no longer occupies a central, privileged place in society. Moreover, being free from the need to defend religious beliefs and practices at all costs, means that the negative influences of religion can be fully exposed. Cox builds on Bonhoeffer's famous allusion to 'religionless Christianity', by making out a case for Christian faith being the antithesis of a religious view of the world.

Arend van Leeuwen takes a similar line by seeking to show that secularization falls within the benevolent providence of God, for it promotes a culture that permits human beings to be free of external compulsions to take on for themselves a full mature responsibility for their lives. In this sense, it builds on Bonhoeffer's prophetic imagination in talking about people 'coming of age'; in other words, acting as fully-grown adults. Van Leeuwen contemplated a world in which secular assumptions and the growth of technologies would increasingly deliver a life freed from superstition and stultifying religious practices. He also believed that secularization would produce a climate worldwide more conducive to Christian faith, seeing that the latter was not dependent on a defence of religion but was at home theologically in a secular environment, which it had been instrumental in bringing about. Karl Hartenstein, in a paper written in 1928,[65] put the contrast between Christian faith and religion in a forceful and uncompromising way:

> He [Hartenstein] defines religion as 'the attempt of man to directly seize God, to bridge the distance between God and man from below.' This results both in the deification of human beings ('you will be like God') and the humanization of God. The deepest nature of human sin reveals itself especially in religion. Therefore Christendom as religion, as empirical experience next to other religions, must be relinquished. 'Christ the revelation of God is opposed to all religions, including Christendom.'[66]

---

[65] Karl Hartenstein, 'Was hat die Theologie Karl Barths der Mission zu sagen?' (Munich: Kaiser Verlag, 1928).

[66] Schuster, 'Karl Hartenstein', p. 62.

The theological assumptions that were expressed in these ways gave rise in ecumenical circles to talk about 'the responsible society', meaning societies built on institutions that allowed maximum consultation and reasoned debate about what the common good should be and how it could be implemented.[67] Religious establishments and thinking would have a place within this debate, but would be given no special privileges. On the contrary, due to their tendency to divide reality falsely into spiritual and material worlds, their contribution has to be received with some suspicion.

In hindsight, the optimism exhibited by these theologians and others about the salutary effects of the secularizing process seems somewhat naive. Some believed that the world stood on the threshold of almost unimaginable revolutionary changes – perhaps the kind of great leap forward depicted in the propaganda of the Soviet Union. For a time groups of Protestant and Roman Catholic theologians met on different occasions with a number of Western Marxists for informal conversations.[68]

Among the interests on the Christian side were: the relationship between the church and society, the meaning of freedom, the demands of radical Christian discipleship in the world, and the connection between hope and utopia.[69]

Probably the most difficult topic to engage with was the relationship between faith and ideology. Berkhof believed that ideology was a necessary tool to be used in the theological task of engaging in Christian mission in a revolutionary age. He argues his case in this way:

> Where general structures are at stake . . . we need general viewpoints to deal with them adequately and effectively. This applies even more when these structures have to be changed. In that case we need an ideology as a set of

---

[67] The kind of discourse that would be ideal in a responsible society is depicted by Jurgen Habermas as 'an ideal speech situation', in which the conditions necessary for interpersonal communication, to be governed by sincerity, truth-telling and rational warrant, would be fulfilled, see *The Theory of Communicative Action* (trans. Thomas Mc Carthy; Boston: Beacon Press, 1984).

[68] See J. Andrew Kirk, *Theology Encounters Revolution* (Leicester: Inter-Varsity Press, 1980), pp. 54–5; Peter Hebblethwaite, *Christian-Marxist Dialogue and Beyond* (London: Darton, Longman & Todd, 1977), pp. 17–37.

[69] This was stimulated by two epoch-making books published during the 1960s: Jurgen Moltmann, *The Theology of Hope* (New York: Harper & Row, 1967); and Ernst Bloch, *Das Prinzip Hoffnung* (1959), translated as *The Principle of Hope* (Oxford: Blackwell, 1986); see also J.C. Hoekendijk, *Horizons of Hope* (Nashville, TN: Tidings, 1970).

general viewpoints, aims and rules, to bring about effectively the necessary change. Christian faith never has developed anything that looks like an ideology of change. Marxism is the only relevant movement which has such an ideology to offer. No wonder that many Christians look for help from this side, particularly because this ideology aims at bringing man out of a situation of self-estrangement to a full realization of his human potentialities. Ideologies are necessary to bridge the gap between mind and matter or thought and action . . . For the Christian the use of ideologies can become an analogy to the work of God who incarnated his mind in a world which is not in accordance with it, and which therefore has to be changed.[70]

These dialogues with some of the leading Marxists of the time gave evidence of a theological trend which found its fullest expression in the theology of liberation of the following decade. This latter will be the subject of the discussion of the next chapter.

The Christian–Marxist conversations came to an abrupt end with the brutal, systematic crushing of the Prague Spring on 21 August 1968. The sight of Warsaw Pact tanks rolling into the centre of one of the most beautiful and cultured cities in the world, to reverse political and economic reforms, caused both left-leaning Christian leaders in Western Europe and senior members of a number of European communist parties to become seriously disillusioned with Soviet-style socialism. This clearly was not the direction from which the coming revolution would spring.

Although hopeful of substantial changes in societies that would make life more human for the vast majority of their citizens, the revolutionary[71] theologians were also aware of the tough obstacles in the way. Revolutionary forces might be oriented towards noble ends, but the means that were used to reach the goals often contaminated the whole process. Moreover resistance to change is powerfully motivated and cunningly manipulated by people who gain much by maintaining the status quo (even whilst speaking the language of revolution!). Hoekendijk hints at the reality of false dawns and unrealistic utopias, when he speaks about Christian hope:

We feel ourselves taken up in a grand 'battle for hope'. In some parts of the world this is evident. There we see 'Christ, our hope' confronted with and

---

[70] Berkhof, 'Re-opening the Dialogue', pp. 293–4. For one of the fullest treatments of the subject, see Juan Luis Segundo, *Faith and Ideologies: Jesus of Nazareth Yesterday and Today* (Maryknoll: Orbis Books, 1984).

[71] The term 'revolutionary' was mentioned both by the report, WCC, *Church for Others*, p. 65, and by the report, Abrecht, 'Responses', p. 452.

challenged by other powers in which people have put their trust with conviction. Opposed to ours we find another articulated eschatology. Therefore, in
this, as in every other Promethean situation, the Christian hope will have to
be proclaimed so convincingly that every other expectation is exposed as
Utopia, every other hope as false hope.[72]

In terms of the kind of theological reflection depicted in this chapter,
the world denies its true destiny, whenever it ceases to be the world, i.e.
when it attempts to convert its true secularity into a total world-view
that in effect denies its human creatureliness. Then the world sets itself
up in opposition to itself as a created order and alleges its 'divinity'
and 'immortality'. In the process a kind of 'resacralization' takes place;
space and time are invested with a different kind of numinous presence,
called the revolution or inexorable progress: 'The historicity of the world
implies its secularity, for in this history with the world God is moving to
bring the world to its destiny, *to make it truly worldly*.'[73]

Conclusion

The aim of this chapter is to give a brief flavour of a particular orientation towards the world on the part of Christian thinkers during the
decades between the late 1950s and the late 1960s. The emphasis has
been on the church discovering in the world the traces of God's creative
and liberating work. So the church is not to focus on itself and its own
expansion as its primary mission, but to discern, in certain 'signs of the
times', God's mission to bring 'all things in heaven and on earth together
under one head, even Christ'.[74] Then the responsibility of Christians is to
engage with secular forces to ensure that the changes necessary to bring
about a world more habitable for human beings do not end up by being
further examples of oppression and injustice.

The motivation for this way of conceiving the *missio ecclesiae* is to
take seriously the world, not so much as the place of opposition to the
will of God, as the arena of God's redemptive and reconciling activity –
the world, which is so much the object of God's care and compassion.
The appropriate image for the church is not that of the ark, a refuge for
people to be safe from the contamination of the world; rather it is that
of salt and yeast, which are effective only when thoroughly mixed into

---

72 Hoekendijk, *Church Inside Out*, p. 58.
73 WCC, *Church for Others*, p. 72 (emphasis added).
74 Eph. 1:10, NIV.

the surrounding matter. The church, therefore, is challenged to rethink fundamentally both its nature and its strategy. It is to be immersed in the world, in order to ensure that the world takes itself seriously as a world fashioned by God and accountable to him.

Hoekendijk expresses this calling well. He begins by pointing out the churches' initial failing: 'When the first stone was laid for the modern industrial cities, the church was absent from the ceremony.' He continues by reminding his readers that, even when the church belatedly recognised its debt to the city, it reversed what should have been the true direction of its mission: 'the church did not let herself be taken up in the missionary movement toward the city, but, the other way around, it has coordinated the city mission, has integrated it in its own work, and so has enclosed it.'

In other words, mission in the city has been absorbed into the static structures of a church traditionally organised around rural village life. It has not been given the freedom to experiment with new forms of ecclesial presence in areas outside the church's normal experience. The problem is that 'We have erected one temple instead of ten tents. And we have carefully delimited the temple area (parish quarters). The mission in the city does not tolerate such immobility . . . The primary thing that is asked of us in this respect is *presence*, to be there, serving without ulterior motives, and for the time being probably without too many words.'[75]

In spite sometimes of the apparent theological recklessness of this pattern of thinking, a rediscovery of the world as the *locus* of God's missionary engagement is an essential compensation for an emphasis on the church as the supreme end and goal of mission. The writers and working groups that we have been considering point to the priority of the kingdom of God over the church as the end point of God's purposes to recreate the inhabited world (*oikoumene*) in true righteousness and peace. Speaking about Hoekendijk's legacy to missiological reflection, Hoedemaker sums up this point by emphasizing that the church is the result of bringing the gospel of the kingdom into the world. Mission takes place between God's kingdom and the world, not between the church and the world. The church should be understood functionally; it is an instrument of God's ultimate plan, not its centre. Therefore, it betrays its *raison d'être*, whenever it becomes settled in a social, cultural or religious status quo.[76]

Nevertheless, this view of church and world does tend to underestimate the central role that the people of God, as a specially convened group of those who consciously commit themselves to trust Christ and

---

[75] Hoekendijk, *Church Inside Out*, pp. 109, 114, 120.
[76] Hoedemaker, 'The Legacy of J.C. Hoekendijk', p. 167.

walk in his ways, has in God's final purposes. By placing the world in the forefront of God's liberating work and relegating the church to the role of a mechanic whose job it is to make sure that the engine is functioning as was intended, this view of the *missio ecclesiae* does scant justice to how the New Testament depicts the church.

The Letters to the Ephesians and the Colossians in particular highlight the centrality of the church. The church is the 'body of Christ', 'the fullness of him who fills all in all' (Eph. 1:23). Christ has been made 'head over all things for the church' (Eph. 1:22). It is clear that 'the one new humanity' (Eph. 2:15) is 'the household of God' (Eph. 2:19), which is also 'a holy temple in the Lord . . . a dwelling place for God' (Eph. 2:21–2). God's reconciling work, bringing together the heirs of the promise and those who were separated from the people of the covenant happens in the church: 'the Gentiles have become fellow-heirs, members of the same body' (Eph. 3:6). Moreover, this work of reunification is the message of the gospel: 'the Gentiles have become . . . sharers in the promise in Christ Jesus though the gospel. Of this gospel I have become a servant' (Eph. 3:6–7). Finally, the church is the Bride of Christ, for whom he gave himself up 'to present the church to himself without a spot or wrinkle or anything of the kind – yes so that she may be holy and without blemish' (Eph. 5:27).

Space does not permit a thorough examination of the way in which the church is presented in the New Testament as fulfilling God's plan of salvation. The church is not merely a sign, foretaste or instrument of God's reign over the universe that will be consummated, when 'all things are put in subjection under his feet . . . so that God may be all in all' (1 Cor. 15:27, 28). It is the gathering of the 'great multitude . . . from every nation, from all tribes, peoples and languages standing before the throne' (Rev. 7:9; 19:1). It is 'the holy city, the new Jerusalem, coming down out of heaven from God, prepared as a bride adorned for her husband' (Rev. 21:2). In other words, the whole biblical narrative of God's great work of bringing salvation to the ends of the earth is consummated in the wedding-feast of the Lamb – Jesus Christ and his bride, God and believing humanity reunited in an unbreakable fellowship of love and adoration.

9

Liberation and the World

Introduction

The last chapter reviewed a significant turning occasioned by a shift (during the 1950s and1960s) in theological thinking from the church to the world as the primary location of God's missionary activity. The present chapter will seek to capture a further shift (that took place during the 1970s) which is, at one and the same time, geographical, theological and ideological in nature. The geographical location moves away from the northern and western hemispheres (West Europe and North America)[1] to the South.[2] The theological move has happened as the result of a change of perspective concerning the motivation, method and meaning of the theological task. The ideological move contemplates a different understanding of the place of ideology as a critical tool in perceiving the church's historical and contemporary role in society. These changes will be explored in the course of discussing the main themes of this chapter.

I will not attempt a general overview of issues related to liberation and justice. This would be beyond both the scope of one chapter and my ability. Rather, I will concentrate on one particular person, José Miguez,[3] an

---

[1] The geography indicates part of a typology that refers to nations with both a certain common history and economic status, and includes therefore Australasia and to some extent South Africa.

[2] This general term alludes to a cluster of nations, formerly called 'the Third World' or the 'Two-Thirds World,' and now usually brought together under the heading of the 'Global South' or 'Majority World'. These are nations that were colonised by European powers and whose present situation may be characterised by the term 'neo-colonialism' with regard to the world economic order. The situation is constantly changing as indicated, for example, by the rise to the status of global economic super-powers of countries like Brazil, India and Malaysia.

[3] He is often given his full name of Jose Miguez Bonino in accordance with the custom in some societies of adding the mother's maiden name to that of the father's.

Argentinian church leader, theologian and theological educator.[4] Writing
out of a specific context, he has done as much as anyone to clarify the
challenges facing the Christian community and its theological reflection
brought about by the realization that endemic poverty for the majority
of a population has its roots in deeply established, long-term, economic,
political and social structures. A major part of his importance lies in the
fact that he is one of only a handful of prominent Latin-American Protestant[5] theologians who identified themselves with particular movements
for liberation and justice. Generally speaking, the best known advocates
of a theology of liberation have come from the Catholic Church. Their
thought and action has been endlessly discussed and analysed.[6] The
Protestant contribution to the debate has not had the same attention.[7]

Naturally, I cannot hope in one chapter to cover the immensely rich
and wide variety of Miguez's thought. I will limit myself to his writings
of the 1970s[8] and to certain specific themes within these that seem to be
most germane to the overall interest in the theme of liberation. These

---

[4] He died on 30 June 2012, at the age of 88.

[5] In Latin America they are usually known in Spanish as *iglesias evangélicas*,
    similar to the use made of the term *evangelische* in German.

[6] I have myself written a full-length book on the use of the Bible in libera-
    tion theology, taking as illustrations the writings of Hugo Assmann, Seve-
    rino Croatto, Gustavo Gutierrez, Jose Miranda and Juan-Luis Segundo: see
    J. Andrew Kirk, *Liberation Theology: An Evangelical View from the Third World*
    (London: Marshall, Morgan & Scott, 1979/1985).

[7] However, at least three major reviews of Jose Miguez's thinking and commit-
    ments have been made in the last twenty years: Rebecca Chopp, *The Praxis
    of Suffering: An Interpretation of Liberation and Political Theologies* (Maryknoll:
    Orbis Books, 1992); S.J. Schubeck, *Liberation Ethics: Sources, Models and Norms*
    (Minneapolis: Fortress Press, 1993); Paul J. Davies, *Faith Seeking Effectiveness:
    The Missionary Theology of José Miguez Bonino* (Zoetermeer, ND: Uitgeverij
    Boekcentrum, 2006).

[8] Specifically, I will deal with the following books: *Ama y haz lo que quieras:
    hacia una ética del hombre nuevo (Love and do what you like: toward an ethic of the
    new person)* (Buenos Aires: La Aurora, 1972); *Doing Theology in a Revolutionary
    Situation* (Philadelphia, PA: Fortress Press, 1975), edition in the UK, *Revolu-
    tionary Theology Comes of Age* (London: SPCK, 1975); *Espacio para ser hombres:
    una interpretación del mensaje de la Biblia para nuestro tiempo* (Buenos Aires:
    Tierra Nueva, 1975), ET, *Room To Be People: An Interpretation of the Message
    of the Bible for Today's World* (Augsburg: Fortress Press, 1979); *Christians and
    Marxists: The Mutual Challenge to Revolution* (London: Hodder and Stoughton,
    1976); ed., *Jesús: ni vencido ni monarca celestial* (Buenos Aires: Tierra Nueva,
    1977), ET, *Faces of Jesus: Latin American Christologies* (Maryknoll: Orbis Books,
    1984); *Toward a Christian Political Ethics* (London: SCM Press, 1983).

include an analysis of reality, the meaning of liberation, the theological task and method, and the church's mission and nature. These encompass a number of sub-topics which, I believe, will reveal the essence of his thinking during this decade. I will not attempt to discuss how Miguez's thought may have developed and changed during the last thirty years of his life. That would be a task for at least another chapter.

The Real World

Pivotal to all Miguez's thinking is the importance of gaining knowledge of the reality of human communities. This cannot come about by an appeal to abstract, universal truths or ideas. The truth of a matter is not measured by its correspondence to an idea, but by its conformity to historical events. Knowledge of the truth is not gained by theoretical contemplation, but by active involvement in historical processes (as, for example, the struggle throughout the 1970s in Latin America to challenge military dictatorships to implement human rights).

The real world is known in the act of engaging in its transformation; though not any kind of transformation, for history has been transformed by ideologues such as Stalin, Hitler, Mao Tse-Tung and Pol Pot. Knowledge has a deep moral content, for the action required must be in harmony with God's ultimate project to create a human world where justice is carried through in all relationships, the intrinsic dignity of every person is respected and the welfare of all provided for. Truth is discovered by people when they work for a society in which poverty, exploitation and violence become matters of the past. It is in the very conditions of change that the truth will be known.

The importance of this viewpoint cannot be exaggerated, for it avoids driving a wedge between theoretical concepts, ideas and principles and the realm of actions, in which the latter is relegated to a second level of discourse, playing the role of being mere deductions from the pure world of theory. Miguez notes three dangers in maintaining this distinction. First, ideas and theories can be discussed without taking into account the concrete historical circumstances out of which they are born. Second, ideas take on a life of their own unrelated to the existence of actual people living in specific, material conditions. Third, a distinction is drawn between an ideal course of action (impossible to implement) and the compromises necessary to make the ideal a reality in ordinary human existence.[9]

---

[9] See Miguez, *Christians and Marxists*, p. 30.

So a right understanding of the real world comes through participation in movements to change it for a better world. In Christian terms it means obedience in following the path that God has set out through his self-communication in historical acts of judgement and promise. Moreover, in answer to the question, how do we know what God requires, Miguez replies that we have to take risks:

> The most profound and decisive matters of life are never guaranteed . . . They are only demonstrated in practice. Those who take no risks, will never know the truth about those aspects of life that make human life human . . . This is what happens in relation to God. The Bible offers us a way; it invites us to belong to a society together with God. Whoever is willing to begin this journey, to commit themselves to this society, will confirm the truth . . . Whatever we hold back without commitment will remain beyond verification.[10]

Analysing the Real World

Although knowledge of reality cannot be obtained outside of a committed, practical engagement in the transformation of human society, it is not self-explanatory. To understand the forces of history that have brought the world to its present state, we need a frame of reference or unified perspective that enables us to interpret the situation in which we find ourselves. Miguez is prepared to use the term ideology, in spite of its negative connotations, to describe this orientation.

The use of ideology

An ideology is a way of seeing the world. It is a set of lenses that can be adjusted for making reality more or less visible. In this sense the term itself is neutral; it all depends on the lenses that are used. The choice of lenses will be largely determined by people's social standing and, therefore, their perceived need either to maintain or change their position in society. Ideologies that are used to keep the status quo more or less intact interpret reality in the interests of perpetuating the privileges and power of those already dominating the structures and institutions of society – for example, government, financial establishments, universities, the media, and the church. Ideologies that are used to advocate and stimulate change claim to interpret reality in the interests of those disadvantaged by the present structural arrangements of society – for example,

---

[10] Miguez, *Espacio para ser hombres*, p. 10.

the low-paid, unemployed, ethnic and religious minorities, immigrants, refugees.

During the 1970s, when the use of ideology as a means of understanding the dynamic movements of contemporary history was at its zenith, it was considered impossible not to be driven by ideologies used in one of these two senses. The luxury of sitting on the fence by not opting for an ideology either of the status quo or of change was deemed wishful thinking. To pretend that one did not have to make a choice was already a choice in favour of the status quo. The debate about ideologies was polarised around the axes of two fundamental possibilities.

Miguez clearly opted for an ideology of change. Along with a small group of leaders of Protestant churches in Latin America and an increasing number of Roman Catholic clergy and lay people, they forged a method for understanding what Christian obedience entailed by reference to an ideological lens, through which the historical forces operating could best be understood. However, not any ideology of change could do the job adequately; only one that uncovered most adequately the economic and social movements that sustained a dysfunctional (unjust and unequal) society. That ideology was Marxism, not as a philosophical position, but as an analytical tool to allow a deeper understanding of economic exploitation and an alternative political option.

The option for Marxism

The turn to Marxism was brought about by a growing dissatisfaction with alternative ways of understanding the historical events unfolding in Latin America during the 1960s. Politically the world at that time was dominated by the ideological conflict between the nations of the West and the Soviet Union, each block seeking to spread its influence across the globe. The Unites States considered the western hemisphere its legitimate area of operation; all that the Soviet Union stood for was alien to its history and heritage. Yet, the Soviet Union had managed to secure a toehold on the continent with the accession to power in Cuba of Fidel Castro. The USA became increasingly obsessed with the presence of a communist state in its back yard, as the Bay of Pigs operation (April 1961) and the missile crisis of 1963 amply demonstrated.

The USA was determined, therefore, to ensure that the 'cancer' of Communism did not spread. The strategy it adopted was twofold: to strengthen the hand of the governments opposed to socialist ideals and to launch a massive development project, known as 'the Alliance for Progress'. In the former case, nation after nation in Latin America abandoned democratic rule as military governments suspended constitutions and governed by diktat. In the second case, huge amounts of aid and investment were pumped into the region in order to try to replicate the development pattern of North America. Neither strategy worked as the USA would have hoped. The military dictatorships fuelled resentment and resistance among large sectors of the population, particularly as elementary human rights were increasingly trampled upon. The economic measures increased poverty and misery, as more capital was sucked out of the continent than was invested in it. As a result, Latin-American economists coined the phrase, 'the development of underdevelopment'.

Some elements of the political class, realizing the chaos caused by the imposition of economic measures imported from elsewhere in the interests of those who had grabbed power, and yet hesitant to advocate a full-scale socialist solution to the crisis, suggested the possibility of adopting a 'third way' between a naked capitalism and a rigorous socialist model of society. This attempt at a compromise between two extreme ideologies was enacted in Chile during Eduardo Frei's presidency (1964–70), under the slogan of 'revolution in liberty'. However, at the end of his period in office, the socialist politician Salvador Allende was voted into power with a popular mandate.

Miguez, along with an alliance known as 'Christians for Socialism', rejected all third ways (*tercerismos*) and promoted a radical transition to an autochthonous socialist society through sustained popular pressure. The problem of 'the third way' was that it was an idealistic solution to an endemic problem that failed to understand the real underlying causes of the crisis. Speaking of the group, he says:

> It is my thesis that as Christians, confronted by the inhuman conditions of existence prevailing in the continent, have tried to make their Christian faith historically relevant, they have been increasingly compelled to seek an analysis and historical programme for their Christian obedience. At this point, the dynamics of the historical process, both in its objective conditions and its theoretical development, have led them, through the failure of several remedial and reformist alternatives, to discover the unsubstitutable relevance of Marxism . . . The failure of Christian democratic Parties – particularly in Chile – convinced these Christians that 'third ways' between capitalism and socialism involving purely idealistic and voluntaristic approaches to structural change were inadequate and ill-fated. The decision for Marxism is therefore an option for structural over against purely individual change, for revolution over against reformism, for socialism over against capitalist development or 'third' solutions, for 'scientific' over against idealistic or utopian socialism.[11]

---

[11] Miguez, *Christians and Marxists*, p. 19.

Marxism appealed as it appeared to provide both a set of analytical tools that uncovered the real causes of inherent poverty, human alienation and violence in society, and a revolutionary theory that could set society on a trajectory towards a community able to grant an equal distribution of the fruit of human labour to all. What particularly attracted the well-educated classes to this mode of analysis was its claim to be scientific.

Scientific methodology

The scientific method can be defined as the process by which the actual nature of the world is laid bare. It adopts a rigorous, testable procedure by which the reality which is observed can be traced back to necessary and effective causes. Normally, science operates within the domain of physical matter through its various disciplines of biology, chemistry, physics and their sub-divisions. However, the methods that are used can also be applied analogically to the world of human society to account for the concrete social, political and economic situation as the result of a demonstrable set of historical factors.

When the word 'scientific' is applied to Marxist modes of analysis it appears to mean that the one overriding reality of modern societies, shaped and driven by the capitalist mode of production, can only be properly explained on the basis of one particular interpretation of the historical development of the forces at work. Once the facts of the matter are uncovered, their truth-value can be confirmed by verifying the consequences or predictions that flow from them.

Miguez quite frequently appeals to the scientific character of the Marxist approach to investigating the nature of historical forces. He contrasts it to idealistic methods of interpretation (such as sociological functionalism) that obscure, rather than expose, the real situation. However, he does not engage much in a discussion of the epistemological assumptions that undergird the use of the term or the debates that continue to exist in the philosophy of science concerning scientific methodology.[12] He rather takes for granted the application of 'scientific' to the Marxist conceptual tools of analysis and the hypotheses that these engender about the future shape of human society. However, he does tend to put the word scientific in brackets, indicating perhaps that there is some controversy over its

---

[12] These are amply portrayed in Martin Curd and J.A. Cover, *Philosophy of Science: The Central Issues* (New York: W.W. Norton, 1998); Alexander Bird, *Philosophy of Science* (London: Routledge, 1998); James Ladyman, *Understanding Philosophy of Science* (London: Routledge, 2002); Alex Rosenberg, *Philosophy of Science: A Contemporary Introduction* (New York: Routledge, 2000).

use in the context of the social sciences.[13] I will return to this discussion further on.

Marxist beliefs

Miguez is well aware of just how controversial for a Christian is the use of Marxist categories to interpret social movements in history. Even more, he understands, within the largely conservative culture of Latin-American Protestantism, the contentious nature of even mentioning language associated with Communism. Thus, when given the opportunity,[14] he constructed a careful assessment of the strong and weak aspects of Marxism as both a particular interpretation of humanity's alienation and a revolutionary theory pointing to how this will be overcome.

First and foremost Miguez was a Christian and a trained theologian.[15] As we will see later, his view of Marxism always passed through the grid of his prior commitment to the good news of Jesus Christ. However, he emphasises the point that the acceptance of certain conclusions arising from a Marxist explanation of history is in no way incompatible with his faith. At the same time, he decisively rejected aspects of the total Marxist world-view because of their dubious philosophical heritage and unscientific speculation. Thus, in reviewing Marx's critique of religion, he says:

'Marx's critique of religion ought to be only "functional", in the sense that it is at most an abstraction of the empirical evidence of how religion has functioned and functions today. As such, atheism cannot be a necessary foundation or postulate of historical materialism. But quite clearly this is not so. Marx seems to claim for his analysis of religion an almost "metaphysical" status.'[16]

So, for Miguez, Marx's exposure of the real workings of the capitalist system of production has to be accepted, in so far as it is true to the reality on which he is commentating. In an attempt to clarify how Christians

---

[13] In relation to Marxism, the philosopher Roy Bhaskar explores briefly the issues that need to be discussed, when Marxists claim that their methods of analysis are scientific; see *A Dictionary of Marxist Thought* (ed. Tom Bottomore: Oxford: Blackwell, 2nd edn, 1991), pp. 491–3.

[14] The opportunity was an invitation from Dr John Stott to deliver the London Lectures in Contemporary Christianity in 1974 on the subject of the Christian–Marxist dialogue.

[15] He says of himself, 'This author is neither a politician nor a sociologist. He is a theologian trying to discharge his political responsibility as a theologian', *Christians and Marxists*, p. 10.

[16] Miguez, *Christians and Marxists*, p. 72.

may legitimately view Marxism without compromising their belief in the truth of Jesus Christ, he argues as follows:

> We must face the multiplicity of meanings of the word 'Marxist' . . . It is possible . . . to consider Marxism exclusively as a set of analytical tools concerning economic activity and its political and social significance. Such tools make it possible to analyse capitalist society and bourgeois culture in a dynamic way and therefore to project a political strategy of change. It is even possible in this respect to receive the Marxist criticism of religion . . . as a valid instrument for understanding and criticizing bourgeois Christianity and therefore as a valuable contribution to a true renewal of the churches . . . In this respect, one may go further and say that Marxist insights, like any other scientific discovery, are now a generally available resource and, as such, it is not only legitimate for the Christian to use it, but he is morally obligated to do so *to the extent that it proves to be scientifically accurate and valuable.*[17]

In so far as the Marxist critique of capitalism is based on sound observation and correct processes of deduction, there is not much to quarrel with. Its value as an explanation rests entirely on its ability to give the best theoretical account of real human social reality. In this respect, Marx's interpretation of the productive processes within the capitalist manufacturing system – namely that they create alienation by depriving the worker of the full fruit of his labour by reserving a considerable part of the wealth created to pay for the capital provided by a non-labouring class (surplus value) – can be discussed as an empirically verifiable occurrence. In this context, one may be able to speak meaningfully of a conflict of classes. The scientific status of other aspects of the Marxist analysis, such as commodity fetishism, labour power, recurrent crises in capitalism, exploitation and reification is also dependent on conforming to empirical evidence, and is thus open to universal criteria of confirmation or refutation.

However, Marxism claims much more for its theories. What has made it a powerful force for revolutionary change is its move from theories of alienation to a programme for de-alienation, i.e. the mapping out of a path that would lead capitalist societies eventually to embrace socialism, understood as the collective ownership of both the means of production and the wealth generated throughout society by labour-power. This in turn, according to the theory, would lead on to an idealised communist society in which human beings would regain their full humanity through the abolition of private property and the division of labour in all their

---

[17] Miguez, *Christians and Marxists*, p. 121–2 (emphasis added).

forms, and in which each person would contribute to society according to their ability and draw from the common stock of material goods according to their needs. Human beings then encounter themselves as they truly are – social beings; alienation is overcome, and the kingdom of freedom arrives.

Is such a society remotely possible? Its projection into the future on the basis of a certain historical determinism – the sequential unfolding of economic and political forces – is certainly not based on empirical data that can be evaluated by testable criteria. The implications of the disjunction between a genuine analysis of present realities and the calculation of future historical processes will be taken up later. They are critical to an assessment of Christian involvement in political and social movements of change.

Liberation

During the decade of the 1970s theological reflection in Latin America mainly centred around the churches' response to a political climate that advocated liberation from social, economic and political arrangements that perpetuated the impoverishment of the majority of working people. Christians involved in ministries of solidarity with the poor began to reflect seriously, using the resources of the Christian faith, on the relationship between liberation from failed human relationships in social terms and liberation from sin and evil, understood as corruptions of an order originally created 'very good'.

The existence of sin and evil

Miguez understands evil to be the result of human beings doing things badly and getting them wrong. It is the consequence of God having made people with the capacity to choose freely what kind of life they wish to create for themselves. It is not his will to intervene every time humans make mistakes, for otherwise they would not be truly human. Like a child given a task to do, the father or mother does not aid the child's learning process by doing the job themselves: 'God never says to the person: "get out of here and I will do it myself", but invites us constantly to begin again; he gives us back the opportunity to make corrections and do (the task) again.'[18]

So evil is seen in the context of the freedom that God has given human beings to be human: 'God wished to have a person that was not part of

---

[18]   Miguez, *Espacio para ser hombres*, p. 22.

himself but another. For that to happen he gave the person space. The world is the space given to people that they may be themselves.'[19]

It follows that sin is due to people's failure to be the human being they were created to be by a God whose desire is invariably their highest wellbeing. Sin is dehumanization, the destruction of the perfect master-piece that God has made. Its fundamental cause springs from the deci-sion by human beings to rebel against the way God has made the world, by rejecting the relationship of mutual love which God has established between himself and his special creation. Sin against God is the prostitu-tion of love by turning it in on oneself. The consequence is that human beings deny their true selves by denying that they are creatures before God and by repudiating the humanity of others. They no longer love others as they love themselves; but they love themselves at the expense of others. So, human beings live in a state of alienation, caused by their self-centredness, and this has repercussions in the social and economic spheres of communities.[20] Marx, it appears, has helped to uncover some of the symptoms, whilst failing to recognise the 'fundamental estrange-ment'.[21]

Another way of understanding the nature of radical evil is by exposing the reality of idolatry, about which the Bible speaks so much. Idolatry manifests itself essentially in the act of substituting the real God for one that can be managed and manipulated by human beings. We attempt to get rid of the God who is, in order to avoid costly commitment to neigh-bours, to strangers, even to enemies. In God's place we manufacture a caricature God who is indulgent of our self-absorption and self-seeking. So, we create a God who does not interfere in our lives, who does not hold us to account according to his demands of justice and love, but can be turned to in times of crisis to give us comfort and healing. This 'God', says Miguez, is a 'God-of-the gaps', for he is utilised as a kind of tran-quiliser at deeply troubling moments of life; for the rest of the time he is ignored, or held at arm's length by elaborate rituals or twisted moral reasoning.

Being set free

To know the fundamental cause and consequences of radical evil is the first step in overcoming the alienation. If the overarching problem with humankind is the distortion of God's creation-plan of love, which has

[19] Miguez, *Espacio para ser hombres*, p. 23.
[20] Miguez, *Espacio para ser hombres*, pp. 40–42.
[21] Miguez, *Christians and Marxists*, p. 109.

severely damaged its humanness, then the remedy has to be to return to the source of that love and allow it to mould all human relationships. This requires a fundamental re-orientation of the human mind and will to set them on a new path of fellowship with God and of selfless service to others.

To know God is to be committed to bringing about a world that protects and seeks justice for those who are abused and damaged by the intrinsically inequitable social arrangements spawned by present economic relations and manipulated by powerful self-interests: 'To know God is equivalent to coming actively to grips with God's concrete demands and actions. Knowing God is being involved in his invitations, commands, judgements . . . We can say that there is no relation to God outside a covenant, an active engagement, the specific content of which is defined by God himself in his own action which seals and ratifies the covenant.'[22]

The terms of the covenant are made plain in the law, and by the prophets speaking on behalf of God's self-revelation. They are made operative in the lives of ordinary humans by the new covenant ratified in the self-sacrifice of God himself to remove all facets of human self-alienation.

In his ministry Jesus sets people free to begin their lives again: 'What he does is take people, who are imprisoned, captive, and set them on their way in the direction of the fullness of life: of health, integration into the community, of their calling . . . in the direction of the kingdom of God which is the fullness of humanity and the world.'[23]

Liberation is a process through which 'a "new man" must emerge, a man shaped by solidarity and creativity over against the individualistic, distorted humanity of the present system.'[24] This process has to incorporate the structures that shape society, for human beings are enmeshed in communal relationships which affect the possibility of their living truly human lives. The liberation, therefore, which Christ brings, has both an inner and an outer dimension. The full liberation of human beings is never effective until both aspects are complete.

Now for Miguez and others immersed in the struggles of 'peasants, workers and students' for a different kind of society, this process of liberation is already underway in Latin America. It was heading in a very specific direction – 'the transformation of Latin American society, through revolutionary change, in the direction of a socialist society'.[25] So liberation

---

[22] Miguez, *Christians and Marxists*, p. 38.
[23] Miguez, *Espacio para ser hombres*, p. 43.
[24] Miguez, *Revolutionary Theology*, p. 40.
[25] Miguez, *Revolutionary Theology*, p. xx

implies the overthrow of the present economic and political system which is organised to favour a small elite by maintaining them in power to the exclusion of the vast majority of the population. It means the expropriation of the wealth of the oligarchic class, so that it can be made to work for the benefit of the hitherto abandoned classes. In Miguez's thinking it is essential that the recovery of love between people and the promotion of justice in their relationships is not left at the level of a theoretical abstraction but is made efficacious through making right the central mechanisms of society. In the next sections we will see how he builds an adequate bridge between commitment to the mission of Christ and to the present situation of real people within societies organised along divisive social lines.

Doing Theology

Christian theological reflection is related to two given realities: God's initiative in revealing his nature and purposes for the world he has created and the concrete context in which he has called the community of Jesus, the Christ, to share in his mission. It has taken many different forms down the ages. The form that it takes in any historical moment will depend on the purpose for which it is undertaken and the situation to which theological thinkers relate. For Miguez, the reality of the poor is the unconditional starting point, for it is the supreme symptom of a dysfunctional human society. Commitment to the struggle to overcome this situation is an absolute ethical demand in the light of what God has shown about himself in concrete historical circumstances.

The double location

Miguez refers to these two realities – the record of God's speaking and acting in a specific history through specially chosen messengers and contemporary history – as a double location. On the one hand, there is an epistemological commitment to the truth about God revealed once for all in climactic events in the history of Israel, Jesus Christ and the first Christian communities. On the other hand, there is a social commitment to the truth about the dynamic workings of current historical processes. Both have to be articulated according to the integrity of their own subject matter. Theology is not a 'sanctified sociology'; nor is sociology subordinate to theology. As we have already seen, social analysis gives us grounds for seeing the workings of human societies as they really are. Theological reflection gives us grounds for choosing to act in a particular way in response to what has been revealed through both locations:

In Latin America . . . we have found it necessary to relate our theology to a commitment to the struggle for liberation, a struggle that has a predominantly social and political dimension; we have therefore found it necessary to take very seriously a socioanalytical mediation for theological thinking. *But we intend to do theology*, not sociology or politics. Moreover, we believe that theological reflection, while it is related to the political praxis of Christians, is not a mere reflection of that praxis . . . We believe that the questions which emerge in the praxis of liberation must be articulated and dealt with within theology's sphere of competence and using the tools of theological thinking.[26]

A hermeneutical key

Just as analysis of a social reality requires a proven methodological mediation, so the self-revelation of the God of creation also needs to be understood in the light of a particular mediation. This is normally referred to as a hermeneutical key. In the case of Miguez's theological reflection different ones have been suggested. In a lengthy discussion of Miguez's theological method, Paul Davies highlights effectiveness as a key to Miguez's thinking.[27] The point of departure for theological reflection has to be missionary obedience and its aim is missionary effectiveness. By the latter Miguez means the role that Christian people and communities have to play in broken societies if they are going to be genuine agents of change. The efficacy of the church's involvement in society is measured by its ability to contribute to the implementation of a new vision of human relations, in which the self-centred exploitation of the many by the few will be eliminated. The task of theology is to hold the church to account by assessing its faithfulness to the creation of a world in which self-giving love ultimately triumphs.

The kingdom of God
The theme of God's kingdom features prominently in Miguez's understanding of theology as both a task and a gift. He emphasises the continuity of human history by using kingdom terminology to link together the original creation and the new creation. In creating the world with its special human inhabitants, God's purpose was to work in partnership with his image-bearers to continue and complete his creative work. Work, therefore, is a key component of what it means to be human:

Whether one deals with the creation stories, with the law, or with the prophetic message, there seems to be in the Bible no relation of man to himself, to his

---

[26] Miguez, *Christian Political Ethics*, p. 43 (emphasis original).
[27] See Davies, *Faith Seeking Effectiveness*, pp. 39–79.

neighbour, or even to God which is not mediated in terms of man's work. His dignity is located in his mission to subdue and cultivate the world. His worship is related to the fulfilment of a law in which the whole realm of his economic and political activity is taken up.[28]

Human beings, however, soon decided to abandon the partnership with God and attempted to launch out on their own. In turning to their own wisdom and seeking to create a world without reference to the Creator they produced an environment not only of grandeur and beauty but of ugliness, destruction and conflict. The core message of the Christian faith is that God did not abandon them to the dire consequences of their choice to reject his sovereign right to rule over his domain. He inaugurated a history that would lead to the establishment of a new creation in which his righteousness would be gladly accepted and put into practice. The kingdom is this new creation:

> The concept of the kingdom of God . . . is concerned with a transformed humanity in a renewed earth. It is the vision of a world in which the creative purpose of God has been finally fulfilled: where hunger, poverty, injustice, oppression, deceit, and finally illness and death itself have been definitively banished. It is the vision of a world from which evil has been uprooted for ever; where God's love is 'all and in all'; where the quality of human life given in Jesus Christ has penetrated the whole of our humanity and, therefore where God's plan to make a humanity that, in solidarity, expresses love in a harmonious world that it works, cultivates and makes fruitful, has been fulfilled.[29]

The kingdom of God, therefore, neither negates the world nor human creative work within it. On the contrary all that is good and beautiful, right and true, in human endeavour will find its appointed place in God's final recreation. In a penetrating study of the relationship of human history to the final reordering of creation, Miguez avoids both a dualistic and a monistic interpretation. The dualistic version asserts that human history is permanently under God's judgement; that it is basically empty of meaning and its achievements worthless. The monistic version asserts that God's specific action in Jesus Christ, to rescue humanity from the destructive consequences of its arrogant desire for complete independence from its Creator, is not foundational to the liberating project, but merely a kind of metaphor or example to inspire human beings to struggle themselves to create a new humanity. This latter uses the language of

[28] Miguez, *Revolutionary Theology*, p. 109.
[29] Miguez, *Espacio para ser hombres*, p. 61.

'love', 'liberation' and 'the new man' but without measuring its content by the specific historical facts of the life, death and resurrection of Jesus.[30] The concepts then can float away from their historical anchor and be filled with the ideological or rhetorical content of the moment. History then becomes God.[31]

The clue to avoiding the two misinterpretations is to view the kingdom of God not as a denial of history, but 'the elimination of its corruptibility, its frustrations, weaknesses, ambiguity – more deeply, its sin – in order to bring to full realization the true meaning of the communal life of man'. Through God's judgement 'which divides, excludes, and cleanses ("burns") that which does not belong in the new age', the kingdom 'redeems, transforms and perfects the "corporality" of history and the dynamics of love that has operated within it'.[32] Miguez is fond of using the phrase 'there is no love that is lost in this world'.[33] In other words, every action that reflects the gift of divine love will endure and be recognised and taken up in the coming kingdom, which has already begun to take shape in the present.

Renewing the earth

Another way of viewing this key hermeneutical tool for evaluating the relationship between ordinary history and salvation-history is through the image of creation renewed. There are several advantages of seeing God's mission in this way. First, the whole cosmos is part of God's salvific work. It is not restricted to an individual's spiritual relationship to God. Second, it takes seriously what some theologians have called the cultural mandate, given in Genesis 1 – 2, to take responsibility for the wellbeing of the whole of creation; work to sustain life and art to enhance and beautify it are essential parts of what it means to be human. Third, it sees human history from creation to the final consummation as one seamless

---

[30] The importance of recovering a genuinely liberating Jesus Christ, interpreted historically within the apostolic tradition, is manifested in the context of the alienating images of Jesus encountered in the history of Latin-American Christianity – the Christ of the conqueror (of the political masters) and of the conquered (of the suffering people, alienated and defeated); see José Miguez Bonino, '¿Quien es Jesucristo hoy en America Latina?' ('Who is Jesus Christ Today in Latin América?') in *Jesus: Ni Vencido Ni Monarca Celestial (Jesus: Neither Defeated Nor Celestial Monarch)*, pp. 9–17; also Samuel Escobar, *En Busca de Cristo en America Latina (In Search of Christ in Latin America)* (Buenos Aires: Ediciones Kairos, 2012), *passim*.

[31] See Miguez, *Revolutionary Theology*, pp. 138–9.

[32] Miguez, *Revolutionary Theology*, p. 142.

[33] Miguez, *Espacio para ser hombres*, p. 58.

whole, interrupted by sin and its destructive power, but not fundamentally pushed in a different direction. This, I believe, is the driving motif of Miguez's theological undertaking. 'How God's action in history . . . is understood and how human action relates to it is the main thrust of his reflections.'[34]

The Church's Mission

Whilst, on the one hand, Miguez relativised the absolutely central role of the church in the mission of God, he was also passionately committed to the church as a body that had been given by God a special mandate in the world. The church is subordinate to God's rule, which extends beyond its boundaries; it cannot be identified with God's kingdom. The liberating work of the Spirit occurs outside, as well as inside, the community called to belong to Jesus Christ. As we have seen, in Miguez's understanding of the unity of human history, wherever in personal and social relationships genuine love and justice are displayed, there is the Spirit of God; there the rule of Christ is taking effect, even though it may not be recognised as such.

Nevertheless, the church is an institution with a long history that exists because its supreme head has commissioned it to make disciples of all nations, by bearing witness to him to the ends of the earth. It has a double responsibility. First, it has to appraise its past history, in order to discern where it has succeeded and where failed in its faithfulness to its high calling. This is particularly important in Latin America where the church has had such a great influence and power in society, and continues to do so. Second, it needs to be able to read the signs of the times, so that it can situate its mission within the urgent needs of the moment and establish its priorities.

If its primary vocation is to aid a process of humanization, i.e. to restore human beings in community to an original nobility, in which the needs of all become the responsibility of all, then it must be part of that body of people who have given themselves to overcoming every destructive force in society and creation: 'Our human vocation is to "humanise" – to put at the service of the community in dedicated love every new possibility that opens up in the dominion and responsible use of the world.'[35]

This is not a matter of right-sounding words; to fulfil the aspiration demands very specific commitments:

---

[34] Davies, *Faith Seeking Effectiveness*, p. 106.
[35] Miguez, *Espacio para ser hombres*, p. 44.

We have to say that every struggle against oppression and injustice has a future. Therefore the struggle against capitalist greed or against bureaucratic and centralizing dehumanization, the substitution of an economy at the service of humans in the place of monopolies and multinationals, the efforts to preserve creation from the destruction and waste of a consumer-society, the efforts to organise human communities politically in real equality . . . is part of human service to Jesus Christ . . . The struggle for the liberation of women from being treated as a thing, one more product of our society, is part of a service to Jesus Christ . . . All this is to fight against sin and thus part of creating the kingdom of God.[36]

The mission of the Christian community has a profound political dimension, once one understands that politics 'is the effort to take back the world for humanity, to free it from the power of irrationality and selfishness . . . and return it to its purpose – to serve the enrichment and fullness of the [whole] human community. This is a fundamental Christian obligation. One cannot be a Christian without accepting it, for one cannot be a person without carrying it out.'[37]

It may be asked whether the Christian has anything distinctive to offer to the cause of liberation. The answer might go in two directions. First, the Christian community is called to be a model of the new creation in its inner life and in its presence in society. Paul Davies gives a useful summary of Miguez's thinking in this matter:

Miguez believes that God works directly in the world to re-establish the Kingdom of God; the church is not the exclusive mediator of God's mission . . . However, he does not want to see the church's role completely relativized. The church is more than just a signpost towards the kingdom of God . . . The church's role is to represent the world giving both a model to the world and enabling the world to become what God originally meant the world to be . . . .He states that the life of the church serves as a model of the quality of fellowship desired by God for the world.[38]

Second, it offers to the world a unique source of motivation and dynamism in the struggle for change – that of unconditional love. Those who love to the highest degree are the ones who know most assuredly that they are loved. Just as, in biblical terms, there is no love for God where love of the neighbour is absent, so there is no sustainable love for the

---

[36] Miguez, *Espacio para ser hombres*, pp. 63–4.
[37] Miguez, *Espacio para ser hombres*, p. 47.
[38] Davies, *Faith Seeking Effectiveness*, p. 140.

neighbour without the empowering love of God filling and taking control of the whole life of a person.

The nature of love is grounded ultimately in the being of God: God is love, pure and simple. 'There is no other reality "behind" or "beyond" the self-assertion that God has given of himself in his own action and Word'[39] that can set the standard for the meaning of love. This love is ontologically ultimate, but it is not abstract. It is manifest 'in the history of God's self-revelation. He is as he has acted – in creation, in Jesus Christ, in the power of his Spirit.'[40] Therefore the love that flows from God into the lives of those who recognise him as Lord and saviour has to be historically concrete and engaged: 'When we speak of love we do not refer to a mere feeling, to an emotion, but to the concrete and effective dedication to the real need of the other.'[41]

It follows that the exhibition of love cannot remain at the abstract level of intention, but requires the choice of a political and economic strategy that will make a difference in meeting those real needs. So love operates in an alienated world by establishing justice, even though this may involve conflict with the entrenched privileges of a social elite: 'Judgment, therefore, is the unavoidable shadow of love as it meets human arrogance and inhumanity. And the seriousness of this judgment is such that it becomes final, ultimate . . . (Matt. 25:41–42,45).'[42]

The potentially conflictual nature of love is manifest often in the life of Jesus:

> The Gospels do not admit an interpretation of Jesus' love for all men as tolerance, compromise, or acceptance of evil or as good-natured, easygoing bonhomie. Did he not love the scribes and pharisees whom he violently and consistently criticized and condemned? Did he not love Herod . . . [and] the rich young ruler? The examples can be multiplied. Either Jesus excluded from his love a very significant number and, what is more important, whole groups of people, or love must be interpreted in such a way that it may include condemnation, criticism, resistance and rejection.[43]

Nevertheless, it is also a characteristic of the Christian understanding of love that it renounces the hatred and bitterness that are so easily engendered by the intensity of a struggle against an implacable enemy. Unless

[39] Miguez, *Christians and Marxists*, p. 105.
[40] Miguez, *Christians and Marxists*, p. 105.
[41] Miguez, *Espacio para ser hombres*, p. 50.
[42] Miguez, *Christians and Marxists*, p. 112.
[43] Miguez, *Revolutionary Theology*, pp. 121–2.

genuine concern for the humanity of others is maintained, even when they oppose all measures to change permanently the living conditions of the victims of injustice, the revolutionary struggle will probably end up by being even more dehumanizing than the regime it seeks to supplant: 'If hatred of the enemy is subordinated to love for the brother and sister, then the struggle is made "functional", and the possibility of affirming the humanity of the enemy during and after the struggle remains open. This is the kind of ethics of liberation which many – Christians and non-Christians – are trying to develop within the project of liberation.'[44]

In this context, Miguez criticises Marxism for its inadequate humanism. Although it may be argued that Marxism offers a verifiable and efficacious way of articulating love historically in the establishment of justice, it is devoid of a prior engagement with love in its eternal, transcendent origin:

> The Christian alliance with Marxist socialism is therefore always an uneasy alliance, in which the fundamental divergence about the source and power of solidary love results in constant questioning in the realm of practice. The source of this criticism is not a rejection of Marxism as social theory but a radical questioning of the philosophical foundation of its ethos – the rejection of the Triune God of love.[45]

There is, therefore, a radical disjunction between Marxist and Christian views of the reality of humanness. For the former, humans are the highest possible form of being; their self-consciousness is the highest divinity. Humans owe to themselves their social, emotional and intellectual existence. Anything else is alienation. For the latter, 'man is constituted as man in a relationship to God and the neighbour which is not "added" to his autonomy *but belongs to his very existence as human*. Love is not a product of man, but man a product of love.'[46]

The Church in the Struggle for Liberation

The church can only be understood in relationship to its missionary obedience. There is, therefore, no ontological being of the church prior to its engagement in the *missio Dei*. It is defined by its calling to a certain kind of praxis. In this sense, the church gradually assumes its identity in the course of its becoming conformed to the reality of God's new order. Its

---

[44] Miguez, *Christian Political Ethics*, p. 113.
[45] Miguez, *Christians and Marxists*, p. 116.
[46] Miguez, *Christians and Marxists*, p. 117 (emphasis added).

being is established eschatologically as a pilgrim people in the fulfilling of its mission to proclaim the good news of the kingdom to the poor.

The reference-point for the true church is not, therefore, to be sought for in some essential being given by its structures, which then have to be manifested in a particular way in each subsequent generation. It does not have an eternal form, which has to be reflected in a particular kind of organization. There is not one, indispensable way of ordering its life. The church has gone seriously wrong in concentrating so much on the exactness of its internal arrangements. These questions have bedevilled attempts at finding ways of uniting different expressions of church.

Miguez is clear that the faithfulness of the church to its nature as church can only be measured by its dedication to the task to which it has been called by its head, Jesus Christ, in the power of the Holy Spirit. Thus the church is the fellowship of those who embrace the historical task of making real God's sovereign rule: 'Miguez . . . [insists] that the very nature of the church is to be found in its attitude and action towards the issues of poverty, injustice and oppression and its identification with the poor.'[47]

The struggle for the true church

This fresh understanding of the church's constitution, being found in its option for a particular praxis as a means of doing God's will in the world, leads Miguez to stress the necessity of struggling for the true church. This has two crucial dimensions. On the one hand, its is a struggle *against* the church in so far as the church is not engaged in working for a transformation of present conditions of existence on behalf of the dispossessed and victimised. In Latin America this refers to all ecclesial bodies who are content to maintain a status quo that, in their opinion, allows the maximum amount of freedom to proclaim a gospel of individual forgiveness and reconciliation without fear of restrictions and sanctions. These are the bodies that would claim that the church has no business to be engaged in political controversies; its mission, basically, is to reproduce itself and hope that enough converts will eventually make a significant impact on society for good by the quality of their changed lives.

On the other hand, Miguez is not content with the implicit or explicit ecclesiology of some of the leading theologians of liberation. They have tended to interpret the boundaries of the church in a way that would include all 'people of good will', precisely those who embrace the praxis of liberation of the poor, though without acknowledging that this has

[47] Davies, *Faith Seeking Effectiveness*, p. 119.

any relationship to a new world that God is creating. There are those theologians inclined to apply the notion of 'anonymous Christians'[48] to such people. Miguez, however, disassociates himself from this line of reasoning. He insists that, despite the often appalling witness given by churches to the reality of God's kingdom, the church is a distinguishable community with a specific calling that cannot be reduced to tactical support for an otherwise secular struggle for the liberation of the poor:

> When the cause of Jesus Christ (and consequently the Church in any missionary understanding of it) is totally and without rest equated with the cause of social and political revolution, either the Church and Jesus Christ are made redundant or the political and social revolution is clothed in a sacred or semi-sacred gown. Non-believing revolutionaries are then baptized as 'latent', 'crypto', 'potential', or 'unknowing' Christians, a new form of Christian paternalism which elicits a quite justified rejection on their part.[49]

So, where is the church to be identified? Miguez gives a tentative answer, using the concepts of 'the covenant of creation' and 'the covenant of redemption'. The church is the concrete embodiment of God's will to restore the whole set of broken relationships which have so damaged his handiwork. Redemption (salvation from the guilt, power and consequences of sin) involves the reordering of all these relationships (to fellow human beings, to nature and to God) in order that human beings may be 'put back again on the road to [their] self-realization' as 'partners in the covenant of creation'.[50] The reordering cannot happen apart from the act of salvation that Jesus Christ has accomplished historically, once-for-all. The church is the only body that believes that this statement is true and has profound consequences for the whole of human existence:

> The Church is itself when it witnesses to God's saving activity in Jesus Christ, that is, when it makes clear God's renewed authorization, commandment, and liberation to man to be human, to create his own history and culture, to love and transform the world, to claim and exercise the glorious freedom of the children of God. The Church's distinct – and certainly scandalous – claim is that the fullness of this humanity is given in the explicit, faithful, and grateful acknowledgement of Jesus Christ.[51]

---

[48] The phrase was first made into a theological catchword by the Swiss theologian Karl Rahner in his *Schriften zur Theologie* (Zurich, 1957) with reference to non-conscious believers in Christ who belonged to other faith traditions.

[49] Miguez, *Revolutionary Theology*, p. 163.

[50] Miguez, *Revolutionary Theology*, p. 165.

[51] Miguez, *Revolutionary Theology*, p. 167.

Miguez finishes his discussion by suggesting that the term 'church' can and should be used of a number of different communities that are 'historical and time-bound "condensations" of the struggle to confess Jesus Christ significantly throughout history'.[52] In other words, the true church is to be located wherever groups of Christians are committed to following the mission of God in the way of the historical Christ, so that human beings (oppressed and oppressors) may be restored again to the full humanity they have lost in refusing to realise their human destiny as planned by God in reciprocal unconditional love for one another: 'Faith in Christ is not, therefore, a step beyond humanity but toward it. "We are not men in order to be Christians, but Christians in order to be men." '[53]

Assessment

In this final section, I would like to offer a brief, personal account of Miguez's thinking. I would reiterate that I have deliberately chosen to consider only one period of his Christian, theological pilgrimage. This is not a judgement, therefore, on his thinking as a whole. To attempt such a task would be impossible in the confines of one chapter. Miguez lived another thirty years after this period, and naturally continued to reflect and write.[54] Others have given a fuller picture of Miguez's thinking up to and including the new millennium. Having stated this caveat, it would also be true to say that there is little indication that Miguez ever fundamentally reconsidered his theological and practical commitments, which were so creatively honed in the period under review.

Strengths

I would highlight three aspects of Miguez's considerable contribution to a creative theological reflection on the relationship of the church to the world.

---

[52] Miguez, *Revolutionary Theology*, p. 173.

[53] Miguez, *Revolutionary Theology*, p. 167. The quote comes from the Dutch theologian Lambert Schuurman.

[54] The most significant writings of this later period are: *Faces of Latin American Protestantism* (Grand Rapids, MI: Eerdmans, 1997) (Spanish original, 1995); *Poder del Evangelio y poder politico* (Buenos Aires: Editorial Kairos, 1999); 'The Protestant Churches in Latin America in the New Millenium' in *Faith in the Millenium* (ed. Stanley E. Porter, Michael A. Hayes and David Tombs; Sheffield: Sheffield Academic Press, 2001); 'Latin America' in *An Introduction to Third World Theologies* (ed. John Parratt, Cambridge: CUP, 2004).

Integration

Miguez achieved a remarkable synthesis in grappling with the difficult problem of combining the biblical witness to God's activity in the world to make concrete his gift of salvation ('salvation-history') and the normal history of human beings engaged in the routine tasks of everyday life. He brought together human history as a reflection of the creation mandate to work, to raise families, to create art and to enjoy the fruit of labour and the history of his special intervention in the life of Israel, Jesus Christ and the church, to create a new community out of a humanity that has lost its way. Miguez has done this by using two complementary images that reunite the original intention of God's perfect creation with the eschatological promise of a new creation: the kingdom of God and humanization.

The kingdom of God is rightly considered to be a principal key to understanding the whole plan and purpose of God. It is the perfect rule of God over his property. It is the intricate design that God has laid down for the full flourishing of his creation. It has, therefore, unmistakeably to do with the whole of life. It is also the anticipation of a full restoration of human relationships within a transformed nature, in which unconditional love for God and the other triumphs over selfishness, greed, hatred and violence. The kingdom of God, therefore, represents both creation as it is intended to be and creation as it will be, when all sin has been eliminated. It is the coming of a whole new order of social arrangements, when the old order of the abuse of power is finally destroyed (1 Cor. 1:20; 2:6). The kingdom, therefore, recapitulates everything in creation that is good, beautiful and true, whilst pointing to the necessary and sufficient liberation from the evil that has pervaded the innermost life of human beings, achieved by the self-sacrifice of the Son of God.

In the idea of God's kingdom, biblically understood, two opposite erroneous views are eliminated. The one sees the life of the church as radically separate from the life of the world, the latter being consigned in its entirety to the scrapheap of history. The other sees little point in emphasizing the particular testimony of the church within the world, since the secular realm is the place where human history is restored. The first view perceives a sharp discontinuity between creation and recreation, because sin and evil has pervaded every aspect of life to its core; the second view considers the two as coextensive, as the failings of humanity will be eliminated in the course of human endeavour itself. Miguez has successfully avoided both distortions of reality.

Humanization, which we have already considered in the context of the secularizing theology of the Western world, is dealt with more adequately in Miguez's thought. Constantly he portrays God's mission in the world in terms of what one might call the re-humanization of people: 'Christ has made it possible for humanity, once again to take up its role as God's partner in creation within those relationships that God originally established. Christ did this through the creation of a new humanity that all people can enter through faith in Christ.'[55]

The purpose of God's acts of liberation is to restore human beings to the fullness of their humanity, measured ultimately by the life and witness of Jesus Christ, the last Adam (1 Cor. 15:45):

> What Jesus Christ puts in this world is a new humanity and a new form of being human. And this new humanity in Jesus Christ does not last or penetrate human history primarily through laws and institutions (that without doubt exist and have value) but rather through a message that ceaselessly engenders new life, and through a community of people 'reborn' and 'resurrected' to a new life, 'redeemed' (that is liberated), and renewed (with a new 'mind' – a totally, radically changed orientation).[56]

Being and doing

Miguez rightly rejoins thought and practice in considering how we may know the truth about reality. These had tended to be separated by the Western tradition of Cartesian dualism that placed the sense of identity in the thinking subject, somewhat divorced from the material world. Reality, however, is not known by contemplating it alone; it is perceived and understood by active experience of the manifold conditions of life. For Miguez this implies commitment to a cause and the taking of risks; above all it indicates the priority of obedience over theoretical knowledge: 'Its [God's word] truth does not consist in some correspondence to an idea but in its efficacy in carrying out God's promise or fulfilling his judgment. Correspondingly, what is required of Israel is not an ethical inference but an obedient participation – whether in action or in suffering – in God's active righteousness and mercy.'[57]

So knowing the truth is a fruitless exercise unless accompanied by doing the truth: 'God is unknown unless man participates in his concrete life through love.'[58]

Liberation thinking has attempted to restore a proper balance between theory and practice. Nevertheless, I will argue below that it tends to slide into an illegitimate, pragmatic notion of truth.

---

[55] Davies, *Faith Seeking Effectiveness*, p. 127.
[56] Miguez, *Ama y haz lo que quieras*, pp. 26–7.
[57] Miguez, *Revolutionary Theology*, p. 89.
[58] Miguez, *Revolutionary Theology*, p. 90.

Missionary theology

Miguez endorses the common perception that Latin-American liberation theology is not intent on raising 'a new theological subject, but a new way of doing theology'.[59] According to Paul Davies, the framework for the whole of Miguez's theology is not the attempt 'to achieve an intellectual understanding of reality, but rather effectiveness in changing reality'.[60] He goes on to interpret Miguez as elaborating a theological methodology which will accompany the church in its mission to change the world. Theology has to be about the *missio Dei*, for God is only revealed as an active subject in the world he has created and redeemed, sustains and transforms. God is not a static, timeless, a-pathetic (immune to suffering), remote being who is best known by those who separate themselves from the world to meditate on an abstract nature. Theology presupposes a community already actively engaged in bringing healing to a broken world, using all the intellectual resources of divine revelation and its historical interpretation to be more effective in its various callings: 'One could précis Marx's eleventh thesis on Feuerbach by saying: "it is not the responsibility of theology to understand the world but rather to change it".'[61]

Weaknesses

Theory and practice

The relationship between belief and action is similar to the question about the chicken and the egg: which comes first? It is undoubtedly a matter of observation that people's theoretical commitments are made within a particular society and culture at a particular time. Beliefs are shaped, and to a certain degree determined, by factors that arise from the circumstances of life. In reflecting upon the adequacy of one's commitments, one's position in society has to be carefully considered for the way in which it may have fashioned unconscious, implicit loyalties to certain belief systems. This is true, not only of individuals, but also of the church. The church is an institution replete with historical practices that have arisen out of centuries of traditional views inherited from the past. Just because it makes truth claims for itself and its message, it is not exempt from the suspicion that its stance on a number of issues is derived from the influence of questionable ideologies.

These general points are admitted by critical historical analysis. However, liberation theologians sometimes seem to slip into a kind of

---

[59] Miguez, *Revolutionary Theology*, p. 62.
[60] Davies, *Faith Seeking Effectiveness*, p. 1.
[61] Davies, *Faith Seeking Effectiveness*, p. 39.

pragmatic determinism that makes committed action into the sole criterion of truth and right. Miguez appears to endorse the position of Assmann and Gutierrez when he states that 'they are saying, in fact, that there is no truth outside or beyond the concrete historical events in which men are involved as agents. There is, therefore, no knowledge except in action itself, in the process of transforming the world through participation in history.'[62]

At one level, this statement is self-explanatory. Truth is believed and lived by human beings embedded in the material conditions of life. It is inevitably related to real historical circumstances. At another level, however, it is profoundly misleading. It is clearly impossible for praxis somehow to precede belief, for praxis (unless it is completely mindless – induced, perhaps, by drugs or drunkenness) is fuelled by what we believe. We engage in an activity, presumably because we think it is good to do so (through a sense of duty or because it gives us pleasure). But the notion of the right thing to do depends on a theoretical articulation of good and right. Thus, to take a preferential option for the poor by struggling for the end of their situation of oppression implies that there is a good reason for committing oneself to changing the situation. The reason does not arise purely out of contemplating or experiencing their lot in life, it has to be justified by reference to a transcendent conviction that this situation is wrong. In other words, the stark analysis of a reality cannot prescribe a course of action; what *ought* to be done does not follow inescapably from what is the case.

The priority of ethical values, which are used as axioms to be justified or refuted in themselves, over practical commitment seems to be accepted by Miguez in his appeal to the hermeneutic mediation of the biblical revelation of God in Jesus Christ. In his discussion of re-humanization, he clearly is already adopting a theoretical scheme (which undoubtedly has to be embedded in real-life circumstances) to understand what it means to be fully human. He quarrels with Marxists at this point for their inadequate conceptualization of humanness, their distorted or limited humanism. The discussion is based on the adequacy, or otherwise, of the source of the respective beliefs. At the very least, Miguez is ambiguous in his appropriation of theories of knowledge. I suspect that, although the chicken-and-egg conundrum cannot easily be solved, there is a danger here of putting the cart before the horse.

The use of Marxist analysis
As I have already indicated, Miguez, along with other liberation theologians, accepts that the Marxist view of capitalist economics is the most

---

[62] Miguez, *Revolutionary Theology*, p. 88.

valid interpretation of global economic life that is available. He credits Marxism with a convincing theory that accounts most adequately for the huge disparities in wealth that have always been a feature of the capitalist system in operation. Marx's theories of class, labour-power, surplus value, accumulation, base and superstructure, alienation and exploitation, give a true account of the social processes at work in the capitalist mode of production. In this sense they are credited with the adjective 'scientific': 'Marx . . . understood the job of theory as the empirically-controlled retroduction of an adequate account of the structures producing the manifest phenomena of socio-economic life, often in opposition to their spontaneous mode of appearance.'[63] In other words, the theories exactly matched the reality on the ground (Marx opposed all forms of idealism).

In one sense, there is nothing surprising in the Marxist analysis. It simply dissects the way that capitalism functions by expropriating the surplus-value of the manufacturing process from the employees and converting it into accumulated capital to be owned by the employers. Marx saw that this process created two classes, whose interests conflicted, and which thereby set up a society divided against itself.

We may respond: so far so good. However, Marxists tend to claim far more for their theoretical position than a mere description of reality. They also lay claim to a revolutionary theory that promises a historical process that will see the end of capitalism (and, therefore, the end of the division of labour and the class system) in a communist society. There the wealth-creators will also be the wealth-owners and, therefore, their labour-power will be returned to them so that they can fulfil their nature as creative artisans. Alienation and exploitation will, in the nature of the case, be eliminated. Human beings will be free from the tyranny of extraneous powers. Marx seemed to think that this process was historically inevitable, for the inherent contradictions of the capitalist system would eventually cause it to collapse. Adopting a Hegelian dialectic schema, he presumed that the negation of the human being under capitalism would itself be negated in a communist community in which human beings recovered their humanity.

It is here that Christians, among others, should react with extreme caution, simply because the Christian faith proposes another analysis of alienation that roots it much deeper in the human self than Marx, or his followers, could ever concede.[64] His vision of the future is utopian, in

---

[63] Bhaskar, *Dictionary of Marxist Thought*, p. 491.

[64] 'There are two interrelated questions . . . which need to be treated separately: they are the questions of the rootedness of alienation and its consequences or extension. On the answer to these questions will largely depend our evaluation of every project for liberation.' Kirk, *Liberation Theology*, p. 171.

the sense that it is a projection of a new form of society in radical discontinuity with the present. Although Marx disassociated himself strongly from a variety of utopian socialisms, by his claim to have uncovered the laws that govern social history, in fact, no such laws exist. If they did, then the prediction of a certain future pattern of events would surely by now have been corroborated.[65] One hundred and fifty years after Marx's most incisive writings, the world is probably further away from the vision of a communist society than when he wrote. This being the case, Miguez's faith in the power and accuracy of Marxist analysis should be modified. Of course, it is easy with hindsight to see the somewhat romantic optimism being engendered within certain quarters in Latin America during the decade of the 1970s. The Christians for Socialism movement was powerful in its exposure of the intrinsic failings of a free-market economy, geared always to enrich the already wealthy (whether individuals or nations). They were right ethically to deplore the oppressive nature of unaccountable, techno-military governments, using the excuse of a war against Communism to repress brutally the aspirations of the people. However, these attitudes were a long way from having any concrete plan for the introduction of a non-absolutist socialist system. When challenged to state how, within the political reality of the time, a socialist regime could be introduced and could flourish, they were always vague and equivocal.

This is surprising in the case of Miguez, given his quite severe criticism of Marxism for its lack of realism concerning the true state of the human condition: 'The Marxist view of the human problem is insufficient – and to that extent misleading – because it does not take seriously enough the depth of man's alienation and consequently of the problems of power, of man's self-interest, of the intractability of human relationships.'[66]

He castigates orthodox Marxism for its unscientific adoption of an all-embracing philosophical materialism that cannot explain the origin of private property, commodity fetishism and class oppression. He accuses it of an idealistic belief in progress, which has no concrete basis in the actual development of the forces of production. One might say that the logic of the Marxist dialectical view of history is a revolutionary fervour built on eschatological day-dreaming! One cannot help but think that Latin-American liberationists bought into the fervour of the time, without an adequate theological critique, built on a profoundly different anthropology from that assumed by Marxism. Marxism cannot provide a convincing reason why the dialectic of history (the negation of the negation) has to end up

---

[65] The alternative, presumably, is an indefinitely suspended eschatology.

[66] Miguez, *Christians and Marxists*, p. 98.

in an ideal communist society. Is it not just as likely (more likely given the Christian view of the corruption of power) to end up in Stalinism? The former prediction is no more than pure speculation, which has turned out to be a mirage in the desert. It has been 'scientifically' disproved by the events of history.[67]

If Marxism is basically right in its description and analysis of present global capitalism, but wrong in its projection of the future, where does that leave reflection on the church's mission within the tensions, conflicts, disappointments and hopes of current global political and economic life? That is far too big a subject to tackle here. Suffice it to say that the church has at its disposal a comprehensive message that is not disposed either to cynicism or to naive optimism. Its strength comes from both its realistic assessment of what God-created, but fallen, human beings are capable of; and its sure hope that the future belongs ultimately to the one and only God whose will is to make all things new.

Soteriology

As would be expected, Miguez, from his Protestant background, is adamant that the crucifixion and resurrection of Jesus Christ supremely reveal both the nature of God and his action in securing salvation for those who trust in him. Curiously, however, he appears to deny the substitutionary nature of Christ's atonement: 'Jesus Christ did not come to substitute for people but to open the way so that they could realise their human task.'[68]

He makes a distinction, in Christ's work of mediation, between the 'substitute' and 'the representative': 'The former replaces and absorbs the person and initiative of those whom he substitutes, the latter takes

---

[67] In this context, it is curious that Alistair Kee in his rather dismissive critique of liberation theology (*Marx and the Failure of Liberation Theology*; London: SCM Press, 1990) should find it surprising that Miguez accepts Marx's critique of religion as an opiate for the poor or as an ideology supporting the rich, but rejects Marx's critique of religion as the supreme example of the inversion of reality. He seems to suggest that Marx's theories have to be taken *en bloque*, or disallowed all together. By what criteria is Marx assumed to be the normative critique of religion? But then Kee appears to being using Marx for another agenda, namely to promote a secularised religion over against one that believes in the existence and activity of a trans-natural, supreme Being; see the closing pages: 278–83. He does not appear to understand why Miguez, and others, accept an active, transcendent God, although the reason is given precisely in his critique of Marx's deficient anthropology and idealistic attachment to the notion of progress.

[68] Miguez, *Espacio para ser hombres*, p. 23.

up the temporarily necessary function of doing, on behalf of the represented . . . that which he cannot do, *in order that they may arrive at the
point at which they may do it themselves.*'[69]

At one level, one can understand in a positive way what he is
saying: namely, that Christ's work of salvation does not nullify the
human person's responsibility 'to grow into the fullness of creativity,
freedom, fellowship which Jesus himself displayed and made available.'[70] On the other hand, he seems to claim that there is nothing unique
and final about Christ's work of salvation, in which he takes the place
of humanity, accomplishing an atonement for sin that human beings
are entirely incapable of achieving for themselves. Thus he says, for
example, 'In His miracles, His merciful healings, in His teaching, in
His unbreakable faithfulness to the poor and unvalued, *above all in His
giving himself on the cross and triumph over death*, He does what the real
humanity should do – He does it in representation of humanity, as its
defender and advocate.'[71]

At face value, this view of the cross and resurrection undermines the
irreplaceable act of substitution in which Jesus Christ bears the sin of
the whole world 'in his body on the cross' (1 Pet. 2:24) as a propitia-
tion (*hilasmos* – 1 John 2:2; 4:10; *hilasterion* – Rom. 3:25) before God, aptly
summed up in the final Servant Song: 'the LORD has laid on him the iniquity of us all' (Isa. 53:6). Now, Miguez hints that he does hold to a substitutionary account of the atonement in saying, 'the mediation of Christ is not
the substitution of man (although substitutive once-for-all aspects are not
excluded)'.[72] However, it is not at the centre of his thinking about salvation. Consequently, his theology of the cross may be inadequate, in that
it does not emphasise sufficiently the total incapacity of human beings to
remove God's righteous judgement on 'human ungodliness (*asebeia*) and
wickedness (*adikia*) of those who by their wickedness suppress the truth'
(Rom. 1:18).

Ultimately, a Christian's understanding of the nature of salvation/
liberation will have an effect on what is believed both about the human
condition and about the whole political process; Miguez (rightly) sees
these as defining for the church's mission in the world.

---

[69] Miguez, *Christians and Marxists*, p. 109 (emphasis original).
[70] Miguez, *Christians and Marxists*, p. 109.
[71] Miguez, *Ama y haz lo que quieras*, p. 52 (emphasis added).
[72] Miguez, *Christians and Marxists*, p. 109.

10

A Peaceable World

Introduction

> Humanity is now living in the dark shadow of an arms race more intense, and
> of systems of injustice more widespread, more dangerous and more costly
> than the world has ever known. Never before has the human race been as
> close as it is now to total self-destruction. Never before have so many lived in
> the grip of deprivation and oppression.[1]

So began one of the public statements of the Sixth Assembly of the World
Council of Churches held in Vancouver in July and August 1983. With
thirty years of hindsight, some might dismiss this declaration as grossly
exaggerated if not scaremongering. The reference is to the decision by
NATO in the late 1970s to allow a new generation of nuclear warheads
(notably Cruise and Pershing missiles) to be stationed in Europe. The
purpose was to counteract the danger that the Warsaw Pact might launch
a military strike against Western Europe with vastly superior conventional
forces. The move had potentially devastating consequences, not only for
the inhabitants of the European continent, but for the whole world.

The decade of the 1980s was notable, among other events, for the
heightened tensions that existed throughout between the liberal, capitalist societies of the West and the communist nations of the Soviet Union
and its East European satellites. There were other significant flash-points,
where regional conflicts could have spilled over into more widespread
conflagrations: the Iran–Iraq War, the Soviet Union's military intervention in Afghanistan, the first 'intifada' launched by Palestinian dissidents
against the occupation of their country by Israel and the continuing
struggle in South Africa to end the apartheid regime and secure a united,
democratic country.

---

[1] WCC Sixth Assembly, 'Statement on Peace and Justice', Ecumenical Review
36 (January 1984), p. 82.

All these events gave rise to an intense public debate about the moral legitimacy of a nuclear deterrence, the proliferation of nuclear arms' capability, increasing militarization through the manufacture, trade and stockpiling of conventional weapons, the nature of national security, disarmament, revolutionary violence and the creation of a just peace. The decade saw many demonstrations against the threat of a nuclear exchange, including the famous 'peace camp' set up outside the military base at Greenham Common in Berkshire, England. The Campaign for Nuclear Disarmament (CND) recruited thousands of members and became increasingly active in its opposition to the deployment of nuclear warheads. The Soviet army, seeking to defend a 'secular' government in Afghanistan against the guerrilla warfare of the Mujahidin, became entrapped in a losing battle. The political and armed wings of the African National Congress in South Africa increased their opposition to and defiance of the white South African government in its implementation of the doctrine of separate homelands for black people.

Amidst the threats, tensions, hostilities and dangers of the decade, Christians of every tradition felt compelled to reflect on their mission in relation to these events. In this chapter, I will endeavour to lay out some of the main issues concerning war and violence and how Christians responded both in theory and practice to some of the major dangers of their generation.

The discussion is of more interest than a mere historical survey of a set of problems and disputes that were burning issues three decades ago; even less is it simply an academic debate about the legitimacy of war and the promotion of peace. The issues remain: in the following two decades, the world witnessed two Gulf Wars, a NATO operation in Afghanistan, events unleashed by the 'Arab Spring' in North Africa and the Middle East, and the reality and threat of 'ethnic cleansing' in Ruanda, Burundi, Sudan, Sri Lanka and Bosnia. They have been further escalated by the widespread occurrence of indiscriminate violence used, ostensibly, in the cause of religiously militant ideologies. In other words, to revisit the controversies sparked off at another time will help the present generation consider its own responses to the current complexities of war and peace. The world 'has moved on'; it is always moving on. However, most of the deep issues that confronted the nations in the 1980s remain to be solved. The Christian church is well advised to scour the past, looking for clues to help it live in the present with a view to the future.

Nuclear Deterrence

The theory behind the deployment of weapons of mass destruction is eminently simple. Their very existence avoids war between the major powers that possess them, as there could be no conceivable gain for any nation, or group of nations, in initiating a war in which their use is conceivable. Nuclear weapons exist; they cannot be dreamed away. In the absence of an agreed policy for the controlled and verifiable reduction, and eventual elimination, of nuclear armaments and a considerable decrease in the size of standing armies and the weapons of war they deploy, nuclear deterrence is justified. Nuclear arsenals do not exist for the waging of war, but precisely to make war less likely. To abandon deterrence does not increase peace and a sense of security; rather, it increases injustice by failing to deal with the threat of oppression.[2]

Some Christian ethicists argue that, given that nuclear weapons are a part of the defence strategy of nations that possess them, for the church to decry their deployment and possible (although highly unlikely) use is to confine itself to the margins of political influence. Such a stance is not credible for a body that believes it has a mission to influence the public affairs of a state. Paul Ramsey, for example, believes that, when the church says no to nuclear deterrence, by virtue of its rejection of a settled public policy, it makes itself into a sect.[3] By this he means, presumably, that the church, by pronouncing itself against a particular strategy, has abandoned its role of supporting the democratically elected government's policy and taken up a non-conformist stance in the political arena. Ramsey argues that religious communities should only be concerned with *perspectives* on politics (such as political doctrine and the structures of common life) not with specific *directives*. When churches try to influence particular policy decisions, they err.[4]

Not many Christian thinkers have followed Ramsey in this opinion. Ronald Preston, for example, is also critical of the ease with which church conferences pronounce on complex moral issues and tend to ignore the cost of the policies they recommend. Nevertheless, he believes that Ramsey makes far too sharp a separation between the elected civil authorities and those who elect them, as if the former somehow lived above the play of political ideologies and moral accountability.[5] Today, there appears to be a much greater consensus among Christians that

---

2   See Jerram Barrs, 'Justice and Peace Demand Necessary Force' in J. Andrew Kirk, ed., *Handling Problems of Peace and War: An Evangelical Debate* (Basingstoke: Marshall Pickering, 1988), pp. 16–18.

3   See Paul Ramsey, 'Who Speaks for the Church?' in *A Textbook of Christian Ethics* (ed. Robin Gill; Edinburgh: T & T Clark, 1995), p. 321. The excerpt is taken from Paul Ramsey, *Who Speaks for the Church? A Critique of the 1966 Geneva Conference on Church and Society* (Nashville, TN: Abingdon Press, 1967).

4   Ramsey, 'Who Speaks for the Church?', pp. 324–8.

5   Ronald H. Preston, *Confusions in Christian Social Ethics: Problems for Geneva and Rome* (London: SCM Press, 1994), p. 65.

democracy works best, not just through periodic elections, but through a continuing engagement by intermediate civic organizations with a government's legislative agenda. This was certainly true of the 1980s decade with regard to questions of war and peace. The nuclear issue was far too urgent and far-reaching to be left to the 'professional' politicians or to the military establishment.

So, for a variety of reasons, the majority of churches have spoken out against the retention of nuclear weapons and the threat to use them in extreme circumstances. The arguments have been well rehearsed. For those convinced that Christians should never, under any circumstances, condone the use of killing, the issue is already settled. For others, although they believe that sometimes war, in spite of its grim repercussions, is justified as a last resort and a lesser evil, a potential nuclear exchange raises serious misgivings.

In the first place, it is clear that a war, in which nuclear weapons were used, would not be a war in any normal sense. They are part of an arsenal (that includes biological and chemical weapons) technically known as weapons of 'indiscriminate effect'.[6] Conventional war, at least in theory, has been conducted in the belief that non-combatant civilians should not be the intended or unintended targets of violence. For this reason, during the war against Nazi Germany, Bishop Bell condemned 'obliteration bombing' (of cities such as Dresden and Hamburg) as not being 'a justifiable act of war'. He is quoted as saying that 'to justify methods inhumane in themselves by arguments of expediency smacks of the Nazi philosophy that might is right'.[7] Nuclear weapons, once released, would kill or mutilate hundreds of thousands of people external to the conflict that triggered off their use.

In the second place, the normal presumption that, as an outcome of a war, there would be a victor and a vanquished, simply could not apply in the case of the use of nuclear warheads. Both sides in the contest would be defeated, due to the utter devastation that their nations would suffer. Nothing, therefore, would have been achieved, in terms of producing a just outcome to a conflict. It is impossible to argue, therefore, that a war in which nuclear weapons were used could possibly achieve 'the vindication of an undoubted right that had been infringed.'[8]

In the third place, the use of nuclear weapons infringes the mandate given to human beings to take care of the earth and to pass it on intact to

---

[6] WCC, 'Statement on Peace and Justice', p. 87.
[7] The quote is taken from John Stott, *Issues Facing Christians Today* (Basingstoke: Marshall, Morgan & Scott, 1984), p. 91.
[8] See Robin Gill, 'The Arms Trade and Christian Ethics' in Robin Gill (ed.), *The Cambridge Companion to Christian Ethics* (Cambridge: CUP, 2001), p. 186.

the next generation. The Life and Peace Conference that met in Uppsala, Sweden (in 1983), under the auspices of the archbishop of that country, called attention to the stark choice facing humanity under the threat of a nuclear exchange:

> The advent of nuclear weapons has ushered in a new age of terror. For the first time in history we human beings, always possessed of limited power to destroy, are now capable of wiping out the civilization which has been built up over the previous centuries. Humanity is face to face with the final choice between life and death. The production and threat to use nuclear weapons capable of annihilating the human race demonstrate an *ultimate arrogance before God*, who alone disposes of life and death.[9]

It may be true that mere survival of the human race is never the over-riding consideration when confronted with massive ethical choices. As Stanley Hauerwas and others have argued,[10] reasoning from the survival of the species is a typically humanist ploy, given that survival, and therefore the passing on of the collective gene pool, is the only possible goal for humanity in an otherwise meaningless universe. Nevertheless, to use such a massively destructive force, knowing the consequences, surely usurps the prerogative of the Creator and Sustainer of all that is; it implies a claim to play the role of God. Therefore, in theological terms, it is idolatry.

It is not surprising that the vast majority of Christians have stated categorically that the use of nuclear weapons could not be justified under any circumstances.[11] Nevertheless, their possession and the threat of their use have raised moral dilemmas of the highest order. If it is immoral ever to use nuclear weapons, how can the threat to use them ever be moral? Some Christians have argued that the possession of weapons is a morally neutral matter. Arms are a form of technology, which can be used properly

---

9   Christian World Conference, 'Message of Life and Peace', *Church and Society* (Sept.–Oct. 1983), p. 68 (emphasis added).

10 Stanley Hauerwas, *Against the Nations: War and Survival in a Liberal Society* (Notre Dame: University of Notre Dame Press, 1992), pp. 143–6.

11 See for example, US Catholic Bishops, 'The Challenge of Peace' in *A Textbook of Christian Ethics*, p. 338; taken from *The Challenge of Peace: God's Promise and our Response: A Pastoral Letter on War and Peace* (Washington, DC: Catholic Truth Society, 1983); Charles Villa-Vicencio, *Theology and Violence: The South African Debate* (Grand Rapids, MI: Eerdmans, 1988), p. 235; Gordon McConville, 'Concerning Starting-Points' in *Handling Problems of Peace and War: An Evangelical Debate* (ed. J. Andrew Kirk; Basingstoke: Marshall Pickering, 1988), p. 118.

or improperly. It is the people that own the arms that act as moral agents, not the arms themselves. If it is legitimate to possess weapons for defensive purposes, then the greater the destructive power the less likely they would ever be used and, therefore, the less likely that a war would ever be started. Their deployment is justified on the grounds that 'the enemy' has no certainty about the intention of the other side in the event of a full-scale conventional war being launched. Therefore, at the least, war is avoided.

However, others have argued that such a stance is inherently unethical in that it rests on deception. In the event of a major war occurring, even a first strike with nuclear weapons, although it would undoubtedly halt any advance, would nonetheless be suicidal, since the enemy would still be capable of retaliating with its own nuclear arsenal. The possession of nuclear arms, therefore, is a bluff, since no sane authority would ever countenance their use. The enemy might, therefore, raise the stakes by calling the bluff and invade another's territory, knowing that the initiation of a nuclear conflagration could not be rational, even as a last resort. So, ultimately, the argument that it works as a deterrence is unproven; it could only do so if the nation that uses it first could also prevent the other side from retaliating. This possibility was the logic behind the development of the Strategic Defence Initiative (SDI), announced by US President Ronald Reagan in March 1983, and aptly called 'Star Wars'. The object was to create an impenetrable shield against incoming nuclear missiles by having the ability to destroy them whilst they were still in mid-air.

Paradoxically, however, it is precisely the ability to neutralise the threat of a nuclear strike by technological means that invalidates the argument that the threat of using nuclear arms acts as an effective deterrence against war. Either way, both 'Mutual Assured Destruction' and SDI are essentially destabilizing realities.[12] They tend to increase the sense of insecurity that abounds where weapons with such massively destructive potential abound. Other ways of avoiding war and creating a stable peace need to be found.

Disarmament

Commenting on the tendency among many African nations to rely on armaments to secure peace, thus squandering limited resources that should be spent on improving health care and providing universal

---

[12] See Bryan Hehir, 'Ethics and Deterrence', in *Power and Peace: Statements on Peace and the Authority of the Churches* (ed. Carl Reinhold Brakenhielm; Uppsala: LPI, 1992), pp. 19–28.

education, and quoting the passage in the prophecy of Isaiah (31:1,3) that speaks of the folly of trusting in military strength, John Pobee (of Ghana) draws the following conclusion:

> The message is clear: seeking peace and security in armaments is not only criminal folly but also a sin insofar as it is a rejection of God the creator and protector of nations and humankind. The lesson of history seems to confirm that seeking security in armaments is a blinding and empty ideology. The theory of deterrence has not helped the world; indeed the continuing escalation of armament research is evidence that despite the theory of deterrence, the world knows no peace.[13]

Mutual Assured Destruction spells MAD, and the notion that national security can ultimately be best served by maintaining a constantly up-dated arsenal of sophisticated weaponry is madness. Attempts have been made to discover ways of reducing the stockpiles of weapons and banning the further testing of nuclear devices. They have had limited success. Unless those nations who possess nuclear weapons are seen to take seriously the urgency of ridding themselves of weapons of indiscriminate use by mutual, controlled and verified disarmament, they can have no moral argument against the proliferation of such weapons. If it is legitimate for any nation to possess certain types of weapons for defensive purposes, it cannot be wrong for other nations to possess them as well for the same reason.[14] For nations with nuclear missile capability to insist on non-proliferation smacks of hypocrisy. It displays an arrogant self-righteousness in assuming that only certain nations can be trusted with such deadly means of destruction.

However complex, challenging and difficult the process may be, real lasting peace will only be achieved through processes of mutual security and confidence-building. Where long-lasting conflicts have been resolved (as in Northern Ireland and South Africa, and hopefully in Burma), certain elements have to be present. The willingness to turn away from treating the adversary as an implacable enemy is a first step. This involves the ability to understand the situation of conflict from the perspective of the opponent. It also requires both sides to desist from comprehensively blaming the other for the adversarial situation. Fixation on the enemy poisons the whole of life.[15] A second step would be the willingness of both sides to relinquish an entirely

---

[13] John S. Pobee, 'Peace, with Justice and Honour, Fairest and Most Profitable of Possessions', in *Power and Peace*, p. 107.

[14] Gill, 'Arms Trade', p. 188.

[15] Bert Hoedemaker, 'Peace Witness and Church Authority: A Reformed Perspective from the Netherlands' in *Power and Peace: Statements on Peace and the Authority of the Churches* (ed. Carl Reinhold Brakenhielm; Uppsala: LPI, 1992), p. 43.

intransigent set of demands. The abandoning of political, ideological, and sometimes religious rhetoric is also required in order to build mutual comprehension.

A third crucial step is the building of confidence and respect between the parties in conflict. It means acknowledging that those formerly considered to be enemies have legitimate concerns about the intentions and good will of the other side. Crucially, it means taking active steps to lessen tensions and to limit possibilities of future hostilities by agreeing a substantial reduction in offensive weapons, standing armies and provocative military manoeuvres. It requires transparency in allowing an open policy of verification. The provisional goal of negotiations for arms reduction would be military stability. This would be achieved by settling for a certain parity in weapons possessed, judged by what is sufficient for defence.[16]

Militarization and the Arms Trade

Apart from the complex notion of ridding the world of the threat of nuclear warfare, there is the continuing scandal of the trade in conventional weapons. At 'the beginning of the 1990s . . . the end of the Cold War was followed by a decline in the production and proliferation of arms'. This tendency lasted until the end of the century.[17] However, an increase in the transfer of arms has picked up from the beginning of the new millennium onwards.

Although there are national laws and international agreements regulating and restricting the official arms trade, 'it is estimated that as much as 90% of all illegal and illicit weapons have once started their circulation on the white (i.e. official) market.'[18] In other words, the final destination of many weapons, especially small arms, is all too often not the originally intended one. The widespread abuse of the arms trade, which presumably is intended to enhance the authority and control of legitimate governments, often has the opposite effect, as the weapons find their way into the hands of militias, self-proclaimed guerrilla groups, drug cartels and other groups of organised crime.[19] Every year approximately 8 million new small

---

[16] See Vladimir Shustov, 'Common Security and Overcoming the Consequences of the Cold War' in Roger Williamson (ed.), *Overcoming the Institution of War* (Uppsala: LPI, 1992), pp. 114–121.

[17] Peter Brune, *The Gothenburg Process: Faith-Based Advocacy for Disarmament* (Uppsala: LPI, 2009), p. 5.

[18] Brune, *Gothenburg Process*, p. 14.

[19] 'Given that there is such huge social investment in the science and technology of war, and that weaponry is transferred around the world in such quantities, it is hardly

arms are produced, whilst only half a million are destroyed. This leaves an annual surplus of 7.5 million. The consequences are horrendous: 'Armed conflicts . . . force people from their homes, kill parents, force children to become soldiers and killers, destroy social networks, use mass violation as an instrument of war, etc. . . . Not only civilians are wounded and affected. So many soldiers, women and men, are traumatised for a life-time by their service on the battle fields.'[20]

Moreover, 'approximately 200,000 people die every year from small arms in places without an ongoing "conflict".'[21] The more weapons that are available on white, black or grey markets, the higher the temptation to solve conflicts through violence, rather than through peaceful negotiation. As the proverb aptly puts it, 'If the only tool you possess is a hammer, everything appears to be a nail.'[22]

Financial resources spent on armaments are entirely non-productive. Their only purpose is to threaten or cause death and injury; in the latter case, the treatment absorbs medical resources that otherwise could be spent on treating and eradicating endemic diseases. Dwight Eisenhower's speech to the American Society of Newspaper Editors on 16 April 1953, with its clear Christian allusions, tragically remains as true today as when he spoke it sixty years ago:

> Every gun that is made, every warship launched, every rocket fired signifies, in the final sense, a theft from those who hunger and are not fed, those who are cold and not clothed. This world in arms is not spending money alone. It is spending the sweat of its labourers, the genius of its scientists, the hopes of its children . . . Under the cloud of threatening war, it is humanity hanging from a cross of iron.[23]

Much of the arms trade is an affront to the dignity of human beings.[24] It is a major reason for the neglect of adequate educational and medical provision for the majority of citizens of numerous countries across the

---

(cont.) surprising that wars continue', Roger Williamson, ed., *Overcoming the Institution of War* (Uppsala: LPI, 1992), p. 22; see also, *Campaign against the Arms Trade, Death on Delivery: The Impact of the Arms Trade on the Third World* (London: CATT, 1989).

20 Brune, *Gothenburg Process*, p. 15.
21 Brune, *Gothenburg Process*, p. 15.
22 Brune, *Gothenburg Process*, p. 21.
23 Brune, *Gothenburg Process*, p. 21.
24 'The only legitimations for arms transfers . . . are the preservation of peace, the defence of human rights and the preservation of life and dignity', Gill, 'Arms trade', p. 193.

globe.[25] It is the cause of corruption, human rights abuses and other forms of oppression and exploitation. There is, therefore, every reason for considering the proliferation of arms to be one of the major crimes against humanity. It is sad that so little seems to be done to hold those responsible to account. Nevertheless, achievements in banning certain weapons, such as anti-personnel mines and cluster munitions, have been made. The campaigns by ordinary people to rid the world of such particularly barbarous weapons show that, with dedication and perseverance, advances in the cause of disarmament can be gained. Other initiatives that show promise are the call for a comprehensive arms trade treaty[26] and the European Union Code of Conduct that became legally binding in 2008.

Revolutionary Violence

The decade of the 1980s witnessed the intensification of the struggle against the policy of apartheid in South Africa. Opposition to the white minority's denial of the black majority's right to determine its own future took a number of directions. As the oppressive nature of rule in South Africa became increasingly clear, so pressures for change from inside and outside the country escalated. Financial sanctions were applied, making it almost impossible for the nation to acquire foreign exchange for the purpose of trade. The boycott of sporting events caused great distress to a community passionate about sport. Embargos on the supply of weapons from abroad weakened the power of the army and police to maintain minority rule by force. One of the most successful strategies for bringing an end to the push for 'separate development' was the policy

---

[25] 'In 2006, one of Sweden's largest arms exports ever (the radar system Erieye) was given the go-ahead. The deal cost Pakistan about US$10 billion, *an amount 12 times Pakistan's yearly budget for water and sanitation*', Brune, *Gothenburg Process*, p. 16 (emphasis added). The South Commission, chaired by Julius Nyere of Tanzania, argued that 'only a few developing countries can rightly claim that their military expenditure is proportionate either to an external threat or to the resources at their disposal', South Commission, *The Challenge to the South: The Report of the South Commission* (Oxford: OUP, 1990), p. 53.

[26] The process of reaching an international binding agreement is ongoing. The latest step in this process was the negotiation of a multilateral treaty at a UN conference held in New York in July 2012. This would have to be considered by all members of the UN, probably modified, and then ratified by each nation before it could become effective.

of disinvestment. The withdrawal of or refusal to renew capital funding by governments and overseas companies caused economic hardship and instability, which affected every sector of the population. In such circumstances, demands for change from within the ruling white community began to split its hitherto ominous solidarity. Alongside all these events, an armed struggle had been going on: its long-term intention was that of neutralizing and overcoming the military forces that held the apartheid regime in power; the short-term plan was to show just how seriously the opposition regarded the need for fundamental change.

The justification of 'counter-force' violence (by definition armed conflict not sanctioned by the state) has always been treated with suspicion by nations with a certain amount of democratic stability. Nevertheless, what liberation theologians in Latin America referred to as 'the second violence' has usually been countenanced in exceptional circumstances. The notion has been supported by appealing to the principles of legitimate self-defence and last resort. When a regime has become totally intransigent, deaf to any appeal for change, when it suppresses all dissent by using methods of extreme brutality, and when all non-violent means for achieving the legitimate aspirations of the majority of the population, there appears to be no other recourse but the resort to arms. The concentration of resources in police and military states makes revolutionary violence appear as one of the last options for removing a government from power.[27]

The Programme to Combat Racism

So it came about that the ecumenical movement, whilst repeatedly calling for disarmament, affirmed the right of oppressed people to resort to revolutionary war as a means of throwing off the bonds of oppression.[28] In 1969, as the result of a mandate from its Fourth Assembly (Uppsala, 1968), the World Council of Churches set up the Programme to Combat Racism (PCR).[29] Through this programme it contributed to the struggle

---

[27] Villa-Vicencio, *Theology and Violence*, p. 237.

[28] Villa-Vicencio, *Theology and Violence*, p. 233.

[29] 'The main aim of the PCR is to define, propose and carry out ecumenical policies and programmes that substantially contribute to the liberation of the victims of racism. Although it attempted to deal with racism as a world-wide problem, much of its attention and energy during the apartheid era was focused on Southern Africa. One of PCR's most effective tools has been a WCC special fund to combat racism, from which annual grants are made to racially oppressed groups and organizations supporting the victims of racism. The fund is supplied by voluntary contributions from

in South Africa against the apartheid policy. The Sixth Assembly of the WCC (Vancouver, 1983) agreed that, among other things,[30] non-military aid should be given to the liberation movement, to support those engaged in the armed struggle. As can be imagined, the PCR caused deep conster-nation among some sectors of the WCC and other Christian groups who were not members. Although funds were given to organizations using violent means to create a racially inclusive society, they were designated strictly for humanitarian aid. Some opponents of the aid argued that, as this released other monies for the purchase of arms, the WCC was tacitly contributing to the armed struggle.

However, the WCC was clear in its argumentation for the PCR's special fund and consistent in its implementation of the help offered. It denied any desire to promote revolutionary violence; rather, it sought to understand how it could arise and in what circumstances it could be warranted. The situation in South Africa seemed to offer a clear-cut case for the justification of a measure of armed resistance to a regime built on and maintained by systematic violence.

The Christian community does not have a happy history with regard to its support for the use of force. So often, as in Latin America during the rule of the military (roughly from 1964–89), many churches have supported forces of oppression, which have been wielded by a ruling elite against the aspirations of the population for proper democratic accountability and political policies that use the nation's resources for the good of all. It is not surprising, therefore, that many within and outside the WCC were extremely wary of a reversal of this procedure in giving support to the victims of violence, when they resorted to violence themselves.

The Purpose of War

There is general agreement that, prior to the 'concordat' between the Emperor Constantine and the Christian church at the beginning of the fourth century, Christians did not participate either in the empire's mili-tary campaigns or in efforts to resist them.[31] Whilst Christianity remained a minority and persecuted faith, it did not compromise with the use of violence as a state policy. However, when Constantine began to diminish

---

(cont.) churches as well as from local ecumenical and support groups all over the world'; see www.idc.nl/faid/448faidb.html (accessed 26 Nov. 2012).

[30] The WCC was one of the first protagonists to withdraw all its investments from companies trading in South Africa.

[31] For example, in the Jewish War of AD 66–73.

the restriction on Christians and eventually turn to the faith they professed, the situation changed dramatically.[32] Henceforth, the Christian church became a defender of the empire as the empire had recently become a defender of the faith. This dramatic shift in its understanding of its mission led the church to rethink its attitude to the use of force and to the participation of Christians in military action.

One of the first recorded discussions of some of the principles that later were incorporated into the 'just-war theory' occurred in the Indian epic, the *Mahabharata*. Five brothers, deprived of their kingdom and intent on winning it back, discuss the ethics of war as to whether the suffering inflicted can ever be justified. Before coming to the conclusion that ultimately war may be justified, they examine arguments about the causes of war, the means of fighting and the outcome. A similar discussion is held in another Indian epic, the *Ramayana*. Ravana, whose kingdom is situated in present-day Sri Lanka, has captured Sita, the wife of Prince Rama, from the Indian mainland. As Ravana contemplates the war that will ensue when Rama seeks to win back his wife, he seeks advice from his ministers. One of his generals tells him how foolish he is to put himself in a situation where war will occur, as 'the only just war is the inner war . . . Violence is condemned if it is due to unresolved inner conflicts, which instead become externalised in bloodshed or in attitudes of anger or hatred which portray one's opponent as an enemy. Such violence is harm not merely pain.'[33]

Augustine was ambiguous about the practice of war. This is, perhaps, not surprising, as he was unclear about the role of political power. He lived at the time of the decline of the Roman Empire, whose new official faith was now Christianity. In his mind these two factors gave rise to two major problems. On the one hand, Rome was under constant military threat from various tribes to the north and east. On the other hand, Christians found themselves without clear guidance as to what military roles their faith would permit. Augustine set out to try to answer two major questions that circumstances had brought to the fore. What responsibility do Christians have towards the state under whose jurisdiction they live? And, can a Christian with a clear conscience before God take up arms to defend the empire? His answers are scattered

---

[32] See for example, A. Kreider, 'Introduction' in *The Origins of Christianity in the West* (ed. A. Kreider, ed., Edinburgh: T & T Clark, 2001) and J. Andrew Kirk, *Civilisations in Conflict? Islam, the West and Christian Faith* (Oxford: Regnum International, 2010), pp. 152–5.

[33] See Francis X. Clooney, 'Pain but not Harm: Some Classical Resources toward a Hindu Just War Theory' in *Just War in Comparative Perspective* (ed. Paul Robinson, Aldershot: Ashgate Publishing, 2003), p. 122.

throughout his writings, and in particular in his major work *De Civitate Dei*.[34]

The views of Augustine may be summed up by saying that, because of the evil effects of original sin on human social relations, war is inevitable. Its legitimate purpose is to bring about a measure of justice by containing or defeating unjust regimes, strategies and actions. It is incumbent upon government, therefore, to ensure that its cause is a just one and that the conflict is waged with due respect for the human dignity of all those involved. He elaborated, in an unsystematic but nevertheless coherent fashion, principles to govern justifiable reasons for embarking on war and permissible ways of conducting it.

Thomas Aquinas elaborated further these two major criteria that made war, whilst always sinful, allowable in certain circumstances. They have become known in the long tradition of the just war as *jus ad bellum* (acceptable precepts in deciding on war) and *jus in bello* (acceptable ways of conducting combat). In the *Summa Theologica* (Secunda Secundæ Partis, Question 40), he set forth three cardinal considerations:

> In order for a war to be just, three things are necessary. First, the authority of the sovereign by whose command the war is to be waged. For it is not the business of a private individual to declare war, because he can seek for redress of his rights from the tribunal of his superior . . . And as the care of the common weal is committed to those who are in authority, it is their business to watch over the common weal of the city, kingdom or province subject to them . . . For this reason Augustine says (Contra Faust. xxii, 75): 'The natural order conducive to peace among mortals demands that the power to declare and counsel war should be in the hands of those who hold the supreme authority.'
>
> Secondly, a just cause is required, namely that those who are attacked, should be attacked because they deserve it on account of some fault. Wherefore Augustine says (QQ. in Hept., qu. x, super Jos.): 'A just war is wont to be described as one that avenges wrongs, when a nation or state has to be

---

[34] For a comprehensive discussion of Augustine's contribution to the just war tradition, see John Mark Mattox, *Augustine and the Theory of Just War* (London: Continuum, 2006). The question of whether Augustine had a settled theory of what would constitute justified violence or whether his discussion amounts only to a rough ethical guidance to practice is dealt with by Mattox in the first chapter of his book. It need not detain us here. What is important is the near universal agreement that Augustine was the first Christian thinker to reflect coherently on the acute predicament of war for the Christian faith; see also John Langan, 'The Elements of St. Augustine's Just War Theory', *Journal of Religious Ethics* 12 (Spring 1984), pp. 19–38.

punished, for refusing to make amends for the wrongs inflicted by its subjects, or to restore what it has seized unjustly.'

Thirdly, it is necessary that the belligerents should have a rightful intention, so that they intend the advancement of good, or the avoidance of evil . . . For it may happen that the war is declared by the legitimate authority, and for a just cause, and yet be rendered unlawful through a wicked intention. Hence Augustine says (Contra Faust. xxii, 74): 'The passion for inflicting harm, the cruel thirst for vengeance, an unpacific and relentless spirit, the fever of revolt, the lust of power, and such like things; all these are rightly condemned in war.'

James Turner Johnson sums up the thinking of both Augustine and Aquinas on the legitimacy of war by referring to the three cardinal ideals for which war may be promoted. They are to maintain order, to serve justice by the punishment of evil and to achieve [an earthly] peace.[35] Aquinas did not elaborate on the criteria for *jus in bello*. Nevertheless he did show some concern for the way in which war should be conducted: 'Wherefore if a man, in self-defense, uses more than necessary violence, it will be unlawful: whereas if he repel force with moderation his defense will be lawful, because according to the jurists . . . "it is lawful to repel force by force, provided one does not exceed the limits of a blameless defense."'

This consideration covers the twin principles of the use of minimal force – the amount of force used must not exceed what is needed to achieve the aim of the war – and proportionality – the violence inflicted must not be greater than that which it intends to end.[36] These, together with the condition of discrimination – force must be directed only against legitimate targets of attack – were elaborated further at a later stage.

Stanley Hauerwas, well-known as a pacifist, attempts a kind of thought-experiment by which he attempts to make out the best possible case for the retention of war as a policy of the state.[37] He begins his discussion by suggesting that, as war seems to be universal and perennial, there might be a moral purpose in its continuing use. In spite of all calls for peace, might it not be possible that, if war was eliminated, we would be morally worse for it?

Following Augustine, Christians have usually insisted that war is always the result of sin, arising from disordered affections and ambitions.

---

[35] James Turner Johnson, 'Just War as it was and is', *First Things* (January 2005).
[36] See J. Andrew Kirk, *What is Mission? Theological Explorations* (London: Darton, Longman & Todd, 1999), p. 149.
[37] Hauerwas, *Against the Nations*, pp. 169–98.

All those who hold to the theory of a just war, whilst urging peace, defend war as a moral possibility. In modern just-war thinking, an emphasis on the justification of war has shifted from the notion of the punishment of evil to that of the defence of the violated. It is self-evident that 'every nation has a right and a duty to defend itself against unjust aggression'.[38] By extension nations also have a responsibility to defend the powerless victims of another nation against internal or external aggression towards them. The declaration of war against Nazi Germany in 1939, as a response to its invasion of Poland, and the intervention of NATO forces in Kosova in the 1990s were both morally good acts in so far as they ultimately helped to prevent a greater moral evil.

The institution of war demonstrates that there are worse situations than those caused by a resort to violence, in order to end the gratuitous violence inflicted on defenceless peoples by the use of unscrupulous military force. The end purpose of war is to preserve the common life of a people, which transcends the individual life of those who sacrifice themselves for a noble cause. So instead of arguing that war can be no more than a lesser evil, it might be possible to defend the position that actually it contributes to a greater good. The good that war protects is cooperation among nations and peoples. Its use is intended to demonstrate that the global community will not tolerate a deliberate policy that fractures human community to preserve the vested interests of one group at the expense of others (as in Ruanda–Burundi, Sierra Leone, Libya and Syria in recent times). So war is not an institution that is necessarily caused by sin, but one that is morally necessary for the protection of the goods of society. Hauerwas ends his thought experiment with a quote from David Hollenbach: 'The ultimate problem for pacifists is that they are willing to tolerate injustice in the limit situation where justice cannot be attained by non-violent means.'[39]

Needless to say, Hauerwas does not accept the premise of his thought-experiment – that war may have a positive moral purpose. He is simply trying to understand the reasoning of those who do. Further on I will review the Christian pacifist objections to war as a conventional way of bringing about peace.

The just-war theory has two principal goals. First, it is intended to promote justice by upholding the rights of peoples not to be victimised by the use of arbitrary power. Thus, in the situation where all other means of attaining a cessation of an excessively violent abuse of citizens or the

---

[38] US Catholic Bishops, *Challenge of Peace*, p. iii.
[39] David Hollenbach, *Nuclear Ethics: A Christian Moral Argument* (New York: Paulist Press, 1983), p. 28.

illegitimate invasion of territory by a foreign nation, it would be permissible for the international community to intervene to halt the aggression. Second, it is designed to set such limits to the justification of war that most wars would be prohibited.

Oliver O'Donovan has made one of the clearest defences of just war theory:

> All actually justified resorts to war combine, in some measure, all the three traditional causes: defence, reparation and punishment . . . To the extent that one takes international authority seriously, one takes the penal cause as the *presenting* cause. *The decisive point* in the crystallising of the cause for war is that international authority must be vindicated. But this does not mean that international authority may command a war to vindicate itself without substantial *underlying* causes of other kinds . . . Without some grave danger from *not* going to war, the danger of going to war will always be unwarranted.[40]

This affirmation presupposes that there is such a reality as an international authority (presumably the UN's Security Council acting to defend the UN Charter and international law). It also assumes that the right and duty of national governments to exercise punitive justice within their borders can be extended to the international scene. Both of these premises are contestable.

O'Donovan defends the exercise of war as a secular form of judgement; in Christian terms it acts as an interim provision of God's common grace: 'armed conflict can and must be re-conceived as an extraordinary extension of ordinary acts of judgement.'[41]

So the just-war principle is not so much a theory as a proposal of practical reason. It spells out in careful detail how competent people may enact just judgements even in a theatre of war. It is the exercise of practical imagination in the service of international justice, rather than national self-defence or self-aggrandisement. It is a doctrine that intends to offer help for those who wish to engage in a praxis of judgement. Judgement is reached through the threefold means of *description* – an analysis of the moral realities of a situation; *discrimination* – a decision about innocence and guilt; and *decision* – what is the right action in the circumstances.

The just-war criteria may be the most objective set of principles that are available to the international community as it seeks to deal with the problem of conflict and aggression. Nevertheless, they are not without

---

[40] Oliver O'Donovan, *The Just War Revisited* (Cambridge: CUP, 2003), p. 134 (emphases original).
[41] O'Donovan, *Just War Revisited*, p. 7.

serious criticism. Hauerwas believes that the criteria are, at best, ambiguous. He highlights the notions of 'declaring war', definitions of 'offensive and defensive war', 'non-combatants' and 'legitimate authority'. He also asks whether all the criteria have to be met before a war can be judged authorised. He maintains that the paradigm from which it is derived is not clear: is it primarily self-defence or defence of the innocent?[42] Thomas Massaro and Thomas Shannon argue that just-war thinking relies too heavily on the use of civil authority and can easily convey the impression that one's own nation is always involved in just wars. They ask what constitutes a competent authority in the event of a surprise attack. In the case of the so-called 'war against terrorism', how would one possibly assess whether victory is likely?[43] Donald Shell sums up one Christian response to just-war thinking:

> The just war doctrine is an interesting attempt to systematise scriptural teaching on the subject. But it is fundamentally artificial, academic and unreal. In so far as it encourages prudent thought about the use of force and instils a cautionary attitude, it is helpful . . . The main problems with the just war doctrine are that its propositions are not operational, and it almost certainly encourages self-delusion.[44]

The fundamental testimony against the just-war tradition is that it fails in practice to stop indefensible acts of war:

> It is pertinent to ask when in practice has the just war theory ever been used to demonstrate the illegitimacy of a particular use of force, in such a way that authorities bent on declaring war have been persuaded to change their mind. The case of the invasion of Iraq by the so-called 'coalition of the willing' is powerful evidence of the failure of the theory. There could not have been a clearer case, according to just war criteria, of the illegitimacy of a pre-emptive strike against the regime of Saddam Hussein. In Britain, even before the highly dubious intelligence reports became publicly known, the Churches were completely unanimous in condemning the action as an unfounded war of aggression against a sovereign nation. None of the major criteria – last resort, self-defence, legitimate authority, proportionate means or improved end result – were present.[45] Nevertheless the British Prime Minister and most

---

[42] Hauerwas, *Against the Nations*, p. 136.
[43] Thomas J. Massaro and Thomas A. Shannon, *Catholic Perspectives on Peace and War* (Lanham, MY: Rowman & Littlefield, 2003), pp. 123, 128.
[44] Kirk, *Handling Problems of Peace and War*, p. 98.
[45] The reasons why the war did not fit the criteria are set out in J. Andrew Kirk, 'Letters to World Leaders', *New Routes: A Journal of Peace Research and Action* Vol. No. 1, 7 (2003), pp. 3–6.

of the Cabinet, on the basis of false information, against the express wish of the Security Council, the advice of the UN inspectors working in Iraq and the overwhelming majority of the population, supported the ill-conceived adventure of President George Bush.[46]

Pacifism

Although the legitimacy of using violence in certain well-prescribed circumstances, to curtail evil and promote justice, has been defended by a majority of Christians down the ages, the rejection of violence as a means to secure these ends has also been a constant witness within sectors of the Christian community. Among pacifists there may be different interpretations of whether force should ever be used to curb evil-doers. Thus, some will define pacifism as any position that renounces (all) violence as a means to secure otherwise legitimate ends.[47] This suggests an absolute prohibition on all use of superior physical power to meet the violence of others. Others consider that a minimal use of force, as long as it does not issue in lethal violence against another human being, may be permitted: thus, 'Pacifism proposes the principle that physical force should not be used beyond the point at which it ceases to be an expression of caring for the enemy.'[48]

Christian pacifists claim that costly discipleship requires a life that is moulded after the example of Jesus Christ. His life was an exemplar of his own command to his disciples: 'Do not resist an evildoer . . . love your enemies and pray for those who persecute you' (Matt. 5:39,44); 'Do good to those who hate you, bless those who curse you, pray for those who abuse you' (Luke 6:27–8). Alexander Webster makes a distinction between non-violence, which requires one to refrain from resorting to lethal force, or perhaps any force, to attain one's ends, and non-resistance, which forbids any attempt to change the oppressor or perpetrator of violence through what he calls, 'active, manipulative opposition'.[49] Christ exhorts his disciples to flee rather than resist the Romans. He himself neither resisted arrest nor tried to escape his passion.

---

[46] J. Andrew Kirk, *Mission Under Scrutiny: Confronting Current Challenges* (London: Darton, Longman & Todd, 2006), p. 140–41.

[47] Hauerwas, *Against the Nations*, p. 134.

[48] Alan Kreider, 'Following Jesus Implies Unconditional Pacifism' in *Handling Issues of Peace and War*, p. 22.

[49] Alexander Webster, *The Pacifist Option: The Moral Argument Against War in Eastern Orthodox Theology* (San Francisco, CA: International Scholars Publications, 1998), p. 246.

In the same tradition, Paul handed on to the Christians in Corinth and Rome, the teaching he had received that 'Christ died for our sins according to the Scriptures' (1 Cor. 15:3). How did Christ die? 'Like a lamb that is led to the slaughter, and like a sheep that before its shearers is silent, so he did not open his mouth. By a perversion of justice he was taken away . . . although he had done no violence . . . he bore the sin of many, and made intercession for the transgressors' (Isa. 53:7b,8a,12c).

So Paul counsels the followers of the Lamb of God: 'Bless those who persecute you . . . do not curse them . . . Do not repay anyone evil for evil . . . so far as it depends on you, live peaceably with all . . . never avenge yourselves . . . "If your enemies are hungry, feed them; if they are thirsty, give them something to drink" . . . overcome evil with good' (Rom. 12:14,17–19,21b).

Peter is aware of the same tradition: 'Christ also suffered for you, leaving you an example, so that you should follow in his steps . . . When he was abused, he did not return abuse; when he suffered, he did not threaten; but he entrusted himself to the one who judges justly' (1 Pet. 2:21b,23).

Imitatio Christi is a powerful motivation for Christians to adopt a consistent non-violent lifestyle. Following in the way of Christ is incompatible with causing physical hurt to others. It is not, however, the only argument that Christian pacifists will use to promote their convictions. It is reinforced by several, general theological principles. Pacifism is not first and foremost a prohibition, but an affirmation that God rules his creation not through violence and coercion but by love. Christians are non-violent not because certain implications follow from their beliefs, but because the very shape of their beliefs fashion them to be non-violent.[50] Christians believe that by being incorporated by faith into the death, burial and resurrection of Christ (Rom. 6:3–11), they have entered on a new life. They have left behind the wisdom, customs and norms of 'this age' (1 Cor. 1:20; 2:6–8; 3:18; 2 Cor. 4:4; Gal. 1:4). They have been delivered from 'the power of darkness' and transferred to 'the kingdom of his beloved Son' (Col. 1:13) This is an objective reality brought about by Christ's act of redemption and the Holy Spirit's act of regeneration. They are called, therefore, to live by the high ethical demands of the rule of Christ (Eph. 4:20–23; Col. 3:1–3): 'The old self, with its practices, has been stripped away' and 'the new self has been put on' [like a permanent change of clothing] (Col. 3:9–15). The new garments consist of virtues that make violence a matter of past history: compassion, kindness, humility, meekness, forgiveness, love and peace.

---

[50] Stanley Hauerwas, 'Pacifism: Some Philosophical Considerations', *Faith and Philosophy* 2 (April 1985), pp. 339–40.

Living according to the standards expected in the realm where Christ rules is not so much a command as a delight. It is the result or fruit of the Spirit working in the inmost being of the believer in Christ (Gal. 5:16ff.). Whoever is 'in Christ' longs to be conformed to the image of Christ (2 Cor. 3:17–18). The life of violence, and the attitudes and affections which cause it – 'enmity, strife, jealousy, anger, quarrels, dissensions, factions and envy' (Gal. 5:20–21) – belong to the old life. This being so, the use of violence is a form of denial of the gift of the Spirit, who has brought believers through death and resurrection to a new level of existence. It is not surprising that Paul exhorts the Christians in Galatia to 'Live by the Spirit', because 'through the Spirit, by faith, we eagerly wait for the hope of righteousness' (Gal. 5:16,5).

Nevertheless, although Christians' citizenship is in heaven (Phil. 3:20) (i.e. in the realm where God's will reigns supreme), they also continue to live in the present world (where God's rule is usually disregarded). In this world, Christians are bound by conscience to be subject to those authorities that God has instituted to uphold good conduct and punish the wrongdoer. They are, therefore, also citizens within the existing order, with obligations to the state – to pay taxes, to respect and honour the authorities and to love the neighbour (Rom. 13:1–10).

Christian pacifists do not necessarily agree about what they 'owe to Caesar' (Mark 12:17). To what extent does their primary obligation to follow Christ, living under his rule, make involvement in civil affairs problematic? The question may not have been too difficult for the first Christians, in so far as they would have been excluded from positions of responsibility in the state, or would have excluded themselves on the grounds that to bear office in the state required the observance of pagan rituals. Twenty-one centuries later, in societies that have been transformed, up to a point, by the same faith, the situation is more complicated.

Some believe that taking any kind of public office (for example, being a magistrate or politician) would inevitably cause a conflict with their pacifist calling. John Elford asks, under what circumstances is responsible citizenship compatible with pacifism in a largely non-pacifist world, where peace and freedom of conscience are largely brought about by military constraint?[51] Alexander Webster believes that the pacifist trajectory implies that the church and its members can only play a restricted role in the social, political and cultural life of a non-Christian community. As the pacifist option follows what he calls 'a maximalist morality of the gospel', rather than 'the minimalising, civilising ethic of natural law', it would be nigh impossible for them to participate in the ordinary affairs of state, where other (pragmatic) moral

---

[51] John Elford, 'Christianity and War' in *The Cambridge Companion to Christian Ethics* (ed. Robin Gill; Cambridge: CUP, 2001), p. 175.

principles are in play.[52] If it is true that the Christian's requirement to love
the enemy is the greatest test of a Christ-like love (Rom. 5:10), then the Christian has no option but to stay clear of the state's judicial function because its
first function is to ensure that retributive justice is carried out. A Christian's
prime concern when wrong is done is to bring reconciliation between victim
and perpetrator and restore the latter to responsible citizenship.

Other pacifists, whilst declining to participate in any activity that
might lead to the use of lethal violence, are prepared to tolerate the use
of minimal force within a carefully controlled legal system for the sake
of restraining a greater violence. The caveat is that the humanity of the
violent person is fully recognised and protected and that a fundamental
change of attitude is the guiding aim of any process of punishment.
Charles Villa-Vicencio challenges Christians to formulate a viable political ethic that seeks not revenge for acts of violence but satisfaction for the
person or community violated and the restoration of a situation marked
by repentance, forgiveness and reconciliation.[53]

This kind of stance opens the possibility for a pacifist Christian to participate in judicial and penal processes that punish an evil-doer by restricting
his or her freedom or oblige them to make restitution to society in general
and to those they have wronged in particular. They would strongly resist
any attempt to impose any kind of penalty that violates the physical integrity of the guilty person or degrades their humanity through the circumstances under which they are forced to serve their sentence.

Towards a Christian Social Ethic of War and Peace

In the debate between pacifists and non-pacifists different approaches
and priorities are in play. Space does not allow a thoroughgoing analysis
of the contrasts between them. However, it may be helpful to list a few
and comment on them briefly. First, there is the question of how Scripture
is to be interpreted and applied. Christians have wrestled and continue
to wrestle with this matter. Sometimes it is relatively straightforward;
often it is complex. Space does not permit an adequate discussion of all
the relevant issues here.[54] In the context of the discussion of this chapter,

---

[52] Webster, *Pacifist Option*, pp. 252, 256.
[53] Charles Villa-Vicencio, *The Art of Reconciliation* (Uppsala: LPI, 2002), pp. 4–5.
[54] As I have already written a book on the subject, I refer readers to my conclusions; see J. Andrew Kirk, *God's Word for a Complex World: Discovering How the
Bible Speaks Today* (Basingstoke: Marshall Pickering, 1987). Although written
over 25 years ago, I believe the general and specific orientation and the case-
studies are sound.

there are one or two specific themes that may be highlighted. One has to do with the relation between the Old and New Testaments.

Since the way in which the Old Testament should be interpreted is defined by its fulfilment in the ministry of Jesus and his apostles, how is the law, the wisdom and prophecy of the Old Testament in the context of the history of Israel to be understood today? Can it ever be approached as the word of God without a specific reference to its completion in the word and works of God through Jesus Christ? Some Christians believe this is legitimate. Thus, the patterns of good government are laid down in all forms of literature in the Old Testament. The meaning of justice in the community largely finds its origin there. The use of force by God's servants is clearly sanctioned in the Old Testament. The notion of nations being held to account for observing or rejecting the law of God is a strong element of the Old Testament's message.[55]

Other Christians point out that the history of Israel was a unique and unrepeatable event. God's relationship with the nations since the coming of Jesus is now through the church as it gives witness to the good news of the kingdom of God which he has inaugurated. Texts of the Old Testament, which were applicable when the people of God were coextensive with one political entity, are no longer apposite in the same way, when the people of God are now scattered through all the nations. In a controversy between nations, which may threaten violence, Christians are likely to be on both sides of the dispute. Richard Bauckham and Gordon McConville argue that instructions about war in the Old Testament are not relevant to issues surrounding war today. As 'holy wars', God required them in specific circumstances for specific ends to show the people that God was serious about evil; frequently they were used against Israel. However, 'The New Testament applies "holy war" language to the Church, but reinterprets it in terms of spiritual warfare, suffering witness and church discipline . . . Two major consequences follow from the new reality of Jesus Christ. Firstly, the Church may not fight crusades. Secondly, no State may consider itself God's people, fighting his wars against his enemies.'[56] Both these errors have been committed by the church and state during the long period in which the Christendom model of church–state relations endured.

Alan Kreider argues that the Christian community must always begin its quest for an understanding of its calling in any generation with Jesus: 'Jesus, I am convinced, should be our hermeneutical key as we read the Old Testament. Similarly in the New Testament we observe Jesus forming

---

[55] See Kirk, *Handling Problems of Peace and War*, pp. 11–12.
[56] Kirk, *Handling Problems of Peace and War*, p. 58.

a movement of men and women who, filled by the Holy Spirit, applied his teachings and lifestyle to the congregations which they founded, and who, in all their behaviour, were determined to "walk in the way in which he walked" (1 John 2:6).'[57]

For Kreider, unconditional love for one's enemies is the hallmark of faithful discipleship. According to Luke's Gospel, it is the first piece of ethical teaching that Jesus gave his disciples (Luke 6:27). It excludes all killing. It was the way of life followed by the early church: 'For three hundred years following Pentecost, the Church expressed this new way of living in the Spirit by teaching and practising the love of enemies. Its leaders forbade the taking of life, in war, in abortion, in gladiatorial games. Their non-violence was a part of the preaching of the gospel and a consequence of conversion to Christ.'[58]

However, Kreider does not tell us how he makes the step from Jesus' command to love the enemy, in the very specific political circumstances of Israel during the time that he was preaching and demonstrating the arrival of God's kingdom (with all its political connotations), and loving one's enemies two thousand years later. In the former case, Jesus prohibited his followers from engaging in a holy war. The model for the kingdom of God was not Judas Maccabeus triumphing over the invaders of 'holy' land through a war of righteousness. The kingdom could not ever be brought about through the use of violence (Matt. 26:52–3; John 18:36). It is doubtful that the Christians would have considered those who persecuted them their enemies. The term would have been applied, with the exception of death (1 Cor. 15:26) and the devil (1 Pet. 5:8), to those who declared themselves to be enemies of the Christians (Rom. 12:20).

By analogical reasoning, Christians have no one they would consider enemies. Other individuals might declare themselves to be their enemies, or the state may regard another hostile nation an enemy, but this does not commit Christians to view them as such. In this way a legitimate distinction can be made between the 'enemy' as a collective whole and 'enemies' as individuals, who may hate and despise Christians, but whom the Christian does not consider an adversary.

If this is a fair interpretation of the contextual nature of the command to love one's enemies, then the command is not broken if and when Christians in extreme circumstances as a lesser evil, a last resort and in self-defence, are confronted with the task of having to kill. The caveat is that these circumstances will almost never apply. The importance of

---

[57] Kreider, 'Following Jesus', p. 76.
[58] Kreider, 'Following Jesus', pp. 24–5.

application by analogy cannot be overestimated. However, this works more by using dynamic equivalents – conveying 'to contemporary readers [of the text], using appropriate forms, means *equivalent* to those understood by the original readers' – than by a formal correspondence – 'whose main concern is to imitate by translating literally'.[59] The point of the exercise is to try to understand and reapply the original injunction, not only to love one's neighbour as oneself, but also those not considered neighbours (Romans, Samaritans, collaborators).

Second, there is the question of participation in or withdrawal from civic society. What is the distinctive witness that Christians should give to the state and what form should their participation in political life take?[60] Most Christians agree that discipleship enjoins a measure of involvement in public life. They take seriously the two metaphors of being the 'salt of the earth' and the 'light of the world'. Christian lives individually and collectively should bring goodness to the communities in which they live.

However, Christians do not necessarily agree about the extent of their engagement in the affairs of this world. For some it will mean the willingness to take on roles, whether in paid employment or as volunteers, in public office as servants of the state – elected politicians, civil servants, magistrates, judges. Others find that this kind of commitment will inevitable involve compromising their Christian convictions. Gordon McConville believes that 'in public life, almost by definition, the Christian's principles are *always* compromised. There is something slightly luxurious about the thought that it will always be possible to resign if Christian principles are offended. This is because, even in modern democracies, culturally influenced by the Christian tradition, at bottom the controlling spirit is not Christian but at best utilitarian.'[61] In largely post-Christian secular societies, adherence to a Christian interpretation of reality as a God-given structure that operates according to laws that ensure human flourishing as designed by God has been largely lost.[62]

The latter group of Christians will confine their participation in society to working in the caring services or simply dedicating spare time to looking after the homeless, welcoming refugees, visiting the elderly, sick and prisoners, supporting young offenders, combating human trafficking or taking

[59] Kirk, *God's Word for a Complex World*, p. 103.
[60] For further reflection on this complex relationships, see Kirk, *Handling Problems of Peace and War*, pp. 102–12; Kirk, *What is Mission?* pp. 150–51; 152–5.
[61] McConville, 'Concerning Starting-Points', p. 119.
[62] The implications and consequences of an accelerated drift away from core Christian beliefs by society as a whole will be explored in the final chapter of this book.

on responsibilities that enhance the wellbeing of their neighbourhoods (Matt. 25:35–40). In this way, they are able to show the kind of compassion and sense of justice that walking in the way of Jesus demands, expressing their call to a servant ministry, whilst not having to make concessions to their core beliefs.

Speaking in broad terms, one will find Christians from a Catholic or Reformed background willing to take on public office as part of their vision of social involvement; whilst those from an Anabaptist peace tradition will refuse the first option, but become fully engaged with the second. I recognise that this is a generalization, for there are different degrees of collaboration with any given state that Christians may embark upon – partly out of the presence or absence of opportunities, partly out of conscience. The point, however, is to highlight the level of participation in public life that diverse Christians are willing to make according to their pacifist or non-pacifist convictions.

There is, of course, another general category of involvement in public life that probably the vast majority of Christians would endorse. It is often referred to as a 'prophetic ministry'. It entails a witness to both the justice and mercy of God in every aspect of society's affairs. It means active participation in debates about every variety of public policy, more particularly the spending of public finances, the enactment of laws, educational and health policies, international relations, human rights, issues of equality and immigration, and those surrounding the beginning and end of life. As servants of the living God, whose concern is that human beings live as humans, Christians have a calling to hold authorities and powers to account. Their witness is to the moral law of righteousness, to its perfecting in the life of Jesus and to its inscription on the consciences of human beings, whether believers or unbelievers.

Just Peacemaking

Disciples of Jesus are called blessed and children of God when engaged in peacemaking (Matt. 5:9; also Rom. 14:19; Jas 3:18). According to Peter Matheson, just peace is a contemporary translation of the biblical concept of *shalom*, 'a communal wellbeing in which God's creation is justly ordered'.[63] Glen Stassen and David Gushee talk of a theory of

---

[63] Peter Matheson, *A Just Peace: A Theological Exploration* (New York: Friendship Press, 1981), p. 9, quoted by Susan Brooks Thistlethwaite, 'Peace Theology and American Protestant Ecclesiology in the 1980s' in *Power and Peace: Statements on Peace and the Authority of the Churches* (ed. Carl Reinhold Brakenhielm; Uppsala: LPI, 1992), p. 139.

just peacemaking that has arisen out of an attempt to move on the stale debate about pacifist and just-war ideas. They call it 'a third paradigm for the ethics of peace and war . . . a worldwide awareness . . . that we must develop effective war-preventing practices.'[64] The logic behind the move to just peacemaking is to substitute *ius ad bellum* with *pax ante bellum* (peace before war) and *pax anti bello* (peace instead of war). It would also incorporate a third factor into just-war thinking, namely *ius/pax post bellum*.

One of the continuing tasks of peacemaking is to promote awareness of the enormous cost of war to all parties involved. When a military campaign is being carried out in another part of the world, even with images being transmitted over numerous media networks, it is not easy to appreciate the devastating effects of violence on both combatants and ordinary citizens. Infrastructures are destroyed, dwellings are demolished, sources of food and water are interrupted, the economy is destabilised, fear and suspicion are multiplied, and the education of young people will be curtailed. Although these may all be unintended consequences of violent conflicts; their likelihood is well known in advance.

War is economically unproductive. Huge amounts of money are spent on military equipment and munitions whose object is to kill and destroy opposing forces and intimidate civilian populations. The money is wasted on causing devastation and chaos. The same amount of money could be spent on solving problems that lead to war. If peacemaking is bringing about change through wholly non-violent means,[65] then in order to create a lasting peace the main causes of conflict have to be dealt with before they create open hostilities. Some of these are: the monopolizing of power by a small elite group within a community or nation; repression of the people, so that the holders of power are not effectively challenged; corruption, in which resources destined for the welfare of all the people are expropriated for the governing bodies; fraudulently conducted elections; the expatriation of a nation's natural wealth to foreign companies, and the refusal to abide by international law.[66]

So, many of the causes of war or internal rebellion (such as have erupted in the acclaimed 'Arab Spring') are the result of economic conditions produced by the factors mentioned above: 'No society may enjoy peace without the guarantee of justice, dignity, minimum comfort for all

---

[64] Glen Stassen and David P. Gushee, *Kingdom Ethics: Following Jesus in Contemporary Context* (Downers Grove, IL: IVP, 2003), p. 169.

[65] Oh Jae-Sik, 'Justice with Peace,' in *Overcoming the Institution of War*, p. 85.

[66] The Israeli government's promotion of Jewish settlements on foreign territory is a classic case; see Kirk, *Civilisations in Conflict?* pp. 47–8.

. . . Peace does not and cannot cohabit with fear, anger . . . disappoint-ments, hopelessness.'[67]

Peacemaking involves tackling these issues head-on. One small way of redressing balances would be for aid-donating countries to channel development funds through grass-roots civil organizations, rather than sending them directly to governments. Such an action would ensure the aid was used by the communities for the communities and would cut out a major opportunity for corruption. Many other sensible and workable suggestions have been made.[68] These initiatives are aimed at creating conditions in which it is in no one's interest to cause instability by resorting to violence.

Attending to the fundamental causes of war is an aspect of estab-lishing a common security. Where economic conditions give populations a chance of living in circumstances of relative wellbeing, hope is kindled and the fundamental threat of deprivation is removed. As a result, governing bodies can themselves feel secure from internal unrest. Conse-quently, governments do not have to spend unsustainable amounts of money (often incurring an ever-increasing debt burden) on trying to secure themselves from internal or external threats. Peacemaking is about creating such a virtuous circle.

Stassen and Gushee list a number of practices that will, if imple-mented, promote peace.[69] Where situations of conflict are endemic (as is the case in the Middle East, parts of Central Asia and the Congo, and was the case in South Africa, Northern Ireland, the Balkans and Liberia, among others), or brewing, it is necessary for independent initiatives to be undertaken to reduce the distrust that hinders support for negotiated settlements. 'Spreading human rights, religious liberty and democracy is effective in building peace. As surprising as it seems, during the entire twentieth century, democracies with human rights fought *no wars* against one another.'[70] The United Nations and other international organizations need to be reformed and strengthened. It cannot be right, and has often proved to be an obstacle to peace, that any one of five nations (out of a total of 193 members) has the power to veto Security Council resolu-tions. On one recent occasion,[71] the veto has had the effect of increasing

---

[67] Pobee, 'Peace, with Justice and Honour', p. 96.

[68] For example by Tomas Tellez, 'The Third World and a New World Order,' in *Overcoming the Institution of War* (ed. Roger Williamson; Uppsala: LPI, 1992), pp. 111–12.

[69] Stassen and Gushee, *Kingdom Ethics*, pp. 170–73.

[70] Stassen and Gushee, *Kingdom Ethics*, p. 171.

[71] The decision by China and Russia to block plans to halt the Syrian regime's systematic programme of intimidation and terror.

violence, killings and refugees. On other occasions,[72] the possibility of serious peace negotiations has been undermined. The veto is an anachronism, inherited from the aftermath of a war (1939–45) concluded nearly seventy years ago.

Stassen and Gushee's final suggestion is to encourage grass-roots peacemaking groups and voluntary associations.[73] They set out a vision that, although often thwarted by specious arguments and bad practices, sustains a realistic hope for a world where everyone's security is dependent on everyone else also feeling secure, so that 'nation shall not lift up sword against nation, neither shall they learn war any more' (Isa. 2:4):

> A transnational network of groups, including church groups, can partially transcend captivity to narrow national or ideological perspectives. They can serve as voices for the voiceless, as they did in churches in East Germany and in women's groups in Guatemala (see Tooley, *Voices of the Voiceless*).[74] They can help to initiate, foster and support transforming initiatives that take risks to break out of the cycles that perpetuate violence and injustice. They can nurture the spirituality that sustains courage when just peacemaking is unpopular, that creates hope when despair and cynicism are tempting, and that fosters grace and forgiveness when just peacemaking fails.[75]

---

[72] The USA's constant opposition to resolutions intending to end Israel's illegal occupation of Palestinian land.

[73] One interesting and influential example of a grass-roots organization that campaigns (through the widespread use of the internet) on issues tending towards the establishing of peace with justice is Avaaz (meaning 'voice' in several European, Middle Eastern and Asian languages). It is a non-governmental, non-party-political, non-ideological, international association that selects political and economic ethical issues on a non-partisan basis where blatant wrongs need to be righted: 'Avaaz empowers millions of people from all walks of life to take action on pressing global, regional and national issues, from corruption and poverty to conflict and climate change. Our model of internet organising allows thousands of individual efforts, however small, to be rapidly combined into a powerful collective force' (taken from its web-site; see www.avaaz.org [last accessed 9 July 2013]).

[74] Michelle, Tooley, *Voice of the Voiceless: Women, Justice and Human Rights in Guatemala* (Scottdale, PN: Herald Press, 1997).

[75] Stassen and Gushee, *Kingdom Ethics*, p. 173.

11

Religious Worlds

The various modes of worship which prevailed in the Roman world were all considered by the people as equally true; by the philosophers as equally false; and by the magistrate as equally useful.[1]

Defining the Indefinable?

In spite of confident predictions that religious beliefs and practices would wither away before the onslaught of reason and science, because, so it is alleged, the latter give an adequate explanation of all human experience within the bounds of the material world, religions continue to thrive, even in the heartlands of belligerently secular societies. It seems curious that, in recent years, vehement atheists, who believe that religious creeds of all kinds are intellectually unfounded and morally objectionable, nevertheless pay so much attention to what they believe must soon pass away.

The term religion seems to be used as though everyone knew intuitively what is meant by it. However, on closer inspection, the reality is hard to identify with any precision. Presumably, to be able to use the term with any assurance, it must be able to include all manifestations that most people would recognise as belonging to the category. Roy Clouser[2] makes one attempt to find a way of defining religious belief that is all-inclusive. He begins by stipulating that two requirements must be fulfilled for a definition to be adequate. First, the characteristics of religion have to apply to every member of the class being defined. Second, the characteristics may not apply to anything that is not a member of the class.

---

[1]   Edward Gibbon, *The Decline and Fall of the Roman Empire* (New York: Modern Library, 1932), vol. I, pp. 25–6.
[2]   Roy Clouser, *The Myth of Religious Neutrality* (Notre Dame: University of Notre Dame Press, 2005).

In the light of these prerequisites, there are a number of potential defi-nitions that fall by the wayside. The view, for example, that religions hold to belief in one supreme being could be correct only if theisms were the only possible religions. Some religions are polytheistic, with no one sovereign being. Some beliefs associated with religion are atheistic (in the sense of denying any reality to a personal deity beyond the universe); this is true particularly of Advaita Hinduism and Theravada Buddhism:

> Traditionally in Europe we have thought of religion as involving belief in God or belief in the gods . . . Such a definition would satisfy many Europeans. But . . . it is too restricted, since it fails to embrace at least one of the world's great religions Buddhism: Buddhism does not centre upon belief in a personal Creator; nor is the supernatural, as commonly understood central to its teachings.[3]

> The notion of revelation is totally foreign to the Buddhists. There is no God . . . Here we should not argue that they give to God another name, because for them there is no God to be named.[4]

Another view sees religious belief as that which inspires or supports worship. Again, such a definition is defeated by Advaita Hinduism and Theravada Buddhism, for worship, as commonly understood, does not feature. Peoples may believe in many gods and yet not worship them. Such was the case of the Epicureans in ancient Greece, and a number of indigenous religions in more recent times. The gods had to be appeased, but because they did not care about humans they were not worthy of worship.

A third possible understanding of religion is that it points to a belief in some supreme value, an ultimate conviction that is worth dedicating one's life to, and perhaps even dying for. This too is inadequate, since in theistic religions God is not seen as a value. Rather, God is the basis for identifying true and false values; values follow a prior belief in God.

Having surveyed some inadequate understandings, Clouser then attempts to give what he considers a satisfactory definition. He starts from the assumption that every religious tradition regards something as divine. There is a consensus among the religions that there is a dimen-sion to the universe that cannot be confined to the material conditions of

---

[3] Ninian Smart, 'The Nature of Religion', *The Listener* (26 November 1964), p. 835.

[4] Yves Raguin, 'Differences and Common Ground' in G. Anderson and P. Stransky, *Mission Trends No. 5: Faith Meets Faith* (Grand Rapids, MI: Eerdmans, 1981), p. 175.

life. There is, however, much disagreement over what is divine. Every religious tradition, he believes, regards as divine that which possesses an unconditional, non-dependent reality; something which is absolute, self-existent, the source of all things and the final reference point for life.

Religious belief is not dependent on agreeing what has divine status. A belief is religious if it is a belief in something as divine, however it is described. It will include beliefs about how the non-divine depends on the divine, and how humans may stand in a proper relationship to the divine, where the meaning of 'divine' is (minimally) anything that has the status of utterly unconditional reality.

This way of looking at the religions also appears problematic. First, the definition appears to be too broad, for it makes beliefs belong to the category 'religious' if they possess unconditional reality. These, presumably, would include metaphysical, logical and scientific theories: for example, the law of non-contradiction, matter, forms, numbers, logical sets, physical laws, etc. All these are ultimate explainers, possessing a final, independent existence. Now Clouser is content to include these as 'religious' beliefs, so long as they can be separated into a distinct category. So religious beliefs can now be divided into two classes: those that occur within a cultic tradition and those that act as ultimate explanations. In both cases something is being accorded the status of divinity.

Second, there are some methodological problems with this interpretation of religion. The first difficulty is in assuming a class of religious beliefs prior to defining the meaning of 'religious'. If there is such a class, it must depend on a prior understanding of religion. This is a circular argument, seeing that something is accorded divinity only in terms of the definition. In ordinary discourse, no one would include some of these beliefs among the religions. The hypothesis appears to have become the conclusion. There is another difficulty in the use of language: unconditional reality may be called 'the metaphysically ultimate' rather than 'divine'. In normal language use these are not equivalents. The first does not belong in the same category as the second, unless included arbitrarily. Who believes that matter, numbers or logical sets have divine status? Religion is being used as a catch-all phrase, and evacuated of its particular meanings.

Third, there is a conceptual confusion. It might, therefore, help to clarify the situation of religious beliefs, if one were to make a fundamental distinction. All religious beliefs are beliefs in some kind of unconditional, self-existing reality. However, not all beliefs in the latter class are necessarily religious.

Origin of the term

Perhaps one of the main explanatory difficulties is that the idea of religions having common features, with a similar core essence, across all particular manifestations is simply the result of a European civilization that in the eighteenth century wished, through the use of precise categories, to bring order and coherence to its understanding of a world that was beginning to open up through the discoveries of the natural sciences. Religions, it was thought, could be treated rather in the same way that Linnaeus (Carl von Linne) produced a taxonomy for plants and animals. The word was invented to describe a phenomenon being encountered across the world by travellers and explorers. It was borrowed from Latin: either from *religionem*, coming to mean 'being tied to the gods', or from *religens*, meaning 'fearing the gods'. In most non-European languages, however, the word does not exist.

Use of the term

In modern usage religion has come to signify a set of convictions that are contrasted to a secular view of life. The latter tends to divide existence into separate compartments: such as work, leisure, family, civic duties, scientific investigation and religion. Religion is then classified as a separate entity, a kind of personal, private leisure activity that is not expected to influence the public life of work, politics, economics, law-making, education or medicine. However, it is a truism to state that no major religion has such a view of life. Religion is an invention of the West's secularizing tendency, intended to distinguish certain beliefs and activities from a life lived as though the only reality was material existence.

Characteristics of religion

In light of my discussion so far, it would seem that all definitions that wish to capture an all-embracing essence of religion fail. As soon as one attempts to discover commonalities that broadly refer to the same reality across all hypothetical religions, exceptions will always be found. Those categories that have been identified, such as the idea of 'the sacred' (Durkheim),[5] 'systems of meaning given to experience beyond the everyday world' (Luckmann),[6] 'faith' and 'cumulative

[5] See Robert Towler, *Homo Religiosus: Sociological Problems in the Study of Religion* (London: Constable, 1974), p. 63.
[6] See Thomas Luckmann, *The Invisible Religion: The Problem of Religion in Modern Society* (New York: Macmillan, 1967).

traditions'(Cantwell Smith),[7] an experience of 'the Ultimately Real' (Hick),[8] are extremely vague; it is hard to distinguish any content that can be recognised as meaningful.

It may be helpful, in the light of the difficulties I have encountered in giving a precise and specific definition to religion in general, to look at the phenomena of religious practices in particular as social entities; in this way I may be able to demarcate boundaries. Then, at least, if a person claims to be non-religious, they have good grounds for being able to say, 'None of the above'!

To qualify as a religion, I would suggest that at least the following elements have to be present:

● *A core message*, which is often written in a sacred text (or handed on orally), said to have been transmitted from a source beyond the human intellect;
● *An experience related to the message*, which takes the form of a fundamental conviction leading to a wholehearted commitment, through a sense of duty or obligation;
● *A group expression based on the message*, i.e. a sense of belonging to a distinct community which follows the same message;
● *A lifestyle which seeks to put the message into practice* through certain rituals, customs and ethical behaviour.

These four elements allow for considerable diversity in naming certain beliefs and practices 'religious'. At the same time, they do not attempt to cover every possible aspect of religion; nor do they pretend that all fundamental beliefs held or core activities practised are religious in some way.

It may be helpful to make a distinction between those belief systems which hold to the existence of 'unseen powers which are said to have an independent existence beyond the human' and those which seem to depend on the innate depths of the human psyche as the source of an existence that transcends the material world. In the first case, the powers do not have to be personal; they could be impersonal forces, just as long as they cannot be reduced to the human world. This distinction may help to clarify the difference between a religious orientation and one that is based on a philosophical system. Strictly speaking, under this categorization, certain interpretations of Buddhism and Hinduism would more

---

[7] See Wilfred Cantwell Smith, *The Meaning and End of Religion: A New Approach to the Religious Traditions of Mankind* (New York: Harper & Row, 2nd edn, 1978).
[8] See John Hick, *An Interpretation of Religion: Human Responses to the Transcendent* (New Haven: Yale University Press, 2nd edn, 2004), *passim*.

naturally fall into the latter group. Probably, phenomena like 'New Age' spiritualities, which appear to derive their energy from an exploration of the depths of human consciousness, would be better defined as a philosophy than as a religion.

It may be noted that the four core elements fit the so-called major world religions, including certain more recent deviations from the norm (e.g. Mormonism and Christian Science). However, at the margins of these religions, or even separate from them, there exists in many different forms what is known as implicit, common or popular religion. According to Towler, these comprise 'those beliefs and practices of an overtly religious nature which are not under the domination of a prevailing religious institution'.[9] The elements involved may vary from place to place and time to time, but generally include at least one of the following: belief in the power of fate, luck and the paranormal (such as astrology, fortune-telling and contact with the dead), rites of passage, a benevolent divine being who will look after humans and accept them on the basis of the balance of their good lives. Common religion is infused with what those adhering to orthodox religious beliefs call superstitions.[10] There exists in them a certain latent magical view of human life,

> based on a set of reasonably clear assumptions: life is governed by chance; the universe as such is (or appears to be) impersonal . . . certain events bring either good or bad luck . . . Good fortune depends on pleasing an unseen world . . . Harmony with the beyond is maintained, or restored, through observing the right rituals (the avoiding of taboos, the use of charms and mascots, incantations, heeding omens, actions associated with the relics or shrines of 'holy' people, pilgrimages, acts of penance).[11]

Common and popular religious expressions do not fit easily into any definition of religion that would include the mainstream, official religious traditions.

The Foundations of Religion

Any study of the phenomenon of religion is interested to discover on what grounds or by what authority religions legitimate themselves to

---

[9]   Towler, *Homo Religiosus*, p. 148.

[10] See Geoffrey Ahern and Grace Davie, *Inner City God: The Nature of Belief in the Inner City* (London: Hodder & Stoughton, 1987).

[11] J. Andrew Kirk, *Loosing the Chains: Religion as Opium and Liberation* (London: Hodder & Stoughton, 1992), p. 24.

their practitioners and to outsiders. The answer seems to be twofold. Some religions appeal to extra-human revelation as the source of their convictions. Kenneth Cragg suggests that this gives a self-warranting assurance to believers. The authority of the divine communication is its finality. It possesses a once-for-all character which secures it against relativity of doctrine. At the same time, it can withstand the accusation of being anachronistic by opening up the revelatory text to diverse interpretations according to different contexts.[12]

Other religions appeal in the first place to experiences of a reality that transcends the mundane. The experience may be described in general terms as an awareness of the divine. It may come as a sense of union, dependence or separateness. In the first instance, a person may experience a kind of cosmic unity that underlies all things: a larger whole into which all particulars, including the believer, are incorporated. Strictly speaking this is not an experience of a personal God, for that would imply a dualistic separation between the universe and a cosmic being; an idea clearly disallowed by monistic faiths. It is certainly a profoundly mystical experience, through which believers are made aware of their inner being as pure selfhood or consciousness, stripped of all particular qualities.[13]

Claims to have encountered some reality that goes beyond sensations of the external world are difficult to assess. The difficulty is in deciding what, if anything, can be inferred from the occurrence of subjective sensations. Is it possible to deduce from the internal images an external cause that exists independently of the believer? Is there any reason to doubt the genuineness of the experiences?[14] These are questions that divide opinion among those who most closely observe the phenomenon of religious faith. I will return to a fuller discussion of the issues surrounding claimed experiences further on.

The Study of Religion

Given the near impossibility of arriving at a satisfactory understanding of religion that does justice to all the intricate, particular manifestations, it is not surprising that the history of its study during the last two and a half centuries has led to widely differing views. The study has been undertaken by a number of different disciplines, each of which seeks to

[12] Kenneth Cragg, *The Christ and the Faiths: Theology in Cross-Reference* (London: SPCK, 1986), p. 7.
[13] See C. Stephen Evans and R. Zachary Manis, *Philosophy of Religion: Thinking about Faith* (Downers Grove, IL: IVP, 2nd edn, 2009), pp. 99–101.
[14] See the discussion in Evans and Manis, *Philosophy of Religion*, pp. 102–14.

assess the phenomena from a particular perspective. In general terms, there have been two main approaches: that of the social sciences and that of religious studies. The first has contented itself largely with attempting to discern the origin and function of religion. As these people claim scientific validity for their methods, they have tended to postulate a naturalist hypothesis to account for all religious incidents. Thus, for example, it has become commonplace to assume that religions arise to serve strong human needs: such as those of providing systems of meaning that will fit all the disparate elements of existence into a unified whole; or those of supplying both a justification and sanctions for moral behaviour; or those which give comfort in the face of adverse circumstances, or those which attempt to control an uncertain future through prediction and supplication.[15] Social scientists are particularly interested in the social, economic and psychological effects of religious beliefs and practices.[16]

Theories from religious studies tend to begin with the assumption that religious experience originates in some real experience of the divine; one which reflects an innate need for some reality greater than the human, and which cannot be fulfilled by any secular substitute. Eliade holds that 'religious man cannot live except in an atmosphere impregnated with the sacred'.[17] Contact with this reality is deemed as much a fundamental need as that for food or water. However, strictly speaking, the discipline of religious studies does not concern itself with the issue of God's existence, but only with the existence of an alleged universal need for a sacred space for life.[18] The question of the truth of the alleged object(s) of religious faith is a matter to be left to the philosophy of religion or philosophical theology.

All theories of religion are in danger of committing a number of fallacies. To ascribe the meaning of religion on the basis of either its assumed origin or the function that it appears to fulfil in society runs the risk of reductionism. Such theories tend to isolate certain aspects and treat the partial as though it accounted for the whole. As soon as sufficient exceptions are discovered to the general rule of thumb, the

---

[15] Richard K. Fenn suggests that 'the perennial origins of religion' are to be found 'in the existential refusal to submit to unbearable loss: religion begins with a conscious rebellion against the passage of time', 'The Origins of Religion' in Richard K. Fenn, *The Blackwell Companion to Sociology of Religion* (Oxford: Blackwell Publishing, 2003), p. 187.

[16] See Robert A. Segal, 'Theories of Religion' in *The Routledge Companion to the Study of Religion* (John R. Hinnells, ed., 2nd edn., Abingdon: Routledge, 2010/2), pp. 75–76, 78.

[17] Mircea Eliade, *The Sacred and Profane* (New York: Harvest Books, 1968).

[18] Segal, 'Theories of Religion', p. 78.

theory breaks down. In arguing that religions arise in order to fulfil needs, the theories tend to commit the fallacy of simply affirming what has been assumed. To ignore claims to ultimate truth for a set of beliefs, or to a realist account of religious experience in a distinct self-existing object, is to commit a methodological fallacy by assuming first that scientific knowledge alone is warranted true belief, and second, that scientific methodology cannot take into account evidence that defies a naturalistic explanation. To refer all religious language to human inter-subjective discourse is to beg a huge question about reference and correspondence.

Comparative Religion

Taking religion to be a distinct expression of human life and noting the extensive variety of religious expressions across the globe, the cross-cultural study of all forms and traditions of religious life has emerged as a significant contribution to the debate about religion. It entails a disciplined and historically informed consideration of the commonalities and differences that exist between these multiple religious displays.[19]

Various approaches have been taken. One common thread that has pervaded the study of religion is 'universalism', i.e. the assumption that all religions refer to the same underlying spiritual reality seen through time-bound cultural forms and articulated in distinct language structures. Fostered initially by the Romantic movement of the late eighteenth century, it is strongly advocated by a 'pluralist theological theory of religions', proposed by writers such as John Hick, Raimund Pannikar, Alonso Pieris and Paul Knitter.[20] Institutional and doctrinal differences are seen as secondary, outward elaborations of a shared, intuitive sense of a mystery that is said to ground the whole of life.[21]

Other scholars have sought to employ a more neutral approach that does not presuppose either the truth or value of any one religion, but sets out to investigate religion as a patterned phenomenon of human culture and behaviour. All religions are studied by the same criteria and none are specially privileged.[22] In a general 'science of religion' approach the attempt is made to organise and collate all data of religious history into groupings or classes of religious expressions, in order to identify an

---

[19] William E. Paden, 'Comparative Religion' in *The Routledge Companion to the Study of Religion*, p. 225.

[20] This theory will be considered later in the chapter.

[21] Paden, 'Comparative Religion', p. 228.

[22] Paden, 'Comparative Religion', p. 229.

overall taxonomy or anatomy of religious life[23] (the equivalent, as I have
suggested already, of Linnaeus's work in the field of botany in the eighteenth century).

These attempts at cross-religious comparison have problems. They
tend to begin with the premise that there exists a common essence that
belongs to every manifestation of religious belief. The search is then on to
discover signs of this essence in the bewildering variety of religious traditions practised around the world. However, the claim that cross-cultural
patterns exist can lead to 'superficial parallels, false analogies, misleading
associations, stereotyping and unscientific, imaginative projections . . .
Religious phenomena are embedded in unique, socio-cultural settings . . .
Cross-cultural categorizations suppress or conceal differences giving the
illusion of homogeneity.'[24]

A proper comparative methodology endeavours to interpret religious traditions from within their own premises, eliciting motives and
clarifications from the practitioners themselves. This will require a deep
listening process that is slow to jump to conclusions about possible
resemblances. Comparisons should be based on carefully defined
aspects, focussing on the exact features being compared. Thus to call
the three major theistic religions – Judaism, Christianity and Islam –
Abrahamic faiths, on the grounds that Abraham is prominent in all
of them, misses the point that the way in which and the purposes for
which the Abraham narrative is told differs markedly in the Genesis
account, in extra-canonical Jewish writings, such as *Jubilees, 1 Maccabees, Sirach*, Philo and Josephus[25] and in the Qur'an.[26] By attending to a
detailed study of the portrayal of Abraham in the different traditions,
it may be shown that similarity does not equate with identity, and that
the alleged commonalities between the faiths boil down to little more
than the name, Abraham. As we shall see later in this discussion, the
implications for inter-religious dialogue of forging a precise and robust
comparative methodology are substantial.

---

[23] Paden, 'Comparative Religion', p. 231.
[24] Paden, 'Comparative Religion', p. 233
[25] See the extended study made by Paul Watson, *Paul and the Hermeneutics of
Faith* (Edinburgh: T & T Clark, 2004), pp. 165–269, of the appropriation of the
Abraham story in post-canonical Judaism.
[26] A detailed comparative study of the various texts of these three religions,
particularly of Genesis and the relevant Qur'anic suras, is forthcoming in a
PhD thesis: George Bristow, 'At Abraham's Table: A Study of Christian-Muslim
Intertextual Encounter in Turkey.'

Critique of Religion

Since the seventeenth century in the Western world, religious claims have been strongly contested from many different angles. Given the turn to the subjective in theories of knowledge, the exaltation of reason and the autonomy of the individual, confidence in methods of empirical research, the prominence given to the interpretative powers of language, the emphasis placed on the contingency of historical events and the weight given to cultural variety and plurality in interpreting human life, the assault on religious beliefs is not surprising.[27]

The most notable theories attack religious convictions as illusions, postulating that they are projections designed to compensate for the sense of finitude, fragility and mortality of the human condition.[28] According to Max Stackhouse, there is a generalised perception, at least among a certain group of intellectual elite, that the sceptics of the last two hundred years have carried the day. 'Educated people' do not believe that religion is decisive and indispensable for personal, communal and civilizational viability, do not consider theology to be a science in any current meaning of the term, and do not think that there is anything 'out there', other than the models we construct out of the partial experiences of historical life.[29]

The 'Masters of Suspicion'

Marx, Nietzsche and Freud, who through their analyses of social and individual alienations earned the epithet above, all had their own specific view of religion as compensation.[30] For Marx, religion amounts to a *projection* of human beings' failure to solve their own problems. It is a factor of *alienation*, as it weakens human beings' resolve to bring about a revolutionary change in their situation of misery and oppression. It is also a *diversion*, in that it gives the wrong explanation for human suffering. Religion represents an inverted world consciousness: 'The abolition of religion, as the *illusory* happiness of men, is a demand for their real

---

[27] A full review of the origin, reasons for and content of the various intellectual movements that have led to assaults on religious belief can be found in J. Andrew Kirk, *The Future of Reason, Science and Faith: Following Modernity and Postmodernity* (Aldershot: Ashgate Publishing, 2007).

[28] See John Habgood, *Church and Nation in a Secular Age* (London: Darton, Longman & Todd, 1983), p. 26.

[29] Max L. Stackhouse, *Apologia: Contextualization, Globalization and Mission in Theological Education* (Grand Rapids, MI: Eerdmans, 1988), p. 82.

[30] I deal with the each one's critique in some detail in *Loosing the Chains*, pp. 32–50.

happiness. The call to abandon their illusions about their condition is a
call to abandon a condition which requires illusions.'[31]

For Nietzsche, religion (he thought mostly in terms of Christian faith)
was an enormous hindrance in the way of the rebirth of civilization, a
'higher' age, in which a 'stronger species of man' would create its 'own
new tables of values: 'a more manly, warlike age . . . which will above all,
bring valour again into honour! . . . An age that will carry heroism into
knowledge, and wage war for the sake of ideas and their consequences.'[32]

Stern sums up Nietzsche's objection to Christianity in the following way:

> The ultimate indictment of Christian belief . . . is that it does not recognise
> man as the master of the universe, since it insists that freedom, authority and
> knowledge, vouchsafed to men, are all relative to an alien, outside decree,
> and rendered intolerable because they are derivative . . . Man cannot reach
> the highest enhancement of his powers until he has destroyed in himself his
> belief in the divine.[33]

For Freud a mythological view of the world found, as a grand theory, in
most religions is nothing other than psychological processes projected
onto the outer world.[34] The purpose of religion is to act as a compensation for a series of psycho-social inadequacies. Freud linked the origin of
the religious impulse to his alleged discovery of the 'Oedipus complex':
'In a study of the beginnings of human religion and morality which
I published in 1913 under the title of *Totem and Taboo* I put forward a
suggestion that mankind as a whole may have acquired its sense of guilt,
the ultimate source of religion and morality, at the beginning of its history, in
connection with the Oedipus complex.'[35]

The 'Oedipus complex' in Freud's thinking is the repressed guilt associated with the shameful and unacknowledged desire of the male child
to eliminate the rivalry of the father and to have sexual relations with the
mother. He came to believe that all religious sentiments were manifestations of guilt and neurosis. God is a human creation whose function is to
assuage the sense of suppressed outrage which the child directs against
itself when it realises the enormity of its fantasies. The need to believe

[31] David McLellan (ed.), *Karl Marx: Selected Writings* (Oxford, OUP, 1977), p. 64.
[32] Frederick Nietzsche, *A Nietzsche Reader* (trans. R.J. Hollingdale) (Harmondsworth: Penguin, 1977), p. 283.
[33] J.P. Stern, *Nietzsche* (London: Collins, 1978), pp. 96–7.
[34] See Robert Banks, 'Religion as Projection: A Re-Appraisal of Freud's Theory'.
Religious Studies 9 (1973), p. 401.
[35] Sigmund Freud, *Introductory Lectures on Psychoanalysis* (Harmondsworth:
Penguin Books, 1973), p. 375 (emphasis added).

in God represents a regression to an immature state of human development. As Freud put it in a notable epithet, 'the ultimate basis of man's
need for religion is infantile helplessness.'[36]

Freud, like Marx and Nietzsche, viewed religion as the major obstacle to
humanity discovering the real causes of its distress and embarking upon
the conquest of a new and more glorious stage of human development:

> The meaning of the evolution of civilization is no longer obscure to us. It must
> present the struggle between Eros and Death, between the instinct of life and the
> instinct of destruction, as it works itself out in the human species. This struggle is
> what all life essentially consists of, and the evolution of civilization may simply
> be described as the struggle for life of the human species. And it is this battle of
> the giants that *our nurse-maids try to appease with their lullaby about Heaven*.[37]

Nearly all subsequent negative evaluations of religion start from a similar
premise to those proposed by these three critical thinkers: religious
beliefs obscure economic, social and psychological realities; religious
practices (such as prayer, worship and ritual routines) act as a recompense for helplessness in the face of oppression, the challenge of freedom
or psychological trauma.

Over two centuries ago, the French philosopher Baron d'Holbach
summarised what has become and remains a truism among the humanist
defamers of religion: 'It is ignorance and fear which have created the gods;
conceit, passion and deceit which have adorned and disfigured them; it is
weakness which adores them, credulity which nourishes them, and tyranny
which supports them in order to profit from the delusions of men.'[38]

It is not only the so-called 'new atheists' who have turned these kinds of
sentiments into profitable publishing ventures; a quick survey of responses
to blogs promoting religious beliefs and ethical values will demonstrate
similar thoughts, though almost certainly not so eloquently put.

A 'postmodern' perspective

The American philosopher, Richard Rorty, combines the postmodern
turn to language[39] with a utilitarian view of ethical behaviour in his

---

[36] See Kirk, *Loosing the Chains*, pp. 44–5.
[37] Sigmund Freud, *Civilization and its Discontents* (New York: Norton, 1961), ch.
6 (emphasis added).
[38] From Baron d'Holbach, *The System of Nature*, quoted in Eduardo Mendieta,
The Frankfurt School on Religion: Key Writings by the Major Thinkers (Abingdon:
Routledge, 2005), p. 217.
[39] See Kirk, *Future of Reason*, ch. 6.

attempt to assign a meaningful role for religious language in the cultural politics of the twenty-first century.[40] He defines cultural politics in terms of acquiring the right beliefs that ensure the optimum amount of human happiness in the world. The question about religious beliefs is not whether they purport to be true and, therefore, conversely could be shown to be false,[41] but what sort of role they should play in advanced democratic societies. Arguments about the relative dangers or benefits that religions represent are the only ones that matter. Attributions of truth or reality are compliments we pay to entities or beliefs that have proved themselves useful and therefore been incorporated into accepted social practices.[42]

Following from this general premise, the question of God's existence is nothing more than the issue of the advantages or disadvantages of using God-talk over alternative ways of talking. He believes that all attempts to name an authority superior to that of society are disguised moves in the game of cultural politics; they are mere assertions ('table-thumping'). Instead of talking about whether God exists, it is better to ask whether anything useful is served by using the language of God: 'Do we want to weave one or more of the various religious traditions together with our deliberation over moral dilemmas, deepest hopes and need to be rescued from despair? . . . Does one or more of these religious traditions provide language we wish to use when putting together our self-image, determining what is most important to us?'[43]

Rorty's argument is not important for its intellectual rigour, but for the fact that it both reflects and shapes an increasingly dominant train of thought among a certain class of communicators in the global transmission of information and opinion. He adopts a circular argument to support his conclusions. When asked, 'Are these desirable norms?' or, 'Is this good social practice?' all we can do is ask, 'By reference to what encompassing social practice are we supposed to judge desirability?'[44] If social practices define desirable norms, then there is no way of deciding whether, for example, the practice of eugenics is acceptable. But the practice of eugenics has to be decided on the basis of prior ethical norms; these are not necessarily already agreed by those who practise it in the absence of such norms.

---

[40] Richard Rorty, 'Cultural Politics and the Question of the Existence of God', in *Radical Interpretation of Religion* (ed. Nancy K. Frankenberry; Cambridge: CUP, 2002), pp. 53–76.

[41] As Marx, Nietzsche and Freud alleged.

[42] Rorty, 'Cultural Politics', p. 57.

[43] Rorty, 'Cultural Politics', p. 71.

[44] Rorty, 'Cultural Politics', p. 74.

Rorty himself acknowledges the trouble with his line of reasoning when he says that it may seem that to acknowledge the ontological priority of the social entails allowing existence to be ascribed to anything that society finds it convenient to talk about. As in all attempts to ground behaviour in a utilitarian ethic, the question is begged: who decides what is *useful* to believe or the content of human happiness? In fragmented societies, where cultural politics are fiercely contested, who decides 'what is most important to us'? I suspect that Rorty's answer might be, 'Well, of course, the most ultra-liberal, politically sophisticated and intellectually successful should have the most votes!'

Judging by trends, an increasing number of people (mainly males?) might say that watching pornography is most important for them. And, as long as this habit did not induce them to abuse children sexually or resort to rape to fulfil their fantasies, why would they be wrong? They are as much justified in defining happiness for themselves as Rorty and his friends.

His proposal comes as the end product of decades when cultural politics has encouraged people to express themselves freely, to allow their subjective feelings to drive their moral sensibilities. Ultimately, it is incapable of giving good reasons for the acceptance of some norms and the rejection of others, because it resolutely refuses to face the question of whether there is a true way for human individuals and societies to flourish, irrespective of personal or majority desires.[45] So, if language about God is nothing more than a projection, a way of endorsing or sustaining whatever a given society may find acceptable, it would be better to throw it away. If it does not refer to a living reality, but only masks human aspirations, better to eliminate it.[46]

Approaches to Religious Diversity

Due mainly to migration, instantaneous communication across the globe and the resurgence of politically motivated religious activists, the impact of multiple religious convictions and practices has penetrated into nearly every corner of the world. Particularly in secular societies, which think that religion should by now have vanished over the horizon, the resurgence of certain forms of religion seems to portray 'the revenge of the gods'.

---

[45] See the extended argument on the implications of Rorty's philosophical and political stance in Kirk, *Future of Reason*, pp. 88–93.

[46] We will return to the question of the use of religious language in the next section.

It is not surprising, therefore, that religion, especially when mixed with political projects deemed subversive of liberal democracies, is receiving enormous attention. The destruction of the twin towers of the World Trade Centre in New York one September morning in 2001 has galvanised action to an unprecedented degree. Universities have gone out of their way to found institutes, centres and chairs in various aspects of religious studies, especially Islam. The religions themselves are being challenged as never before to give an account of the diversity in relation to their own truth claims. Here, I will survey briefly some of the more recent responses that have been given from within the Christian tradition to the plurality of religious beliefs and practices.

Epistemological issues

Before embarking on the survey, it should prove helpful to consider some of the prior issues that address an adequate approach to the subject. Kenneth Cragg points out that there is no starting-point for comparison, unless each faith possesses a trustworthy core of beliefs: 'There can be no *fiducia* if there is no explicitness, no certitude, no dependable meaning institutionalised in creed and symbol.'[47]

How and where are these to be recognised? Who has the authority to speak on behalf of a religion? Perhaps, the best we can do is to refer to the meticulous study that goes into writing handbooks and dictionaries on contemporary religions.[48] At least at the level of the theory of the different religions, including many of their sub-groups, there is a large measure of agreement about the core beliefs.

Cragg mentions another problem. Given that, at least in the case of religions of the book – those that derive their teaching from a revelation, disclosed once for all to chosen people – the text is fixed, how much room is available for different interpretations of the text in response to widely diverse contexts? Is there, as has been emphasised in the Catholic tradition of Christianity, a surplus of meaning (*sensus plenior*) in the text not necessarily envisaged by the original writers, but nevertheless deducible as a response to contemporary situations? These legitimate questions cannot be discussed within the confines of this work, but they are recognised as posing the problem of ascertaining when certain beliefs and practices may be said to have passed over from the orthodox to the heterodox.

---

[47] Cragg, *Christ and the Faiths*, p. 329.
[48] Such as John R. Hinnels, ed., *A Handbook of Living Religions* (London: Penguin Books, 1985); John R. Hinnels, ed., *The Penguin Dictionary of Religions: From Abraham to Zoroaster* (London: Penguin Books, 1984); John L. Esposito, *The Oxford Dictionary of Islam* (Oxford: OUP, 2003).

A major issue concerns enquiry into the truth status of religious claims. Assuming that all propositional statements are about some reality, whether it is about the external world, the inner human world of experience or a being existing outside matter, by what criteria can we judge whether they are true or mistaken? As Kenneth Cragg recognises, 'there is no feasible or agreed arbiter to adjudicate their claims'.[49]

Various suggestions have been made. Since the Enlightenment, reason seems to be a good candidate. However, in practice, it often means, 'if you think like me, you will come to see the truth'. Unfortunately, the desire to convince others that my beliefs are true can lead to bias, distortion and self-delusion. Given the fickle nature of human judgement, reason alone is an unreliable instrument for deciding between conflicting claims.

Others have suggested that the presence of (a sufficient number of?) saintly characters or an ability to endure through many adversities vindicates a particular religion. Intuition, feeling, emotion, capacity for idealism, capacity for realism, coherence of belief or psychological serviceability might all offer decisive evidence. Yet, all of them are themselves on trial.[50] This seems to leave us with two further possibilities: revelation and experience.

Revelation indicates a disclosure about the great questions of life that human beings, beginning with their own unaided reason and the knowledge gained from the natural world, could never answer. On the one hand, it is perfectly plausible to claim that, without a trustworthy unveiling of knowledge that comes in addition to what humans can discover for themselves, the ultimate mysteries of life would remain unanswered. On the other hand, there is the small matter of adjudicating which claims to revelation are true; if, indeed, any are. The argument adduced against the authenticity of any claim to revelation is that 'the multiplicity of belief systems precludes a self-disclosure by a rational god, for such a God would have revealed himself clearly without the possibility of such a diversity of perceptions. The variety of belief engenders confusion and, therefore, points to the hiddenness of God. The only true knowledge is one that is based on principles universally acknowledged and accessible.'[51]

In other words, it is alleged that all claims to revelation break down on the grounds that they are self-excluding. The argument assumes that God (if there is one) would have communicated with his creation in an unmistakeable manner, so that there could be no basis for ambiguity, doubt or disputation. There is also the complex matter of understanding

[49] Cragg, *Christ and the Faiths*, p. 338.
[50] See Cragg, *Christ and the Faiths*, p. 339.
[51] Kirk, *Future of Reason*, p. 53.

revelation aright. If, as seems to be generally recognised, all knowledge is partial and revisable, how can we be sure that we have heard the 'word of God' aright? 'Because, it may be said, all purported revelation has to be accepted and judged by humans, will not teaching arising from it be infected by the same human weakness that is liable to taint all our judgements? . . . The bridge between humans and God that revelation allegedly provides then becomes as clouded in fog as any other human advance towards knowledge.'[52]

To judge the credibility of religious claims we appear, therefore, to be left with religious experience. Religious experience on its own, however, can only be convincing to the believer because it is self-validating. Its reality can be challenged on the grounds that the experience is a self-induced illusion. There is no other evidence available that can help to support the conviction that the experience is authentic and to quell the suspicion that it is the result of a false impression. This is particularly true for experiences claimed within a monistic world-view, which dissolves the dualism between mind and matter, the external world and internal consciousness and exalts the undifferentiated unity of all things.

There seems to be no way of deciding the likely cause of experiences which are intensely individual to the believer who claims to have had them. As with revelation, the content of the experience may differ enormously across the various religious traditions. Moreover, it (e.g. the experience of suffering) will be interpreted within the parameters of the tradition to which the believer belongs, thus begging the question about the reality of contradictory experiences. Experience may be entirely convincing to the person concerned; however, it is an unreliable guide to the truth of religious claims, however intense it may seem.

There is one other possible way of deciding whether some religious claims may be true and others false. It is the ability to explain in the most plausible way possible the whole of reality in which human life is immersed. A theory is true to the extent that it is able to accomplish four tasks: be self-consistent; give credible answers to social and personal problems; reflect accurately all life's experiences and enable people of every kind of background to live by it.

One of the main methodological tools used by the experimental sciences for assessing outcomes of research-work is given the technical name of *abduction*.[53] Abduction is also known by the term *inference to the*

---

[52] Roger Trigg, *Rationality and Religion: Does Faith Need Reason?* (Oxford: Blackwell, 1998), p. 186.

[53] See James Ladyman, *Understanding Philosophy of Science* (London: Routledge, 2002), p. 47.

best explanation (henceforth IBE). It is a tool used by reason for settling disputes about the truth of a matter; it is evidence-based.

There are two particular mechanisms by which the method proceeds. The first works by way of contrast: 'best' implies the most persuasive among a number of alternative hypotheses; it seeks to answer the question 'why *this* account of reality rather than *that*?' The second is to keep a distinction between what Lipton calls 'the likeliest' and 'the loveliest' explanation, i.e. a 'distinction between the explanation most warranted by the evidence . . . and the explanation which would, if true, provide the most understanding'.[54]

IBE, as both a method of dialogue and a research method, appears to offer prima facie a potentially effective way of resolving the impasse created by contradictory claims to know the truth.[55] It is already used as a method of both discovery and confirmation in the experimental sciences and, therefore, by inference can be applied (with caution) to issues in areas of philosophy (such as epistemology and moral reasoning) and inter-religious encounter (such as giving explanations of suffering and evil) with a view to testing hypotheses and tentative claims about the nature of reality. So, in answer to the question, 'what is true?' in the context of the religious smorgasbord of contemporary societies, IBE offers potentially an excellent method for deciding between contradictory views. It assumes that conversation and discussion, in an atmosphere of openness and trust, will enhance understanding of the nature and veracity of religious claims.

This is an enormous assumption, given the tenacity with which people adhere to religious beliefs and practices. If IBE were to work satisfactorily in the field of religious convictions, as it does in that of the material sciences, it would mean that theories that could not account for certain realities in the world would have to be given up for more adequate ones. However, with regard to religious beliefs there are levels of human existence that do not respond so easily to rational persuasion. Nevertheless, IBE as a way of conversation about acute differences of opinion should be non-threatening to those willing to engage with its method, and possesses a good prospect of moving the question of truth-claims to a valid resolution.

---

[54] Peter Lipton, *Inference to the Best Explanation* (London: Routledge, 2nd edn, 2004), p. 207.

[55] I set out in much more detail the reasons for this claim (in the context of Christian witness in a secular society) in J. Andrew Kirk, *Christian Mission as Dialogue: Engaging the Current Epistemological Predicament of the West* (Nijmegen: Nijmegen Institute for Mission Studies, 2011). This is also available in electronic form from the Radboud University, Nijmegen, The Netherlands.

Inclusivist proposals

The threefold division of Christian theological reflection on other faiths – inclusivist, exclusivist and pluralist – has become commonplace. Although it is not wholly satisfactory, being too schematic and not open enough perhaps to subtle nuances, nobody yet has found a better way of classifying different approaches.

In an important document, published on behalf of the Church of England, inclusivism is described as follows:

> While holding firmly to the belief that God was supremely manifest in Jesus, inclusivist theories also affirm the universal presence of God's Spirit through the whole of Creation. God's saving power and presence is defined in the life, death and resurrection of Jesus, but it is not confined to him. Through his Logos or his Spirit, God is operative beyond Christian culture, bringing salvation to other peoples and cultures who may not even know the name of Jesus.[56]

> According to this view, where people respond to the spiritual illumination they have (provided, it is understood that the agent is the eternal logos who 'brings light to all people' (John 1:4)), seeking in their religious practices God's mercy and forgiveness and attempting to live out a life of peace, reconciliation and justice, God's salvation in Christ is available to them. Or, to put the matter the other way round, those who do these things already demonstrate God's salvific grace at work in their lives.[57]

Timothy Yates points to an article by Oliver Quick as seminal for the inclusivist way of thinking.[58] In it Professor Quick believes that other religions should be seen in the light of the Christian gospel, revealed for the first time in their own best and truest colours; and, by being thus revealed, enhance and enrich the glory of the gospel itself. Under such a proposal, to find a point of contact, even in a corrupt religion, was not to be relativist or syncretist. Rather, it is to find Christ (as ever unexpectedly) at Nazareth, despised for not being orthodox. For Quick such manifestations of true values as the Muslim's emphasis on universal brotherhood or the

---

[56] Church of England, *Towards a Theology for Inter-Faith Dialogue* (General Synod 625) (London: Church Information Office, 1984), paragraph 18.

[57] J. Andrew Kirk, *What is Mission? Theological Explorations* (London: Darton, Longman & Todd, 1999), p. 129.

[58] Oliver Quick, 'The Jerusalem Meeting and the Christian Message', *International Review of Missions* 17 (1928): pp. 445–54.

Buddhist's sympathy for pain and suffering were tints of light, picked up by the light of the gospel and brought into a new and truer relief.[59]

In brief, the inclusivist proposal suggests that salvation is accessible to people who are followers of any of the religious traditions, but it is mediated through the universal Christ, whose work of redemption covers all who are looking for an escape from a life of oppression and suffering through the gift of God. These have, as it were, become aware intuitively that salvation is by grace alone, even though they do not know directly what its source might be.

Exclusivist proposals

The exclusivist position postulates a radical break between the message of the gospel of Jesus Christ, as found in the New Testament, and all religious manifestations. Whereas inclusivism allows for some continuity between the different faiths, exclusivism, in the famous riposte of Karl Barth, says No![60] According to Ninian Smart, for example, Theravada Buddhism is convinced of the incompatibility of Buddhism and theism as understood in the West. Smart adds his own comment: 'the gulf between the two systems does indeed seem a large one.'[61]

From the beginning of 'the Way', the name given to the community of the first followers of Jesus,[62] Christian discipleship was exclusive. Thus, for example, combining Christian baptism and initiation into a mystery cult would not have been tolerated. Those who sought baptism into Christ were required to renounce all other allegiances.

Lesslie Newbigin, speaking about Muslim and Hindu converts to Christ says that at the point of crisis, Jesus appeared to them as one who threatened all that was most sacred to them. He goes on to say, the unique historic deed of the cross stands as a witness against all claims of religion to be a means of salvation.[63] Religion is not the means of salvation. Indeed, in the

---

[59] See Timothy Yates, *Christian Mission in the Twentieth Century* (Cambridge: CUP, 1996), pp. 102–3.

[60] This is the general tenor of Barth's approach to the notion of religion in 'God's Revelation and the Abolition of Religion' in *Church Dogmatics*, I/2, Section 17. For a critical dialogue with Barth's uncompromising position, see Hendrik Vroom, 'Karl Barth and the Nature of False and True Religion', *Studies in Interreligious Dialogue*, 22, 2012, 1, pp. 74–84.

[61] Ninian Smart, *Beyond Ideology: Religion and the Future of Western Civilization* (Gifford lectures) (New York: Harper & Row, 1981), pp. 112 and 105.

[62] See Acts 9:2; 19:9,23; 22:4, 24:14,22.

[63] Lesslie Newbigin, 'The Gospel among the Religions', *Mission Trends No. 5: Faith Meets Faith* (ed. G. Anderson and P. Stransky; Grand Rapids, MI: Eerdmans, 1981), p. 13.

debate about salvation and the religions, the testimony of converts from other religions is often ignored. Their experience of a reality (salvation in the name of Jesus) they are convinced was not available to them through the religion they grew up in is deemed irrelevant to the discussion. Carl Braaten argues strongly that exclusive claims about Jesus Christ are not a footnote to the Gospel; they are the gospel. If Jesus Christ is the unique and universal saviour, there is no salvation in non-Christian religions; if there is, Jesus Christ is not the universal saviour.[64]

Brian Hebblethwaite makes the philosophical point that, if God is going to make himself known in a personal and specific way, it has to be through a particular story; personal self-revelation and an atoning act cannot be replaced by a universally available set of truths.[65] One of the principal problems with all non-exclusivist claims concerning the mediation of salvation is that they make such generalised assertions, intended to fit exceptionally diverse religious concepts, that they end up by being vague in the extreme.[66]

It has been pointed out that, logically speaking, it is impossible to avoid being exclusivist, for the very denial of exclusivism rests on an exclusivist proposition: in both other theological theories of the relationship between religions, by definition exclusivism has to be excluded. As a corollary to this conclusion, it is also pointed out that all religions tend inevitably to their own form of exclusivism. Each religion not only maintains that its teaching and practice is unique, in the sense that it is *sui generis* (one and only), but that it is unique in understanding how the fullness of spiritual life may be appropriated. In this sense, each one makes a claim to possessing an unrivalled insight into the mysteries of human life in the universe, and also to being normative for assessing the claims of other faith traditions.

Pluralist proposals

The third distinct position that Christians take towards other faith traditions starts from the assumption that, as Kenneth Cracknell puts it, the plurality of religious traditions is within the gracious purposes of God and God's gracious presence is found among people of other faith.[67] Some

---

[64] Carl Braaten, 'The Uniqueness and Universality of Jesus Christ', *Mission Trends No. 5: Faith Meets Faith* (ed. G. Anderson and P. Stransky; Grand Rapids, MI: Eerdmans, 1981), pp. 75, 78.

[65] Brian Hebblethwaite, 'Religious Language and Religious Pluralism', *Anvil* 4 (1987), p. 107.

[66] This point will be taken up again in the next section on pluralist proposals.

[67] Kenneth Cracknell, *Towards a New Relationship: Christians and People of Other Faith* (London: Epworth Press, 1986), p. 110.

people argue that for God to have confined himself to one particular historical trajectory, leaving billions of human beings outside his salvific purposes, would negate his absolute justice. For them this notion would dishonour God, and leave his character stained by a series of immoral acts.

A second assumption asserts that the acts of faith made within other religious exercises lead to authentic visions of God. Religions differ in the way in which they portray religious experience, because of divergent cultural histories. Nevertheless, behind the variety of expressions of faith and cultic practices lies the same ultimate reality. This may be communicated by an intensely personal apprehension of the divine, or it may be conveyed through the medium of mystical encounter.[68]

Christians, because their own core faith centres on the atoning sacrifice of Jesus Christ for the sins of the whole world (1 John 2:2; 4:10,14), are concerned about how salvation may be appropriated by those for whom Christ is an unknown figure. Pluralists postulate that, for all religions, salvation (liberation, transformation or enlightenment) is achievable through the practical disciplines that they teach. The genuineness of their spiritual life is a guarantee that significant changes are taking place. Christians need to go beyond the idea of 'salvation history' focussed entirely upon the scheme of election, promise and fulfilment in the life of Israel, Jesus Christ and the church. There is a mystery of salvation at work in the nations, where the grace of God is operative when Brahmins, Buddhists or Muslims read and put into practice the injunctions of their own Scriptures.[69]

Raimundo Pannikar has put forward the notion of homology to explain how pluralists come to their conclusions about the equivalence of all religions. There is a correlation between the points of two different systems, so that the point of one corresponds to the point in another. The notions in the different religious projects play equivalent roles; they occupy homologous[70] places within the respective systems. In the case of Brahmin and Yahweh, for example, though the context and contents of their appearing are utterly different, and not mutually translatable, each plays a similar role in a different cultural setting. They both refer to a highest value and an absolute term.[71]

---

[68] See Smart, *Beyond Ideology*, pp. 112ff.

[69] George Khodr, 'The Economy of the Holy Spirit' in *Mission Trends No. 5: Faith Meets Faith* (ed. G. Anderson and P. Stransky; Grand Rapids, MI: Eerdmans, 1981), pp. 43–5.

[70] Taken from the biological sciences, it refers to items 'having the same relative position, proportion, value, structure, etc.' *Concise English Dictionary* (London: Cassell, 1993), p. 652.

[71] Raimundo Pannikar, 'The Rules of the Game' in *Mission Trends No. 5: Faith Meets Faith* (ed. G. Anderson and P. Stransky; Grand Rapids, MI: Eerdmans,

Another assumption made by many pluralists is that religious language functions in a particular way: it does not intend to assert propositions about objective realities; rather it is picture language whose purpose is to express religious commitment and moral and spiritual ideals. Religious language, therefore, is culturally shaped by particular historical traditions, yet yields the same apprehension of the transcendent.[72]

Charles Davis, in a book that caused much controversy when first published, called for a radical reinterpretation of the Christian faith in order to make room for religious plurality. He finds the way forward in the modern concept of symbol: 'Each concrete social form of religious faith is centred, so it seems, not upon a list of propositional beliefs, but upon a set of symbols . . . A complex of symbols lies at the heart of every religious tradition . . . at the centre of Christianity is the symbol Jesus Christ.'[73] Davis defines symbols in the following way: 'symbols are the images that express the dynamic thrust of man towards the unknown and yet to come . . . they reach out to this mysterious reality and include it within their meaning by becoming analogies.'[74] He draws the following conclusion: 'Divergence at the interpretive or doctrinal level does not constitute a fundamental religious difference . . . The symbols are presented as a series of stories or myths stressing that religious language in its fundamental form is figurative, analogical, existential, rather than plain, literal and direct.'[75]

A Theology of Religions

As the pluralist case is the one that has been most systematically advanced in recent years, I will endeavour to explore the theological (and philosophical) thinking that undergirds it and engage with it from the perspective of its many critics. In this way it is to be hoped that the main theological issues will be exposed.

Charles Davis's use of symbols is a pertinent place to begin. He begins with the assumption that the first flowerings of a critical response to the

---

(cont.) 1981), pp. 118–19 (originally ch. 3 of *The Intrareligious Dialogue* (New York: Paulist Press, 1978).

[72] See Brian Hebblethwaite, 'Religious Language and Religious Pluralism', *Anvil* 4 (1987), pp. 101–2. Brian Hebblethwaite is not himself a pluralist, but here describes a pluralist viewpoint.

[73] Charles Davis, *Christ and the World Religions* (London: Hodder & Stoughton, 1970), p. 104.

[74] Davis, *Christ and the World Religions*, p. 108.

[75] Davis, *Christ and the World Religions*. We will pick up the consequences of Davis's understanding of religious symbols in the next section.

dominance of technical reason in the aftermath of the Enlightenment, which accompanied the student rebellions of the late 1960s, presaged a new desire for a religious interpretation of the world. However, in the 'making of a counter-culture',[76] the revival of religion will not be that of the traditional forms, but a reappraisal of religion as such. The problem with many studies of religion is that they are dealing with theoretical categories, lumped together under the titles of Buddhism, Christianity, Hinduism, Islam or whatever. To a large degree they ignore religious practice in its manifold forms. In a multi-religious world the religion of the textbooks is esoteric; it does not reflect the beliefs and practices of common religious observance.

Thus, if we stick with a phenomenological approach to specific religious practices, we will discover that 'each concrete form of religion is centred upon a set of symbols. The central symbolic complex is always primary: propositional beliefs are derived from that. So . . . there have been and are many religions according to the cluster of symbols which predominate for the persons concerned.'

He goes on to assert that this new consciousness of the reality of religion on the ground means that 'there can be a free regrouping of religious persons according to different types of religion'. The mission of Christianity is 'to provide the symbolic resources needed in the reawakening of (the) religious consciousness of the West'.[77] In other words, if the religious or spiritual dimension of human life is to be recaptured from out of the tedious and exhausted secularism of modernity, 'let a thousand religious blossoms bloom'.

Here we have one example – one of the first in the recent past – of an attempt to arrest the onward march of a thoroughly materialist, reductionist account of the world by affirming what everyone knows in their own experience, that the human being 'cannot live by bread alone'. At the same time, it allows free experimentation in spiritual practices and good reasons for not being tied to the formalised structures of official belief-systems.

'The Ultimately Real'

Naturally such an approach to a new counter-culture means, among other things, a thorough reinterpretation of the Christian faith (and other

[76] See Theodore Roszak, *The Making of a Counter-Culture: Reflections on the Technocratic Society and its Youthful Opposition* (Oakland, CA: University of California Press, 1968).

[77] Charles Davis, 'Religious Pluralism and the New Counter-Culture', *The Listener* (9 April 1970): p. 480.

traditional religions). In the last few decades those who have set their hand to such a task have not been lacking.

The most prolific and influential has been John Hick. His own spiritual pilgrimage is reflected in the development of his theological outlook. Beginning with a commitment to an orthodox Christian faith in the evangelical tradition, he has subsequently moved from a christocentric account of God to a generalised theism, which in the opinion of some has left him dangerously exposed to the accusation of a tacit atheism.[78]

It is difficult to do justice to Hick's main thesis in a short space; nevertheless, it is worth trying, as it represents one of the most substantial attempts to construct a universally valid account of religious belief as a common experience in all cultures. There is an ultimate reality (beyond the universe), says Hick, which he refers to as the Real. Although itself beyond the range of our human conceptual systems, its universal presence is humanly experienced in the various forms made possible by our linguistic systems. This Real is ineffable, i.e. it is beyond the possibility of any human language to express its nature or character. For this reason it is illegitimate to use statements of this reality that imply that it is personal, rather than being impersonal, good or evil, just or unjust, because these concepts do not apply.[79] The ultimately Real does not possess properties or attributes that would tie it down to any one tradition of understanding (for example, monotheism).

The Real exists in itself (Hick insists that his epistemological assumption is critical-realist), but it can only be experienced through the phenomena of religious 'appearances to consciousness as formed by different religious traditions'. This means that all religious beliefs are equally warranted; in the words of Thomas Aquinas, 'the thing known is in the knower according to the mode of the knower'. The test by which people of faith may judge the authenticity of their religious experience is in its moral and spiritual fruit in human life. When people are moved by their beliefs and practices from self-centred existence to a Reality-centred existence they are on the way to salvation. No one religion can claim any final truth about existence; for, on the basis of empirical observation, the adherents of no one religion stand out as morally or spiritually superior to the rest of the human race.

As said above, Hick's general theory entails both a denial of mainstream Christian teaching on the person and work of Christ and the reconstruction

---

[78] For example, Sumner B. Twiss, 'The Philosophy of Religious Pluralism: A Critical Appraisal of Hick and His Critics', *Journal of Religion* 70 (1990): pp. 533–63; J. Andrew Kirk, 'John Hick's Kantian Theory of Religious Pluralism and the Challenge of Secular Thinking', *Studies in Interreligious Dialogue* 12 (2002): pp. 23–35.

[79] Hick, *Interpretation of Religion*, pp. xixff.

of a Christology that fits the pluralist hypothesis.[80] According to Hick, Christians, when they refer to their object of worship, refer to *their distinctively Christian image* of ultimate reality as Trinity. This belief is derived from experience, where Christian faith begins, coming originally from the contagion that Jesus transmitted to his followers of being in the presence of the Heavenly Father of whom he spoke.[81] A statement about the divinity of Christ is not to be taken literally, but is nevertheless mythologically true, i.e. it sets us on the true path of transformation.

Hick's approach to the origin of Christian belief in the writings of the early church requires him to make a thoroughgoing distinction between what Jesus taught about the kingdom of God, and what the church taught about the divine nature and unique sacrifice of the Christ. It is based on a sceptical opinion about the historical reliability of the gospel accounts of Jesus' ministry and teaching. It also involves a selective approach to Jesus' teaching, rejecting as not original all claims, alleged to have been made by him, that allude to his divine nature. So, to make his theory work, either he has to hold fast to a revisionist interpretation of early Christian history, for which there is little substantial evidence,[82] or he has to postulate a symbolic reinterpretation of Jesus' claims, making them signify something other than what they expressly connote.

Hick admits that his theory appears to run into the difficulty of not dealing adequately with conflicting truth-claims. His response to this problem,[83] however, lands him in an impossible contradiction. He appears to be advocating two different understandings of truth: a critical-realist account and a pragmatic view. On the one hand, something is true if it corresponds to the way things are ultimately. Thus, he believes in the objective ontological reality of the ultimately Real (i.e. its existence, independent of all our thoughts and imaginings), even though nothing can be said about it. On the other hand, a belief or practice is true, if it is

---

[80] This was attempted in *The Myth of God Incarnate* (J. Hick, ed., London: SCM Press, 1977).

[81] Hick, *Interpretation of Religion*, p. xxx.

[82] It appears that Hick bases his interpretation of the New Testament documents on historical-critical methods of a former era, now judged to be mainly speculative and question-begging. Today, many scholars are convinced that the first disciples transmitted the events and teaching of Jesus faithfully through carefully controlled oral traditions; see James D.G. Dunn, *Christianity in the Making, vol. 1, Jesus Remembered* (Grand Rapids: Eerdmans, 2003); James D.G. Dunn, *A New Perspective on Jesus: What the Quest for the Historical Jesus Missed* (London: SPCK, 2005); Richard Bauckham, *Jesus and the Eyewitnesses: The Gospels as Eyewitness Testimony* (Grand Rapids, MI: Eerdmans, 2006).

[83] Hick, *Interpretation of Religion*, pp. 363ff.

soteriologically effective: i.e., if it brings about 'the realisation of a limit-lessly better possibility for human existence'.

I think that ultimately Hick's theological account of religion is inco-herent, just because he desires to have his cake and eat it! He wishes to maintain that something (not someone!) exists ultimately. It cannot be known in itself, only in its assumed manifestations in completely different guises in people's religious experiences; nevertheless, religion is not pure projection of human aspirations or anxieties onto a mythological figure that does not exist except as a human invention. At the same time, he appears to be saying that the essence of religion is contained only in deep linguistic structures that have become the vehicle for articulating a level of human consciousness and ethical behaviour that probes a long way beyond the mundane; no more can be said about any other reality.[84] His claimed realism vanishes (like the Cheshire cat – not even the smile is left) in the intrinsically unidentifiable and unknowable mysticism of the Ultimately Real;[85] it is swallowed up by an ethical idealism that always begs the question, what does it mean to be good, and how can we know?

Hick's attempt to convince others that he has constructed an adequate philosophical-theological framework for concluding that all religious expressions[86] can be unified, in spite of their seeming disparities, is ship-wrecked on the immovable rock of the truth question. As Roger Trigg[87] and others have cogently argued, an adequate theology of religions can only be based on a robust realism concerning the ability to discover the truth about all matters pertaining to the world, belief and action. Hick claims to be a critical-realist; in fact, in so far as he replaces talk about a hypothet-ical transcendent reality by talk about different religious beliefs and prac-tices, all of which are culturally and socially shaped to such an extent that they make contradictory claims about what is ultimate, he is an anti-re-alist. A realist is one who believes that 'the objective character of reality, independent of judgements, beliefs, concepts, language and so on' is acces-sible to human cognition. In this sense atheists, who do not believe there is anything existing outside of material existence are realists; they are making an assertion about the whole of reality as they perceive it. 'An anti-realist

[84] For a thorough analysis and critique of what he calls Hick's traditional prop-ositional-realist view of religion and his cultural-linguistic view, see Twiss, 'Philosophy of Religious Pluralism', *passim*.
[85] Wittgenstein's *bon mot*, 'a nothing would serve just as well as a something about which nothing could be said' (*Philosophical Investigations* (Oxford: Blackwell, 1953), # 304), seems to capture the dilemma appropriately.
[86] Does he really mean all? Or, does he mean the enduring world religions of which he approves?
[87] Trigg, *Rationality and Religion*, pp. 59–69.

would on the other hand change the subject of what a belief is about to the general character of the belief.'[88] In other words, in Hick's thinking, religion is about commitment to something (faith) beyond the empirically testable and a movement 'from self-centredness to love and compassion towards our fellow human beings';[89] it is not about understanding the true nature of the Ultimately Real (UR).

A thought experiment

Now supposing that one were to start from a different hypothesis, namely that the UR is personal and defines the meaning of being personal. And suppose that this ultimately personal is of such a nature that he/she desires to create a material universe out of nothing and to place in it beings with which he/she can communicate. Is it not probable that he/she would choose one group of people to be the vehicle of this communication, so that they could capture the essence of this transcendent being and the revelation of his/her purpose in creation? Moreover, is it not highly plausible that this being would seek not only to speak through chosen messengers, but also in person, and to do so by entering the world as a human being? These suppositions of the Judeo-Christian faith are just as reasonable and credible as Hick's belief that religious phenomena are experiences of, but do not ultimately refer to, this UR, which cannot be known 'in-itself'.

From this discussion, a logical conclusion should be drawn: one or the other premise in the two thought experiments is correct, or they are both incorrect; they cannot both be correct. This means that Hick's view is only one among other options for elaborating a coherent and conceivable theology of religions. It is, therefore, just as exclusive as those which he denigrates as exclusive theories of religious diversity. The problem of the truth-content and truth-value of religious claims cannot be evaded.

Testing truth claims

As outlined above, as a way of approaching the question of the truth of affirmations made about religious life, I have suggested and elaborated an adaptation of the heuristic method known as inference to the best explanation.[90] By a comparative analysis of different propositions and theories, there is a probability that one gives a better explanation of the wealth of

---

88 Trigg, *Rationality and Religion*, p. 65.
89 Kirk, 'John Hick's Kantian Theory', p. 24.
90 Kirk, *Christian Mission as Dialogue*; see also Kirk, *Future of Reason*, pp. 125–6, 204–5, 207ff., 226–8.

human experience both of the external world and the internal world of human consciousness, conscience, rationality, emotions, personal relationships, and so on, than others. This is the claim that is made by Christian theism, one which has to be argued for against alternative interpretations. It is not possible, for both logical and empirical reasons, to accept that mutually exclusive explanations could somehow all be part of a wider truth. A choice has to be made. My expectation is that most spokespeople for other religious traditions would say, 'and so say all of us!'

Dialogue and/or Mission?

In modern mission theory, dialogue has come to mean a mutually respectful conversation between equal partners concerning deep questions of belief, commitment and ethical action. From the Christian side the concept and practice has been elaborated almost entirely in relation to the five generally recognised 'world' religions[91] – Buddhism, Hinduism, Islam, Judaism and Sikhism – each with many centuries of existence. I have suggested elsewhere that the following principles usually motivate and guide the practice of dialogue:[92]

- Respect for the dignity and integrity of all human beings. Given that religious belief and practice are central to the lives of the majority of humanity, respect entails taking seriously what other people say matters most to them, irrespective of whether I share their ideas or not.
- The need to represent other people's views fairly. It is dishonest and unjust to rely exclusively on outsiders' interpretations of the meaning and implications of a particular faith. Careful listening to practitioners is a precondition for overcoming caricatures and stereotypes.
- The need to hear and consider what others say about our beliefs and practices. Convictions, when held intelligently, are open to criticism leading to the possibility of conversion and change.
- The call to work together in common projects that seek justice and reconciliation in society, such as the implementation of human rights, community development and the overcoming of community strife.
- Mutual witness. For some this is the most controversial aspect of dialogue. However, there is a sense in which all religions are 'evangelistic' in intent,

---

[91] The World Council of Churches has also promoted dialogue with representatives of contemporary ideologies, most explicitly with Marxism and other forms of socialism; see *Guidelines on Dialogue with People of Living Faiths and Ideologies* (Geneva: WCC, 1979).

[92] Kirk, *Mission Under Scrutiny*, pp. 28–9.

in that they see themselves as the guardians of crucial insights into the nature and meaning of life itself and how it should be conducted, which they have an obligation to share. Dialogue:

> assumes that the partners in dialogue have basic beliefs that are distinguish-able in principle from contingent, cultural forms of them, that there are points of contact between different belief systems that enable a genuine intellectual engagement to take place, that the parties to the dialogue . . . believe that they may have something to learn as well as to give in the exchange, that the opin-ions we do not share are fairly represented, and finally that the issues under discussion are significant matters not only for theoretical considerations, but also in daily living.[93]

Dialogue does not mean that one has to concede the validity of another religion's world-view.[94] It does not mean that one is necessarily working towards a mutually acceptable synthesis of beliefs or common actions. It does not mean that those in conversation are forbidden *ab initio* from trying to persuade the others of the wisdom of believing as they do, as long as this is done in gentleness, without coercion, and with the highest regard for the humanity of the other. It does not mean that one is obliged to put one's own fundamental convictions in parenthesis, whilst engaged with the core beliefs of others. Above all, it does not mean that one has to accept *a priori* an all inclusive (pluralist) position on other faiths, in order for dialogue to be fruitful. Indeed, it can be cogently argued that the exclusivist may well engage in a more rewarding dialogue than people who hold other perspectives, just because all religions are exclusive to a large degree, and their adherents will therefore understand one another much better.

In the New Testament, dialogue has its own distinctive meaning. It is used quite frequently in the book of Acts by Paul's companion, Luke, to describe Paul's method of teaching in the synagogues (of the Jewish dias-pora), being translated by the NRSV as 'argue', 'have a discussion', 'hold a discussion', 'talk', 'dispute' and 'discuss' (e.g. Acts 17:2,17; 18:4,19; 19:8ff.; 20:7, 9; 24:12, 25):

> Paul more than any other New Testament figure actually engaged in inter-faith dialogue in practice and reflected on it theologically. He related both to the sophisticated scriptural faith of his own background – Rabbinic Judaism

---

[93] Kirk, *Christian Mission as Dialogue*, p. 128.
[94] As Kenneth Cracknell says, all religious traditions are 'all-inclusive systems and theories of life rooted in a religious basis', *Towards a New Relationship*, p. 91.

– and to Greek polytheism in both its developed philosophical form and its primitive paganism. In Acts we see him seeking to persuade Jews to see in Jesus their Messiah (e.g. 13:16–41), and to persuade Greeks to see in Jesus the Saviour appointed by their Creator (14:14–17), and their Judge (17:31).[95]

For reasons I have already hinted at, dialogue is not exclusive of mission. Dialogue cannot be authentic, unless it issues in an invitation to consider the truth claims that the other is committed to. In spite of the false methods that have, all too often, been used in taking the good news of Jesus Christ to people of different faiths (for example, material inducements to convert, coercion, harassment, propaganda and subjugation), Christian people have an obligation to share sensitively and appropriately the truth, as they see it, as it is in Jesus (Eph. 4:21; Rom. 1:14–15; 1 Cor. 9:16): 'Dialogue with people of other faiths and ideologies is misunderstood if it is presented as the only way of mission or if it is represented as being complacent and tolerant in the face of evil nonsense . . . we share in dialogue because we want to share in the blessings of the gospel.'[96]

Of course, it may be possible to build on other religions' genuine insights into the ultimate nature of reality, as is the case of the personal piety of the Indian bhakti poets with their emphasis on divine mercy and grace or the struggle to identify one personal God in the case of Ramanuja.[97] However, this has to be done with caution, just because the distinctive message of God's singular acts of salvation through the cross and resurrection of Jesus Christ, the one and only Messiah and Redeemer, tends to be absorbed into an alien pattern of thought and thereby transformed from a gift of God into another human work.

In the last analysis, dialogue is an activity that goes on among people, not religions. It is more a matter of relationships than debate.[98] To convey the wonder and beauty of the story of Jesus as told and interpreted by Jesus' first followers (which is the essence of evangelism) one needs to enter as deeply as possible into the material, affective and intellectual world of the other and build bridges of understanding. So dialogue without mission betrays fundamental Christian convictions about truth; but mission without dialogue betrays an indifference to the human integrity of the person with whom we wish to share the story.

[95] Chris Wright, 'Inter Faith Dialogue', *Anvil* 1 (1984), p. 252.
[96] Cracknell, *Towards a New Relationship*, p. 29.
[97] See Hendrik Kraemer, *The Christian Message in a Non-Christian World* (London: Edinburgh House Press, 1938), p. 372.
[98] See Stanley J. Samartha, 'Partners in Community: Some Reflections on Hindu-Christian Relations Today', *Occasional Bulletin of Missionary Research* 4 (April 1980), p. 78.

12

Secular Worlds

Now all the Athenians and the foreigners living there would spend their time in nothing but telling or hearing something new.[1]

Defining the Indefinable?

Secular

The terminology that surrounds the concept of secular – *secularization, secularity, secularism* – is often related, by immediate association and by way of contrast, with religion. To what extent this pairing is fair or illuminating I will explore in the course of this chapter. Whatever the conclusion, the terminology shares almost the same amount of ambiguity as religion.

In its origin, secular meant, 'belonging to this present world' and 'civil' in contrast to 'ecclesiastical'. Only at a later date did it acquire an anti-religious connotation: 'nothing but this world' and 'civil rather than ecclesiastical'. It is right, therefore, at least to begin my survey with the unprejudiced version; not least because, at a time of increasing tension between religious and secular viewpoints, it points to several positive changes secured for contemporary societies.

A secular society has come to represent an entrenching in law of the freedom of conscience. A space has been created in which human beings are free from moral and legal pressures to act in certain ways by conforming to other people's expectations. In Western nations, this freedom was initiated largely by nonconformist Christian campaigning.[2] In the first instance, it touched on religious beliefs, then later on gender, economic status and ethnic identity. It was argued that none of these

---

[1] Lukas, *Acts of Apostles* (c.70 AD), chapter 17, verse 21.
[2] See Owen Chadwick, *The Secularization of the European Mind in the Nineteenth Century* (Cambridge: CUP, 1985), pp. 26–7.

should be considered as constituting a ban on any of the benefits of full citisenship (the rights, for example, to education, work, and participation in public life). Max Stackhouse, in his historical survey of the rise of a concern for human rights,[3] demonstrates the strong Christian roots of this sense of the absolute call of conscience.[4]

The theoretical grounding for a breakthrough in the struggle against absolute regimes comes in two complementary convictions. First, human beings, by virtue of bearing the image of God, possess an intrinsic dignity and worth that no amount of human repression or arbitrary legislation can efface. Their value is guaranteed by the simple virtue of having been born. Therefore, each person enjoys an equality of importance and esteem. This fact implies that no one has the right to treat another as simply a means to his or her ends. Further, it also presupposes that the state or other powerful institutions have a burden of proof to justify the curtailing of freedoms. Second, beliefs by their very nature should be the result of free acts of the intellect. If they are held out of fear, due to the imposition of a superior force, they no longer reflect the authentic convictions of the individual. David Martin, in a penetrating observation on the logic of the Christian message, says, 'The separation of Caesar and God, nation and religion is paradoxically, the end of religion, but the essence of Christianity.'[5]

In this sense, secular stands for the abolition of coercive practices that seek to force people to hold certain types of belief, whether religious, ethical, political or ideological. The converse was medieval Catholicism, seen at its worst in the enforced conversion of the indigenous peoples in Latin America in the sixteenth century.[6] As we have seen in the case of the Anabaptist movement in the same century,[7] the magisterial Reformation adopted stringent measures against dissenters. The attempt to impose religious conformity in Britain in the seventeenth century led to the colo-nization of North America, to denominationalism and to the separation of church and state.

In modern times, Fascism and Communism have been notorious for their brutal repression of dissidents. Muslim leaders from early on in the spread of Islam imposed a system of discrimination on minority peoples who would not convert to the faith. Today, in many Islamic-constituted

---

[3] Stackhouse, Max L. *Creeds, Society and Human Rights: A Study in Three Cultures* (Grand Rapids, MI: Eerdmans, 1984).

[4] We have already traced one strand of this Christian tradition in Chapter 5.

[5] This could be considered a theological interpretation of the sociological theory of differentiation (see below); see David Martin, *A General Theory of Seculariza-tion* (Oxford: Blackwell, 1978), pp. 69–82.

[6] See Chapter 5.

[7] In Chapter 6.

nations, it is a crime with harsh penalties to try to persuade Muslims to change their beliefs.

This freedom of conscience is a value eminently worth preserving against all attempts to enforce, by means of physical, psychological or moral pressure, any kind of arbitrary conformity to the beliefs and actions of others. This freedom is enshrined in Articles 18 and 19 of the universal Declaration of Human Rights:

> Everyone has the right to freedom of thought, conscience and religion; this right includes freedom to change his religion or belief, and freedom either alone or in community with others and in public or private to manifest his religion or belief in teaching, practice, worship and observance. (Article 18)

> Everyone has the right to freedom of opinion and expression; this right includes freedom to hold opinions without interference and to seek to receive and impart information and ideas through any media and regardless of frontiers. (Article 19)

The interpretation of freedom given in these two articles is currently in danger of being eroded in the interests of 'political correctness' and the elimination of 'hate speech' and 'incitement to violence', even in societies that pride themselves on their secular status.

Secularization

The thesis

Particularly since the 1960s many commentators have attempted to understand and interpret a social trend that has gathered force in the latter part of the twentieth century. Everyone is agreed that in highly industrialised, urbanised and economically advanced nations with a certain stability of democratic government and judicial processes remarkable changes have taken place in a short period of time with regard to shared core beliefs. The place of religion in society, in terms of individual convictions, participation in activities and the influence of religious bodies on public decision-making, has diminished strikingly. There has been an increasing tendency to challenge statements about belief and behaviour based on an unquestionable authority, especially if the authority is said to rest on a supernatural reality.[8]

The process of secularization is characterised by an increasing preoccupation with temporal affairs and the overall pursuit of happiness in

---

[8] See Alan D. Gilbert, *The Making of Post-Christian Britain: A History of the Secularisation of Modern Society* (Harlow: Longman, 1980), p. 23.

this life. The 1960s generation became increasingly inarticulate with regard to religious ideas and ideals. Christian faith in Western European nations gradually lost its drawing power and, therefore, its sway over the minds and consciences of huge swathes of the population. Immoral acts (such as cohabiting, homosexual liaisons and abortion), formerly considered by Christian teaching to be sins against a holy God, became acceptable. The generation born immediately after the Second World War increasingly defied convention. Religion was deemed to be an activity that belonged to the past; its beliefs and demands considered quaint and curious remnants from a bygone age.[9] Indeed, Callum Brown dates the loss of what he calls the definitive Christian protocols to 1963, specifically between the end of the ban on the publishing of D.H. Lawrence's *Lady Chatterley's Lover* and the Beatles' first LP!

The course of secularization followed both intellectual and social paths.[10] As belief in the guiding power of revealed truth faded, so reliance on human powers of unaided rational thinking took centre stage. Laws were no longer supposed to have emanated from an all-knowing deity; rather, it seemed obvious historically that laws have always been created by humans in their own interests. For a considerable time past, communities that have liked to think of themselves as emancipated from speculative myths about another world have believed that their ability to define standards of good and evil is superior to past efforts:

> A kind of de-conversion experience has taken place by which, over several centuries, religious beliefs have become marginal to life, where to be irreligious is to be normal, where religious beliefs, where they do exist, have been relocated from the public world to the private, inner experience of the divine or sacred. Holy days, when the sacred (and 'secular') reality of the Saviour of the world has been celebrated, have become holidays (celebrations of the secular values of rest and relaxation) . . . Meanwhile moral ideas of good and evil, right and wrong, are disconnected from the demands of a personal God and seen to rest on the foundation of natural rights, evolutionary advantage or utility.[11]

So human beings are alone as agents in a search for an understanding of life's meaning. They have replaced God to become the creators of their

---

[9] See Callum Brown, *The Death of Christian Britain* (London: Routledge, 2001), pp. 180–85.

[10] See David Lyon, 'Secularisation', *Third Way* (July/August 1984): p. 24.

[11] J. Andrew Kirk, 'Christian Mission in Multifaith Situations' in *Theology and the Religions: A Dialogue* (ed. Viggo Mortensen; Grand Rapids, MI: Eerdmans, 2003), pp. 155–6.

own destiny. Only what can be established rationally on the basis of conclusive empirical evidence should be believed.[12]

At the same time, due to the huge changes brought about by the industrial revolution, societies became fragmented. The reality of *differentiation* most adequately sums up the secularization process.[13] The various spheres of human activity became separated into different domains.[14] Specialization in a variety of disciplines (such as education, social welfare, law, economic management, physical and psychological health and the various sciences) became more pronounced. Industrialization demanded a division of labour, in which people became experts in an increasingly specialised range of activities in an ever more complex set of manufacturing and financial sectors. The cohesive, interdependent rural communities of the past were largely dissolved: 'In the modern industrial concern, the organization of a complex series of tasks is essential . . . Some must have the authority to direct and organise the activities of others . . . Thus a highly specialised division of labour tends to generate a hierarchy of authority and a system of rules.'[15]

The main consequence, according to Max Weber, was the bureaucratization of society. The trained and highly qualified specialists in the different areas of life became the authorities who set the rules and patrolled them. Laws increased exponentially in order to regulate working practices and a career-oriented civil service came into being to supervise and ensure compliance.

Another consequence of differentiation was the creation of a pronounced stratification of society into different 'classes'. Space precludes an adequate discussion of a complex set of different realities, whose interpretation is often determined by particular ideological commitments.[16] Suffice it to say that both job specification and unequal financial rewards for employment opportunities in the new enterprises created severe disparities in social status. These were aligned to the ownership of the means of production and the balance of power between salaried workers and the capitalist entrepreneurs.[17]

Industrialization caused considerable disruption to the life of Christian churches, since 'geographical and social mobility erodes stable religious

---

[12] See Colin D. Greene, *Christology in Cultural Perspective: Marking out the Horizons* (Carlisle: Paternoster Press, 2003), p. 75.

[13] Martin, *On Secularization*, p. 17.

[14] Martin, *On Secularization*, p. 123.

[15] M. Haralambos, *Sociology: Themes and Perspectives* (Slough: University Tutorial Press, 1980), p. 279.

[16] The various analyses are dealt with at some length in Haralambos, *Sociology*; see pp. 24–97.

[17] We will explore the origins of secularization in another section.

communities organised on a territorial basis . . . it also contributes to a rela-tivization of perspectives through extended culture contact'.[18] The churches were obliged to adapt their corporate life and mission to an unfamiliar urban scene. However, it could be argued that, even until the present time, they have never wholly outgrown a residual rural mentality.

Secularism

David Martin distinguishes between *secularization*, described as a histor-ical development, which brought about diachronically the changes described in the previous section; *secularity*, which he treats as a condi-tion (i.e. the changes seen synchronically from a particular point in time); and *secularism*.[19] The latter he calls an ideology. As this terminology is usually used in a critical sense, the notion needs to be explored sepa-rately. An ideology is a 'theory or system of ideas that leads to particular kinds of political or social action'. In a positive sense, it may 'provide justifications for political or social schemes deemed by its adherents to promote justice, equality and the dignity of all human beings'. In a nega-tive sense, 'an ideology is often said to defend and promote the vested interests of a sector of a given population . . . irrespective of the effect its implementation may have on other groups in society'.[20]

When a certain position on the benefits of a thoroughly secular society becomes a strong campaigning strategy against the remnants of a reli-gious view of the world, it can be said to have taken on ideological elements. There are two distinct components to secularism as an ideolog-ical strategy. These can be illustrated by reference to the stated purposes of two well-known secular organizations: the National Secular Society (NSS) and the British Humanist Association (BHA).[21]

The NSS states (on its web-site) as its aim to:

> campaign from a non-religious perspective for the separation of religion and state and promote secularism as the best means to create a society in which people of all religions or none can live together fairly and cohesively. The NSS sees secularism – the position that the state should be separate from religion – as an essential element in promoting equality between all citizens. We work in the UK and Europe to challenge the disproportionate influence of religion on governments and in public life. We provide a secular voice in the media,

---

[18] Martin, *General Theory*, p. 3.
[19] Martin, *On Secularization*, p. 81.
[20] J. Andrew Kirk, ' "God is on Our Side": The Anatomy of an Ideology', *Trans-formation* 27 (2010): pp. 239–40.
[21] See www.secularism.org.uk, and www.humanism.org.uk.

defending freedom and equality as a counterbalance to the powerful religious lobby and some of the more destructive religious impulses that can threaten human rights worldwide.

It explicitly rejects the assumption that it must be opposed to the practice of religious beliefs as such. As long as these take place as leisure activities in the private sphere of individual citizens, they are legitimate expressions of people's freedom of belief. Its concern is to free every public activity from religious interference and pressure, and to free religious practices from the intrusion of the state. It clearly rejects the notion that it is seeking to promote atheism: 'Secularism is not atheism. Atheism is a lack of belief in gods. Secularism simply provides a framework for a democratic society. Atheists have an obvious interest in supporting secularism, but secularism itself does not seek to challenge the tenets of any particular religion or belief, neither does it seek to impose atheism on anyone.'

The BHA, on the other hand, as well as promoting the same aims as the NSS, is committed to a humanist agenda. However, it is not easy to discover a comprehensive explanation of humanism on its web-site. The closest definition of what it means to be a humanist is found in the following passage:

> Humanist is used today to mean those who seek to live good lives without religious or superstitious beliefs . . . Humanists believe that moral values follow on from human nature and experience in some way. Humanists base their moral principles on reason (which leads them to reject the idea of any supernatural agency), on shared human values and respect for others. They believe that people should work together to improve the quality of life for all and make it more equitable. Humanism is a full philosophy, 'life stance' or worldview, rather than being about one aspect of religion, knowledge, or politics.

The difficulty of understanding the meaning of humanism as used by humanists is that it is couched in concepts, many of which religious people would also endorse, not least the emphasis on the use of reason (which, for the latter, is a God-given gift). It may be helpful, therefore, to state (on behalf of humanists) the basic tenets. First, scientific methods of establishing facts about the real world are the only sure path to true belief about the real world. They alone can produce data universally believable, in that they alone are open to both verification and falsification.

Second, therefore, rational enquiry into human existence should exclude the idea of revelation. There is no agent external to the universe that can communicate information not available through human experimentation and reasoning. Nature, not the message of the Bible, is really real. Human reason is the measure of all that it is.

Third, the world can only be explained uncontroversially in terms of cause and effect; not in terms of purpose. The first can be demonstrated scientifically; the second is a matter of personal opinion. Human beings can be explained in terms of their biological origins; the meaning of life, however, has to be created by each person individually. Humanists claim to be able to explain *how* human beings have come into being, but not *why*. The evolutionary process seems to be blind and haphazard; the only controlling principle is survival and reproduction of the gene pool. It would seem to follow, therefore, that, in order for human communities to be able to arrive at shared values, evolutionary theory by itself is inadequate. Scientific explanations of how the world *is* cannot prescribe how human beings *ought* to live. Ethical norms have to be derived by breaking into the mechanistic chain of biological determinism.[22]

Humanists proclaim that religious beliefs not only are not true, but are harmful: they distort reality, provide false hopes, justify harmful practices and often hinder what humanists conceive to be moral advancement. So the advocacy of the secular becomes a weapon of war, first to discredit and then to banish any idea of a personal reality beyond the senses to which we are accountable. Human beings are alone in the universe. They are, therefore, responsible to themselves alone. They have to resolve their problems on their own. They need to learn to live without God (or gods). They should be educated out of an allegiance to a religious view of life, in order to be freed from superstition and the conflicts engendered by unprovable beliefs, to work for genuine justice, equality and harmony in society.

Origins

If one had the space to write fully on the subject of the historical causes of secularization, no doubt the influences would be traced back to ancient times – both the Hebrew prophets and Greek philosophers proclaimed beliefs and ideas that contained seeds that in the right historical contexts would germinate into secular values. However, that would require a volume running to several hundred pages.[23]

---

[22] See the full discussion of this issue in Holmes Rolston, III, *Genes, Genesis and God: Values and Their Origins in Natural and Human History* (Cambridge: CUP, 1999), ch. 5: 'Ethics: Naturalized, Socialized, Evaluated.'

[23] Charles Taylor's celebrated *A Secular Age* (Cambridge, MA: Harvard University Press, 2007) runs to 851 pages. No doubt he would say that it is incomplete!

In this brief summary, I can do no more than point to two hugely influential social, political and cultural moments in European history: the Reformation and the Enlightenment. They are both codes for a great variety of different modes of thinking and acting. I will seek to distil a few core precepts from these monumental events.

The Reformation

The major reformers provoked three major breaks from the cultural and religious assumptions of the medieval period. First, the individual's conscience is inviolable.[24] Second, every individual human person has the opportunity to enjoy an unmediated fellowship with God (by 'faith alone'). Third, the Bible, as a source of knowledge, independent of the church's teaching, and made available in the language of the people, stands above the church as its authoritative judge in all matters of faith and action. It is self-interpreting ('Scripture alone').

Although these new emphases may seem to be esoteric, over a period of time they unleashed huge social, political and spiritual consequences. We may note four. First, the official leadership of the formerly unified church began to lose its authority to interpret and control religious belief and practice. At the same time, the recapture in Protestant circles of the biblical emphasis on the priesthood of all believers led to a rejection of a specialist priesthood that mediated God's grace to ordinary believers through the sacraments. Every Christian had equal access to all the benefits of salvation. The individual was no longer dependent on the services of an elite clerical cohort.

Second, the distinction between what Juan Luis Segundo has called 'heroic religion'[25] and the practice of the masses became unsustainable. A hierarchical grading of different vocations, some considered superior to others, also disintegrated. From now on every legitimate occupation was deemed to be of equal value if it was fulfilling a genuine call from God.

Third, although only gradually, the notion that belonging to the church and the state were coextensive dwindled. The notion that membership of the church was territorially assured was undermined by the rediscovered gospel message that the benefits of salvation were appropriated by an individual act of faith alone, not by virtue of birth and infant baptism. The extensive proclamation of such an idea led to a plurality of religious options within one state. The notion of a sacred order tying together an

---

[24] We have seen in Chapter 5, however, that advocacy of freedom of conscience antedates the Reformation period and its defence is not confined to the Protestant faith.

[25] See Juan Luis Segundo, *Masas y Minorias en la dialéctica divina de la liberación* (Buenos Aires: La Aurora, 1973).

entire people in a defined jurisdiction by means of their religious affilia-
tion began to disintegrate.

Fourth, this creeping toleration of different interpretations of the
Christian faith, although strongly resisted by both political and ecclesial
powers for a long period, in time was extended to those who wished
to repudiate all religions. The logic is spelt out by Grace Davie: 'If it is
possible to tolerate a variety of religious views within one society, can
any of these views be considered an embodiment of the truth? In other
words, once more than one "truth" is permitted, *all* religions necessarily
lose their plausibility, not to mention their capacities to discipline the
faithful.'[26]

Together these repercussions opened the way for a number of significant cultural shifts in the Western world: for example, an emphasis
on the priority of the individual over the community in matters of
belief, the questioning of all statements based solely on the traditional
authority of an institution, a critical approach to hitherto accepted
doctrines, the elimination of a false dichotomy between the alleged
sacred and profane by the sanctifying of all aspects of life, the end of
attempts by the state to enforce religious conformity. Charles Taylor
elaborates on the effects of the 'disenchantment' and what he calls 'the
rage for order' provoked by the Reformation. One of his main theses
is that these changes resulted eventually in an exclusive humanism, in
which nature became the new focal point for understanding human life
and the human task.[27]

The Enlightenment

The intellectual movement of the eighteenth century that is also referred
to as the 'Age of Reason' carried forward, through an emphasis on free
thinking, both the notion of disenchantment and the rationalization of
knowledge and social order.

Disenchantment
In the birth of modern science,[28] the natural world gained independence
from the supernatural. The two 'books' of revelation and nature, alluded

---

[26] Grace Davie, *Europe: The Exceptional Case; Parameters of Faith in the Modern
World* (London: Darton, Longman & Todd, 2002), p. 15.
[27] Taylor, *Secular Age*, pp. 77–88.
[28] For a brief overview of both the necessary and sufficient causes of the rise
of modern science see J. Andrew Kirk, *The Future of Reason, Science and Faith:
Following Modernity and Postmodernity* (Aldershot: Ashgate Publishing, 2007),
ch. 2: 'An Enquiry into the Origins of Modern Science.'

to by Francis Bacon, were understood to be using entirely different tools to understand human life in the world. Nature became increasingly less mysterious and under human control. At the beginning, the main impulse to explore the natural world came from a fresh understanding of the implications of nature being created by a God who also had endowed human reason so that it could understand and interpret its surroundings. Later, it gradually came to be accepted that religious faith was not essential to being a good scientist. Scientific research progressively became preoccupied with the minutiae of the mechanical processes of natural objects. By the mid-nineteenth century, Paley's teleological argument for design by a personal Creator was considered by many in the academic community to have been refuted by Darwin's account of the origin of species by natural selection. The latter theory was alleged to have given a perfectly plausible explanation for the evolution of life through wholly natural causes. The scientist, at least, no longer had need of a God-hypothesis to fill in gaps of understanding where knowledge was not yet available.

A second area of disenchantment was provoked by the prolonged religious wars of the seventeenth century. In the struggle for domination between rulers aligned to either the Protestant or Catholic faiths, European nations became increasingly intolerant of dissent. The cost in individual human lives and the disruption of societies across the continent, because of competing versions of Christian faith, became immense. A growing realization took hold that, if religious views could be contained within the private world of the individual and its divisive influence banished from the normal concourse of nations, communities did not have to be subjected to this kind of violence.

Rationalization

Disenchantment of nature and the success of scientific prediction and technological application led to a growing confidence in the ability of the scientific enterprise to explain reality and the power of human reason to overcome inherent human problems. It was alleged that human reason alone had been able to develop the powers necessary to discern and control adverse social forces and promote healthy ones. It was believed that more and more of life could be reduced to forces potentially under full human control.

So scientific understanding began to be expanded from the world of the natural sciences to all things human – the economy, morality, ideas and beliefs. Once understood, all aspects of human endeavour could be directed rationally towards the increasing wellbeing of the whole of society. Enlightenment spelt emancipation from nonsensical superstitions and harmful dogmas that had no place as guiding principles in a rational world. Enlightenment also spelt progress; access to sound knowledge would open the doors to a new age of collaboration in the conquest of all that enslaves human life.

Charles Taylor refers to the outcome of the struggle between religion and the new version of rationality as the new framework in which 'human beings [form] societies under the normative provisions of the Modern Moral Order, and [fulfil] their purposes using what Nature provides, through the aid of accurate knowledge of this Nature, and the contrivances of what we will later call Technology'.[29] He concludes, 'the development of *the disciplined, instrumentally rational order of mutual benefit* has been the matrix within which the shift could take place. This shift is the heartland and origin of modern "secularization".'[30]

Other aspects of the history of secularization

It is worth considering briefly some other features of secularization that Taylor analyses in his study, seeing that he has explored the phenomenon in greater depth than almost all other writers on the subject.

The rise of the disciplined society

Congruent with his belief that secularization has religious antecedents, Taylor links *the turn to nature* to the new religious interest in the lay world. People began to turn their attention from heaven and life after death to this world and life before death. They became interested in nature for its own sake, not just in relation to God. This movement also coincided with and was partly instrumental in stimulating the natural sciences.

Now, just as science was conceived as the way to control nature for the material benefit of humankind, so began attempts to discipline the whole population: 'The drive to reconstruction was not inseparable from the move to mechanism . . . the practice of self-refashioning is applied to society as a whole, when the nascent state becomes more and more an engineer of morals and social practice.'[31]

Hitherto, people generally believed that only God's power makes this high moral attainment possible. Now, however, the righteous enlightened have acquired the competence to enforce the changes:

---

[29] Taylor, *Secular Age*, p. 294. The use of capital letters in the sentence presumably is intended to heighten the absolute nature of the new set of core modern beliefs.

[30] Taylor, *Secular Age*, p. 295 (emphasis added).

[31] Taylor, *Secular Age*, p. 114.

The goal of order is redefined as a matter purely of human flourishing. We no longer see the pursuit of it as a way of following God, let alone glorifying him . . . The power to pursue it is no longer something that we receive from God, but is a purely human capacity . . . The new understanding is frequently expressed in terms of 'nature', following the philosophical tradition which comes down to us from the ancients.[32]

Civility

Taylor refers to this new perception of the human calling to subdue nature and train human nature as civility. Civility is understood as a refined life in contrast to the savage existence of life in the wild. It is rational and morally excellent, and resists abandoning life to uncontrolled desires. The demand for self-discipline and self-control were guided by a new range of manners and conventions in the forming of good habits: ' "Civilised" societies, as the very word implies, were governed in an orderly way; they had a state, law and order, internal peace, unlike "savage" tribes.'[33]

We might say that the great enemy of the drive for a civilised life is anything deemed wild, primitive, turbulent or untamed, and therefore outside of the bound of what can be controlled, made to function and put to good use.

Imminence and exclusive humanism

The history of secularization can be described in part as a radical, intellectual and cultural shift: from a God who, being an ever-present reality in human affairs, brings salvation from sin, order out of chaos and the healing of body, mind and soul, to a God that has created an intricate and balanced natural order, from which he has stepped back and told his creatures they are in charge and can find the route map to their providential destiny within the imminent order itself. It is not surprising that the final destination of this train of thought is the disposal of God altogether; God is an unnecessary hypothesis, as he himself has allegedly authorised his creatures to work out their own salvation.

What is now becoming evident is that for many the latter view is taken as a default position. What Taylor calls 'closed world structures' are taken as obvious and unchallengeable. In other words, in a highly secularised intellectual climate, the burden of proof has now shifted on to those who wish to claim that there is another reality beyond the material that impinges directly upon the physical one. This position represents a clever manipulation of the discussion away from what we have a right to assume.

---

[32] Taylor, *Secular Age*, p. 84.
[33] Taylor, *Secular Age*, p. 394.

God has been replaced by nature and the highest living organism within the natural world (which is the only world) is the human being. Therefore, there is no possibility of transcending ordinary human experience. This is where exclusive humanism takes the stage. We can still talk about morality and spirituality, but only as internal, imminent resources. There is simply nothing there beyond the powers of human reason, self-love, the moral will and rightly guided education: 'Conditions have arisen in the modern world in which it is no longer possible, honestly, rationally, without confusions, or fudging, or mental reservation, to believe in God. These conditions leave us nothing we can believe in beyond the human – human happiness, or potentialities, or heroism.'[34]

Consequences of the Advent of Secular Worlds

Indifference towards and ignorance of Christian faith

In one sense secularization is itself defined by the consequences it has brought. The most conspicuous is the decline in formal religious adherence, both in belief and practice. Closely related to a reduced conviction that Christian faith represents the truest picture of reality comes an increase in new forms of religion. The search for a personally meaningful faith has latched on to 'New Age' cults.[35] This may be one way of attempting to satisfy the quest for identity through what some have referred to as 'peak experiences'.[36]

Secularization has occasioned an increasing unfamiliarity with the main tenets of the Christian faith: 'We are now faced by an ignorance in the elite which is certainly one indication of the possibility of a secular society.'[37]

This illiteracy is the result in part of the media's focus on the sensational views of a small group of unrepresentative scholars and uninformed novelists and librettists concerning Christian origins. Thus, the Jesus, consistently portrayed in the New Testament's accounts of his public ministry and last days as the Messiah (the Son of God) promised by the

---

[34] Taylor, *Secular Age*, p. 560.
[35] See Brown, *Death of Christian Britain*, p. 196; Lars Johansson, 'Mystical Knowledge, New Age, and Missiology' in *To Stake a Claim: Mission and the Western Crisis of Knowledge* (ed. J. Andrew Kirk and Kevin Vanhoozer; Maryknoll: Orbis Books, 1999), pp. 172–204.
[36] See Greene, *Christology in Cultural Perspective*, pp. 382–3, citing Z. Bauman's analysis in *Postmodernity and its Discontents* (Cambridge: Polity Press, 1997), pp. 179–81.
[37] David Martin, *Tracts against the Times* (London: Lutterworth Press, 1973), p. 179.

prophets of the Hebrew Bible, is recreated as a 'crypto-revolutionary', or a wandering teacher and practitioner of lofty moral values or a sage proclaiming ancient wisdom. The true dynamic of his confrontation with political and religious leaders and his significance as the Suffering Servant who gave his life to deal with the fundamental problem of evil is completely lost. Instead he is turned into an innocuous protagonist of general ethical principles or a failed schismatic dissenter.

This growth in the misrepresentation of its core beliefs has accompanied an escalation of direct attacks on Christian conscience and participation in public policy-making. The so-called 'new atheists' have been exposed for their failure to engage with a sophisticated account of what Christian faith is about. It is, perhaps, a sign of the times that these people prefer their own dogmatic misinterpretations rather than grapple with the beliefs of well-informed Christians.

Impermanence

Following Zygmunt Bauman's ingenious description of the postmodern individual as a nomad, vagabond or tourist,[38] David Martin, quoting Stewart Sutherland,[39] suggests that human beings do not have a 'chief end', they only come to an end: 'Pilgrims have been replaced by tourists who are lovers of sights and sounds, dealers in experience for its own sake, *going* nowhere.'[40]

Essentially tourists are not engaged with any permanent reality. They are not seeking 'the city of the living God . . . a kingdom that cannot be shaken' (Heb. 12:22,28) but a transitory, fleeting experience of a pleasure-filled interlude in their normal, routine lives.

Bauman calls the present a heterophilic age,[41] meaning that people support in principle openness to a wide variety of ways of interpreting life's experiences. As individuals seek to take control of their identities, so they tend to reject rigid expectations and opt for flexibility. This allows a maximum opportunity to change their own self-image, either by choice or under pressure from others. One of the mantras of the age is the tolerance of difference. However a person chooses to live their life, and as long as they are genuinely sincere, others should respect their decision.

---

[38] In Z. Bauman, *Postmodern Ethics* (Oxford: Blackwell, 1993), pp. 240–43.

[39] Stewart Sutherland, 'Nomad's Progress', *Proceedings of the British Academy* 131 (2005): pp. 443–63.

[40] David Martin, *The Future of Christianity: Reflections on Violence and Democracy, Religion and Secularization* (Aldershot: Ashgate Publishing, 2011), p. 193 (emphasis in the original).

[41] Bauman, *Postmodernity*, pp. 30–31.

In the secular world, where many of the old boundaries have been erased, life appears to be volatile and unpredictable. Economic realities mean that most employees will change jobs with much greater frequency than in more stable times; many will undergo retraining several times in their work experience, even shifting from one profession to another. In social relationships, long-term commitments are considered to be too burdensome. It is now accepted practice that two people attracted to one another will live together some time before they seriously think about getting married. Sometimes these relationships last for years; in the case of younger couples, often the formality of public marriage is delayed until the first child is on the way. Yet,

> Choosing to cohabit rather than get married is a pale reflection of what the marriage relationship could and should be . . . It signifies a weak commitment, because the mutual consent on which it is based is something into which the couple may have drifted without going through a similar process of decision-making associated with engagement and getting married. A limited time-span . . . is also likely if the couple tacitly accept that their relationship is a limited experiment which can be (relatively easily) ended if it appears not to be working.[42]

Cohabitation cannot be seen as a 'trial marriage', since marriage cannot be tested until it is a lived experience. It is a different kind of relationship with a different kind of connection to the wider community. It reflects precisely the belief that permanence is no longer attainable, even if it were to be an ideal. In an age of experimentation and the search for serial adventures, long-term commitments may be considered too risky or too restrictive.

Pluralism

As beliefs proliferate and tolerance becomes a major value, ethical values and lifestyle choices also multiply. The contribution of religion to social and individual morality is undermined by the common conviction that beliefs are ultimately all created by human beings to respond to changing circumstances and are, therefore, relative to time and place.[43]

John Gray has set out an impassioned argument in defence of value-pluralism in regard of ethical choices.[44] He appears to be saying that there is no way ultimately of resolving what he calls the incommensurability of ethical

---

[42] J. Andrew Kirk, *The Meaning of Freedom: A Study of Secular, Muslim and Christian Views* (Carlisle: Paternoster Press, 1998), p. 218.

[43] See David Lyon, 'Secularization: The Fate of Faith in Modern Society', *Themelios* 10 (Sept. 1984), p. 18.

[44] John Gray, *The Two Faces of Liberalism* (Cambridge: Polity Press, 2000).

choices and practices. Therefore, the world would be a far better place if different cultures could learn to live alongside one another by accepting that different ways of living are equally morally acceptable according to contexts and circumstances. To admit incommensurable values means tolerating contradictions. The supposition is that they must belong to forms of life that have no categories or concepts in common.[45] Against what he considers a destructive form of liberalism, namely the insistence on universal concepts such as justice and human rights, he advocates a *modus vivendi* pact to forestall the imposition of only one version of moral righteousness.[46] He accuses the modern project of being a secular form of an imperious form of religion: 'Enlightenment thinkers like to see them-selves as modern pagans, but they are really latter-day Christians: they too aim to save mankind.'[47]

Curiously, Gray rejects the notion that he is advocating a wholly subjective and relativistic notion of what is good and evil. And yet that is exactly what he is doing in defending a notion of life in which 'no one view of good has overall priority over all others'.[48] He actually commends the supreme value of pursuing compromises when incompatible claims clash. He argues that consistency in applying universal moral standards leads to impoverished lives. However, he does not face the likelihood that compromise will do so even more. In so far as he is prepared to draw an ultimate line against some practices (e.g. torture, female genital mutilation, forced marriages, the prohibition of women's education, the sexual abuse of young people), he shows that he does not really believe in a blanket *modus vivendi*. If he is really prepared to negotiate compro-mises, so that these practices can continue in some form, how can he have any handle on moral worth? If he stands against them, is he not as much a moral absolutist as any 'latter-day Christian'?

Legislation

In the absence of an agreed basis on which laws can command popular assent, government legislation can often appear arbitrary. In practice in a secular society changes to or the addition of laws are often the result of the lobby that can exert most influence. Whoever can persuade a majority of elected political representatives to vote in a particular way can force laws onto the statute books. Once laws are passed they have

---

[45] Gray, *Two Faces of Liberalism*, p. 51.
[46] Gray, *Two Faces of Liberalism*, pp. 13–21.
[47] J. Gray, *Al Qaeda and What it Means to be Modern* (London: Faber & Faber, 2003), p. 104.
[48] Gray, *Two Faces of Liberalism*, p. 135.

a tendency to confirm society in a particular attitude. This has been the case, for example, with the laws on abortion, embryo experimentation and civil partnerships. There is growing pressure to curtail freedom of speech in certain instances through legislation on so-called 'hate crimes'. In drafting laws, there often appears to be little discrimination between active incitement to violence and the expression of deeply held convictions about what is morally right and wrong.

So legislation may be founded on the flimsy basis of what may, or may not, be emotionally acceptable to the public at any one time. After a time outraged feelings die down, people become bored with the issue, and a practice that once was condemned as unacceptable becomes a normal part of life.[49] The law becomes dependent on a prevailing consensus.[50] Moreover, in the administration of the law, partly because of the widespread recourse to judicial reviews, the courts are given 'an almost unfettered discretion to decide how a society may operate. They are not constrained by the law, since they are in control of interpretations of it. They decide how far rights extend, and even what is a right.'[51]

Education

The question of what should be taught in a fully-rounded school curriculum is a matter of constant debate. In a society that prides itself on being secular, meaning in this case one that does not accord particular privileges to any set of beliefs or world-view, the issue takes on perplexing dimensions, for almost every subject, including the natural sciences, presupposes some view of the whole of reality. Let us take two examples to show that what children are taught is going to be influenced ultimately by background metaphysical assumptions. These examples encapsulate the predicament caused when attempts are made to interpret secularism in terms of a campaign to banish any set of core beliefs from the public domain.

First, how are children going to be helped to understand their place in the world as part of a vast universe? What will be said about the origin of the universe and the emergence of life, particularly self-conscious life characteristic of the human species? A secular society that has consigned religious belief to the realm of private opinion and that relies on scientific data-gathering and experimentation for true knowledge is likely to favour the teaching of evolutionary theory as

---

[49] Jerram Barrs, 'Christian Standards in a Puralistic Society', unpublished paper presented to a Consultation on Christian Social Action (November 1988), p. 8.
[50] Roger Trigg, *Religion in Public Life: Must Faith be Privatized?* (Oxford: Oxford University Press, 2007), p. 170.
[51] Trigg, *Religion in Public Life*, p. 153.

the approved explanation concerning the beginnings of life on earth. Which theory, however, will be taught? Presumably the one that has gained the ascendency, i.e. macro-evolution – the belief that all life has one single point of origin and has gradually diversified over millions of years into the huge variety that is seen today. It is said that this theory has the overwhelming support of all serious scientists working in the field. Therefore, it can be taught to children with absolute confidence. However, a minority of scientists have cast doubts on the theory, because of the paucity of evidence for the cross-mutation of species and because of the nature of the data on which the whole theory has been constructed. These would assert that really convincing evidence only allows us to affirm the more modest theory of micro-evolution, i.e. development within species.

The problem is not one that can safely be left to scientists as scientists, for there are immense human implications involved in what is said, and left unsaid, that affect the whole human race. Macro-evolution is usually presented as an impersonal, purposeless process driven on purely by the need of living beings to survive and reproduce. As a purely instinctive and involuntary movement, it is intrinsically unable to explain how consciousness, self-awareness, rational thought, conscience, moral perceptions and the intuition of eternity have come into existence. When science as such has had its say, nothing of ultimate significance has been clarified. It is incapable of bridging the gap between an account of how material forces have worked and the much profounder questions of existence:

> The idea that God and biological evolution are mutually exclusive alternatives implies . . . that God and evolution belong to the same category of explanation. But this is plainly false . . . A category mistake is being committed. Evolution purports to be a biological mechanism, and those who believe in God regard him as a personal Agent who, among other things, designs and creates mechanisms.[52]

Only two major alternatives appear to be possible: either the universe has been brought into existence and subsequently shaped by a personal Creator who, at all times, is intimately involved in its mechanisms, or the universe exists by absolute chance in a way that has no ultimate explanation. In the first case, one may assume deliberate intention and therefore an overall purpose is built into life; in the second case, there is no aim, no plan, no design and no goal.

---

[52] John Lennox, *God's Undertaker: Has Science Buried God?* (Oxford: Lion Hudson, 2009), p. 89.

Now, if these are the only genuine options, what is to be taught to children? Common sense would suggest that both alternatives should be laid out. In reality, in a truly secular society, neither option appears to be acceptable. The notion of personal creation and design takes us into the realm of religion, which, because it cannot be publically demonstrated, should only be taught as a matter of private belief. The view that life has come about by a wholly random procedure and of itself makes no sense is much too bleak and depressing a creed to teach children of an impressionable age. The dilemma is the result of a secularist approach to education that perpetuates the myth that science and religious faith cannot be reconciled, or that science alone has access to true knowledge and understanding. In fact, by privileging science, secularists betray their own stated conviction that no core belief should be given precedence over any other; belief that scientific research can uncover reality is itself a metaphysical act of faith.

Second, on what basis are children going to be taught the nature of right and wrong, good and evil? A reasonable answer would seem to be on the basis of who they are. To know what makes human life human, we need to know what it means to be human. According to the discussion on origins and meaning, humans are either the result of millions of years of accumulated random mutations, naturally selected for the one purpose of surviving, or they are the special creation of a personal God who has brought them into the world to enjoy fellowship with him and the fruits of the natural world.

In the first case, moral values will have to be created out of nothing, since a chance process geared to survival gives no clue about why certain actions would be right and others wrong, except on the one utilitarian principle that they either aid or negate survival. Such a view, however, gives no explanation why survival itself should be considered a virtue. On this account, the 'underlying structure of the natural world appears to be a form of ego-centric determinism', so there appear to be no grounds for 'the altruistic, self-sacrificing and voluntaristic virtues' inherent in the Christian account of the common good.[53] In the second case, the distinction between right and wrong is given in the nature of the One who has created all things, and continues to guide people who will listen into the ways of justice, mercy and peace.

So, when it comes to education in moral values and social and civic virtues, what should be taught? The secularist will say that to teach religious beliefs as true is indoctrination; it puts undue pressure on vulnerable minds and is, therefore, a form of unacceptable coercion. But what is the alternative: to teach that the naturalist view of the

---

[53] Greene, *Christology in Cultural Perspective*, p. 92.

world is true? If so, is that not also indoctrination, since such a view is not in any way entailed by scientific fact, but is a metaphysical hypothesis? But a choice has to be made.

One might say, well then, both views should be taught, and the children left to decide. This is wholly unreal as a strategy. In the first place, teachers will find it almost impossible to be wholly impartial between the two options, since they will have their own convictions. Second, how are young children, or even adolescents, expected to decide between such contested views? In practice most educational policies fudge the issue. In Western nations, heavily influenced by Christian teaching, whose laws and legal practices are based on a distinctively Christian understanding of justice, basic Christian ethics are assumed, even when they are transmuted into some form of natural law and rights. At the same time, the corollary that Christian ethical principles actually reflect what is true about the universe cannot be taught because secular dogma decrees that a supposed neutral educational system must teach that all traditions are of equal relevance.[54] The inherent problems in trying to promote a secularist agenda in education will continue to run and run. The idea that there is an unbiased, neutral 'humanist's-eye view' of reality is a wholly unfounded, although constantly perpetuated, fiction.

A Post-Christian Society?

In analysing the current state of Western societies, is it helpful to evaluate them in terms of how far they have drifted from a commonly shared acceptance of Christianity as the tacit belief system by which communities order their lives? Is the long-standing implicit assent to the Christian religion as the principle that sets the guidelines for a civilised standard of life now over? These are questions debated in Christian and non-Christian circles as contemporary Western nations consider what set of fundamental beliefs and values is going to hold peoples together in a progressively more pluralist, multicultural and sceptical age.

Callum Brown certainly thinks that Christianity has had its day. He speaks of the death of Christian culture, of the ways in which people re-imagine themselves that completely ignore the Christian heritage of the past, of the cancellation of a mass subscription to the Christian

---

[54] For an illuminating discussion of the quandaries and ambiguities in according religious beliefs and values a place in a contemporary curriculum in a secular state, see Roger Trigg, *Religion in Public Life: Must Faith be Privatized?* (Oxford: OUP, 2007), ch. 9, 'Religion in State Education'.

Page 314 The Church & the World

discourse.[55] Alan Gilbert observes that we live in an age in which to be irreligious is to be normal, and to act in secular ways conventional. Each generation inherits less of a consciousness that Christianity has been the main force that has shaped the way we think and act.[56] David Millikan, reflecting on life in Australia, quotes the opinion of Jonathan King[57] that the daily life of most Australians has little spiritual foundation and God seems irrelevant.[58] In the East German context, Hartmut Barend talks of the unchurched masses in a telling phrase as those 'who have forgotten that they have forgotten God'.[59] 'These unchurched people come along with an atheism, which is deep but not necessarily aggressive. This atheism comes with a far-reaching indifference for the whole religious interpretation of life.'[60]

According to David Martin, the last great effort to increase the practice of Christian faith in post-Enlightenment times lasted from the early nineteenth century to the mid–twentieth century, when it was overwhelmed 'by the flood-waters of the natural, the primitive, the ahistorical and the primordial'.[61] He adds that the official norms of the church in matters of sexuality and family life (most recently in the debate about same-sex marriage) have a decreasing influence on secular law. The ability of religious bodies to make a telling contribution to public debate on matters such as housing, migrants, economics and war has declined markedly in recent years.[62]

Churches are allowed a minor, though emotionally significant, role in presiding over grief for the death of a celebrity or major public figure and over mourning in the event of some tragedy. And yet, faced with death, the Christian interpretation of the end of this life and what follows after is not comprehended. Funeral services tend to express the sentimental notion that the deceased has just passed next door, is still part of the family and is automatically enjoying a better existence. The aspect of accountability and judgement for what has transpired in this life is largely absent. The notion that those content enough to live without God before death

[55] Brown, *Death of Christian Britain*, p. 193.
[56] Gilbert, *Making of Post-Christian Britain*, p. ix.
[57] Jonathan King, *Waltzing Materialism* (Sydney: Harper & Row, 1978), p. 131.
[58] David Millikan, 'Secularism, Social Change and the Role of Christians in Australia,' *Zadok Occasional Paper*, 1978.
[59] Hartmut Barend, *Kirche mit Zukunft:Impulse fur eine missionarische Volkkirche* (Giessen, 2006), p. 43, quoted by Michael Herbst in *Mission and Postmodernities* (Rolv Olsen [ed.], Oxford: Regnum Books, 2011), p. 44.
[60] Olsen, *Mission and Postmodernities*, p. 47.
[61] Martin, *On Secularization*, p. 6.
[62] Martin, *Future of Christianity*, p. 107.

might feel incredibly uncomfortable when confronted with the reality of God after death does not seem to be reckoned with. The crucial issue of whether the individual has centred his or her life on seeking God's will and walking in his ways does not seem to be contemplated. Studied indifference towards the things of God is a high-risk venture; it makes Pascal's wager an odds-on favourite!

So the funeral service becomes a charade, focussed on the achievements of the dead person, but singularly avoiding the ultimate question of eternal destiny. Christian hope, given in the resurrection of Jesus Christ as the triumph over death (physical and spiritual), although formally present in a Christian liturgy, rarely becomes the central reality to be celebrated at this crucial time.

Grace Davie, in a series of writings, tries to analyse the dynamic changes in society that have left official Christian institutions and their teachings in such a weak state. She propounds a number of possible theories to account for the rapid de-Christianization of society.[63] One theory is that, as long as a faithful few can maintain the ritual obligations on behalf of the many, the general populace no longer believes it necessary to practise religion; practising Christians are the surrogates who maintain a certain degree of stability for the social fabric as a whole. Another theory, which attempts to explain the difference between the European experience and that of North America (equally secular in its institutions), argues that the churches of Europe have failed to adapt to changing circumstances and reinvent themselves and the product they are seeking to sell. In Europe the churches are severely hampered by their long alliance with the establishment and their tendency to opt for being a spiritual tranquiliser for the disoriented and guilt-ridden middle-classes. In America, they have capitalised on the free market in religious goods and have found convincing ways of meeting spiritual needs.

Davie also expounds the 'amnesia thesis'. In Europe, in particular, religion has been a matter of forging a coherent identity that has held together both national and local communities. It has been the most significant element in linking the present to the past of a nation. It has thrived on being able to keep intact and pass on, from one generation to another, significant traditions. However, over time, people are no longer being nurtured in these traditions. They are no longer aware of the role played by Christian faith in shaping social existence. They have forgotten why faith has played such an important role in defining life. Thus, 'modern societies are not less religious because they are increasingly rational, but

---

[63] See Grace Davie, *Religion in Modern Europe: A Memory Mutates* (Oxford: OUP, 2000); and Davie, *Europe: The Exceptional Case*.

because they are less and less capable of maintaining the memory which lies at the heart of their religious existence.'[64]

Whatever the merits of these theories, and others that have been advocated, some observers do not believe that the decline in religion is nearly as pervasive as the various secularization theses propound. They are inclined to believe that what is being described is the death-throes of Christendom. Stuart Murray interprets the present situation as one in which 'Post-Christendom . . . culture . . . emerges as the Christian faith loses coherence within a society that has been definitively shaped by the Christian story and as the institutions that have been developed to express Christian convictions decline in influence'.[65]

He characterises the phenomenon as a series of transitions: from being a majority to being a minority; from being sojourners, at home in a culture shaped by the Christian story, to being exiles in a culture felt to be increasingly alien; from privilege to plurality; from control over society to influence by witness alone.[66] He explicitly rejects the notion that we are living in a post-Christian age. Such a characterization would imply that Christendom reflected the epitome of Christian faithfulness, rather than a decline in serious Christian discipleship. He also believes that grasping the reality of the present post-Christendom context gives the church an enormous opportunity to reinvent itself as the humble, but bold bearer of good news to a restless, cynical and bewildered culture.

Christian Mission in a Secular Age

In defence of the secular

It would be foolhardy in the extreme to pretend that the task of Christian communities in secular societies of the twenty-first century is straightforward. The first challenge is to attempt to understand the social forces at work; no easy undertaking. Although, from a Christian perspective, there is much to criticise and deconstruct in the cultures that have come to rely on human wisdom alone in setting and pursuing communal goals, it is well to begin by recognizing the positive aspects of the secular agenda.

Freedom from the coercive powers of the state to enforce adherence to one set of beliefs, whether religious or ideological, is a precious commodity.

---

[64] Davie, *Europe: The Exceptional Case*, p. 18.
[65] Murray, Stuart. *Post-Christendom: Church and Mission in a Strange New World* (Milton Keynes: Paternoster Press, 2004), p. 19.
[66] Murray, *Post-Christendom*, p. 20.

Few people would consider life in a dictatorship, ruled by the whim of an unelected, unaccountable elite, who impose arbitrary, unchallengeable laws on the citisens, is an ideal to be sought after. With few exceptions, until the determined campaigning of minorities to be allowed to dissent from the hitherto assumed order of things, this has been the lot of humanity throughout history. A secular society, at its best, has the assignment of maintaining the prerogative of minorities to protest against and resist any state-imposed uniformity. The statement, attributed to Voltaire, 'I disapprove of what you say, but I will defend to the death your right to say it',[67] sums up admirably the cherished principle of the freedom of speech, which accompanies other freedoms, such as freedom of association.

The implication of this view of secularity is that no one institution or set of beliefs is accorded a privileged position in society. For centuries the Christian church's monopoly on fundamental beliefs about the reality of human life on earth was protected and promoted by the civil powers. Non-adherence to the officially promulgated state religion brought persecution, repression and civic disadvantages. It is now recognised by most Christians that the church betrayed its own fundamental belief that the kingdom of God could not be instituted by the power of the kingdoms of this world by seeking a concordat with Caesar. It exists, neither by permission nor by the patronage of the state, but by the grace and power of Jesus Christ in whom alone it trusts.

Having made the principle clear, it may be that certain concessions, such as church schools in the state sector, which are the result of historical circumstances (in this case the dominance of the church in the introduction of universal education in the nineteenth century), are legitimate. However, in a secular society the continuance of such institutions cannot be claimed as an absolute entitlement. Their continuing warrant depends on the desire of the majority to preserve their status on the grounds that they make a positive contribution to education.

Part of the church's mission may well be to defend and promote a right view of secularity against an encroaching will to dominance by self-appointed 'evangelists' for secularist beliefs and conformist behaviour.[68] Under a misguided understanding of the meaning and implications of equality, permissible forms of difference and discrimination are being denied. Thus, for example, in the highly controversial contemporary debate

---

[67] In S.G. Tallentyre (pseudonym of Evelyn Beatrice Hall), *The Friends of Voltaire* (London: Putnam's Sons, 1907), p. 199.
[68] Evidence of a creeping state and judicial interference in the freedom of belief and practice is documented in Roger Trigg, *Equality, Freedom and Religion* (Oxford: OUP, 2012), *passim*.

about same-sex marriage, the notion of 'equal marriage' is assumed to trump all other arguments. Not to allow people attracted to their own sex the right to be married appears to deny them equal treatment and diminish their dignity.

A parallel is drawn to the issue of racial discrimination. It is inconceivable that today anyone could justify discrimination against people on the basis of the family they happened to be born into. However, the parallel is inexact, for same-sex attraction is ultimately a matter of choice, whereas the colour of one's skin or one's gender certainly is not. Moreover, there is no equivalence between the relationship of a man and a woman, sealed in marriage, and the relationship between two people of the same gender. The reality that men and women are different and that the difference is celebrated in a marriage bond that enhances a reciprocal and complementary relationship simply cannot apply to same-sex couples.

Hence, the argument from equality is not applicable. In the case of race and gender (and, for slightly different reasons, of disability) equality is based on equal humanity (a notion firmly embedded in the Christian doctrine of creation). In the case of marriage to appeal to equality is to confuse categories. Whatever status society eventually agrees to give to people of the same sex living together, Christians, and others, are right to object strongly to the attempt to manipulate an ancient institution by spuriously exploiting and misapplying the noble concept of equality. This is but one example of the care that has to be taken in ensuring that the very notion of secular is not hijacked in the interests of false ideological claims.

A critique of secularism

When the secular is turned into a pervasive world-view, Christians are called to witness against both the belief system and its concrete manifestations. It may be that Christian mission appears to be so ineffective in some secular nations because Christians have been afraid to challenge the tacit intellectual belief that religious faith is rationally untenable. However, as a result of the recent onslaught on the supposed delusion of religious faith, a number of Christian apologists[69] have responded with

---

[69] Such as Keith Ward, *The God-Conclusion: God and the Western Philosophical Tradition* (London: Darton, Longman & Todd, 2009); Keith Ward, *Is Religion Irrational?* (Oxford: Lion Hudson, 2011); Roger Trigg, *Rationality and Religion: Does Faith Need Reason?* (Oxford: Blackwell, 1998); Alister E. McGrath, *Dawkins' God: Genes, Memes and the Meaning of Life* (Oxford: Blackwell, 2005); Lennox, *God's Undertaker*.

vigour, demonstrating that the alleged irrationality of faith belongs to their accusers more than it does to their own beliefs.

Undoubtedly, the most difficult part of this aspect of Christian witness is being able to engage in a meaningful discussion, in which secularists are willing to listen to both a reasoned advocacy of Christian faith and a substantial critique of their own views. Methodologically, at this level of dialogue, I have myself developed the procedure known as inference to the best explanation (IBE).[70]

It is a mode of reasoning employed whenever we infer the truth of a situation on the grounds that a particular hypothesis offers the best explanation of the greatest amount of evidence germane to the case. So, in medical science, for example, a particular diagnosis of an illness is adopted, because it offers the best explanation of the symptoms manifested. Usually the diagnosis will follow a certain procedure. A doctor will come to a preliminary conclusion on the basis of an initial consultation with the patient. Sometimes the diagnosis is immediate as the symptoms are clear; on other occasions, however, a second, or even third opinion, may be necessary. This is required just because there could be more than one cause. Further tests will, hopefully, eliminate some possible explanations in favour of the one that best accounts for all the evidence. In brief, IBE makes the assumption, based on logical reasoning and evidence, that 'Beginning with the evidence available to us, we infer what would, if true, provide the best explanation of that evidence.'[71] 'Best' implies the most persuasive among a number of alternative hypotheses.

This method of reasoning is an excellent, indeed the most adequate, way of engaging in a dialogue between Christian faith and secular faith. It has the advantage of being recognised as a fruitful way of arriving at knowledge of the truth in scientific experimentation. It also proceeds in ways substantially similar to the processes of the law-courts, which aim to discover, 'beyond all reasonable doubt', what is the truth of the matter in the case of someone accused of a crime. By means of the sifting of forensic evidence, the testimony of witnesses and deductive reasoning, the court proceeds to make a judgement about the best explanation regarding the circumstances surrounding a particular offence.

---

[70] J. Andrew Kirk, *Christian Mission as Dialogue*, pp. 123–32. What follows in this section is taken from the conclusion of this study. I have also referred to this way of entering into dialogue, in the context of inter-religious discussion; see pp. 218–219.

[71] Peter Lipton, *Inference to the Best Explanation*, p. 1.

This method may become a missiological project in which the Christian faith can be shown to be the best of all possible explanations of our unique experience of the universe as human beings: one which offers the most coherent, consistent and complete account. The theory's explanatory power is measured by its observational success in accounting for data already accepted as veridical, and for new data. It also scores well in its predictive ability with regard to human behaviour (i.e. what is likely to happen, if certain courses of action are followed).[72] The model takes account of universally available evidence and proven categories of rational argument. The truth-claims that are made are related to self-awareness, human experience of the world, the universal concourse of alternative traditions, ideas and explanations and are open to a critical exchange of views. Therefore, when it comes to assessing rival interpretations of the origins, meaning and future of human existence in the universe, it has great missiological potential.

IBE offers a method for rationally considering all claims to know the ultimate reality that lies behind the experience of being human. No claim to know the ultimate meaning of life is excluded *a priori*. All beliefs can be part of the dialogue, which proceeds by way of testing the various claims against one another and against the stubborn facts of human life in the world. Naturally, there is no final human arbiter. Each person or group has to decide for itself how far its intuition, common sense, philosophy of life (home-spun or borrowed), ideology or religion is best able to make sense of the widest spread of the reality of life. The process is one of advocacy in which alternative explanations are promoted, discussed and judged. It is assumed that where there are conflicting claims, they cannot all be valid.

A response to a secular age

The need for sensitive and exceedingly well-informed advocates of the truth of Christian belief has never been more acute. In one sense, and contrary to received opinion, what is at stake is nothing less than the defence of a sound rationality and a trustworthy scientific enterprise against their modern and postmodern detractors. It may seem a curious

---

[72] An example of explanatory prediction might be a prognosis of the consequences that will inevitably follow a deficit of proper care, security and affection (e.g. in the case of the absence of a father) for the emotional stability of children. The ability to anticipate certain behavioural outcomes in these circumstances is derived from an understanding of how human beings are created to function best within a stable and cherishing family environment.

reversal of what some secularists wish to portray, namely that Christian faith is opposed to reason and the findings of science. In reality, it lays the foundation for considering both reason and science to be warranted, feasible and intelligible.[73]

However, it is probably true that most people for most of the time are not anxious about sophisticated metaphysical questions. Their concerns and needs are more mundane. Christian witness is perpetually challenged to find ways of engaging with people's fairly ordinary joys, sorrows, delights, fears and regrets and connecting them appropriately with the Christian story of creation and redemption. Most people are secular in the sociological sense that God, salvation and one's eternal destiny do not remotely enter into ordinary discourse or the calculations about relationships, work, finance and leisure. They are not unbelievers in a technical sense, nor are they unspiritual (many record spiritual experiences and times of prayer), but the God and Father of Jesus Christ is not a central reality in their lives. They may not consider themselves religious when confronted by a survey or census questionnaire, understanding this to mean the habitual practice of recognised religious observances; but nor are they militantly anti-religious. Culturally and subconsciously they think of themselves as tone-deaf to religious interests. They may feel that religion for them is an unnecessary intrusion into a life that is complicated enough without introducing into it an unseen world. At the same time, they may admire other people's confident faith in God, and even be a touch wistful that they do not share it.

There are, of course, other factors involved. Indifference to things concerning God can be interpreted theologically as the general human disinclination to allow anything or anyone, except themselves, to govern their lives; it is a natural aversion to outside interference, as they see it. A bad experience of some aspect of religious life may make them cautious about being entangled again. Reports of failings by religious leaders (particularly in the case of child abuse, whether practised or covered up) will undoubtedly have a negative impact on any possible, hesitant interest in religious faith.

In spite of the widespread phenomenon of cultural secularity, or more probably because of it, human beings are missing a whole dimension of life that makes their lives truly human. Charles Taylor offers a clue, in the notion of human flourishing, to the best way of connecting the good news of God's gift of new life through Jesus Christ to the evident failings of a secular reductionist account of what it means to be human. This

---

[73] See Roger Trigg, *Rationality and Science: Can Science Explain Everything?* (Oxford: Blackwell, 1993).

concept is a place where the Christian faith can engage with contemporary culture with a starting point that both sides can agree is significant. Taylor, nevertheless, is not wholly convinced, mainly because he believes that the idea has already been hijacked by exclusive humanism and interpreted in terms of the secular values of life, liberty and the pursuit of happiness. The latter in particular, he believes, is often pursued in deliberate contradiction to the Christian notion of what makes a human being human: 'The pursuit of happiness has come to seem not only not to need a restrictive sexual ethic and the disciplines of deferred gratification, but actually to demand their transgression in the name of self-fulfillment.'[74]

Even where there might appear to be common ground for dialogue with secular people, Christians are in fact struggling against a relentless tide. One of Taylor's basic concerns is to convince our secular age that human flourishing cannot be achieved by releasing humanity from outmoded taboos, in order to justify self-indulgent sensuality; rather it is the consequence of the transformation of human nature by the costly grace of God. In other words, our mission engagement with a secular age is executed initially by showing rationally, spiritually and practically how it is incapable of offering genuine human flourishing or fulfilment: 'There is a crucial point where many come to rest in our civilization, defined by a refusal to envisage transcendence as the meaning of this fullness. Exclusive humanism must find the ground and the contours of fullness in the immanent sphere, in some condition of human life, or feeling or achievement. The door is barred against further discovery.'[75]

Before the good news, comes the 'bad news': a warning that a secular faith leaves humanity sold helplessly short on the true meaning of life and on the fullness of its living expression. Maybe a crucial part of the contemporary challenge for mission in a secular culture is to find ways, in 'bold humility',[76] to prise open the door. This will mean understanding the origins, nature and manifestations of secular culture, engaging vigorously with its destructive tendencies, offering the good news that there is another, God-given, matchless way of being human, and above all showing it in the practice of an integrated life and in costly service to vulnerable members of society.

---

[74] Taylor, *Secular Age*, p. 493.
[75] Taylor, *Secular Age*, p. 769.
[76] A phrase coined by the South African missiologist, David Bosch; see *Transforming Mission*, p. 489.

Epilogue

The theme of this book has been the church in the world seeking to fulfil the assignment given to it by the Trinitarian God who has called it into being. Its focus has been the sphere of human life beyond itself; called to be immersed in the immense variety of activities that make up the life of human social groups across the globe.

It has aimed to look at the world from the perspective of God's living word transmitted through prophet and apostle, on which the church is founded, Jesus Christ being both the corner-stone and the coping-stone (Eph. 2:20). Throughout its history the church has been most faithful to its mission calling when it has paid most attention to the foundation documents which record the many dimensions of God's mission in the world he created. Conversely, it has erred and strayed from God's paths, whenever it has neglected the Scriptures, or when it has manipulated the text in the interests of its own privileges and power or under pressure to comform to cultural influences. Part I of this study is an attempt to do justice to the biblical account of God's intentions for and action within the world he has created for humans to enjoy in fellowship with him.

In the course of our study, we have found both faithful fulfilment and disobedient exploitation of the Bible's message. The history of the church in mission is, to say the least, highly ambiguous. It is easy to interpret it in terms of its many failings to live up to its high calling. The first colonial adventure on the continent to the west of Europe and the brutal suppression of Christian groups, for political ends, during the period of the Reformation are cases in point. These have been highlighted in Part II. The latent paternalism, triumphalism and lack of sensitivity to non-European nations and Christians manifest at the Edinburgh 1910 conference is another example of a failure to read the Scriptures adequately. Finally, as touched on in Part III, the church of the last half century has made a number of serious mistakes: the naive theological optimism in the progress achieved by Western civilization shown in the two decades after the Second World War; the misplaced confidence invested in certain ideological movements in the 1970s; the failure to deal adequately with nationalistic instincts during the period of the 'Cold War' (and its imme- diate aftermath), and the consequent defects in confronting the rhetoric of militarism at the time; and the lack of prophetic leadership in tackling the contemporary slide to an amoral individualism in the West, resulting in compromises with an increasingly godless society.

All these are examples of the church's failure to heed properly the voice of the One who created it and sustains it daily, and there are many more. None of these should be forgotten; nor should the church fail to read carefully 'the signs of the times' in the light of the eternal gospel. At the same time, it would undermine its mission if it allowed itself to be paralysed by a constant fear of betraying its calling.

There is a side to human nature which seems to delight in recording and dwelling on adversity, misfortune and tragedy; it is called *schaden-freude*. The church often appears to take a perverse pleasure in recalling the sins of its past and publicly asking to be forgiven. Whereas acknowl- edgement of evil committed, penitence and, where applicable, restitution is part of its understanding of the message it lives by, sometimes contri- tion for the past takes highly questionable forms. However symbolic and pragmatically beneficial it may be, a contemporary act of official repentance for the Crusades, past examples of Christian neo-colonialism and racism, or the denigration of the status and gifts of women seems misplaced and masochistic. On the other hand, it is appropriate to apol- ogise sincerely and profusely for the ways in which, for example, the contemporary church has covered up its complicity in the physical and emotional abuse of young people. Repenting for the sins of our Christian forebears is not an action we can legitimately take; asking forgiveness for our own misdemeanours is highly befitting and essential.

So, the church in all ages has an enormous responsibility to monitor carefully its mission motives and activities, to ensure that they comply with the ethics of its own proclamation of God's righteous rule. It also has the joyous task of calling attention to those mission practices which truly show forth the compassion and justice of God, and call forth his words of commendation, 'Well done, good and trustworthy servant!' (see Matt. 25:21).

Rights and Freedoms

This book has also recorded some of these. The prolonged efforts of Fray Anton de Montesino, Fray Bartolome de las Casas, Bishop Antonio de Valdivieso and other missionaries in the Americas in the sixteenth century to protect the indigenous populations, in respect of God-given freedoms, against their merciless exploitation by Spanish settlers is, for the time, a remarkable example of the exercise of justice. With the support of theologians and jurists at the University of Salamanca, they began to carve out the first systematic articulation of basic human rights.

In order to carry this forward, they had to defy the vested interests of ruthless compatriots, both plantation owners and the secular clergy (Valdivieso was assassinated in 1550). Bearing in mind that the colonists had plenty of friends in high places at the Spanish court, they also had to persuade the supreme authorities in Spain of the rightness of their campaign. Sadly, although some symbolic gains were made in the passing of laws to prohibit slavery, in the end the colonists prevailed. In reality the Spanish crown was powerless to impose sanctions against groups who lived so far away, once they had succeeded in drawing the local governors to their cause.

Back in Europe, at the same time, a small group of people, stirred by the rediscovery of the biblical message of freedom in Christ, began to organise themselves separately from the state-supported churches of Catholic and Protestant Christendom. Eventually separation also became opposition to what these new believers judged was unfaithfulness to and compromise with the plain teaching of Scripture on the part of the magisterial reformers and their political backers. Although their protest was largely peaceable, they were persecuted and martyred in their thousands. Nevertheless, under great duress, they maintained their independence, stressing that Jesus Christ alone was the supreme head and ruler of the church. They were the latest in a line of 'Nonconformists', those who refused to accept the doctrines and practices of a corrupt church.

Under the influence of extreme apocalyptic beliefs, some on the margins of the Anabaptist movements resorted to violence as a way of anticipating the final battle between purity and corruption. Nevertheless, these were condemned by the leaders of the majority groups, who began to develop a coherent doctrine of Christian pacifism. According to the Anabaptists, Luther's famous words about standing on the teaching of Scripture alone were not carried through thoroughly enough. In the end, for the sake of political stability and the defence of the territorial integrity of the princes, he was judged to have substituted the programme of the kingdoms of this world for that of God's kingdom.

For the following two centuries the Anabaptists and other nonconforming groups were harassed by the establishment (church and state). Eventually, their determination not to be subjugated to what they considered to be merely human-made laws and their willingness to suffer abuse for their convictions was probably the single most important contributory factor in the gradual implementation of rights and freedoms in modern societies.

Neither the Dominican friars of the 'New World' nor the Anabaptists of the 'Old' may have developed a sophisticated theory of political involvement, in which the gospel was applied to the *realpolitik* of the day. Nevertheless, the stand they took for the supremacy of individual conscience in deciding the priorities and limits of government has had an enormous impact on subsequent history. It continues to be a burning issue in the contemporary implementation of rights and freedoms against the tendency of states to demand increasing powers over its citisens.

Mission as Evangelization

The misconceptions of those gathered for the missionary conference in Edinburgh in 1910 have been well-documented. It has been commonplace for subsequent generations in hindsight to criticise quite severely the kind of outlook on the world typical of Christians of that era: their categorization of civilizations according to the measure of the European nations (considered the most advanced); their confidence that new technologies would help promote the Christian faith globally; their belief that the world religions would go into decline, when confronted by the gospel of Jesus Christ; their use of military metaphors to describe the task of world evangelization; their failure to invite more than a handful of participants from the emerging churches outside Europe and North America; and their neglect of the 'Christianised' continents as legitimate spheres for mission.

Nevertheless, there is plenty of evidence in the documents of a mature and sophisticated approach to the task of spreading the gospel. The approach to people of other faiths, through the idea of fulfilment, suggests sensitivity in attempting to find genuine points of contact, rather than emphasizing another religion's weak points. The acknowledgement that the task of evangelism across the globe would fall increasingly to indigenous evangelists showed an incipient recognition of the importance of local initiatives. The discussion of the relation between foreign missionaries and regional political authorities demonstrated a thoughtful approach to issues of sovereignty, perceived interference and the accusation of covert imperialism. The conference did not hesitate to criticise the many failings of Western nations, both in terms of their own moral values and social achievements and the way they treated peoples in their overseas territories. The conference became the main inspiration for much closer cooperation between the various ecclesial bodies that constituted the universal church. The ecumenical movement, which has striven to remove barriers of hostility and suspicion between churches and denominations and to find ways of moving to an ever greater degree of agreement, cooperation and unity, has its origin in the conference.

Finally, the conference displayed a passion for evangelism that recalls the enthusiasm and intensity of the apostolic church. In spite of a certain naïveté with regard to the possibility of finishing the task of making the good news of Jesus known throughout the world, it exhibited its commitment to the primary task of the church in every generation – to make faithful disciples of Jesus Christ who would act as salt and light within a humanity troubled by disease, disabilities, despair, disputes, (natural and human caused) disasters and (premature) death.

Mission Engagement

To slightly misquote the end of John's Gospel, 'There are also many other things that Jesus does (through his disciples); if every one of them were written down, I suppose that the world itself would not contain the books that would be written' (see John 21:25). Here, I will mention only a small sample to illustrate the Christian community operating faithfully in accordance with its greatest mandate to love and serve God and neighbour. I am personally aware of most of these examples.

Throughout the world, from the marginalised peoples of the high Andes to the slum dwellers of Nairobi, Mumbai and Manila, Christians have been involved in alleviating poverty through organizing and running schemes to enable children to be educated and families to own their own businesses. They have (and are) working hard to eradicate child-trafficking for sexual exploitation and forced labour. They run many projects to care for abandoned and traumatised children. They are in the forefront of efforts to overturn the humiliating cultural practice of female genital mutilation. They are engaged in programmes of education concerning the effects of drug-taking, alcohol abuse, sexual promiscuity and gambling addiction. They are also heavily involved in projects designed to liberate people from adherence to such destructive practices.

Christians have been fully committed to treating people with highly stigmatised diseases like AIDS and leprosy as well as serving the needs of people with all kinds of illnesses, especially in areas where there is no public health system in operation. They are engaged in health education and preventative medicine. There are wonderful examples of Christians working for the treatment, rehabilitation and acceptance of people with both permanent and temporary disabilities. I can think, for example, of inspiring projects in Lima (Peru), Santo Domingo (Ecuador) and Iringa (Tanzania).

Christians have played a leading role in attempts on both a global and a local scale to 'make poverty history'. The Jubilee campaign of the end of the twentieth century was an imaginative way of encouraging debt-relief for nations burdened by excessive borrowing. As the name suggests, the inspiration behind it was the provisions for cancelling debt set out in the laws of the Year of Jubilee (Lev. 25). The more recent campaign called 'If' has been heavily supported by Christian organizations. It calls for a renewed commitment to provide sufficient aid to stop people dying of hunger, for governments to stop big companies dodging tax in poor countries and to be transparent about their efforts to eradicate poverty, and to end poor farmers being forced off their land in the interests of growing commercial crops that provide beef and fuel for rich countries.[1]

Likewise, Christian agencies are involved in many schemes for setting up micro enterprises, acquiring funds for starting small-scale businesses that give unemployed (and otherwise unemployable) people the chance to earn a living and to offer work opportunities for others. Christians are dedicating their lives to helping to improve the agricultural techniques of impoverished communities and to finding markets for their products that give a fair return. The Christian organization, Habitat for Humanity, has a proven record in enabling communities to build permanent, solid houses with adequate sanitary facilities.

Last, but not least, Christians have been extensively involved in peace and reconciliation initiatives. These include running workshops on grass-roots involvement in highly inflammatory regions of the world, such as Central America in the 1980s, the Southern Philippines, Palestine, the Horn of Africa, and the Democratic Republic of Congo; the rehabilitation of child-soldiers; the control and limitation of the arms trade; the monitoring of the practices of war; and doing research into the causes and the resolution of conflict.

Most of these mission activities are done out of the spotlight. By and large they do not hit the headlines, with the exception of the large-scale campaigns that focus on pressurizing leading nations, like the G8 group, to bring about change for the benefit of the vulnerable, discarded poor. They are done below the horizon for the joy and privilege alone of serving those in desperate need, and seeing some improvement in their chances of living a fruitful and dignified life. They seek to follow Jesus who served humanity by identifying himself with the needs of the poor and distressed, sacrificing his life to make possible the end of hatred,

---

[1] See www.enoughfoodif.org

greed, violence, hypocrisy and self-assertion by reconciling humanity to the one and only true source of goodness, the Creator and Saviour of all who put their trust in him.

One of the most gratifying aspects of the contemporary church is its rediscovery of its identity as a body in mission. Mission in the world is not just one aspect of its being; it is the very heart of its existence. The relevance of the church is identical with the relevance of its mission. Understanding and carrying out God's objectives in the world is its highest calling.

Bibliography

Abrecht, Paul. 'Responses to the World Conference on Church and Society 1966'. *Ecumenical Review* 20 (Oct. 1968).

Ahern, Geoffrey and Grace Davie. *Inner City God: The Nature of Belief in the Inner City* (London: Hodder & Stoughton, 1987).

Ahonen, Risto. *Mission in the New Millenium* (Helsinki: Finnish Evangelical Lutheran Mission, 2006).

Allen, Roland. *Missionary Methods: St. Paul's or Ours?* (Grand Rapids, MI: Eerdmans, 2001 [original, 1912]).

Anderson, G. and P. Stransky. *Mission Trends No. 5: Faith Meets Faith* (Grand Rapids, MI: Eerdmans, 1981).

Anderson, Gerald et al. eds. *Mission Legacies: Biographical Studies of Leaders of the Modern Missionary Movement* (Maryknoll, NY: Orbis Books, 1994).

Arias, Mortimer and Alan Johnson. *The Great Commission: Biblical Models for Evangelism* (Nashville: Abingdon Press, 1992).

Baez-Camargo, Gonzalo. 'The Place of Latin America in the Ecumenical Movement'. *Ecumenical Review* 1 (1948–9): pp. 311–19.

Bailey, Kenneth E. *Jesus through Middle Eastern Eyes: Cultural Studies in the Gospels* (London: SPCK, 2008).

Balia, Daryl. *Make Corruption History* (London: SPCK, 2009).

Banks, Robert. 'Religion as Projection: A Re-Appraisal of Freud's Theory'. *Religious Studies* 9 (1973): pp. 401–26.

Barend, Hartmut. *Kirche mit Zukunft. Impulse fur eine missionarische Volkkirche* (Giessen: 2006).

Barrs, Jerram. 'Christian Standards in a Puralistic Society'. Unpublished paper presented to a Consultation on Christian Social Action, Nov. 1988.

Barrs, Jerram. 'Justice and Peace Demand Necessary Force'. Pages 16–18 in *Handling Problems of Peace and War: An Evangelical Debate* (ed. J. Andrew Kirk; Basingstoke: Marshall Pickering, 1988).

Barton, Stephen C. 'The Epistles and Christian Ethics'. Pages 63–71 in *The Cambridge Companion to Christian Ethics* (ed. Robin Gill; Cambridge: Cambridge University Press, 2001).

Bauckham, Richard, ed. *Bible and Mission: Christian Witness in a Postmodern World* (Carlisle: Paternoster Press, 2003).

Bauckham, Richard. *Jesus and the Eyewitnesses: The Gospels as Eyewitness Testimony* (Grand Rapids, MI: Eerdmans, 2006).

Bauman, Z. *Postmodern Ethics* (Oxford: Blackwell, 1993).

Bauman, Z. *Postmodernity and its Discontents* (Cambridge: Polity Press, 1997).

Beasley-Murray, George R. *John* (Word Biblical Commentary 36) (Milton Keynes: Word Books, 1991).

Bender, Harold. *Conrad Grebel* (Goshen: Mennonite Historical Society, 1950).

Berkhof, Hendrikus. 'Re-Opening the Dialogue with the "Horizontalists"'. *Ecumenical Review* 21 (Oct. 1969).

Bevans, Stephen B. and Roger P. Schroeder. *Constants in Context: A Theology of Mission for Today* (Maryknoll, NY: Orbis Books, 2004).

Bieringer, Reimund, ed. *Anti-Judaism in the Fourth Gospel* (Assen: van Gorcum, 2001).

Biesecker-Mast, Gerald. *Separation and the Sword in Anabaptist Persuasion: Radical Confessional Rhetoric from Schleitheim to Dordrecht* (Scottdale, PA: Herald Press, 2006).

Bird, Alexander. *Philosophy of Science* (London: Routledge, 1998).

Blauw, Johannes. *The Missionary Nature of the Church: A Survey of the Biblical Theology of Mission* (Guildford: Lutterworth Press, 1974).

Bloch, Ernst. *Das Prinzip Hoffnung* (1959), trans. as *The Principle of Hope* (Oxford: Blackwell, 1986).

Blocher, Henri. *In the Beginning* (Leicester: Inter-Varsity Press, 1984).

Boer, Harry R. *Pentecost and Missions* (Grand Rapids, MI: Eerdmans, 1961).

Bonhoeffer, Dietrich. *Letters and Papers from Prison* (London: SCM Press, 1971).

Bosch, David J. *Transforming Mission: Paradigm Shifts in Theology of Mission* (Maryknoll, NY: Orbis Books, 1991).

Bottomore, Tom, ed. *A Dictionary of Marxist Thought* (Oxford: Blackwell, 2nd edn, 1991).

Bowen, Roger. *So I Send You: A Study Guide to Mission* (London: SPCK, 1996).

Braaten, Carl. 'The Uniqueness and Universality of Jesus Christ'. *Mission Trends No. 5: Faith Meets Faith* (ed. G. Anderson and P. Stransky; Grand Rapids, MI: Eerdmans, 1981).

Brakenhielm, Carl Reinhold, ed. *Power and Peace: Statements on Peace and the Authority of the Churches* (Uppsala: LPI, 1992).

Brawley, Robert L., ed. *Character Ethics and the New Testament: Moral Dimensions of Scripture* (Louisville: Westminster John Knox Press, 2007).

Brown, Callum. *The Death of Christian Britain* (London: Routledge, 2001).

Brown, Raymond E. *An Introduction to the Gospel of John* (New York: Doubleday, 2003).

Brune, Peter. *The Gothenburg Process: Faith-Based Advocacy for Disarmament* (Uppsala: LPI, 2009).

Cahill, Lisa Sowle. 'The Bible and Christian Moral Practices'. In *Christian Ethics: Problems and Prospects* (ed. Lisa Sowle Cahill and James F. Childress; Cleveland: Pilgrim Press, 1996).

Caird, G.B. *Paul's Letters from Prison* (Oxford: Oxford University Press, 1976).

Campaign against the Arms Trade. *Death on Delivery: The Impact of the Arms Trade on the Third World* (London: CATT, 1989).

Cantwell Smith, Wilfred. *The Meaning and End of Religion: A New Approach to the Religious Traditions of Mankind* (New York: Harper & Row, 2nd edn, 1978).

Cardenal, Rodolfo. 'The Church in Central America'. Pages 243–70 in *The Church in Latin America: 1492-1992* (ed. Enrique Dussel; Tunbridge Wells/Maryknoll, NY: Burns & Oates/Orbis Books, 1992).

Carter, Warren. *John: Storyteller, Interpreter, Evangelist* (Peabody: Hendrickson, 2006).

Chadwick, Owen. *The Secularization of the European Mind in the Nineteenth Century* (Cambridge: Cambridge University Press, 1985).

Chaney, Charles L. *The Birth of Missions in America* (Pasadena, CA: William Carey Library, 1976).

Chopp, Rebecca. *The Praxis of Suffering: An Interpretation of Liberation and Political Theologies* (Maryknoll, NY: Orbis Books, 1992).

Christian World Conference. 'Message of Life and Peace'. *Church and Society* (Sept.–Oct. 1983).

Church of England. *Towards a Theology for Inter-Faith Dialogue* (General Synod 625) (London: Church Information Office, 1984).

Clooney, Francis X. 'Pain but not Harm: Some Classical Resources toward a Hindu Just War Theory'. In *Just War in Comparative Perspective* (ed. Paul Robinson; Aldershot: Ashgate Publishing, 2003).

Clouser, Roy. *The Myth of Religious Neutrality* (Notre Dame: University of Notre Dame Press, 2005).

Cochrane, Arthur C. *The Church's Confession Under Hitler* (Philadelphia: Westminster Press, 1962).

Collins Dictionary of the English Language (Glasgow: Collins, 1979).

Cooper, David E. *World Philosophies: An Historical Introduction* (Oxford: Blackwell, 1996).

Copan, Paul and Paul K. Moser, eds. *The Rationality of Theism* (London: Routledge, 2003).

Cox, Harvey. *The Secular City: Secularization and Urbanization in Theological Perspective* (New York: Collier Books, 25th anniversary edn, 1990).

Cox, Harvey. 'The Secular City 25 Years Later'. *Christian Century* (7 Nov. 1990).

Cracknell, Kenneth. *Towards a New Relationship: Christians and People of Other Faith* (London: Epworth Press, 1986).

Cragg, Kenneth. *The Christ and the Faiths: Theology in Cross-Reference* (London: SPCK, 1986).

Cragg, Kenneth. *Sandals at the Mosque: Christian Presence and Islam* (London: SCM Press, 1959).

Craig, William Lane. 'The Cosmological Argument'. Pages 112–31 in *The Rationality of Theism* (ed. Paul Copan and Paul K. Moser; London: Routledge, 2003).

Curd, Martin and J.A. Cover. *Philosophy of Science: The Central Issues* (New York: W.W. Norton, 1998).

Daly, Robert J. *The Moral World of the First Christians: From Biblical Revelation to Contemporary Christian Praxis: Method and Content* (Ramsey, NJ: Paulist Press, 1984).

Davie, Grace. *Europe: The Exceptional Case: Parameters of Faith in the Modern World* (London: Darton, Longman & Todd, 2002).

Davie, Grace. *Religion in Modern Europe: A Memory Mutates* (Oxford: Oxford University Press, 2000).

Davies, Eryl. *The Immoral Bible: Approaches to Biblical Ethics* (London: T & T Clark, 2010).

Davies, Paul J. *Faith Seeking Effectiveness: The Missionary Theology of José Miguez Bonino* (Zoetermeer, ND: Uitgeverij Boekcentrum, 2006).

Davis, Charles. *Christ and the World Religions* (London: Hodder & Stoughton).

Davis, Charles. 'Religious Pluralism and the New Counter-Culture'. *The Listener* (9 April 1970).

Deppermann, K. 'Melchior Hoffman'. Pages 178–83 in *Profiles of Radical Reformers* (ed. H.G. Goertz; Scottdale, PA: Herald Press, 1982).

Dowsett, Rose. 'Cooperation and the Promotion of Unity: An Evangelical Perspective'. Pages 250–62 in *Edinburgh 2010: Mission Then and Now* (ed. David A. Kerr and Kenneth R. Ross; Oxford: Regnum Books International, 2009).

Dunn, James D.G. *Christianity in the Making, vol. 1, Jesus Remembered* (Grand Rapids, MI: Eerdmans, 2003).

Dunn, James D.G. *A New Perspective on Jesus: What the Quest for the Historical Jesus Missed* (London: SPCK, 2005).

Dussel, Enrique, ed. *The Church in Latin America: 1492-1992* (Tunbridge Wells/Maryknoll, NY: Burns & Oates/Orbis Books, 1992).

Dussel, Enrique. *Historia de la Iglesia en América Latina* (Barcelona: Nova Terra, 2nd edn, 1972).

Elford, John. 'Christianity and War'. Pages 171–80 in *The Cambridge Companion to Christian Ethics* (ed. Robin Gill; Cambridge: Cambridge University Press, 2001).

Eliade, Mircea. *The Sacred and Profane* (New York: Harvest Books, 1968).

Engels, Friedrich. 'The Peasant War in Germany'. Pages 397–482 in the *Collected Works of Karl Marx and Friedrich Engels: Volume 10* (New York: International Publishers, 1988).

Escobar, Samuel. *En Busca de Cristo en América Latina* (*In Search of Christ in Latin America*) (Buenos Aires: Ediciones Kairos, 2012).

Escobar, Samuel. 'Mission from Everywhere to Everyone: The Home Base in a New Century'. Pages 185–200 in *Edinburgh 2010: Mission Then and Now* (ed. David A. Kerr and Kenneth R. Ross; Oxford: Regnum Books International, 2009).

Escobar, Samuel. *The New Global Mission: The Gospel from Everywhere to Everyone* (Downers Grove, IL: InterVarsity Press, 2003).

Escobar, Samuel. *Tiempo de Mision: America Latina y la misión cristiana hoy* (Bogota, Ciudad de Guatemala: Ediciones Clara-Semilla, 1999).

Esposito, John L. *The Oxford Dictionary of Islam* (Oxford: Oxford University Press, 2003).

Estep, William R. *The Anabaptist Story: An Introduction to Sixteenth-Century Anabaptism* (Grand Rapids, MI: Eerdmans, 3rd edn, 1996).

Evans, C. Stephen and R. Zachary Manis. *Philosophy of Religion: Thinking about Faith* (Downers Grove, IL: InterVarsity Press, 2nd edn, 2009).

Evans, Craig A. and Stanley E. Porter. *Dictionary of New Testament Background* (Downers Grove, IL: InterVarsity Press, 2000).

Fenn, Richard K. *The Blackwell Companion to Sociology of Religion* (Oxford: Blackwell, 2003).

Fenn, Richard K. 'The Origins of Religion'. Pages 176–96 in *The Blackwell Companion to Sociology of Religion* (ed. Richard K. Fenn; Oxford: Blackwell, 2003).

Fernández, Isacio Pérez. *El anónimo de Yucay frente Bartolomé de las Casas* (Cusco: Centro Bartolomé de las Casas, 1995).

France, R.T. *Matthew* (Leicester: Inter-Varsity Press, 1985).

Francis-Dehqani, Guli E. 'Adventures in Christian-Muslim Encounters since 1910'. Pages 125–38 in *Edinburgh 2010: Mission Then and Now* (ed. David A. Kerr and Kenneth R. Ross; Oxford: Regnum Books International, 2009).

Frankenberry, Nancy K. *Radical Interpretation of Religion* (Cambridge: Cambridge University Press, 2002).

Freud, Sigmund. *Civilization and its Discontents* (New York: Norton, 1961).

Freud, Sigmund. *Introductory Lectures on Psychoanalysis* (Harmondsworth: Penguin Books, 1973).

Friedmann, Robert. 'Community of Goods'. *Global Anabaptist Mennonite Encyclopedia Online* (1953) http://www.gameo.org/encyclopedia/contents/C6593ME.html

Friedmann, Robert. 'Wideman, Jakob (d. 1535/6)'. *Global Anabaptist Mennonite Encyclopedia Online* (1959) http://www.gameo.org/encyclopedia/contents/wideman_jakob_d._1535_6

Friesen, Abraham. *Erasmus, the Anabaptists and the Great Commission* (Grand Rapids, MI: Eerdmans, 1998).

Fromm, Eric. *The Fear of Freedom* (London: Routledge & Kegan Paul, 1960).

Fuson, Robert H., ed. *The Log of Christopher Columbus* (London: Tab Books, 1992).

Gibbon, Edward. *The Decline and Fall of the Roman Empire* (New York: Modern Library, 1932).

Gilbert, Alan D. *The Making of Post-Christian Britain: A History of the Secularization of Modern Society* (London: Longman, 1980).

Gill, Robin. 'The Arms Trade and Christian Ethics'. Pages 186–193 in *The Cambridge Companion to Christian Ethics* (Cambridge: Cambridge University Press, 2001).

Gill, Robin, ed. *The Cambridge Companion to Christian Ethics* (Cambridge: Cambridge University Press, 2001).

Gnanakan, Ken R. *Kingdom Concerns: A Biblical Exploration towards a Theology of Mission* (Bangalore: Theological Book Trust, 1989).

Godin, H. and Y. Daniel. *France, pays du mission?* (Paris: Editions du Cerf, 1943).

Godwin, Colin. *Baptizing, Gathering, Sending: The Significance of Anabaptist Approaches to Mission in the Sixteenth-Century Context* (University of Wales, unpublished PhD dissertation, 2010).

Goertz, H.G., ed. *Profiles of Radical Reformers* (Scottdale, PA: Herald Press, 1982).

Goheen, Michael. 'The Future of Mission in the World Council of Churches: The Dialogue between Lesslie Newbigin and Konrad Reiser'. *Mission Studies* 21 (2004).

Gonzalez, Ondina E. and Justo L. Gonzalez. *Christianity in Latin America: A History* (Cambridge: Cambridge University Press, 2008).

Goodall, N., ed. *Missions under the Cross* (London: Edinburgh House Press, 1952).

Grams, Rollin G., I. Howard Marshall, Peter F. Penner and Robin Routledge, eds. *Bible and Mission: A Conversation between Biblical Studies and Missiology* (Schwarzenfeld: Neufeld Verlag, 2008).

Gray, John. *Al Qaeda and What it Means to be Modern* (London: Faber & Faber, 2003).

Gray, John. *The Two Faces of Liberalism* (Cambridge: Polity Press, 2000).

Grayling, Anthony. *What is Good? The Search for the Best Way to Live* (London: Wiedenfeld & Nicolson, 2003).

Greene, Colin D. *Christology in Cultural Perspective: Marking out the Horizons* (Carlisle: Paternoster Press, 2003).

Gunther, Wolfgang. 'The History and Significance of World Mission Conferences in the 20th Century'. *International Review of Mission* 92 (2003): pp. 521–37.

Gutierrez, Gustavo. ' "If you were Indios . . ." Bartolome de Las Casas'. *Concilium* 5 (2009).

Gutierrez, Gustavo. *Las Casas: In Search of the Poor of Jesus Christ* (Maryknoll, NY: Orbis Books, 1992).

Habermas, Jurgen. *The Theory of Communicative Action* (trans. Thomas McCarthy; Boston: Beacon Press, 1984).

Habgood, John. *Church and Nation in a Secular Age* (London: Darton, Longman & Todd, 1983).

Haralambos, M. *Sociology: Themes and Perspectives* (Slough: University Tutorial Press, 1980).

Harder, Leland, ed. *The Sources of Swiss Anabaptism: The Grebel Letters and Related Documents* (Classics of the Radical Reformation, Vol. 4) (Scottdale, PA: Herald Press, 1985).

Hart, Trevor A., ed. *The Dictionary of Historical Theology* (Carlisle: Paternoster Press, 2000).

Hartenstein, Karl. 'Was hat die Theologie Karl Barths der Mission zu sagen?' (Munich: Kaiser Verlag, 1928).

Hauerwas, Stanley. *Against the Nations: War and Survival in a Liberal Society* (Notre Dame: University of Notre Dame Press, 1992).

Hauerwas, Stanley. 'Pacifism: Some Philosophical Considerations'. *Faith and Philosophy* 2 (April 1985): pp. 339–40.

Hawking, Stephen and Leonard Mlodinow. *Grand Design: New Approaches to the Ultimate Questions of Life* (London: Bantam Press, 2010).

Hawthorne, Gerald F., Ralph P. Martin and Daniel G. Reid, eds. *Dictionary of Paul and His Letters* (Downers Grove, IL: InterVarsity Press, 1993).

Hays, Richard B. *The Moral Vision of the New Testament: A Contemporary Introduction to New Testament Ethics* (New York: Harper Collins)

Hebblethwaite, Brian. 'Religious Language and Religious Pluralism', *Anvil* 4 (1987).

Hebblethwaite, Peter. *Christian-Marxist Dialogue and Beyond* (London: Darton, Longman & Todd, 1977).

Hehir, Bryan. 'Ethics and Deterrence'. Pages 19–28 in *Power and Peace: Statements on Peace and the Authority of the Churches* (ed. Carl Reinhold Brakenhielm; Uppsala: LPI, 1992).

Hick, John. *An Interpretation of Religion: Human Responses to the Transcendent* (New Haven: Yale University Press, 2nd edn, 2004).

Hick, John, ed. *The Myth of God Incarnate* (London: SCM Press, 1977).

Hinnells, John R., ed. *A Handbook of Living Religions* (London: Penguin Books, 1985).

Hinnells, John R., ed. *The Penguin Dictionary of Religions: From Abraham to Zoroaster* (London: Penguin Books, 1984).

Hinnells, John R., ed. *The Routledge Companion to the Study of Religion* (Abingdon: Routledge, 2nd edn, 2010).

Hoedemaker, Bert. 'The Legacy of J.C. Hoekendijk'. *International Bulletin of Missionary Research* (1 Oct. 1995).

Hoedemaker, Bert. 'Peace Witness and Church Authority: A Reformed Perspective from the Netherlands'. Pages 32–54 in *Power and Peace: Statements on Peace and the Authority of the Churches* (ed. Carl Reinhold Brakenhielm; Uppsala: LPI, 1992).

Hoekendijk, J.C. *The Church Inside Out* (London: SCM Press, 1967).

Hoekendijk, J.C. *Horizons of Hope* (Nashville, TN: Tidings, 1970).

Hogg, William Richey. 'Edinburgh 1910 – Ecumenical Keystone'. *Religion in Life* 29 (1959–60): pp. 339–51.

Hollenbach, David. *Nuclear Ethics: A Christian Moral Argument* (New York: Paulist Press, 1983).

Jackson, Timothy P. 'The Gospels and Christian Ethics'. Pages 42–62 in *The Cambridge Companion to Christian Ethics* (ed. Robin Gill; Cambridge: Cambridge University Press, 2001).

Johansson, Lars. 'Mystical Knowledge, New Age, and Missiology'. Pages 172–204 in *To Stake a Claim: Mission and the Western Crisis of Knowledge* (ed. J. Andrew Kirk and Kevin Vanhoozer; Maryknoll: Orbis Books, 1999).

Johnson, James Turner. 'Just War as it was and is'. *First Things* (January 2005).

Jones, David Clyne. *Biblical Christian Ethics* (Grand Rapids, MI: Baker Books, 1994).

Jones, Gareth. 'The Authority of Scripture and Christian Ethics'. Pages 16–28 in *The Cambridge Companion to Christian Ethics* (ed. Robin Gill; Cambridge: Cambridge University Press, 2001).

Joseph, M.P. 'Missionary Education: An Ambiguous Legacy'. Pages 105–20 in *Edinburgh 2010: Mission Then and Now* (ed. David A. Kerr and Kenneth R. Ross; Oxford: Regnum Books International, 2009).

Josephus. *The Jewish Antiquities* in *Works* (Cambridge, MA: Harvard University Press, 1929–65).

Kaiser, Walter. *Toward Rediscovering the Old Testament* (Grand Rapids, MI: Zondervan, 1987).

Kalu, Ogbu U. 'To Hang a Ladder in the Air: An African Assessment'. Pages 91–104 in *Edinburgh 2010: Mission Then and Now* (ed. David A. Kerr and Kenneth R. Ross; Oxford: Regnum Books International, 2009).

Karotemprel, Sebastian, ed. *Following Christ in Mission: A Foundational Course in Missiology* (Boston: Pauline Books, 1996).

Kasdorf, Hans. 'The Anabaptist Approach to Mission'. Pages 55–62 in *Anabaptism and Mission* (ed. Wilbert R. Shenk; Scottdale, PA: Herald Press, 1984).

Kaye, Bruce and Gordon Wenham, eds. *Law, Morality and the Bible* (Downers Grove, IL: InterVarsity Press, 1978).

Kaye, Bruce. 'Law and Morality in the Epistles of the New Testament'. Pages 72–97 in *Law, Morality and the Bible* (ed. Bruce Kaye and Gordon Wenham; Downers Grove, IL: InterVarsity Press, 1978).

Kee, Alistair. *Marx and the Failure of Liberation Theology* (London: SCM Press, 1990).

Kerr, David A. and Kenneth R. Ross, eds. *Edinburgh 2010: Mission Then and Now* (Oxford: Regnum Books International, 2009).

Khodr, George. 'The Economy of the Holy Spirit'. Pages 43–5 in *Mission Trends No. 5: Faith Meets Faith* (ed. G. Anderson and P. Stransky; Grand Rapids, MI: Eerdmans, 1981).

Kidner, Derek. *Psalms 73–150: A Commentary on Books III, IV and V of the Psalms* (Leicester: Inter-Varsity Press, 1975).

King, Jonathan. *Waltzing Materialism* (Sydney: Harper & Row, 1978).

Kirk, J. Andrew. 'Apologetics'. Page 22 in *Dictionary of Mission Theology: Evangelical Foundations* (ed. John Corrie; Nottingham: Inter-Varsity Press, 2007).

Kirk, J. Andrew. *Christian Mission as Dialogue: Engaging the Current Epistemological Predicament of the West* (Nijmegen: Nijmegen Institute for Mission Studies, 2011).

Kirk, J. Andrew. 'Christian Mission in Multifaith Situations'. Pages 153–163 in *Theology and the Religions: A Dialogue* (ed. Viggo Mortensen; Grand Rapids, MI: Eerdmans, 2003).

Kirk, J. Andrew. *Civilisations in Conflict? Islam, the West and Christian Faith* (Oxford: Regnum International, 2010).

Kirk, J. Andrew. 'An Enquiry into the Origins of Modern Science.' Ch. 2 in *The Future of Reason, Science and Faith: Following Modernity and Postmodernity* (Aldershot: Ashgate Publishing, 2007).

Kirk, J. Andrew. *The Future of Reason, Science and Faith: Following Modernity and Postmodernity* (Aldershot: Ashgate Publishing, 2007).

Kirk, J. Andrew. ' "God is on Our Side": The Anatomy of an Ideology', *Transformation* 27 (2010): pp. 239–40.

Kirk, J. Andrew. *God's Word for a Complex World: Discovering How the Bible Speaks Today* (Basingstoke: Marshall Pickering, 1987).

Kirk, J. Andrew, ed. *Handling Problems of Peace and War: An Evangelical Debate* (Basingstoke: Marshall Pickering, 1988).

Kirk, J. Andrew. 'How a Missiologist Utilises the Bible'. Pages 246–68 in *Bible and Mission: A Conversation between Biblical Studies and Missiology* (ed. Rollin G. Grams, I. Howard Marshall, Peter F. Penner and Robin Routledge; Schwarzenfeld: Neufeld Verlag, 2008).

Kirk, J. Andrew. 'John Hick's Kantian Theory of Religious Pluralism and the Challenge of Secular Thinking'. *Studies in Interreligious Dialogue* 12 (2002): pp. 23–35.

Kirk, J. Andrew. 'Letters to World Leaders'. *New Routes: A Journal of Peace Research and Action* 7 (2003): pp. 3–6.

Kirk, J. Andrew. *Liberation Theology: An Evangelical View from the Third World* (London: Marshall, Morgan & Scott, 1979/1985).

Kirk, J. Andrew. *Loosing the Chains: Religion as Opium and Liberation* (London: Hodder & Stoughton, 1992).

Kirk, J. Andrew. *The Meaning of Freedom: A Study of Secular, Muslim and Christian Views* (Carlisle: Paternoster Press, 1998).

Kirk, J. Andrew. *Mission Under Scrutiny: Confronting Current Challenges* (London: Darton, Longman & Todd, 2006).

Kirk, J. Andrew. *Theology Encounters Revolution* (Leicester: Inter-Varsity Press, 1980).

Kirk, J. Andrew. *What is Mission? Theological Explorations* (London: Darton, Longman & Todd, 1999).

Kirk, J. Andrew and Kevin Vanhoozer, eds. *To Stake a Claim: Mission and the Western Crisis of Knowledge* (Maryknoll, NY: Orbis Books, 1999).

Kool, Anne-Marie. 'Changing Images in the Formation for Mission: Commission Five in Light of Current Challenges – A World Perspective'. Pages 158–80 in *Edinburgh 2010: Mission Then and Now* (ed. David A. Kerr and Kenneth R. Ross; Oxford: Regnum Books International, 2009).

Kostenberger, Andreas J. *The Missions of Jesus and the Disciples According to the Fourth Gospel* (Grand Rapids, MI: Eerdmans, 1998).

Kraemer, Hendrik, *The Christian Message in a Non-Christian World* (London: Edinburgh House Press, 1938).

Kreider, Alan. 'Following Jesus Implies Unconditional Pacifism'. Pages 22–40 in *Handling Problems of Peace and War: An Evangelical Debate* (ed. J. Andrew Kirk;. Basingstoke: Marshall Pickering, 1988).

Kreider, A. 'Introduction' in *The Origins of Christianity in the West* (ed. A. Kreider; Edinburgh: T & T Clark, 2001).

Kreider, A., ed. *The Origins of Christianity in the West* (Edinburgh: T & T Clark, 2001).

Ladyman, James. *Understanding Philosophy of Science* (London: Routledge, 2002).

Langan, John. 'The Elements of St. Augustine's Just War Theory'. *Journal of Religious Ethics* 12 (Spring 1984): pp. 19–38.

Las Casas, Bartolomé de. 'Historia de los Indios' (in *Obras Escogidas*) (Madrid: BAE, 1957–8).

Las Casas, Bartolomé de. *Obras Completas* (Madrid: Alianza Editorial, 1992).

Le Grys, Alan. *Preaching to the Nations: The Origins of Mission in the Early Church* (London: SPCK, 1998).

Lehmann, Paul L. 'The Missionary Obligation of the Church'. *Theology Today* 9 (1952): pp. 20–38.

Lennox, John. *God and Stephen Hawking: Whose Design Is It Anyway?* (Oxford: Lion Hudson, 2011).

Lennox, John. *God's Undertaker: Has Science Buried God?* (Oxford: Lion Hudson, 2009).

Lipton, Peter. *Inference to the Best Explanation* (London: Routledge, 2nd edn, 2004).

Littell, Franklin Hamlin. *The Anabaptist View of the Church* (Boston: Starr King Press, 1958).

Locher, Gottfried W. 'Zwingli and Erasmus' in *Zwingli's Thought: New Perspectives* (Leiden: E.V. Brill, 1981), pp. 233–55.

Locher, Gottfried W. *Zwingli's Thought: New Perspectives* (Leiden: E.V. Brill, 1981).

Loserth, Johann. 'Hutter, Jakob (d. 1536)'. *Global Anabaptist Mennonite Encyclopedia Online* (1959) http://www.gameo.org/encyclopedia/contents/H887.html

Luckmann, Thomas. *The Invisible Religion: The Problem of Religion in Modern Society* (New York: Macmillan, 1967).

Lyon, David. 'Secularisation'. *Third Way* (July/August 1984).

Lyon, David. 'Secularization: The Fate of Faith in Modern Society'. *Themelios* 10 (Sept. 1984).

MacIntyre, Alasdair. *After Virtue: A Study in Moral Theology* (Notre Dame: University of Notre Dame Press, 1981).

Maggay, Melba. *Transforming Society* (Oxford: Regnum/Lynx, 1994).

Maluleke, Tinyiko Sam. 'Christian Mission and Political Power: Commission Seven Revisited'. Pages 204–16 in *Edinburgh 2010: Mission Then and Now* (ed. David A. Kerr and Kenneth R. Ross; Oxford: Regnum Books International, 2009).

Marshall, I. Howard. *Acts: An Introduction and Commentary* (Leicester: IVP, 1980).

Marshall, I. Howard. *The Gospel of Luke: A Commentary on the Greek Text* (Exeter: Paternoster Press, 1978).

Marshall, I. Howard. 'Paul's Mission According to Romans,' in *Bible and Mission: Christian Witness in a Postmodern World* (ed. Richard Bauckham; Carlisle: Paternoster Press, 2003).

Marshall, I. Howard. 'Using the Bible in Ethics'. Pages 37ff. in *Essays in Evangelical Social Ethics* (ed. David F. Wright; Exeter: Paternoster Press, 1979).

Martin, David. *The Future of Christianity: Reflections on Violence and Democracy, Religion and Secularization* (Aldershot: Ashgate Publishing, 2011).

Martin, David. *A General Theory of Secularization* (Oxford: Blackwell, 1978).

Martin, David. *On Secularization: Towards a Revised General Theory* (Aldershot: Ashgate Publishing, 2005).

Martin, David. *Tracts against the Times* (London: Lutterworth Press, 1973).

Massaro, Thomas J. and Thomas A. Shannon. *Catholic Perspectives on Peace and War* (Lanham, MD: Rowman & Littlefield, 2003).

Matheson, Peter. *A Just Peace: A Theological Exploration* (New York: Friendship Press, 1981).

Matthey, Jacque. 'God's Mission Today: Summary and Conclusions'. *International Review of Mission* 92 (2004).

Mattox, John Mark. *Augustine and the Theory of Just War* (London: Continuum, 2006).

McConville, Gordon. 'Concerning Starting-Points'. Pages 116–119 in *Handling Problems of Peace and War: An Evangelical Debate* (ed. J. Andrew Kirk; Basingstoke: Marshall Pickering, 1988).

McGrath, Alister E. *Dawkins' God: Genes, Memes and the Meaning of Life* (Oxford: Blackwell, 2005).

McGrath, Alister E. *Surprised by Meaning: Science, Faith and How We Make Sense of Things* (Louisville: Westminster John Knox Press, 2011).

McLellan, David, ed., *Karl Marx: Selected Writings* (Oxford: Oxford University Press, 1977).

Meeks, Wayne A. *The Moral World of the First Christians* (Philadelphia: Westminster Press, 1987).

Mendieta, Eduardo. *The Frankfurt School on Religion: Key Writings by the Major Thinkers* (Abingdon: Routledge, 2005).

Messer, Neil. *Christian Ethics* (London: SCM Press, 2006).

Miguez Bonino, Jose. *Ama y haz lo que quieras: hacia una etica del hombre nuevo* (*Love and Do What You Like: Toward an Ethic of the New Person*) (Buenos Aires: La Aurora, 1972).

Miguez Bonino, Jose. *Christians and Marxists: The Mutual Challenge to Revolution* (London: Hodder & Stoughton, 1976).

Miguez Bonino, Jose. *Doing Theology in a Revolutionary Situation* (Philadelphia, PA: Fortress Press, 1975); UK edn: *Revolutionary Theology Comes of Age* (London: SPCK, 1975).

Miguez Bonino, Jose. *Espacio para ser hombres: una interpretacion del mensaje de la Biblia para nuestro tiempo* (Buenos Aires: Tierra Nueva, 1975); ET: *Room To Be People: An Interpretation of the Message of the Bible for Today's World* (Augsburg: Fortress Press, 1979).

Miguez Bonino, Jose. *Faces of Latin American Protestantism* (Grand Rapids, MI: Eerdmans, 1997) (Spanish original, 1995).

Miguez Bonino, Jose, ed. *Jesus: ni vencido ni monarca celestial* (*Jesus: Neither Defeated Nor Celestial Monarch*) (Buenos Aires: Tierra Nueva, 1977); ET: *Faces of Jesus: Latin American Christologies* (Maryknoll, NY: Orbis Books, 1984).

Miguez Bonino, Jose. 'Latin America'. Pages 2–25 in *An Introduction to Third World Theologies* (ed. John Parratt; Cambridge: Cambridge University Press, 2004).

Miguez Bonino, Jose. *Poder del Evangelio y poder politico* (Buenos Aires: Editorial Kairos, 1999).

Miguez Bonino, Jose. 'The Protestant Churches in Latin America in the New Millenium'. Pages 20–31 in *Faith in the Millenium* (ed. Stanley E. Porter, Michael A. Hayes and David Tombs; Sheffield: Sheffield Academic Press, 2001).

Miguez Bonino, Jose. '¿Quien es Jesucristo hoy en America Latina?' ('Who is Jesus Christ Today in Latin America?'). Pages 9–17 *Jesus: Ni Vencido Ni Monarca Celestial* (*Jesus: Neither Defeated Nor Celestial Monarch*) (Buenos Aires: Tierra Nueva, 1977), pp. 9–17.

Miguez Bonino, Jose. *Toward a Christian Political Ethics* (London: SCM Press, 1983).

Millikan, David. 'Secularism, Social Change and the Role of Christians in Australia'. *Zadok Occasional Paper* (1978).

Moltmann, Jurgen. *The Theology of Hope* (New York: Harper & Row, 1967).

Morris, Leon. *Jesus is the Christ: Studies in the Theology of John* (Grand Rapids, MI: Eerdmans, 1989).

Mortensen, Viggo, ed. *Theology and the Religions: A Dialogue* (Grand Rapids, MI: Eerdmans, 2003).

Mott, John R. *Addresses and Papers*, Vol. V (New York: Association Press, 1947).

Mott, John R. *The Evangelization of the World in This Generation* (London: Student Volunteer Movement, 1902).

Mott, Stephen Charles. *Biblical Ethics and Social Change* (Oxford: Oxford University Press, 1982).

Murray, Stuart. *Post-Christendom: Church and Mission in a Strange New World* (Milton Keynes: Paternoster Press, 2004).

Nazir Ali, Michael. *From Everywhere to Everywhere: A World View of Christian Mission* (London: Collins, 1991).

Nazir Ali, Michael. *Mission and Dialogue: Proclaiming the Gospel Afresh in Every Age* (London: SPCK, 1995).

Newbigin, Lesslie. 'The Gospel among the Religions'. *Mission Trends No. 5: Faith Meets Faith* (ed. G. Anderson and P. Stransky; Grand Rapids, MI: Eerdmans, 1981).

Newbigin, Lesslie. *The Open Secret* (London: SPCK, 2nd edn, 1995).

Nietzsche, Frederick. *A Nietzsche Reader* (trans. R.J. Hollingdale; Harmondsworth: Penguin, 1977).

Nissen, Johannes. 'Mission in the Fourth Gospel: Historical and Hermeneutical Perspectives'. Pages 213–31 in *New Readings in John: Literary and Theological Perspectives* (ed. Johannes Nissen and Sigfred Pedersen; Sheffield: Sheffield Academic Press, 1999).

Nixon, Robin. 'Fulfilling the Law: The Gospel and Acts'. Pages 53–71 in *Law, Morality and the Bible* (ed. Bruce Kaye and Gordon Wenham; Downers Grove, IL: InterVarsity Press, 1978).

O'Donovan, Oliver. *The Just War Revisited* (Cambridge: Cambridge University Press, 2003).

O'Donovan, Oliver. *Resurrection and Moral Order: An Outline for Evangelical Ethics* (Leicester: Inter-Varsity Press, 1986).

Okure, Teresa. 'The Church in the Mission Field: A Nigerian/African Response. Pages 59–73 in *Edinburgh 2010: Mission Then and Now* (ed. David A. Kerr and Kenneth R. Ross; Oxford: Regnum Books International, 2009).

Okure, Teresa. *The Johannine Approach to Mission: A Contextual Study of John 4.1-42* (Tubingen: J.C.B. Mohr, 1988).

Olsen, Rolv, ed. *Mission and Postmodernities* (Oxford: Regnum Books, 2011).

Paden, William E. 'Comparative Religion'. Pages 225–33 in *The Routledge Companion to the Study of Religion* (ed. John R. Hinnells; Abingdon: Routledge, 2nd edn, 2010).

Padilla, René. *Mission Between the Times: Essays on the Kingdom* (Grand Rapids, MI: Eerdmans, 1985).

Pannikar, Raimundo. 'The Rules of the Game' in *Mission Trends No. 5: Faith Meets Faith* (ed. G. Anderson and P. Stransky; Grand Rapids, MI: Eerdmans, 1981), pp. 118–19 (originally ch. 3 of *The Intrareligious Dialogue* (New York: Paulist Press, 1978).

Parratt, John, ed. *An Introduction to Third World Theologies* (Cambridge: Cambridge University Press, 2004).

Pearse, Meic. *The Great Restoration: The Religious Radicals of the 16th and 17th Centuries* (Carlisle: Paternoster Press, 1998).

Penner, P.F. 'The Use of the Book of Acts in Mission Theology and Praxis'. Pages 74–95 in *Bible and Mission: A Conversation between Biblical Studies and Missiology* (ed. Rollin G. Grams, I. Howard Marshall, Peter F. Penner and Robin Routledge; Schwarzenfeld: Neufeld Verlag, 2008).

Peskett, Howard and Vinoth Ramachandra. *The Message of Mission* (Leicester: Inter-Varsity Press, 2003).

Pettegree, Andrew. *The Reformation: Critical Concepts in Historical Studies*, Vol. II (London: Routledge, 2004).

Pinckaers, Servais. *The Sources of Christian Ethics* (Edinburgh: T & T Clark, 1995).

Pipkin, H. Wayne and John H. Yoder, eds. *Balthasar Hubmaier: Theologian of Anabaptism* (Scottdale, PA: Herald Press, 1989).

Pobee, John S. 'Peace, with Justice and Honour, Fairest and Most Profitable of Possessions'. Pages 93–110 in *Power and Peace: Statements on Peace and the Authority of the Churches* (ed. Carl Reinhold Brakenhielm; Uppsala: LPI, 1992).

Porter, Stanley E., Michael A. Hayes and David Tombs, eds. *Faith in the Millenium* (Sheffield: Sheffield Academic Press, 2001).

Preston, Ronald H. *Confusions in Christian Social Ethics: Problems for Geneva and Rome* (London: SCM Press, 1994).

Quick, Oliver. 'The Jerusalem Meeting and the Christian Message'. *International Review of Missions* 17 (1928): pp. 445–54.

Raguin, Yves. 'Differences and Common Ground'. Page 175 in *Mission Trends No. 5: Faith Meets Faith* (ed. G. Anderson and P. Stransky; Grand Rapids, MI: Eerdmans, 1981).

Rahner, Karl. *Schriften zur Theologie* (Zurich, 1957).

Ramachandra, Vinoth. *The Recovery of Mission: Beyond the Pluralist Paradigm* (Grand Rapids, MI: Eerdmans, 1997).

Ramachandra, Vinoth. 'A World of Religions and a Gospel of Transformation'. Pages 139–54 in *Edinburgh 2010: Mission Then and Now* (ed. David A. Kerr and Kenneth R. Ross; Oxford: Regnum Books International, 2009).

Ramsey, Paul. 'Who Speaks for the Church?' Pages 321–8 in *A Textbook of Christian Ethics* (ed. Robin Gill; Edinburgh: T & T Clark, 1995).

Ramsey, Paul. *Who Speaks for the Church? A Critique of the 1966 Geneva Conference on Church and Society* (Nashville, TN:Abingdon Press, 1967).

Randall, Ian M. *Communities of Conviction: Baptist Beginnings in Europe* (Schwarzenfeld: Neufeld Verlag, 2009).

Redekop, Benjamin W. and Calvin W. Redekop. *Power, Authority and the Anabaptist Tradition* (Baltimore: John Hopkins University Press, 2001).

Richey, Lance Byron. *Roman Imperial Ideology and the Gospel of John* (Washington: Catholic Biblical Association of America, 2007).

Roberts, David E. 'Barmen Declaration (1934)'. Pages 52–3 in *The Dictionary of Historical Theology* (ed. Trevor A. Hart; Carlisle: Paternoster Press, 2000).

Robinson, Paul, ed. *Just War in Comparative Perspective* (Aldershot: Ashgate Publishing, 2003).

Rogerson, John. 'The Old Testament and Christian Ethics'. Pages 31–9 in *The Cambridge Companion to Christian Ethics* (ed. Robin Gill; Cambridge: Cambridge University Press, 2001).

Rolston III, Holmes. 'Ethics: Naturalized, Socialized, Evaluated'. Ch. 5 in *Genes, Genesis and God: Values and Their Origins in Natural and Human History* (Cambridge: Cambridge University Press, 1999).

Rorty, Richard. 'Cultural Politics and the Question of the Existence of God'. Pages 53–76 in *Radical Interpretation of Religion* (ed. Nancy K. Frankenberry; Cambridge: Cambridge University Press, 2002).

Rosenberg, Alex. *Philosophy of Science: A Contemporary Introduction* (New York: Routledge, 2000).

Ross, Kenneth R. and David A. Kerr. 'The Commissions after a Century'. Pages 307–18 in *Edinburgh 2010: Mission Then and Now* (ed. David A. Kerr and Kenneth R. Ross; Oxford: Regnum Books International, 2009).

Roszak, Theodore. *The Making of a Counter-Culture: Reflections on the Technocratic Society and its Youthful Opposition* (Oakland, CA: University of California Press, 1968).

Routledge, Robin. 'Mission and Covenant in the Old Testament'. Pages 8–41 in *Bible and Mission: A Conversation between Biblical Studies and Missiology* (ed. Rollin G. Grams, I. Howard Marshall, Peter F. Penner and Robin Routledge; Schwarzenfeld: Neufeld Verlag, 2008).

Rowland, Christopher. *Christian Origins: The Setting and Character of the Most Important Messianic Sect of Judaism* (London: SPCK, 2nd edn, 2002).

Ruston, Roger. *Human Rights and the Image of God* (London: SCM Press, 2004).

Samartha, Stanley J. 'Partners in Community: Some Reflections on Hindu-Christian Relations Today'. *Occasional Bulletin of Missionary Research* 4 (April 1980): p. 78.

Satyavrata, Ivan M. *God Has Not Left Himself Without a Witness* (Oxford: Regnum Books International, 2011).

Schaufele, Wolfgang. 'The Missionary Vision and Activity of the Anabaptist Laity'. Pages 82–6 in *Anabaptism and Mission* (ed. Wilbert R. Shenk; Scottdale, PA: Herald Press, 1984).

Scherer, James A. *Gospel, Church and Kingdom: Comparative Studies in World Mission Theology* (Minneapolis: Augsburg, 1987).

Schleitheim Confession, The (Crockett, KY: Rod & Staff Publishers, 1985).

Schnabel, Eckhard. *Early Christian Mission* (2 vols; Downers Grove, IL: InterVarsity Press, 2004).

Schnabel, Eckhard. *Paul the Missionary: Realities, Strategies and Methods* (Nottingham: Inter-Varsity Press, 2008).

Schoonhoven, Evert Jansen. 'Tambaram 1938'. *International Review of Mission* 67 (1978).

Schreiter, Robert J. 'Prologue'. Pages xi–xii in *The Biblical Foundations for Mission* (Donald Senior and Carroll Stuhlmueller; London: SCM Press, 1983).

Schubeck, S.J. *Liberation Ethics: Sources, Models and Norms* (Minneapolis: Fortress Press, 1993).

Schuster, Jurgen. 'Karl Hartenstein: Mission with a Focus on the End'. *Mission Studies* 19 (2002).

Segal, Robert A. 'Theories of Religion'. Pages 75–78 in *The Routledge Companion to the Study of Religion* (ed. John R. Hinnells; Abingdon: Routledge, 2nd edn, 2010).

Segundo, Juan Luis. *Faith and Ideologies: Jesus of Nazareth Yesterday and Today* (Maryknoll, NY: Orbis Books, 1984).

Segundo, Juan Luis. *Masas y Minorias: en la dialectica divina de la liberación* (Buenos Aires: La Aurora, 1973).

Senior, Donald and Carroll Stuhlmueller, eds. *The Biblical Foundations for Mission* (London: SCM Press, 1983).

Shenk, Wilbert R., ed. *Anabaptism and Mission* (Scottdale, PA: Herald Press, 1984).

Shustov, Vladimir. 'Common Security and Overcoming the Consequences of the Cold War'. Pages 114–21 in *Overcoming the Institution of War* (ed. Roger Williamson; Uppsala: LPI, 1992).

Simons, Menno. *Complete Writings of Menno Simons* (trans. Leonard Verduin; Scottdale, PA: Herald Press, 1958).

Smart, Ninian. *Beyond Ideology: Religion and the Future of Western Civilization* (Gifford lectures) (New York: Harper & Row, 1981).

Smart, Ninian. 'The Nature of Religion'. *The Listener* (26 November 1964).

Snyder, C. Arnold. *Anabaptist History and Theology: Revised Student Edition* (Kitchener, Ontario: Pandora Press, 1997).

Soto, Domingo de. *De justitia et jure* (5 vols; Madrid: Instituto de Estudios Politicos, 1967–8).

Soto, Domingo de. *Deliberacion en la causa de los pobres* (Madrid: Instituto de Estudios Politicos, 1965).

South Commission, *The Challenge to the South: The Report of the South Commission* (Oxford: Oxford University Press, 1990).

Stackhouse, Max L. *Apologia: Contextualization, Globalization and Mission in Theological Education* (Grand Rapids, MI: Eerdmans, 1988).

Stackhouse, Max L. *Creeds, Society and Human Rights: A Study in Three Cultures* (Grand Rapids, MI: Eerdmans, 1984).

Stanley, Brian. 'The World Missionary Conference (1910: Edinburgh, Scotland)'. *Expository Times* 121 (2009): pp. 325–31.

Stanley, Brian. *The World Missionary Conference, Edinburgh 1910* (Grand Rapids, MI: Eerdmans, 2009).

Stassen, Glen and David P. Gushee. *Kingdom Ethics: Following Jesus in Contemporary Context* (Downers Grove, IL: InterVarsity Press, 2003).

Stayer, James. 'The Anabaptist Revolt and Political and Religious Powers'. Pages 50–71 in *Power, Authority and the Anabaptist Tradition* (ed. Benjamin W. Redekop and Calvin W. Redekop; Baltimore: John Hopkins University Press, 2001).

Stern, J.P. *Nietzsche* (London: Collins, 1978).

Storkey, Alan. *Jesus and Politics: Confronting the Powers* (Grand Rapids, MI: Baker Academic, 2005).

Stott, John. *Issues Facing Christians Today* (Basingstoke: Marshall, Morgan & Scott, 1984).

Sutherland, Stewart. 'Nomad's Progress'. *Proceedings of the British Academy* 131 (2005).

Tallentyre, S.G. *The Friends of Voltaire* (London: Putnam's Sons, 1907).

Tan Yak-Hwee. *Re-Presenting the Johannine Community: A Postcolonial Perspective* (New York: Peter Lang, 2008).

Taylor, Charles. 'Foreword' to David Martin, *On Secularization: Towards a Revised General Theory* (Aldershot: Ashgate Publishing, 2005).

Taylor, Charles. *A Secular Age* (Cambridge, MA: Harvard University Press, 2007).

Taylor, J.V. *The Primal Vision* (London: SCM Press, 1965).

Tellez, Tomas. 'The Third World and a New World Order'. Pages 111–12 in *Overcoming the Institution of War* (ed. Roger Williamson; Uppsala: LPI, 1992).

Tennent, Timothy. *Invitation to World Missions: A Trinitarian Missiology for the Twenty-First Century* (Grand Rapids, MI: Kregel Publications, 2010).

Thiessen, Gerd. *Biblical Faith: An Evolutionary Approach* (London: SCM Press, 1984).

Thistlethwaite, Susan Brooks. 'Peace Theology and American Protestant Ecclesiology in the 1980s'. Pages 131–47 in *Power and Peace: Statements on Peace and the Authority of the Churches* (ed. Carl Reinhold Brakenhielm; Uppsala: LPI, 1992).

Thomas, Norman E., ed. *Classic Texts in Mission and World Christianity* (Maryknoll, NY: Orbis Books, 1995).

Thomson, Garrett. *On Locke* (Belmont, CA: Wadsworth, 2001).

Tooley, Michelle. *Voice of the Voiceless: Women, Justice and Human Rights in Guatemala* (Scottdale, PN: Herald Press, 1997).

Towler, Robert. *Homo Religiosus: Sociological Problems in the Study of Religion* (London: Constable, 1974).

Trigg, Roger. *Equality, Freedom and Religion* (Oxford: Oxford University Press, 2012).

Trigg, Roger. *Rationality and Religion: Does Faith Need Reason?* (Oxford: Blackwell, 1998).

Trigg, Roger. *Rationality and Science: Can Science Explain Everything?* (Oxford: Blackwell, 1993).

Trigg, Roger. *Religion in Public Life: Must Faith be Privatized?* (Oxford: Oxford University Press, 2007).

Trigg, Roger. 'Religion in State Education'. Ch. 9 in *Religion in Public Life: Must Faith be Privatized?* (Oxford: Oxford University Press, 2007).

Twiss, Sumner B. 'The Philosophy of Religious Pluralism: A Critical Appraisal of Hick and His Critics'. *Journal of Religion* 70 (1990): pp. 533–63.

US Catholic Bishops, *The Challenge of Peace: God's Promise and Our Response: A Pastoral Letter on War and Peace* (Washington, DC: Catholic Truth Society, 1983).

Van Leeuwen, Arendt. *Christianity in World History: The Meeting of the Faiths of East and West* (London: Edinburgh House Press, 1964).

Villa-Vicencio, Charles. *The Art of Reconciliation* (Uppsala: LPI, 2002).

Villa-Vicencio, Charles. *Theology and Violence: The South African Debate* (Grand Rapids, MI: Eerdmans, 1988).

Vitoria, Francisco de. *Political Writings* (ed. Anthony Pagden and Jeremy Lawrance; (Cambridge: Cambridge University Press, 1991).

Voillaume, R. *Seeds of the Desert: the Legacy of Charles de Foucauld* (London: Burns & Oates, 1955).

Vroom, Hendrik. 'Karl Barth and the Nature of False and True Religion'. *Studies in Interreligious Dialogue* 22 (2012): pp. 74–84.

Waite, Gary. 'The Anabaptist Movement in Amsterdam and the Netherlands, 1531–1535: An Initial Investigation into its Genesis and Social Dynamics'. Pages 140–55 in *The Reformation: Critical Concepts in Historical Studies*, Vol. II (ed. Andrew Pettegree; London: Routledge, 2004).

Walls, Andrew. 'Afterword: Christian Mission in a Five-Hundred-Year Context'. Pages 193–204 in *Mission in the 21st Century: Exploring the Five Marks of Global Mission* (ed. Andrew Walls and Cathy Ross; London: Darton, Longman & Todd, 2008).

Walls, Andrew. 'Commission One and the Church's Transforming Century'. Pages 27–40 in *Edinburgh 2010: Mission Then and Now* (ed. David A. Kerr and Kenneth R. Ross; Oxford: Regnum Books International, 2009).

Walls, Andrew. 'David Livingstone, 1813–1873: Awakening the Western World to Africa'. Pages 140–48 in *Mission Legacies: Biographical Studies of Leaders of the Modern Missionary Movement* (ed. Gerald Anderson et al.; Maryknoll, NY: Orbis Books, 1994).

Walls, Andrew. *The Missionary Movement in Christian History: Studies in the Transmission of Faith* (Maryknoll, NY: Orbis Books, 1996).

Walls, Andrew and Cathy Ross, eds. *Mission in the 21st Century: Exploring the Five Marks of Mission* (London: Darton, Longman & Todd, 2008).

Ward, Keith. *The God-Conclusion: God and the Western Philosophical Tradition* (London: Darton, Longman & Todd, 2009).

Ward, Keith. *Is Religion Irrational?* (Oxford: Lion Hudson, 2011).

Watson, F. *Paul and the Hermeneutics of Faith* (Edinburgh: T & T Clark, 2004).

Weaver, J. Denny. *Becoming Anabaptist: The Origin and Significance of Sixteenth Century Anabaptism* (Scottdale, PA: Herald Press, 2nd edn, 2005).

Webster, Alexander. *The Pacifist Option: The Moral Argument Against War in Eastern Orthodox Theology* (San Francisco, CA: International Scholars Publications, 1998).

Wenham, David. *Paul: Follower of Jesus or Founder of Christianity?* (Grand Rapids, MI: Eerdmans, 1995).

Wenham, Gordon. 'Grace and Law in the Old Testament'. Pages 3–23 in *Law, Morality and the Bible* (ed. Bruce Kaye and Gordon Wenham; Downers Grove, IL: InterVarsity Press, 1978).

Williams, George Hunston. *The Radical Reformation* (Philadelphia: Westminster Press, 1962).

Williams, George Hunston and Angel M. Mergal. *Spiritual and Anabaptist Writers* (Philadelphia: Westminster Press, 1957).

Williamson, Roger, ed. *Overcoming the Institution of War* (Uppsala: LPI, 1992).

Wittgenstein, Ludwig. *Philosophical Investigations* (Oxford: Blackwell, 1953).

Woods, Thomas. *How the Catholic Church Built Western Civilization* (Washington: Regnery Publishing, 2005).

World Council of Churches Fourth Assembly. 'Renewal in Mission: the Report as Adopted by the Assembly'. *International Review of Mission* (April 1969).

World Council of Churches Sixth Assembly. 'Statement on Peace and Justice'. *Ecumenical Review* 36 (January 1984).

World Council of Churches. *The Church for Others: Two Reports on the Missionary Structure of the Congregation* (Geneva: WCC, 1967).

World Council of Churches. *Guidelines on Dialogue with People of Living Faiths and Ideologies* (Geneva: WCC, 1979).

World Council of Churches. *Mission and Evangelism: An Ecumenical Affirmation* (Geneva: WCC, 1983).

World Missionary Conference. *The Church in the Mission Field, Report of Commission* II (Edinburgh and London: Oliphant, Anderson & Ferrier, 1910).

World Missionary Conference. *Cooperation and the Promotion of Unity, Report of Commission* VIII (Edinburgh and London: Oliphant, Anderson & Ferrier, 1910).

World Missionary Conference. *The History and Records of the Conference* (Edinburgh and London: Oliphant, Anderson & Ferrier, 1910).

World Missionary Conference. *The Missionary Message in Relation to Non-Christian Religions, Report of Commission* IV (Edinburgh and London: Oliphant, Anderson & Ferrier, 1910).

Wright, Chris. 'InterFaith Dialogue'. *Anvil* 1 (1984): p. 252.

Wright, Christopher J.H. Appendix, 'What about the Canaanites?' Pages 472–80 in *Old Testament Ethics for the People of God* (Leicester: Inter-Varsity Press, 2004).

Wright, Christopher J.H. *The Mission of God: Unlocking the Bible's Grand Narrative* (Nottingham: Inter-Varsity Press, 2006).

Wright, Christopher J.H. *Old Testament Ethics for the People of God* (Leicester: Inter-Varsity Press, 2004).

Wright, Christopher. 'The World in the Bible'. *Evangelical Review of Theology* 34 (2010).

Wright, David F., ed. *Essays in Evangelical Social Ethics* (Exeter: Paternoster Press, 1979).

Wright, N.T. *Jesus and the Victory of God* (London: SPCK, 1996).

Yates, Timothy. *Christian Mission in the Twentieth Century* (Cambridge: Cambridge University Press, 1996).

Zumstein, J. 'The Farewell Discourses (John 13.1–16.33) and the Problem of Anti-Judaism'. In *Anti-Judaism in the Fourth Gospel* (ed. Reimund Bieringer; Assen: van Gorcum, 2001).

General Index of Authors and Subjects

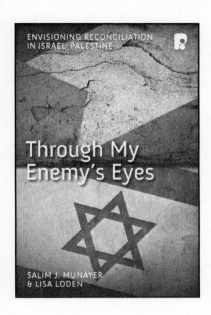

Through My Enemy's Eyes

Envisioning Reconciliation in Israel–Palestine

Salim Munayer and Lisa Loden

This unique book addresses reconciliation in the context of the Israeli Messianic Jewish and Palestinian Christian divide. This remarkable work, written in collaboration by a local Palestinian Christian and an Israeli Messianic Jew addresses head-on divisive theological issues (and their political implications); land, covenant, prophecy, eschatology. The struggle for reconciliation is painful and often extremely difficult for all of us. This work seeks to show a way forward.

'This is a unique conversation in which each partner gives full expression to all that they are and think and feel about themelves and the conflict in their land. Above all we come to share the hope and courage that shines through the pain and struggle.' *Christopher Wright, Langham Paternership.*

'Given the divides between their communities, this book is a remarkable achievement, a cry of hope from the land where Jesus walked.' *Chris Rice Duke Divinity School, US.*

Salim Munayer is on the faculty of Bethlehem Bible College, Bethlehem, Palestine and director of Musalaha Ministry of Reconciliation, Jerusalem, Israel. Lisa Loden is on the faculty of Nazareth Evangelical Theological Seminary, Nazareth, Israel, and Director of Advancing Professional Excellence, Israel.

978-1-84227-748-5 (e-book 978-1-84227-859-8)

Paternoster:
thinking faith

We trust you enjoyed reading this book
from Paternoster. If you want to be informed
of any new titles from this author and other
releases you can sign up to the Paternoster
newsletter by contacting us:

By Post:
Paternoster
52 Presley Way
Crownhill
Milton Keynes
MK8 0ES

E-mail
paternoster@authenticmedia.co.uk

Follow us: